3⁹⁹
CASH

D1130594

Trollope

Trollope
Living with Character

Stephen Wall

HENRY HOLT AND COMPANY
NEW YORK

Copyright © 1988 by Stephen Wall

All rights reserved, including the right
to reproduce this book or portions thereof
in any form.

Published in the United States in 1989 by
Henry Holt and Company, Inc., 115 West 18th Street,
New York, New York 10011.

Published in Canada by Fitzhenry & Whiteside Limited,
195 Allstate Parkway, Markham, Ontario L3R 4T8.

Originally published in Great Britain under the title
Trollope and Character.

Library of Congress Catalog Card Number: 88-81790

First American Edition

Printed in Great Britain
10 9 8 7 6 5 4 3 2 1

ISBN 0-8050-0923-X

Contents

Author's Note

Quotations from Trollope's *Autobiography* and from individual novels are followed by the number in roman numerals of the chapter in which they appear.

I am grateful to Penguin Books Ltd for their permission to reprint parts of my introduction to the Penguin English Library edition of *Can You Forgive Her?*. I have also drawn on my articles 'Trollope, Balzac, and the Reappearing Character' (*Essays in Criticism*, January 1975, Vol. XXV, No. 1) and 'Trollope, Satire, and *The Way We Live Now*' (*Essays in Criticism*, January 1987, Vol. XXXVII, No. 1). Quotations from Trollope's *Letters* are taken from the edition by N. John Hall, 2 vols. (Stanford University Press, 1983), by kind permission of the publishers.

I
Living with Characters

The *Autobiography*

Trollope's revelations about his working methods would have been suicidal had they not been posthumous: that, at least, has been the usual verdict. The familiar details – the old groom paid extra to wake him up early, the three hours at the desk before breakfast, the regular production of so many words against the clock – were first published in the *Autobiography* in 1883, the year after Trollope's death. Since then the mechanical industriousness of such a regime has often been taken to imply a deplorable indifference to the finer literary considerations. Despite strenuous modern attempts to vindicate Trollope's authorial integrity, Henry James's complaint that as an artist Trollope never took himself seriously enough has continued to seem a reasonable inference.

In 1875 James had crossed the Atlantic in Trollope's company and had seen for himself what has been called 'the Novel-Machine' in practice.[1] 'The season was unpropitious, the vessel overcrowded, the voyage detestable; but Trollope shut himself up in his cabin every morning . . . [and] drove his pen as steadily on the tumbling ocean as in Montague Square.' James was impressed, but also censorious:

> The power to shut one's eyes, one's ears (to say nothing of another sense), upon the scenery of a pitching Cunarder and open them upon the loves and sorrows of Lily Dale or the conjugal embarrassments of Lady Glencora Palliser, is certainly a faculty which could take to itself wings . . . [but] with his extraordinary gift, there was always in him a certain infusion of the common. He abused his gift, over-worked it, rode his horse too hard.

James's masterly essay on Trollope (in which these phrases occur

3

and which, like the *Autobiography*, first appeared in 1883) expresses with classical lucidity the unease of serious readers in the face of a fertility that struck the American writer as 'gross' and 'importunate'.

Nothing could be more professional in its way than James's own attitude to his *métier*, and he had no objection to copiousness in itself: 'almost all the greatest writers have been abundant'. The twenty years of Balzac's productive career had bequeathed a body of work that was 'immense, heroic, to this day immeasurable'. If Trollope had been really good, how could one have had too much of him? The trouble was that Trollope did not sufficiently respect the nature of his medium and accepted too complacently the limitations of his material. Although James's acknowledgements of Trollope's local merits are often surprisingly handsome, the younger novelist could not finally forgive the older one his lack of artistic pretension. The piece-work accumulation of two hundred and fifty publishable words every fifteen minutes (not in itself a negligible accomplishment) might have been tolerable as the necessary means of realizing some grandiose project such as the *Comédie Humaine*, but although Trollope's fiction may approach Balzac's in bulk, it was not comparably ambitious. In the last pages of the *Autobiography* he waives any title to literary excellence and contents himself with the fact that he has at least published more than Voltaire and over twice as much as Carlyle.

This apparently philistine claim comes just before Trollope's celebrated table of his literary earnings down to 1879. With the modest confidence of a man who knows his own class, he describes the total – nearly £70,000 – as 'comfortable, but not splendid'. (XX) Given the value of Victorian money, such a sum may now look more reassuring than it seemed to Trollope at the time, but for all his industry he made less than Dickens, and even at the peak of his popularity was never paid as much for a single novel as George Eliot was. Although Trollope was far from being grasping in his actual dealings with publishers, his totting-up has fitted in with his clock-watching productivity with disastrous plausibility. He solicits you to think of him as merely a straightforward artisan who takes a justifiable pride in getting the appropriate reward for honest toil with a pertinacity that seems almost perverse. He insists that writing fiction is mainly a matter of getting down to it, arguing that if he finishes *Doctor Thorne* one day and begins *The Bertrams* the next, he is behaving as properly as a man who, having made one pair of boots, starts immediately on another. (Why Trollope so often cites shoemakers as patterns of industry remains unclear.)

Trollope's 'determination to excel, if not in quality, at any rate in quantity' (VII) does not sound like the resolve of a hero of art, and it is characteristic of his outlook that despite his admiration of George Eliot as a novelist and his reciprocated affection for her as a friend he should nevertheless have thought that 'she struggles too hard to do work that shall be excellent'. (XIII) He refused to concede that his own work would have been better had he taken longer over it. The pages were clocked up with little apparent anguish and passed to the printer with relatively little revision. The number of words in the completed manuscript was invariably the quantity previously bargained for: as a scrupulous tradesman, Trollope prided himself on never giving short weight. Altogether, the *Autobiography* contains all the materials necessary for a portrait of the artist as a conscientious hack.

It also contains enough evidence to suggest quite another picture, revealing Trollope not so much as a man who overworked and abused his gift but as one surrendered to it and was enslaved by it. The process clearly started in his youth. Trollope's early years were often wretched. Unhappy and ostracized at school, hovering uncertainly between gentility and destitution at home, separated for long periods from his mother and left with a morose and incompetent father, he had to make his lonely way with little moral or economic support. The *Autobiography*'s narrative of this period has sometimes been thought self-pitying, but a comparison with Dickens's description of his days in the blacking warehouse makes Trollope's account of his sufferings seem almost laconic. Indeed, Trollope finally refuses to gratify any expectation of complete candour on the grounds that no one, not even Rousseau, can hope to tell the whole truth about himself. The argument is both typical of Trollope's hatred of cant and a convenient justification of his endemic reserve. However, the bare facts of Trollope's case and such comments as his reticence does allow through are enough to indicate that he was driven to fantasy by misery, and that out of fantasy came fiction.

Between the ages of fifteen and twenty-five he kept a journal –

shamefacedly destroyed in 1870 as no doubt too embarrassing to preserve. Had it survived it might have given us more insight into the period of Trollope's life which we know least about but which was probably the most formative. Trollope says that the journal taught him facility of expression, and certainly his later literary career would hardly have been feasible without an extreme readiness of phrase. More important for the future novelist, however, was the development of the habit of making up stories for himself. The mature Trollope felt obliged to condemn such self-indulgence – 'there can, I imagine, hardly be a more dangerous mental practice' – but he saw that without it he might never have become a novelist. In these sagas of his early days, Trollope was of course his own admirable hero, but there was more to them than the normal wish-fulfilling dreams of adolescence. As he continued to elaborate these consolatory fantasies – not only as a boy, but well into his twenties, when he became a scruffy and insubordinate clerk in the General Post Office – he instinctively evolved a narrative discipline:

> Nor were these efforts in architecture spasmodic, or subject to constant change from day to day. For weeks, for months, if I remember rightly, from year to year, I would carry on the same tale, binding myself down to certain laws, to certain proportions, and proprieties, and unities. Nothing impossible was ever introduced, – nor even anything which, from outward circumstances, would seem to be violently improbable . . . I learned in this way to maintain an interest in a fictitious story, to dwell on a work created by my own imagination, and to live in a world altogether outside the world of my own material life. (III)

The controls which the day-dreaming Trollope exercised over his fantasies are prophetically consistent with some of the constraints he was to put upon his fiction: eschewing the speciously sensational, he found his essential interest in the ways in which probable characters move through normal time in an ordinary world. Similarly, he thought of the world of his novels as autonomous, discontinous with his own life, and free from autobiographical undertow.

Thus what was begun by Trollope as a consolatory alternative to life developed its own reality. In his maturity, this imaginative

activity became addictive. Once he had started writing novels he
could not stop: at the time of writing the *Autobiography* he had three
completed books in his bottom drawer as well as another in the
process of publication. In a touching late letter to his eldest son (21
December 1880) he says: 'I finished on Thursday the novel I was
writing, and on Friday I began another. Nothing really frightens
me but the idea of enforced idleness. As long as I can write books,
even though they be not published, I think that I can be happy.'
Such plangent accents are hardly those of an industrious
shoemaker, and indeed, from a purely commercial point of view,
Trollope's inordinate over-production (forty-seven novels in
thirty-seven years) glutted his own market. Trollope was quite
aware that his name 'was too frequent on title-pages'. The daily
stint came to serve deeper and obscurer needs than the simple wish
to keep profitably busy.

Trollope was able to write so much so quickly because he lived
with his characters so closely. Throughout the *Autobiography* it is
taken as axiomatic that a writer cannot create an interest in his
characters unless he himself knows them inside out. This notion
may now look almost quaint, and often seems to be disregarded by
modern critics – or at best tolerated as an inevitable embarrassment.
Nevertheless, it is expressed by Trollope with an unobtrusive
intensity perhaps encouraged by the fact that – under the shelter of
a recommendation to others – he could here confidently allude to
the inner creative life that elsewhere he rarely does much more than
hint at. In a passage often quoted by writers on Trollope, but rarely
given sufficient weight, he says that the novelist must live with his
characters

> in the full reality of established intimacy. They must be with
> him as he lies down to sleep, and as he wakes from his
> dreams. He must learn to hate them and to love them. He
> must argue with them, quarrel with them, forgive them, and
> even submit to them . . . And as, here, in our outer world, we
> know that men and women change, – become worse or better
> as temptation or conscience may guide them, – so should these
> creations of his change, and every change should be noted by
> him. On the last day of each month recorded, every person in
> his novel should be a month older than on the first. (XII)

When Trollope writes of living with his characters in this way, his prose assumes an authority and an energy that is missing when he discusses such topics as the construction of complex plots (which he took little trouble over) or the ethical wholesomeness of English fiction (about which his opinions are conventional if frequently reiterated). In life, Trollope was noted for being assertive to the point of bluster, and taken in isolation the following claim about his characters might seem characteristically overbearing:

> There is a gallery of them, and of all in that gallery I may say that I know the tone of the voice, and the colour of the hair, every flame of the eye, and the very clothes they wear. Of each man I could assert whether he would have said these or the other words; of every woman, whether she would then have smiled or so have frowned. (XII)

Each man? *Every* woman? Trollope had produced getting on for forty novels when he wrote this, and it is natural to be sceptical. Did Trollope really retain so clear a perception of, say, a minor character in *The Bertrams* seventeen years after creating him or her? Perhaps he did. Although he does sometimes make mistakes in continuity, he says in another late letter (5 December 1881) that 'the writer never forgets', claiming that there is not a passage in *Barchester Towers* that he does not remember. In 1859 he had to put *Castle Richmond* aside because Thackeray wanted a novel for the new *Cornhill* (Trollope obliged with *Framley Parsonage*), but he says in the *Autobiography* that he could have completed the book fifteen years later had it been left half-finished. As it was, having two novels in mind at the same time created no more difficulty than having simultaneously two separate sets of friends. As he revealingly comments, 'In our lives we are always weaving novels, and we manage to keep the different tales distinct'. (IX)

To understand what living with his characters meant for Trollope would be to understand what mattered most to him and what still matters most about him as a novelist, and this book is primarily an extended essay on the implications of the phrase. Recent discussions of Trollope have tended to defend him on other grounds, partly no doubt because of a general loss of confidence in the theoretical legitimacy of those ideas about literary character which Trollope shared with his original audience in so untroubled a way. The modern preoccupation with the self-consciousness of the text is obviously hard to reconcile with an assumption that fictional characters have a life beyond it. Nevertheless, Trollope himself worked on such a basis, and the pages that follow here offer not that fully comprehensive, chronological, and critical account of his *œuvre* that we still need but, more modestly, an attempt to assess some of the consequences of that assumption by examining some of his novels.

It is clear from the *Autobiography* that the intimacy of the relationship between novelist and character was encouraged rather than inhibited by rapid composition. When 'at some quiet spot among the mountains', for instance, and thus able to treble his average quota by writing sixteen pages a day seven days a week,

> I have been able to imbue myself thoroughly with the characters I have had in hand. I have wandered alone among the rocks and woods, crying at their grief, laughing at their absurdities, and thoroughly enjoying their joy. I have been impregnated with my own creations till it has been my only excitement to sit with the pen in my hand, and drive my team before me at as quick a pace as I could make them travel. (X)

It is a pity that Trollope does not say which novels or parts of novels were in fact written under such conducive conditions, but the enthusiasm of the passage – though unusual – is again more than would be expected from a merely conscientous craftsman. In the same passage, however, Trollope enters an important qualification: 'the rapidity has been achieved by hot pressure, not in the conception, but in the telling of the story'. In itself, the implication that though birth was quick, gestation may have been prolonged is hardly surprising: novelists commonly brood over their fictions for long periods. However, Trollope wrote not intermittently but continuously. He was always at it: voyages – as James testifies and as Trollope himself records – were an opportunity rather than an obstruction; even railway journeys were turned to advantage with the aid of a specially made 'little tablet'. When this incessant composition is put beside his other activities – his energetically if not always tactfully discharged duties as an increasingly important Post Office official with ultimately high responsibilities, his compulsive hunting, his considerable journalism, his lengthy travel-books, and for that matter his clubmanship and his whist – there does not seem much time left to incubate the Jamesian germ in the notebook-filling way appropriate to the dedicated artist. But where there is little room for deliberate thought there is always time for fantasy, and much of Trollope's imaginative life must have been devoted to his characters' lives rather than his own – and as a matter of personal habit and predilection as much as of deliberate authorial policy.

The *Autobiography* indicates that Trollope's relationships with his characters were not only governed by their current usefulness. He would keep them in mind whether he was writing about them or not. He notes, as a general tendency of his imagination, that 'my mind is constantly employing itself on the work I have done'. (IX) Of course, Trollope was only able to reap the full novelistic benefit of this retrospeculation with characters who appear in more than one novel and, supremely, in the Palliser series. He remarks of the main figures in that group that 'So much of my inner life was passed in their company, that I was continually asking myself how this woman would act when this or that event had passed over her head, or how that man would carry himself when his youth had become manhood, or his manhood declined to old age'. (XVII) This dwelling on his imagined world naturally extended to the physical environment of his characters. It is true that, despite some interesting exceptions, Trollope's novels are not remarkable for their descriptions of places; since he was nearly always writing about modern life, he was often content to refer his readers to their own observation of it. Nevertheless, he significantly says of the fictitious places in the Barset series that he knew of them 'all the accessories, as though I had lived and wandered there'. (VIII) The map of the county which he made for himself has often been reproduced (and even, one must admit, corrected). His communion with the Barset world clearly continued outside and beyond those pages which chronicle its doings, as the well-known case of Mrs Proudie demonstrates. Trollope overheard two clergymen at his club complain that she had become a bore. With typical impetuosity Trollope promised he would kill her off before the week was out, and he was not the sort of man to go back on a publicly announced intention. But although her public career ends in Chapter LXVI of *The Last Chronicle of Barset*, Trollope himself had not finished with her: 'I have never dissevered myself from Mrs Proudie, and still live much in company with her ghost.' He did so not because she could be of any further use to him nor because she was herself lovable, but because he understood her: 'so great was my delight in writing about Mrs Proudie, so thorough was my knowledge of all the little shades of her character'. (XV) Trollope's remorse over the death of 'his old friend' seems to be accompanied by a sense of a prematurely suspended and therefore unfulfilled relationship.

For Trollope a novel was nothing unless not only the reader but also the author sympathized with his characters. It is the main and it sometimes seems the only criterion he brings to bear on his contemporaries. Dickens, although often guilty of dispensing with human nature, lived with his characters 'in his best days'; those parts of George Eliot's work in which the portrait-painter prevails over the philosopher are to be preferred; Bulwer is inferior, for all his gifts, because he never knew his own personages; *Jane Eyre* is certain to last because of the intensity of Charlotte Brontë's feeling for Rochester and the governess – 'she lived with those characters, and felt with every fibre of her heart, the longings of the one and the sufferings of the other'. (XIII) Such observations may now look simple-minded, but they clearly indicate the kind of fictive life that Trollope looked for, and they are consistent not only with his own practice but with the advice he gave to others. In Trollope's view a first novel will come easily enough, since there is bound to be some story or individual that has impressed the would-be writer strongly enough to get him going. But what he writes later will be weary or wooden if he does not give his hand to 'that work of observation and reception from which has come his power'. This work is not merely something a man does at his desk; it should continue 'in all his walks abroad, in all his movements through the world, in all his intercourse with his fellow-creatures'. (XII) This labour may be carried on unconsciously for the most part, but without it a novelist dries up, or dries out. This prescription is quite consistent with that incessant activity of the imagination already noted. Despite their origin in fantasy, Trollope's interior speculations about the development and behaviour of his imaginary characters would naturally involve a continuous monitoring of the world they lived in; they could not be fully envisaged except as part of the society in which they moved, constrained by things as they were.

His record of things as they were is often assumed to be Trollope's main claim to attention and he has increasingly been presented as a penetrating analyst of his age. It can hardly be denied that his fiction gives a true picture of at least the milder and more presentable aspects of mid-Victorian life when it was just this accuracy that was so often noted by his original reviewers, who were after all in a good position to check. Trollope's novels may not now strike us as the last word in realism, but the word 'photographic' crops up too often in the reviews for his accuracy to be doubted (it was of course a new word then). In describing, for instance, the action of *The Belton Estate* in a notice of 1866, Henry James remarks that

> the three persons whom we have mentioned are each a character in a way, and their sayings and doings, their comings and goings, are registered to the letter and timed to the minute. They write a number of letters, which are duly transcribed; they make frequent railway journeys by the down-train from London; they have cups of tea in their bed-rooms; and they do, in short, in the novel very much as the reader is doing out of it.

The implication of this admittedly grudging testimony (as of other contemporary comments) is that the world created by Trollope's imagination was eminently recognizable to his first readers as their own.

But because Trollope's novels have come to have such great documentary value, it does not follow that they were mainly intended as works of social criticism and historical record (as modern critics often assume), and to treat them as such can easily lead us to ignore what is most remarkable about them. Trollope did not propose to himself (as Balzac had done in the 1842 *Avant-propos* to the *Comédie Humaine*) the idea of becoming the secretary of his period. Trollope was an opinionated man and in his later years a public figure, and even without such explicit social commentary as his *The New Zealander* (written 1855–6 but not published until 1972) it would not be difficult to make out from journalistic and other sources his views on many of the questions of the day. Indeed, his ideas are sometimes obtruded into the novels in a quite

12

unfictionalized form: *Castle Richmond*, for instance, contains Trollope's reflections on the Irish famine which he had seen at first hand. Such widespread and undeserved distress was likely to prompt unease about God's purposes and justice in a man of Trollope's generation, and the question is openly rehearsed by him in Chapter VII ('For myself, I do not believe in such exhibitions of God's anger,' etc.). Nevertheless, *Castle Richmond* is not a dramatized debate about how and why God works through history or a fictionalized defence of the Government's relief measures. Again, the first edition of *The Three Clerks* contains material on the Civil Service which Trollope took over from the unpublished *New Zealander* (as its editor N. John Hall shows), but it was subsequently dropped, so that the primary purpose of the novel can hardly have been to express anxieties about public administration. Similarly, although the indigent situation of Mr Crawley illustrates Trollope's concern for clergymen who had to keep themselves and their families respectable on stipends beneath the contempt of a competent tradesman – a concern also voiced in his sketches of clergymen of the Church of England – *The Last Chronicle of Barset* was not written to make a public point out of Mr Crawley's private agonies.

In fictional practice, Trollope always puts the particular life of the private individual before public considerations, even in the Palliser novels which partly derive from Trollope's own frustrated political ambitions. Palliser's meditation on equality in *The Prime Minister* clearly expresses Trollope's own thoughts on the matter, but – as a later chapter will hope to show – Palliser is presented as a fully human rather than a narrowly political animal. Both in the novels sometimes called 'political' and elsewhere the life and value of Trollope's work does not depend on an analytic intelligence that has evolved certain ideas about the world which are then dramatized, as a number of modern studies have tended to imply. It comes rather from a prolonged communion with the characters in his imagination who, like real people, are not to be reduced to category or sample without an unacceptable violation of what makes them individual. Of course Trollope must in some sense control his characters in order to write a novel at all, but they do not seem subject to his will because it is clear that they are not there just to demonstrate something that he wants proved. They do not appear to owe their existence and careers to an ulterior authorial purpose; they are not functional. As Walter M. Kendrick puts it, the Trollope novel 'is not supposed to have *meant* life, to have pointed to life like a sign; it is supposed to have *been* life . . . absorbed into the reader's character as any other experience of reality would be'.

Trollope was sometimes said to be satirical by his earlier reviewers, and a satirical novel conveys its author's views on society by dragooning its characters into animating his thesis. Trollope, however, was distinctly unhappy about the way satire obliges its creator to distort what it portrays, as both his comments in the *Autobiography* and a reasoned letter to Alfred Austin (2 May 1870) indicate: 'the vices implied are coloured so as to make effect rather than to represent truth'. (XX) Moreover, the motives of the satirist are liable to become corrupt as he warms to his work: he leaves the impression that he wants revenge rather than justice. It is therefore not surprising that even when Trollope sets out with an avowedly satirical intention the force of the authorial argument weakens as the complexities in the characters assume priority. As we shall see, this is what happens in *The Way We Live Now*, although it was initially conceived, according to Trollope himself, as an attack on contemporary commercialism. And since his characters tend to take matters into their own hands, any ideas which the author might wish to express through them have to exist on sufference; what the characters decide to do may leave little room for the author's argument and may even contradict it. As Trollope put it in a sentence already quoted, the author must be prepared to argue with his characters, 'quarrel with them, forgive them, and *even submit to them*'.

However, the power of reconciling the claims of the objective normal world with the demands of his characters for their freedom did not come soon or easily to Trollope. His career as a novelist shows no early leap to success; recognition did not come until he was in his forties. It took him a considerable time to develop the kind of novel which would allow the activity of his imagination to have free creative play. His early work derives too much of its material from what was in the public domain for it to benefit very much from the energies latent in Trollope's interior life. The first three novels (*The Macdermots of Ballycloran*, *The Kellys and the*

O'Kellys, and the historical romance *La Vendée*) were written in Ireland, following Trollope's posting there as a Post Office official and his subsequent marriage. The emotional security which marriage seems to have brought must ultimately have helped to release the accumulated fantasy of his miserable London youth and make it available for fictional use, but no doubt time was needed for it to do so.

The impulse behind *The Macdermots of Ballycloran* (written 1843–5; published 1847) was Trollope's accidental discovery of a ruined house in a particularly melancholy part of Ireland; according to the *Autobiography*, the plot was fabricated there and then. Not surprisingly, this external impetus produced a conventional narrative apparatus involving the seduction of a local girl by a police Captain and his murder by her brother, together with her death during the latter's trial. Trollope attempts to make this melodramatic material satisfactorily serve the wider and estimable purpose of portraying Irish conditions of life to a genteel English audience not expected to have much knowledge of them. Chapters like the one describing the wretched little town of Mohill ('Look at that mud hovel on the left . . .' etc.) and reporting with fatiguing fidelity the conversation at Mrs Mulready's shebeen shop ('"Sorrow to your sowl then, mother Mulready; d'ye think I'm so bad already then, that they haven't left me the price of a glass?"') (IX) anticipate the kind of dogged diligence in writing things up on which Trollope was to rely in his travel books.[2] Nevertheless, his understanding of the hopeless economic situation of Thady Macdermot, endlessly hunting for rents which cannot be paid because the land itself is too impoverished, and of the endemic lawlessness and latent violence which such conditions encourage, shows what Trollope called in a later letter (1 May 1874) 'a certain tragic earnestness'; the tolerant treatment of Catholic parish priests is also notable. But the plot does not sufficiently integrate Thady's social position with his personality, and occasional passages of considerable psychological interest – the process by which Thady drifts towards deciding to kill the Captain, and especially his demoralization by inactivity when he takes refuge in the hills (XXIII) – are not elaborated by the inexperienced novelist in the way that they might have been later.

Trollope's mature ability to isolate and treat what were for him the areas of real interest in even so standard a situation can be seen in the much later *An Eye for an Eye* (written in a month in 1870, published 1878–9). The material is again melodramatic: a doomed love affair between an English gentleman and a poor but honest Irish girl, with her mother as the indigenous revenger who finally pushes the seducer over the six-hundred-foot cliffs of Moher. But here Trollope concentrates his attention on the two crucial psychological states – that of the mother, shown from the beginning as regarding the lovers' relationship with an obsessional intensity that is barely under control and which finally escapes it – and of the hero who finds himself through weakness in a dilemma which gradually but remorselessly tightens its grip. The social context in which this drama takes place is deliberately attenuated, and although the remote location on the west coast of Ireland is appropriately romantic, the local colour is limited to what is immediately relevant to the protagonists' states of mind, so that although the field of view is more limited the treatment is psychologically more searching. This reworking, after twenty-five years, of a situation that clearly had for Trollope some sort of human truth in spite of its sensational elements, is characteristic – indeed, some of the story's essential features were again recycled less than a year later in an English setting in *Lady Anna* (discussed below). Such recurrences indicate part of what is implied by Trollope's remark that his mind was constantly employing itself on the work he had done. Repetition was a fundamental part of his authorial practice, and was therefore inextricably bound up with his desire to live with his characters in 'the full reality of established intimacy'.

II

Reappearing Characters

———————————

Barsetshire Revisited

The Warden

The Warden (written 1852–3, published 1855) was the fourth novel Trollope wrote but remains the first that now seems fully characteristic, and it inaugurates the series by which he is still probably best known. As a series, however, the Barsetshire novels are more diverse in nature and inconsistent in quality than is often assumed. The unity given by its West Country setting (which is in fact intermittently deserted for London life) is more apparent than real, and should not be taken to imply a corresponding evenness of execution. Indeed, it would be unreasonable to expect it: *The Last Chronicle of Barset* was not written until 1866, after Trollope had launched his second – and artistically superior – group of interconnected novels with *Can You Forgive Her?*. He was distracted in both series by the intermittent composition of a considerable number of other novels. For all their subsequent celebrity, *The Warden* and *Barchester Towers* are often self-conscious and tentative; by the time he came to write *The Small House at Allington* and *The Last Chronicle* Trollope had found something like his full power. To study the Barsetshire novels in sequence is to see his essential nature as a novelist emerge, and in that process one form of fictional repetition – the reappearing character – is put to ever more rewarding use.

Trollope's account of the origins of *The Warden* makes it clear that, like *The Macdermots*, its location was partly due to his response to a particular place – in this case, the cathedral close at Salisbury (*Autobiography*, V). The physical decay of Hiram's Hospital after Mr Harding resigns his office as its Warden (described in the last chapter) provides a modified English echo of the ruin of the Irish house, but such elegiac approaches were not fundamentally in keeping with Trollope's temperament. Nor is the tendency towards a Sternean or Goldsmithian sentimentalism in the portrayal of the Warden himself (especially in his pastoral and cello-playing capacities) something which Trollope had the stylistic finesse to manage with comfort at this stage. In fact, the book's tone is always liable to become slightly embarrassing. The discrepancy between natural spontaneity and clerical demeanour – 'the bishop did not whistle: we believe that they lose the power of doing so on being consecrated . . . but he looked as though he would have done so, but for his apron' (III) – is one that Trollope exploits with a heavy hand in *The Warden* and its sequel *Barchester Towers*. Both novels are prone to lapse into mock-heroics when dealing with subjects such as evening parties with music and cards or bishops' receptions, and the language employs distant reminiscences of Pope and Cowper in a manner too derivative to be more than fitfully amusing. Rhetorical questions, fine writing, apostrophes to the gentle reader, indifferent parodies of Carlyle and Dickens – all contribute to an instability in the prose that reveals Trollope's twinges of uncertainty in his relationships with his characters and his audience.

It may have partly been a similar lack of assurance that led Trollope to base his plot on a conflict of interests suggested by recent public controversies (referred to several times in the text) over the alleged misappropriation of ecclesiastical charities.[1] His first idea was not an individual but an issue. He had not yet developed that confidence in his characters' ability to look after themselves which was to make plot-making in any rigorous and pre-planned sense unnecessary. Nevertheless, the way in which Trollope viewed the issue is highly characteristic of the even-handed justice of his creative mind. Even though he was prepared to believe that the Church was guilty of diverting funds which should have been used for charitable purposes into its own pocket, he refused to have anything to do with what might have been the Dickensian corollary – 'a bloated parson, with a red nose and all other iniquities, openly neglecting every duty required from him, and living riotously on funds purloined from the poor'. (*Autobiography*, V) Such a resort to caricature to make the case would have involved an unacceptable degree of distortion: 'Satire, though it may exaggerate the vice it lashes, is not justified in creating it in order that it may be lashed.' Thus, the particular clergyman that

Trollope presents as enjoying the doubtful emoluments is not a monster of rapacity but a mild and gentle man who has never thought to question whether his stipend is properly received but who is in his meek way a credit to his order. The attacks on him by the newspaper the *Jupiter* (i.e. *The Times*) are therefore correct in principle, since the abuse is real, but cruel in application, since their object is inoffensive. Characteristically, Trollope saw that there are two sides to every question, both of them reasonable.

What gives *The Warden* its permanent interest is that settlement of the public argument is adjourned in favour of study of the private individual. Archdeacon Grantly, the Warden's son-in-law and as the Bishop's son the effective power in the diocese, sees the attacks of the reformers as an assault on the Church itself, and the *Jupiter* certainly regards the matter as bringing its whole character into modern question. But Mr Harding takes things out of their hands and effectively shelves the issue by resigning his office. He does so because he feels that the reformers' case is sufficiently substantial to make him uneasy in his conscience about living on money to which he may possibly not be entitled. Nevertheless, he does not go over to them, and indeed steadily if somewhat inconsistently supports the Bishop's authority. His extreme step, taken against the advice of most of his friends and relations, is the last thing that he or they would have expected. It comes about because of the pressure put on Mr Harding by the dilemma in which events conspire to place him.

Being in a dilemma is perhaps the most important recurring situation in Trollope's fiction, and *The Warden* is the first of his novels in which its possibilities begin to appear. It is because the Warden has to decide which course of action to take in a state of affairs in which some action must be taken that he, and we, and, one suspects, Trollope himself, discover what he is really like. Strictly, a dilemma is a situation which allows of two possible resolutions, both of them objectionable. One horn of Mr Harding's dilemma is simply that if he is ejected from Hiram's Hospital he and his unmarried daughter will lose £800 a year and a pleasant house and will be reduced to the £150 due to him as vicar of Crabtree Parva. That is a matter of circumstance. The alternative is to stay in office and defy the *Jupiter* and its allies to do their worst. That too is objectionable to Mr Harding – though it might not be so to another – as a matter of temperament. He simply cannot bear it. He finds, as Trollope's heroes are so often to do, that a false position is intolerable. He has, as Trollope's heroes so often have, a thinness of skin which makes the mere discussion of his situation humiliating. It is part of *The Warden*'s argument that newspapers have too much power over private individuals; 'fifty lines of a narrow column' in the *Jupiter* can destroy a man's reputation and equanimity overnight without anyone knowing who wrote them or being able to call their author to account. It is a point that Trollope was to make a number of times in later novels. But any further discussion of the rights and wrongs of the matter is in this case hopelessly compromised by the fact that, of all the men who might be attacked on such grounds, Mr Harding seems to be the most vulnerable; his excessive sensitivity means that he can hardly be taken as a fair sample, a representative case. It is that hyper-sensitivity in the character rather than any late-eighteenth-century sensibility in the author's treatment of him that makes Mr Harding worth attention. This is most fully – and quite unexpectedly – developed in the chapter 'A Long Day in London', which is by far the most absorbing in the novel. Mr Harding has sneaked away from Barchester and the overpowering presence of the Archdeacon in order to explain his intentions to Sir Abraham Haphazard, the legal adviser retained by Dr Grantly. Sir Abraham is the Attorney-General and a busy man, and he cannot be seen before ten o'clock at night. Mr Harding has therefore the whole day to kill and not the least idea how to do it. He is cut off from the conventionally idyllic world of the hospital in its untroubled days and cannot be presented by the author in a context of picturesque prospects and becalmed ecclesiastical retreats. Mr Harding gravitates towards Westminster Abbey, but finds that he is looked at a little oddly as he whiles away the hours; he has a chop at a dirty supper-house that stinks of fish, simply because he can't think where else to go and remembers passing it; and finishes up having a nap over his coffee in, of all places, a 'cigar divan' during which he has some curious dreams. Here, as nowhere else in this novel but in a way that anticipates some of his best work, Trollope follows with sustained concentration the hour-by-hour experience of the character, exposed as he is to all those random impressions and small contingencies that impress themselves so sharply on the mind at times of crisis. The details haven't the hallucinatory reality that Dickens might have given them by metaphoric transmutation, but they are observed with an intensity that perhaps owes something to him.

He found the house easily – just as he had observed it, between the trunks and the cigars. He was rather daunted by the huge quantity of fish which he saw in the window. There were barrels of oysters, hecatombs of lobsters, a few tremendous-looking crabs, and a tub full of pickled salmon; not, however, being aware of any connection between shell-fish and iniquity, he entered, and modestly asked a slatternly woman, who was picking oysters out of a great watery reservoir, whether he could have a mutton chop and a potato.

The woman looked somewhat surprised, but answered in the affirmative, and a slipshod girl ushered him into a long back room, filled with boxes for the accommodation of parties, in one of which he took his seat. In a more miserably forlorn place he could not have found himself: the room smelt of fish, and sawdust, and stale tobacco smoke, with a slight taint of escaped gas; everything was rough, and dirty, and disreputable; the cloth which they put before him was abominable; the knives and forks were bruised, and hacked, and filthy; and everything was impregnated with fish. He had one comfort, however: he was quite alone; there was no one there to look on his dismay; nor was it probable that any one would come to do so . . .

Unknowing as Mr Harding was in the ways of London, he felt that he had somehow selected an ineligible dining-house, and that he had better leave it. It was hardly five o'clock – how was he to pass the time till ten? Five miserable hours! He was already tired, and it was impossible that he should continue walking so long. He thought of getting into an omnibus, and going out to Fulham for the sake of coming back in another: this, however, would be weary work, and as he paid his bill to the woman in the shop, he asked her if there were any place near where he could get a cup of coffee. Though she did keep a shell-fish supper-house, she was very civil, and directed him to the cigar divan on the other side of the street . . .

The place seemed much more suitable to his requirements than the room in which he had dined: there was, to be sure, a strong smell of tobacco, to which he was not accustomed; but after the shell-fish, the tobacco did not seem disagreeable. There were quantities of books, and long rows of sofas. What on earth could be more luxurious than a sofa, a book, and a cup of coffee? An old waiter came up to him, with a couple of magazines and an evening paper. Was ever anything so civil? Would he have a cup of coffee, or would he prefer sherbet? Sherbet! Was he absolutely in an Eastern divan, with the slight addition of all the London periodicals? He had, how-ever, an idea that sherbet should be drunk sitting cross-legged, and as he was not quite up to this, he ordered the coffee.

The coffee came, and was unexceptionable. Why, this divan was a paradise! The civil old waiter suggested to him a game of chess: though a chess player he was not equal to this, so he declined, and putting up his weary legs on the sofa, leisurely sipped his coffee, and turned over the pages of his Blackwood. He might have been so engaged for about an hour, for the old waiter enticed him to a second cup of coffee, when a musical clock began to play. Mr Harding then closed his magazine, keeping his place with his finger, and lay, listening with closed eyes to the clock. Soon the clock seemed to turn into a violoncello, with piano accompaniments, and Mr Harding began to fancy the old waiter was the Bishop of Barchester; he was inexpressibly shocked that the bishop should have brought him his coffee with his own hands; then Dr Grantly came in, with a basket full of lobsters, which he would not be induced to leave downstairs in the kitchen; and then the warden couldn't quite understand why so many people would smoke in the bishop's drawing-room; and so he fell fast asleep, and his dreams wandered away to his accus-tomed stall in Barchester Cathedral, and the twelve old men he was so soon about to leave for ever. (XVI)

The comic but unnerving sense of displacement experienced by Mr Harding in this chapter may seem to run counter to the general snugness of the earlier Barchester novels, where part of the appeal is in the easy adjustment between characters and their environment. But in the longer fictional run Mr Harding's insecurities were to be more productive for Trollope than those too consciously touching moments when father and daughter console each other through their tears or when the Warden bids farewell to his aged bedesmen. In the latter cases, Trollope may well have found the scene affecting himself but he is also clearly manipulating it for effect; the result is bound to seem rhetorical. But in the presentation of the Warden's lonely London wanderings, the gap between narrator and character seems effectively closed. Trollope has become too absorbed in Mr Harding's doings to think about his own. It may be significant that it is *after* this passage of identification that Trollope gives verbatim the two letters of resignation – one formal, one informal – that Mr Harding writes to the Bishop. These are early examples of many such letters that will be written in Trollope's fiction, and, like them, they are convincing because they seem authentic. They sound as if the character had dictated them and Trollope were merely his secretary. Moreover, it seems, in the case of *The Warden*, as if once the understanding between character and author has become complete enough to allow the latter to write the former's letters for him, the novel itself has reached a point of rest. The public issues with which it began have become peripheral; the intimacy with the private man has become paramount; the establishing of that relationship turned out to be what the novel was for. Admittedly the relationship is not sustained in exactly these terms in the later Barsetshire novels, in which Mr Harding tends to revert to type. But it is doubtful if those novels were already in Trollope's head when he wrote *The Warden* – and in any case he did not fully develop the ability to stay in close interior contact with a character for more than one novel until the last two novels in the sequence.

Barchester Towers

The apparent subject of *Barchester Towers* (written 1855–6, published 1857) is a continuation of the ostensible theme of *The Warden*: what is to happen about Hiram's Hospital? But in the second novel the issue is even more decisively handed over to the characters. Trollope no longer looks to them to articulate his own point of view but becomes increasingly content to view the matter through theirs. Hiram's Hospital ceases to be the means of discussing a matter of topical public interest and becomes a nexus of conflict between fictional characters. The question of the Wardenship becomes entangled with the question of who shall be the effective power in Barchester. It continues to be a matter over which the established Tory, high-and-dry Church party in the diocese, embodied in Archdeacon Grantly, is in conflict with the new liberal regime at the Bishop's Palace. But it also becomes the ground over which the Bishop's ambitious chaplain Mr Slope and the Bishop's domineering wife Mrs Proudie struggle for mastery over the abject incumbent. Mr Slope tries to use his influence to reinstate Mr Harding so that he, Mr Slope, shall have a better chance of succeeding with Mr Harding's daughter, now an eligible widow. Mrs Proudie has decided that the office ought to go to the haplessly fecund Quiverfuls, with their fourteen children. The preferment thus gets inextricably entangled with personal relationships and the struggle for personal ascendancy. Trollope here sees for the first time the extraordinarily rich possibilities offered to the novelist by the systems of patronage, as they operated in his time. It is an area in which private motives have clear and immediate public effects, and it was a valuable discovery for a novelist so absorbed in the ways in which the twin pressures of social reality and inner nature combine to direct a man's course.

This more pragmatic approach to the questions raised in *The Warden* gives *Barchester Towers* greater freedom of movement; there is almost a sense of release. This is partly because Trollope now had three volumes at his disposal rather than one. His later one-volume works sometimes show an impressive concentration, but they tend to feel claustrophobic. In *Barchester Towers* Trollope's world has become much wider than it was in *The Warden*, with a larger number of fictive options available to him. He shows a new ease in moving from one centre of interest to another – from the Proudies to the Grantlys, to the Stanhopes, to the Thornes, and so on – while remaining confident of their interconnectedness. The public issues of the day impinge on rather than dominate these people, and the slackening of pressure allows Trollope to bring in a range of characters who are included simply because they interested him. The introduction of the Stanhope family, for instance (briefly mentioned in *The Warden*) shows an urbanity of tone which seems to indicate the author's strengthening confidence in the creative possibilities of his intuitions. It is true that Dr Stanhope has to bring his reluctant family back from their long absence in Italy because he is recalled by a new bishop who will not tolerate such absenteeism, and that this makes a kind of public point. But at the end of the novel, they push off again, so that not very much comes of it. What really interests Trollope is the characters of two of the younger Stanhopes (introduced at some length in Chapter IX). Bertie Stanhope has some artistic talent which he is too indolent to exploit; his bohemianism is offset by his good nature, so that although he has no principles to speak of, he does not become vicious. His cosmopolitanism has made him immune to English inhibition, and the resulting ensemble is both absolutely unreliable and charmingly straightforward. The lives of such useless people were often to absorb Trollope, even when the appeal came to wear rather thin. His appalled fascination with states of endemic idleness – a fascination which may have had much to do with his own inert youth and his fortunate discovery of the life-saving powers of his own industry – is at this early stage touched in lightly. The other interesting member of the family is Bertie's distractingly beautiful sister, who absurdly styles herself 'La Signora Madeline Vesey Neroni' on the strength of what sounds like a shotgun marriage with a shifty Italian captain. She is fond of claiming that the blood of the last of the Neros flows in the veins of their overdressed child; Madeline herself has become crippled in some obscure way, possibly owing to the violence of the decamped husband, and exploits the disability in a way that is both ruthless and rather game. She again is an early example of a type to which Trollope returned in such studies as Madalina Demolines in *The Last Chronicle of Barset* and supremely in Lizzie Eustace in *The Eustace Diamonds*. Although his own explicit morality is always healthily orthodox, Trollope saw that the absence of principle can both charm and be of considerable advantage, and Madeline's enslavement of all the men within eyeshot of the sofa on which she decoratively reclines is here a largely comic indication of the havoc that can be caused by unscrupulous sexual appeal. But although Trollope is quite clear about the inadequacies of the Stanhopes, they are not condemned or even moralized over very much, as one might have expected. It is not just that their absurdities are intended to amuse: they are also allowed to have the qualities of their defects. Bertie is too guileless as well as too indolent to pursue Eleanor Bold and her £1000 a year with the tenacity of genuine self-interest; La Signora, having had as much kick as she wants and is likely to get out of reducing the high-minded Mr Arabin to stammering admiration, resigns him to Mrs Bold out of sheer good nature.

Such a forestalling of the easy judgement becomes a cardinal principle of Trollope's fiction, and his treatment of the Archdeacon at the beginning of *Barchester Towers* is a classical example of it. Dr Grantly is kneeling at the bedside of his dying father trying to stop himself from calculating his chances of succeeding him as bishop. In the event, through the collapse of the government likely to be favourable to him, political change frustrates private ambition. His struggles are viewed by Trollope with sympathy – a sympathy perhaps increased by the fact that, at the end of *The Warden*, he had apologized for the poor light in which the Archdeacon had hitherto been seen; the feeling that Dr Grantly was a better man than that novel was quite able to give him credit for is characteristic of Trollope's sense of his characters' claims. Anticipating protest from severe readers against the heartless worldliness of the Archdeacon's speculations, Trollope says 'Many will think that he was wicked to grieve for the loss of episcopal power, wicked to have coveted it, nay, wicked even to have thought about it, in the way and at the moments he had done so.' His reply is sturdily evasive in a manner with which readers of Trollope become very familiar: 'With such censures I cannot profess that I completely agree.' His defence of the Archdeacon is based on the premise that it is natural for men in any line to be ambitious and it would be inhuman to expect clergymen to be exempt from such feelings. 'If we look to our clergymen to be more than men, we shall probably teach ourselves to think that they are less, and can hardly hope to raise the character of the pastor by denying him the right to entertain the aspirations of a man." (I) The argument is turned back – 'Our archdeacon was worldly – who among us is not so?' – in a way that is not admonitory, but which rather implies that Dr Grantly is no more guilty than the reader feels himself to be. To say that Dr Grantly is simply like us is in effect to establish his innocence: we know that *we* mean no harm.

The confidence with which his readers come to expect Trollope to be not merely narrowly just but broadly humane towards his characters is one of the reasons why they find his fiction so reassuring. In *Barchester Towers* Mr Slope is in a sense the villain of the piece; not only do his machinations provide much of the narrative momentum but he is also clearly meant to be objectionable. When introduced, he is presented in unpleasant terms that do not differ greatly in technique from, say, Dickens's portrayal of Mr Chadband's physical appearance – 'His nose . . . is pronounced straight and well-formed; though I myself should have liked it better did it not possess a somewhat spongy, porous appearance, as though it had been cleverly formed out of a red coloured cork.' (IV) The authorial intrusion here – 'I never could endure to shake hands with Mr Slope' – is gauche, and the tone less generous than it later becomes. In fact, by Chapter XV Mr Slope is being apologized for on lines very similar to those which Trollope uses to exculpate the Archdeacon: 'And here the author must beg it to be remembered that Mr Slope was not in all things a bad man. His motives, like those of most men, were mixed; and though his conduct was generally very different from that which we would wish to praise, it was actuated perhaps as often as that of the majority of the world by a desire to do his duty.' Trollope never comes to like Mr Slope nor are we meant to do so, but the necessity for the purposes of the novel of seeing things as he saw them gradually enforces some understanding. Admittedly, Mr Slope has indignities visited on him by both author and character: his ear is boxed by Mrs Bold, and his letter and proposal to her in the tender-pious vein are too close to burlesque for comfort. They give him a degree of fatuity that is hard to reconcile with the scenes in the Bishop's study, where Mr Slope battles it out with Mrs Proudie with a resourcefulness that says much for his shrewdness and penetration as well as everything for his sense of self-interest.

Mr Slope's discomfiture at Mrs Bold's hands occurs at the Ullathorne party, the full account of which occupies eight chapters; it has been preceded by a comparable but earlier incident at Mrs Proudie's less lavishly described reception, in which Bertie Stanhope's attempt to move the sofa on which his sister is reclining ends disastrously when the castor catches Mrs Proudie's lace train and carries away 'there is no saying how much of her garniture'. In both cases Trollope has recourse to the kind of mock-epic figures already employed in *The Warden* in order to underline the comedy of the situations. The idiom, as used by the author – 'So, when a granite battery is raised . . . But, anon, a small spark is applied to the treacherous fusee . . .', and so on – is too weary to have any force and moreover diminishes the characters. Oddly enough, however, it works well enough when the characters themselves are driven to it:

> 'Unhand it, sir!' said Mrs Proudie. From what scrap of dramatic poetry she had extracted the word cannot be said; but it must have rested on her memory, and now seemed opportunely dignified for the occasion.
>
> 'I'll fly to the looms of the fairies to repair the damage, if you'll only forgive me,' said Ethelbert, still on his knees.
>
> 'Unhand it, sir!' said Mrs Proudie, with redoubled emphasis, and all but furious wrath. This allusion to the fairies was a direct mockery, and intended to turn her into ridicule. So at least it seemed to her. 'Unhand it, sir!' she almost screamed.
>
> 'It's not me; it's the cursed sofa,' said Bertie, looking imploringly in her face, and holding up both his hands to show that he was not touching her belongings, but still remaining on his knees. (XI)

Mrs Proudie's 'Unhand it' has a Lady Bracknell-ish inevitability beside which Trollope's own earlier invocation of the wrath of Juno seems gratuitous.

At such times Trollope is still inclined to fuss; his remarks after Eleanor's battery of Mr Slope are quite flustered – 'it is to be feared that every well-bred reader of these pages will lay the book down with disgust . . . She is a hoyden, one will say . . .' (XL) The mock-heroic is again resorted to ('But how shall I sing the divine wrath of Mr Slope') and is again a sign of a momentary loss of control, an uncertainty of tone. It is partly that Trollope is not yet always sure how his audience will react to a given situation, and partly because he has not yet written himself so deeply into the situation as to have become indifferent to considerations of effect. The uneasy edging of both incidents into something that momentarily approaches farce was not to be Trollope's best way.

Similarly, his nervous reprimanding of his characters too often seems unnecessarily anxious. Authorial comment on the thoughts and doings of his personages was always to remain part of the Trollopian method, but it later becomes more subtle and less supervisory. In *Barchester Towers* the habit of apostrophizing the characters is still liable to appear, and this too is really another form of chivvying.

Nevertheless, the extended treatment of the Bishop's reception and of the Ullathorne sports represent a marked technical advance for Trollope in some respects. They show his emerging ability to bring disparate groups of characters into contact with each other, to envisage their encounters dramatically, and to cope with the logistics of a great social occasion. These became important assets to him as a novelist, and they help greatly to substantiate the sense of Trollope's created world as thickly populated. Some of the guests at Ullathorne – the Lookalofts and the Greenacres – are too obviously extras hired for the day, but they do not seriously compromise Trollope's success in bringing together elements of what appears to be a genuine community. Moreover, it is one that, even in the novel's third volume, seems to be full of possibilities. *Barchester Towers* contains many narrative hints that Trollope was later to take up and whose potential was no doubt obscure to him at this time. 'The poor curate of a small Cornish parish' who keeps Arabin on the *via media* of Anglicanism at a time when he is tempted to follow Newman to Rome must be the first mention of the there unnamed figure that was to grow into that of Mr Crawley, hero of *The Last Chronicle of Barset*; the Archdeacon's daughter Griselda (now the elder, although the younger in *The Warden*) catches Trollope's eye briefly here, before becoming an important figure later; Lady de Courcy makes an aristocratic appearance at the Ullathorne sports, and the Thorne estate itself is clearly ripe for development. To extend the Barsetshire series Trollope had only to dip into these densely peopled pages to find abundant material.

But *Barchester Towers* not only gives us for the first time that sense of a social world which is multifarious and proliferating in a way that plausibly imitates the real world (in which we know, as Henry James put it in the Preface to *Roderick Hudson*, that 'really, universally, relations stop nowhere'). It also begins to evolve a vocabulary for charting the states of mind of the individuals in that world which can effectively register Trollope's perceptions of them. As was to become customary with him, Trollope refuses to base the appeal of his novel on suspense: 'what can be the worth of that solicitude which a peep into the third volume can utterly dissipate?' He candidly reveals in Chapter XV that Eleanor Bold is not destined to marry either Mr Slope or Bertie Stanhope (there is usually, as here, a certain disingenuousness in such disavowals: the man whom Eleanor does finally marry is not named, nor can he easily be since he has not yet been introduced). When, however, Trollope says that 'Our doctrine is, that the author and the reader should move along together in full confidence with each other', he seems really to mean not merely that circumstantial facts should not be kept back, but also that psychological facts should be made fully available. Such suspense as *Barchester Towers* affords is partly caused by the struggle for power between Mrs Proudie and Mr Slope and is partly due to our interest in the stages by which Eleanor and Arabin come together. These developments are not perceptible to their friends and relations, so that their engagement causes much surprise. It is no surprise to us because each stage of the relationship has been monitored by Trollope. The kind of language which he now finds useful in this task indicates a significant development.

When Eleanor is first introduced to Mr Arabin 'they were soon on comfortable terms together; and *had she thought about it, she would have thought that* . . . Mr Arabin would not have been a bad addition to the Stanhope family party'. (XXI) Trollope is clearly trying to get at a level of reaction that is subliminal rather than conscious. A few chapters later, Eleanor is piqued when Arabin pays attention to the Signora. She is not in love with him – the idea has not even crossed her mind; she is in a state when 'she could not but like him . . . And yet she could not quite like him.' (XXIV) At any rate she is certainly less devoted to the memory of her late husband. In registering this small shift of feeling, Trollope comments in a casual aside which yet prophetically marks out part of the territory which he was to explore as perhaps no previous English novelist had yet done: 'How many shades there are between love and indifference, and how little the graduated scale is understood!' When Mr Slope writes to Eleanor virtually promising her father's reinstatement as Warden of the Hospital, he recalls the day when he found her at home with her hair dishevelled through playing with her child, and adds a postscript on her 'beautiful long silken tresses'. Gentlemen, as Trollope reminds us, do not write to ladies about their tresses. Trollope's account of Eleanor's reaction to the letter again tries to indicate reactions that hardly form themselves as conscious responses:

> Lastly she arrived at the tresses and felt a qualm of disgust. She looked up in the glass, and there they were before her, long and silken, certainly, and very beautiful. I will not say but that she knew them to be so, but she felt angry with them and brushed them roughly and carelessly. She crumpled the letter up with angry violence, and resolved, almost without thinking of it, that she would not show it to her father. She would merely tell him the contents of it. (XXVIII)

However repulsive Mr Slope is to Eleanor, she finds the suspicion that he is not so almost harder to bear. The conviction of the Grantly party and even of Arabin that her commonplace civility to the objectionable chaplain signifies a covert predilection creates in her an intolerable sense of injury and injustice; she can no more bear being put in a false position in private life than her father could in the more public circumstances of *The Warden*. But she is stung into an articulacy that makes matters worse by the fact she already perceives that Arabin loves her. Nevertheless 'Eleanor could not bring herself to abandon her revenge. She did not ask herself whether or not she would ultimately accept his love. She did not even acknowledge to herself that she now perceived it with pleasure.' (XXX) The negatives here clearly tell their suppressed tale. When the Signora summons Eleanor to tell her that she has something interesting to say about Arabin, Eleanor's reaction is revealingly physical: 'Her blood was rushing about her body she knew not how or why. She felt as though she were swinging in her chair; and she knew that she was not only red in the face, but also almost suffocated with heat.' (XLV) And the final agreement of the lovers – overlaid as it is by the embarrassments of 'When the ivy has found its tower . . .' (XLIX) etc., is recorded as much through their touchingly tentative gestures and looks as through their language. The moment is satisfying not so much for sentimental reasons as because it is the final stage in a process of feeling which the author has registered with sufficient delicacy to convey its human truth. This process is made possible in *Barchester Towers* by allowing the characters concerned to live off such meagre scraps of plot as the author throws in their way from time to time while leaving them largely free to their own devices.

Doctor Thorne

Too strong a direction from a pre-ordained plot allows the character less freedom to follow the emerging logic of his or her own nature, and in the next novel in the Barsetshire series, the increasing psychological subtlety of Trollope's method has to struggle with a certain element of coercion in the form of a predetermined story. The story of *Doctor Thorne* was not in fact Trollope's own but his brother's, and it is an indication of his continuing diffidence that he should have been prepared after fourteen years of authorship to adopt it (the novel was written in 1857 and 1858, partly while on a journey to Egypt on Post Office business, and published in the latter year). The bare bones of the plot have a stronger 'period' feeling than is usually the case with Trollope, whose novels are so often so immersed in their own time that, paradoxically, they swim all the more effortlessly free of it. The central theme is of the kind hearts and coronets type (the phrase is after all Tennyson's). As Trollope explains in a more than usually clumsy exposition (for which he apologizes), Mary Thorne is the illegitimate daughter of an emigrated mother, brought up by her natural uncle Dr Thorne. Despite some egalitarian tendencies, the doctor is the trusted friend and adviser of the Greshams of Greshamsbury, the first com-moners of Barsetshire and related by marriage to the grand de Courcys. Frank Gresham, the son and heir, is enjoined to marry money to restore the depleted family fortunes, but he wants Mary, despite her obscure birth and lack of cash. Her origins are finally made up for by her inheritance of the wealth made by Sir Roger Scatcherd, the railway millionaire, when both he and his feeble son successively die of drink. Frank has a few faint twinges of dis-loyalty to Mary – at the behest of his mother he half-heartedly pursues Miss Dunstable, an agreeable heiress though not in the first flush of youth – but he nowhere shows the kind of agonies of indecision and uncertainties of principle that make such later heroes in similar positions (as Frank Greystock in *The Eustace Diamonds*) reasonably interesting. Frank Gresham has one striking moment of aggression – an assault on Mr Moffat who has jilted his sister – but this violence is quite unrelated to anything else in his character. The outcome of the story is visible early on, and it is hard not to feel that by the third volume Trollope has been driven to delaying tactics in order to keep the novel going until the allotted space is filled. Mr Oriel is introduced as a 'new character' as late as Chapter XXXII, but proves not to have very much mileage in him. A chapter of letters (XXXVII) which seem half-heartedly to parody the old epistolary novel procedure – and which certainly do not have the impress of their writers in the way that Mr Harding's letters did – helps to pad things out, but time tends to hang heavily in the novel's later pages. The characters seem too often to be repeating gestures that they have already made: Mary's readiness to renounce Frank if he should wish it in Chapter XLII simply endorses what she has formerly confessed to Frank's sister in Chapter XXXIII – ' "I am pledged to him; but he is not pledged to me." '

The relative listlessness of some of the writing may well be due to the fact that Trollope's received plot inhibited his imagination because it restricted the possibilities open to his characters. It substituted one kind of suspense which seemed to Trollope factitious for another kind which contributes everything to the life of his fiction. The crude narrative question that *Doctor Thorne* poses is: how long will it be and what do the characters have to go through before the hero gets the heroine and the heroine gets the money? The kind of question Trollope preferred to consider would be more like this: the circumstances being what they are and the protagonists being as they are, what is the logical and psychological effect produced by the combination? Michael Sadleir suggested, in his strangely enthusiastic critique of the novel, that Mary Thorne embodies 'the true essence of the Trollope heroine', but she seems rather an early prototype of the species – deceptively demure, fiercely loyal, passionately conventional.[2] She is not an individual in the manner of the best of her successors, and her approximation to an ideal of her period is almost bound to deprive her of personality.

Mary's uncle, the novel's eponymous hero, is in effect her father,

and there are some sentimental moments in which the emotion of
his quasi-paternal function is made the most of – again, very much
in the manner of the period. But the situation into which he is put
by the plot is one which condemns him to a passivity or at least to a
waiting game which is at odds with his own nature, as far as
Trollope conceives it. He seems most himself when intermittently
foreshadowing the combative resistance to authority that Trollope
was later to relish in such figures as Dr Wortle of *Dr Wortle's School*.
In his duel with Lady Arabella in Chapter XXVI Dr Thorne
expresses himself with the heady articulacy that often comes to
Trollope's characters when they experience the luxury not only of
being in the right but also of finding the right words at the right
time.

> 'I will allow no one to interfere with her; no one, Lady
> Arabella. She has suffered very greatly from imputations
> which you have most unjustly thrown on her. It was, how-
> ever, your undoubted right to turn her out of your house if
> you thought fit; – though, as a woman who had known her
> for so many years, you might, I think, have treated her with
> more forbearance. That, however, was your right, and you
> exercised it. There your privilege stops; yes, and must stop,
> Lady Arabella. You shall not persecute her here, on the only
> spot of ground she can call her own.'
>
> 'Persecute her, Doctor Thorne! You do not mean to say
> that I have persecuted her?'
>
> 'Ah! but I do mean to say so. You do persecute her, and
> would continue to do so did I not defend her. It is not
> sufficient that she is forbidden to enter your domain – and so
> forbidden with the knowledge of all the country round – but
> you must come here also with the hope of interrupting all the
> innocent pleasures of her life. Fearing lest she should be
> allowed even to speak of your son, to hear a word of him
> through his own sister, you would put her in prison, tie her
> up, keep her from the light of day –'
>
> 'Doctor Thorne! how can you –'
>
> But the doctor was not to be interrupted.
>
> 'It never occurs to you to tie him up, to put him in prison.
> No; he is the heir to Greshamsbury; he is your son, an earl's

grandson. It is only natural, after all, that he should throw a few foolish words at the doctor's niece. But she! it is an offence not to be forgiven on her part that she should, however unwillingly, have been forced to listen to them! Now understand me, Lady Arabella; if any of your family come to my house I shall be delighted to welcome them: if Mary should meet any of them elsewhere I shall be delighted to hear of it. Should she tell me tomorrow that she was engaged to marry Frank, I should talk over the matter with her, quite coolly, solely with a view to her interest, as would be my duty; feeling, at the same time, that Frank would be lucky in having such a wife. Now you know my mind, Lady Arabella. It is so I should do my duty; – you can do yours as you may think fit.'

Lady Arabella had by this time perceived that she was not destined on this occasion to gain any great victory. She, however, was angry as well as the doctor. It was not the man's vehemence that provoked her so much as his evident determination to break down the prestige of her rank, and place her on a footing in no respect superior to his own. He had never before been so audaciously arrogant; and, as she moved towards the door, she determined in her wrath that she would never again have confidential intercourse with him in any relation of life whatsoever.

The appeal of such scenes (of which the greatest is Mr Crawley's interview with the Proudies) perhaps relates to the common fantasy – sometimes known as *esprit d'escalier* – in which one reorganizes and rehearses the unsatisfactory and recalcitrant dialogues of real life into idealized exchanges more soothing to the ego. But in Dr Thorne's case the adumbrated internal conflict between his democratic impulses and his secret pride nevertheless at the Thorne family connection (he is a cousin of the Thornes of Ullathorne) comes to nothing much, and indeed, his difficulties in behaving with a proper degree of scruple over his duties as Sir Roger's executor are presented by Trollope with some repetitiveness and little dramatic resource. A satisfactory balance between conflicts of will with the external world (rival medical practitioners included) and internal doubts is never securely established.

The doctor is certainly not studied with any kind of searchingness in his professional capacity. He arouses local opposition because – unlike Lydgate in *Middlemarch* – he insists on dispensing as well as prescribing his medicines – but his professional life and views are not philosophically pondered and related to their effect on his immediate society as Lydgate's are. Indeed, the description of Greshamsbury itself, 'the fine old English gentleman's seat', in the opening chapter and the complacent accompanying digression on the superior character of English landed interests, demonstrate how undistinguished Trollope's exposition is. His power of relating the individual landscape or habitation to the general experience was never to be great, although he came to write powerfully of the owner's attachment to his own land. His perfunctory treatment of Greshamsbury's architectural features does not suggest a fine awareness of the historical dimension or a more than conventional aesthetic sense. A comparison, again, between the opening chapter of *Felix Holt* and the uneasily Carlylean passage in *Doctor Thorne* in which Trollope expatiates on the decline of the town of Courcy due to the coming of the railway (Chapter XV) hardly shows him to advantage, even when the difference in literary pretension is allowed for.[3]

The figure of Sir Roger Scatcherd might seem to offer a favourable opportunity to ponder social significances: as a self-made millionaire who began as a mason and seized the opportunity to get rich through the huge contracts offered by the development of the railway network through provincial England, Scatcherd had clear contemporary analogues. But Trollope treats his career more as a recognized fact of life than as a prophetic portent of the age. The plot requires Scatcherd to have made a great deal of money which he cannot live to enjoy because it must go to Mary Thorne. He is put out of the way by delirium tremens. His dying words sound the kind of awful warning that would be expected in contemporary melodrama of a Cruikshankian cast:

> 'And, doctor, when you see a glass at his mouth, dash it down; thrust it down, though you thrust out the teeth with it. When you see that, Thorne, tell him of his father – tell him what his father might have been but for that; tell him how his father died like a beast, because he could not keep himself from drink.' (XXV)

Nevertheless, as with Dr Thorne himself, there are moments when Scatcherd's situation oddly anticipates states of mind that were to interest Trollope later. Scatcherd's account of the personal isolation his success has brought him and the way it has led him to the reliable friendship of the bottle (Chapter X) is momentarily impressive; it connects with the characteristic Trollopian terror of social alienation. Scatcherd's extraordinary career, fathered on him by Tom Trollope's plot, does not prevent him from expressing that common longing to feel at home in a society in which one has a recognized place which Anthony Trollope understood so well. This is why Scatcherd minds so intensely (although he affects not to) his unseating through a petition following his election to Parliament. For him, as much later for Melmotte in *The Way We Live Now*, being in the House at least offsets the self-made man's sense of being, when all is said and done, a social leper.

Miss Dunstable is the daughter of a self-made man, and Mr Moffat – who is briefly the intended of one of the Gresham girls – is the son of a tailor. Miss Dunstable has got her money from a product called the Oil of Lebanon, but although she herself clearly offers possibilities as a personality (taken up in the next Barsetshire novel), the sources of her money are not investigated; both Trollope and Miss Dunstable are studiously vague about what the oil is claimed to do and how it is made and sold – omissions that would not have satisfied the Balzac who in *César Birroteau* studied the decline and fall of a *marchand-parfumeur* with such close attention to production processes and market considerations. Trollope is prepared to take an interest (usually jocose in tone) in tradesmen when they provide services (as Mr Neefit, the maker of riding breeches, does in *Ralph the Heir*) because this puts them in a personal relationship with those they serve, but none of his novels deals directly with manufacture.

What is clearly under some scrutiny in *Doctor Thorne* is the question of misalliance. Frank's marriage with Mary is theoretically a misalliance, but it is all right in the end because of the money she brings, and because the love between them is the real thing. As Frank points out, there is nothing in theory to choose between someone of his rank marrying Mary and marrying Miss Dunstable – or between one of his sisters marrying either the socially climbing Mr Moffat or the respectable attorney that she finally does accept.

Lady Arabella's more extreme anxieties on behalf of rank are certainly disapproved of by the novelist, but she herself – insofar as she is genuinely activated by maternal feeling and conditioned by her environment – is not made to look absurd. However, the only clear line that can be got from *Doctor Thorne* on such questions of social disparity is simply that one ought to trust one's best moral feelings. Mary realizes that the worldly considerations that animate Lady Arabella do have some force, the world being what it is, and although she stoutly opposes them in the show-down between the two women in Chapter XLII, she acknowledges their cogency by incorporating them in spirit in her subsequent letter to Frank, offering to release him from the engagement should he find it prudent. But the fact that the world is the world does not in her view absolve her from the obligation of acting according to the highest standards of disinterestedness, and it is in the effects of this integrity that the interest of her situation – sketchily developed as it is – lies.

Framley Parsonage

The struggle within the personality created by the conflicting pressures of social aspirations, emotional desire, and the wish to preserve one's integrity are presented much more subtly in *Framley Parsonage*, the next novel in the Barsetshire series (written 1859–60, published 1861). The book was written under great pressure: it was commissioned at very short notice for the first number of the new *Cornhill*, edited by Thackeray. Unlike Thackeray or Dickens, Trollope did not make a practice of beginning to serialize a work before he had finished writing it, but this opportunity was clearly too good to be missed. Trollope concedes in the *Autobiography* that publication in instalments made him particularly aware of the need to maintain the reader's interest, and the texture of *Framley Parsonage* is noticeably more even than that of its predecessors. It also seems likely that it positively benefited from lack of fore-thought.

There was no time to work out an elaborate plot – Trollope began writing the book on the train back to Ireland after making his deal with George Smith, the publisher of the *Cornhill* – and

Trollope's account of the way the book's materials were assembled shows how open-ended the whole affair was:

> I had got into my head an idea of what I meant to write, – a morsel of the biography of an English clergyman who should not be a bad man, but one led into temptation by his own youth and by the unclerical accidents of the life of those around him. The love of his sister for the young lord was an adjunct necessary, because there must be love in a novel. And then by placing Framley Parsonage near Barchester, I was able to fall back upon my old friends, Mrs Proudie and the Archdeacon. Out of these slight elements I fabricated a hodge-podge in which the real plot consisted at last simply of a girl refusing to marry the man she loved till the man's friends agreed to accept her lovingly. Nothing could be less efficient or artistic. (VIII)

A comparison of these points of departure with the completed novel indicates how far Trollope was from anticipating some of the book's most interesting developments: there is nothing in this sketchy scenario about the man who actually leads the clergyman astray, Mr Sowerby; nothing about the eventual alliance between Miss Dunstable and Dr Thorne; nothing about the plight of Mr Crawley; it isn't even clear that it is the young lord's mother rather than merely his friends who has to accept the girl of his choice. As it turned out, the situation of the tempted clergyman was not so much the principal subject as the point of entry into a fictional world in which his affairs are bound up with and therefore lead us on to the affairs of others in a way that seems plausibly to reflect the natural interconnectedness of life.

Such transitions were made easier by Trollope's renewed refusal to regard clergymen as a race apart. In *Barchester Towers* Mr Arabin had made the mistake of thinking that, as far as he was concerned, 'happiness in this world is not a necessity', and had tried to remain indifferent to the appeal of the good things of the world – promotion, rich livings, a wife and children, comfort, 'the allotted share of worldly bliss'. But 'at the age of forty he discovered that he was not fit to work in the spirit of an apostle'; he found he wanted what other people wanted. Such desires earn Trollope's sympathy, not his censure. He says in *Framley Parsonage* that 'Clergymen are subject to the same passions as other men; and, as far as I can see, give way to them, in one line or in another, almost as frequently.' (IV) The point is not made satirically but in order to deflect unrealistic expectations. Trollope's view that worldliness is normal and not necessarily something to be ashamed of means that when he shows clergymen with their minds on earthly things he registers the inconsistency but does not appear to be catching them out (except when they themselves insist on being pharisaical). As a result, the troubles of his clerical characters are not ones which we can comfortably dissociate ourselves from on the grounds that they are not as other men, and certainly not like us.

Mark Robarts, the vicar of Framley, appears at the beginning of the story to have all those advantages for which Arabin sighed: a good living (£900 p.a.), a pretty parsonage with a dutiful wife to go in it, a bountiful patron in Lady Lufton – and all by his mid-twenties. A little cloyed by such felicities and becoming aware of a larger social theatre beyond the parish boundaries, he accepts invitations from Mr Sowerby and then from the Duke of Omnium. These contacts do indeed prove rewarding, since through them he adds to his living a stall at Barchester (another £600 p.a.). But, as his boyhood friend Lord Lufton has found, such men as Sowerby are dangerous, and Robarts – under the joint pressure of Sowerby's personal ascendancy and his own covert social ambition – signs a couple of bills on Sowerby's behalf, which leave him not only deeply in debt but also with the understandable feeling that he has betrayed his calling. He certainly feels keenly the rebuke of Mr Crawley, a fellow pastor, and at one point is worried lest he be considered guilty of simony, a specifically ecclesiastical offence. But it is also the case that when Robarts finally refuses to put his name to any more bills, he upbraids Sowerby for not living up to his position in the world. Sowerby should have remembered that 'the resentment of a gentleman is terrible to a gentleman'; he has let Robarts down because he has failed to act with a true gentleman's sense of scruple and honour; he does not deserve his status. There is nothing inherently clerical about Robarts's protest, no special appeal on behalf of the cloth; the dialogue between them in Chapter XXXIII could be between any two Trollopian characters with the necessary means and education. Indeed, their dealings prefigure many subsequent transactions in Trollope's fiction, made in entirely secular contexts.

A contemporary reader, led by the title to expect an earnest scene of clerical life, might well have felt that Trollope's treatment of Mr Robarts's situation was – considering his pastoral obligations – almost flippantly negligent. But although he was adamant about the healthy and morally uncontaminating tendency of his fiction, Trollope avoided the sort of exemplary situation that is obviously contrived by didactic purpose. Like *Doctor Thorne*, *Framley Parsonage* provides the materials for and to some extent functions as a thorough critique of worldliness, but the later novel is the more successful – and the more characteristically Trollopian – because the study of personality so evidently comes to prevail over the demands of theme. Miss Dunstable's situation is a case in point. It is clear from the vitality of her first appearance (Chapter III) – when she is allowed to air and share Trollope's own indignation at the inequalities of clerical incomes – that he has become thoroughly familiar with her manner and tone. But it is not simply a question of reviving a style of chat first evolved for Miss Dunstable's parrying of Frank Gresham's faint-hearted advances in *Doctor Thorne*; she is not here on show as an example of the sort of thing that is meant by marrying money. The analysis of her situation at the end of Chapter XVII has a clarity of exposition that shows that Trollope now fully understands her particular internal dilemma:

> Miss Dunstable was by nature kind, generous, and open-hearted; but she was living now very much with people on whom kindness, generosity, and open-heartedness were thrown away. She was clever also, and could be sarcastic; and she found that those qualities told better in the world around her than generosity and an open heart. And so she went on from month to month, and year to year, not progressing in a good spirit as she might have done, but still carrying within her bosom a warm affection for those she could really love. And she knew that she was hardly living as she should live, – that the wealth which she affected to despise was eating into the soundness of her character, not by its splendour, but by the style of life which it had seemed to produce as a necessity. She knew that she was gradually becoming irreverent,

scornful, and prone to ridicule; but yet, knowing this, and hating it, she hardly knew how to break from it. She had seen so much of the blacker side of human nature that blackness no longer startled her as it should do. She had been the prize at which so many ruined spendthrifts had aimed, so many pirates had endeavoured to run her down while sailing in the open waters of life, that she had ceased to regard such attempts on her money-bags as unmanly or over-covetous. She was content to fight her own battle with her own weapons, feeling secure in her own strength of purpose and strength of wit.

Some few friends she had whom she really loved, – among whom her inner self could come out and speak boldly what it had to say with its own true voice. And the woman who thus so spoke was very different from that Miss Dunstable whom Mrs Proudie courted, and the Duke of Omnium fêted, and Mrs Harold Smith claimed as her bosom friend. If only she could find among such one special companion on whom her heart might rest, who would help her to bear the heavy burdens of her world! But where was she to find such a friend? – she with her keen wit, her untold money, and loud laughing voice. Everything about her was calculated to attract those whom she could not value, and to scare from her the sort of friend to whom she would fain have linked her lot.

Her position is in fact an inversion of the staple Trollope problem – how to reconcile the demands of one's social self with one's inner emotional needs. The usual temptation is to sacrifice love in order to get on in the world. Miss Dunstable's vast wealth means that she has already got on; does that mean giving up ideas of love? Her London evening party, which is attended by a substantial Barsetshire contingent from the Duke of Omnium downwards and by such influential London figures as the editor of the *Jupiter*, represents a clear pinnacle of social success. At the end of it she is torn between a sense of gratification and an urge towards self-condemnation – divided feelings that, significantly, she discusses with Dr Thorne. Miss Dunstable is shrewd enough to realize that her only way out of her dilemma is to marry someone who is entirely indifferent to her money, who neither wants it for himself

nor is put off by it. The only available candidate with the right
degree of disinterestedness is Dr Thorne, also brought forward
from the previous Barsetshire novel though not here developed so
interestingly. His already established integrity shows itself as
inhibition – how can he bear the imputation of chasing one
of the richest women in England? – and the couple have to be
manoeuvred into matrimony by the doctor's daughter. Miss Dunstable's acceptance of Dr Thorne's proposal is dramatized almost
laconically by Trollope (Chapter XXXIX). By this time he does
not need to spell out the heiress's internal feelings: we can fully
imagine them because she herself is now fully imagined by her
creator.

The other candidate for Miss Dunstable's cash is Mr Sowerby,
who needs it badly. In theory, he is the 'rogue' of the novel, since it
is he who leads Mark Robarts astray and has been guilty of some
sharp dealings with Lord Lufton. He certainly exhibits a callousness
informed by all the energy of self-preservation. At the same time,
he is capable of great good nature 'and willing to move heaven and
earth to do a friend a good turn' – as indeed he does in getting Mark
Robarts his prebendal stall. Trollope's sense of human reality
would not allow him to be satisfied with melodramatic motivation,
and the conflicting internal impulses of his 'villains' are allowed to
benefit from his scrutiny just as fully as those of his 'heroes' –
indeed, in much of his best work such labels come to have a merely
nominal significance. There is a fascination about Sowerby which
accounts both for his power over Robarts and his appeal for the
novelist. Trollope here grasps the Balzacian truth that debt is
exhilarating: 'The habitual debtor goes along jaunty and with elas-
tic step, almost enjoying the excitement of his embarrassments.
There was Mr Sowerby himself; who ever saw a cloud on his
brow? It made one almost in love with ruin to be in his company.'
(XII) Sowerby's fecklessness gives him style: even when financial
collapse is imminent, he still takes a cab rather than walk from one
side of Oxford Street to the other. Nevertheless, what impresses
Trollope most about Sowerby's self-imposed ruin is not how disgracefully improvident he has been or how sparklingly resilient,
but how wretched he must feel. Sowerby's misery and sense of
deprivation at the loss of Chaldicotes, the estate that has been in his
family for centuries, is studied with particular intentness in Chapter

XXXVII, in which Sowerby spends a couple of days in the old house alone.

There were no lights in the windows now, and no voices came from the stables; no dogs barked, and all was dead and silent as the grave. During the greater portion of those two days he sat alone within the house, almost unoccupied. He did not even open his letters, which lay piled on a crowded table in the small breakfast parlour in which he sat; for the letters of such men come in piles, and there are few of them which are pleasant in the reading. There he sat, troubled with thoughts which were sad enough, now and then moving to and fro the house, but for the most part occupied in thinking over the position to which he had brought himself . . .

It was a melancholy, dreary place now, that big house of Chaldicotes; and though the woods were all green with their early leaves and the garden thick with flowers, they also were melancholy and dreary. The lawns were untrimmed and weeds were growing through the gravel, and here and there a cracked Dryad, tumbled from her pedestal, and sprawling in the grass, gave a look of disorder to the whole place. The wooden trellis-work was shattered here and bending there, the standard rose-trees were stooping to the ground, and the leaves of the winter still encumbered the borders. Late in the evening of the second day Mr Sowerby strolled out, and went through the gardens into the wood. Of all the inanimate things of the world this wood of Chaldicotes was the dearest to him. He was not a man to whom his companions gave much credit for feelings or thoughts akin to poetry, but here, out in the Chace, his mind would be almost poetical. While wandering among the forest trees, he became susceptible of the tenderness of human nature: he would listen to the birds singing, and pick here and there a wild flower on his path. He would watch the decay of the old trees and the progress of the young, and make pictures in his eyes of every turn in the wood. He would mark the colour of a bit of road as it dipped into a dell, and then, passing through a water-course, rose brown, rough, irregular, and beautiful against the bank on the other side. And then he would sit and think of his old family: how they had roamed there time out of mind in those Chaldicotes woods, father and son and grandson in regular succession, each giving them over, without blemish or decrease, to his successor. So he would sit; and so he did sit even now, and, thinking of these things, wished that he had never been born.

The moral of Sowerby's ruin could not be more obvious and unexceptionable, but, in the face of this attentive registration of his feelings, the moral hardly seems to matter.

A more plausible area in the book in which to look for those 'clever' touches which Trollope's early reviewers particularly noted would be that dealing with the continued fortunes of the Grantly family. The Archdeacon himself is in subdued form in *Framley Parsonage*, partly as a consequence of the novel's metropolitan leanings – he is bound to be a smaller man in the capital than down in Barchester – but chiefly because his wife emerges as the more purposefully worldly of the two, since she has a daughter to marry. Griselda Grantly's statuesque beauty and cool style are highly marketable, and her mother is encouraged to feel that Lord Lufton is no more than her due – a sentiment shared by Lady Lufton who sees in Griselda a suitably aristocratic ornament to preside over her son's patrician board. The plan comes to nothing because although Lord Lufton's affections are engaged elsewhere the possibility of his rivalship stings the normally undemonstrative Lord Dumbello into an offer which he honours despite a curious little trip to Paris before the happy day (the episode is perhaps chiefly there to provide a small flurry of activity to fill out the later chapters). Dumbello is broadly treated by Trollope, but Griselda is looked at in a more inconclusive way, as if Trollope – though sure enough of the type involved – did not yet quite know what to make of this example of it.

Part of Trollope's difficulty in getting at Griselda may lie in her lack of intensity; she only shows animation when dancing (when it is difficult to suppress it entirely), when considering personal appearance, and when scoring off the Grantlys' old rivals, the Proudies. Trollope says in a revealing aside that Griselda 'never troubled herself much in thinking about other people's thoughts', but her egotism is not rebuked by authorial sarcasm. It is as if

Trollope were not yet sure how damaging her self-centredness would turn out to be. The real Griselda is only seen by glimpses, as in the brilliant touch at the end of Chapter XX. Lufton and Dumbello have showed themselves as public rivals for her hand on the dance-floor and Lady Lufton has intimated, in a late-night tête-à-tête, that she would be happy if her son should pop the all-important question. An exciting enough evening for most girls newly out of a country parsonage, but 'Griselda kissed [Lady Lufton] with the utmost composure, and betook herself to her own bedroom. Before she retired to sleep she looked carefully to her different articles of dress, discovering what amount of damage the evening's wear and tear might have inflicted.' When she is about to set off on her honeymoon, her principal anxiety appears to be whether 'Jane can put her hand at once on the moire antique when we reach Dover'. Trollope does not seem to light on such details in a spirit of satirical hostility, but rather as sharing Mrs Grantly's puzzlement at her daughter's 'lack of something'.

The continuation of the Barsetshire series meant that he was able to come back to Griselda. Another character who later reappears but who already makes a much larger claim on our attention in *Framley Parsonage* is Mr Crawley. It is typical of the increasingly improvisatory freedom of Trollope's creative manner that he should initially propose to study the situation of an affluent clergyman, and end up with a portrait of another clergyman in conditions of exceptional indigence which far transcends the original subject in intensity and interest. The introduction of Mr Crawley presents us with a man made 'morose, silent, dogged' by having to sustain his gently-nurtured wife and children on a pittance. Trollope is eloquent on the agonies suffered by the genteel when they lose status and the refinements of life in a way that probably reflects his personal sense of the degradations suffered by the Trollopes when he was a boy. (In this novel, however, the bailiffs appear at Mark Robarts's house rather than Crawley's – the memory of what happened to his own family being spread over both figures in the novel.) The account of Mr Crawley begins by being rather theoretical, as if the conditions of Hogglestock were bound to produce the Job-like complaints of its incumbent, but as Mr Crawley is brought into contact with other characters in the novel, Trollope is obliged to envisage him more dramatically. By the time we have reached Chapter XXXVI, Trollope has located and can reproduce in Crawley's dialogue those mingled notes of resentment, scrupulous courtesy, suspicion, pride, pedantry of expression, and morbid sensitivity that make his utterance so recognizable and so revealing. Even though his wife is critically ill with typhus and he is himself incompetent to nurse her, Crawley cannot tolerate any suggestion of charity and finds neighbourly assistance hard to bear even though his children (whom he loves intensely but with whom he finds it hard to communicate) are clearly at risk. They have, in fact, to be kidnapped, and Arabin, Crawley's old college friend and now the prosperous Dean, lures him out of the way while this is done. Their dialogue shows a remarkable leap in Trollope's imaginative understanding of his character. Arabin attributes Crawley's refusal of help to pride:

> 'You look at it, Arabin, from one side only; I can only look at it from the other. It is very sweet to give; I do not doubt that. But the taking of what is given is very bitter. Gift bread chokes in a man's throat and poisons his blood, and sits like lead upon the heart. You have never tried it.'
>
> 'But that is the very fault for which I blame you. That is the pride which I say you ought to sacrifice.'
>
> 'And why should I be called on to do so? Is not the labourer worthy of his hire? Am I not able to work, and willing? Have I not always had my shoulder to the collar, and is it right that I should now be contented with the scraps from a rich man's kitchen? Arabin, you and I were equal once and we were then friends, understanding each other's thoughts and sympathizing with each other's sorrows. But it cannot be so now.'
>
> 'If there be such inability, it is all with you.'
>
> 'It is all with me, – because, in our connection the pain would all be on my side. It would not hurt you to see me at your table with worn shoes and a ragged shirt. I do not think so meanly of you as that. You would give me your feast to eat though I were not clad a tithe as well as the menial behind your chair. But it would hurt me to know that there were those looking at me who thought me unfit to sit in your rooms.'
>
> 'That is the pride of which I speak; – false pride.'

'Call it so if you will; but, Arabin, no preaching of yours can alter it. It is all that is left to me of my manliness. That poor broken reed who is lying there sick, – who has sacrificed all the world to her love for me, – who is the mother of my children, and the partner of my sorrows and the wife of my bosom, – even she cannot change me in this, though she pleads with the eloquence of all her wants. Not even for her can I hold out my hand for a dole.' They had now come back to the door of the house, and Mr Crawley, hardly conscious of what he was doing, was preparing to enter. (XXXVI)

Crawley's admission – 'it is all that is left to me of my manliness' – is both abject and unanswerable. He has assumed responsibility for his family's poverty – a responsibility not really his – with a perverse integrity that makes it feel like guilt. He makes their misery his fault even as he protests against his lot. It would therefore be wrong, in Mr Crawley's logic, for anyone else to deprive him of the responsibility for that poverty by their charity: it would be lessening the burden which is properly his alone. It is some such complex of feelings that gives Crawley's self-lacerations a certain moral magnificence, even though – as he is the first bitterly to recognize – others must pay for it as well as himself. It is not surprising that Trollope felt that so remarkable a psychological discovery warranted the further investigation he gave it in *The Last Chronicle of Barset*.

The nursing of his wife is taken out of Mr Crawley's hands by Lucy Robarts, and the force of her will extracts from him in the end a typically courtly acknowledgement. Trollope thought, by the time he wrote the *Autobiography*, that 'Lucy Robarts is perhaps the most natural English girl that I ever drew ... Indeed I doubt whether such a character could be made more lifelike than Lucy Robarts.' (VIII) Lucy is made lifelike not by the physical picture of her we may form (the description in Chapter X at least avoids the faintly succulent tone that sometimes accompanies Trollope's female introductions) but by the knowledge of her inner nature that the novel gradually reveals. Although only 'the little girl from the parsonage', she turns out to have far more force of character than anyone else in her circle; in her conduct towards others she shows a degree of scrupulosity coupled with an almost ferocious insistence on her own integrity which gives her something in common with Mr Crawley. That Trollope should think of her temperament as 'natural' indicates his own preoccupation with such emotions.

Lucy's story is essentially a reworking of the *Doctor Thorne* situation in which an obscure girl catches the heart of a man of rank to the intense disapproval of his aristocratic mother. This element of repetition may be due to the pressure under which *Framley Parsonage* was written, but Trollope may also have felt that he had not done full justice to the possibilities of such a situation. Indeed, the tension likely to arise when a person's sexual predilection proves socially or familially unacceptable was something that Trollope was never to tire of investigating. What Lucy Robarts has in common with Mary Thorne is her determination not to yield to the man she knows she is in love with until asked to do so by the hostile parent. Lucy's situation is the more successfully presented because it is more delicately interiorized – and not only on her side. The confession of her love for Lord Lufton is accompanied by a barrage of ironies at her own expense which effectively indicates her physical agitation (Chapter XXVI), and after her second rejection of him her suffering is movingly conveyed by the precision of seen gesture:

> She sat herself down on a low chair, which stood at the foot of her bed, and, throwing back her head, held her handkerchief across her eyes and forehead, holding it tight in both her hands; and then she began to think. She began to think and also to cry, for the tears came running down from beneath the handkerchief . . . (XXXI)

The barely suppressed violence of her feelings makes her sister-in-law's comment 'To my thinking she is a girl who might almost die for love' seem not extravagant. The accumulated intensity of her experience both in love and in looking after the Crawleys gives Lucy a marked ascendancy in her scene with Lady Lufton in Chapter XXXV: she knows her conduct has been impeccable in refusing a marriage which Lady Lufton would have regarded as harmful to her son, and she compensates for the internal pain which that refusal has caused her by an aggressive assertion of her own propriety. Lady Lufton cannot but concede her case, and one can sense the shift in power that is occurring even as the ultimately stronger

51

side seems to acquiesce in its own apparent weakness. The successful defiance of authority on authority's own terms is usually agreeable because it permits a kind of aggrandizement of the self which at the same time puts the self in the clear. One shares Lucy's triumph (even though she herself regrets it) rather as one enjoys the discomfiture of Lady Catherine de Burgh at the hands of Elizabeth Bennet (Trollope had decided at an early age that *Pride and Prejudice* was the best novel in the language).

Lady Catherine may be an old dragon guarding the shades of Pemberley from pollution, but there is nothing monstrous about Lady Lufton, although she is masterful in her sphere and deeply conservative in her principles. A society based on the deferential acknowledgement of degree seems right and proper to her:

> Nobody liked clergymen better than Lady Lufton or was more willing to live with them on terms of affectionate intimacy, but she could not get over the feeling that the clergyman of her own parish, – or of her son's, – was a part of her own establishment, of her own appanage, – or of his, – and that it could not be well that Lord Lufton should marry among his own dependants. Lady Lufton would not have used the word, but she did think it. (XXXV)

Nevertheless, Trollope shows by a number of touches (from her payment of his debts to the way she touches his hair) that, widowed as she is, Lady Lufton will always give in to her son in the end because she cannot do without his affection. So that when Trollope concludes, analysing her thoughts as she debates whether Lucy might after all be fit for Ludovic, that 'love was the food chiefly necessary for the nourishment of Lady Lufton – the only food absolutely necessary. She was not aware of this herself, nor probably would those who knew her best have so spoken of her' (XLIII) – when Trollope makes this claim to superior insight, we grant it because it has already been shown to be true. It is this need in her which precipitates her final capitulation, when she goes to Hogglestock (where Lucy is still with the Crawleys) to ask Lucy to be her son's wife, exactly as Lucy has asked. The scene between the two of them in the carriage is obviously sentimental and even lachrymose in a way, but it is more concerned with an almost minute-by-minute fidelity to the current of Lucy's feelings as she tries to absorb the new situation than with being affecting:

'He is the best of sons, and the best of men, and I am sure that he will be the best of husbands.'

Lucy had an idea, by instinct, however, rather than by sight, that Lady Lufton's eyes were full of tears as she spoke. As for herself she was altogether blinded, and did not dare to lift her face or to turn her head. As for the utterance of any sound, that was quite out of the question. 'And now I have come here, Lucy, to ask you to be his wife.'

She was quite sure that she heard the words. They came plainly to her ears, leaving on her brain their proper sense, but yet she could not move or make any sign that she had understood them. It seemed as though it would be ungenerous in her to take advantage of such conduct and to accept an offer made with so much self-sacrifice. She had not time at the first moment to think even of his happiness, let alone her own, but she thought only of the magnitude of the concession which had been made to her. When she had constituted Lady Lufton the arbiter of her destiny she had regarded the question of her love as decided against herself. She had found herself unable to endure the position of being Lady Lufton's daughter-in-law while Lady Lufton would be scorning her, and therefore she had given up the game. She had given up the game, sacrificing herself, and, as far as it might be a sacrifice, sacrificing him also. She had been resolute to stand to her word in this respect, but she had never allowed herself to think it possible that Lady Lufton should comply with the conditions which she, Lucy, had laid upon her. And yet such was the case, as she so plainly heard. 'And now I have come here, Lucy, to ask you to be his wife.' How long they sat together silent, I cannot say; counted by minutes the time would not probably have amounted to many, but to each of them the duration seemed considerable. Lady Lufton, while she was speaking, had contrived to get hold of Lucy's hand, and she sat, still holding it, trying to look into Lucy's face, – which, however, she could hardly see, so much was it turned away. Neither, indeed, were Lady Lufton's eyes perfectly dry. (XLVI)

53

This kind of attentiveness – to physical position and gesture, to the sense of time passing, to the release of emotion through tears – allows the two women to become reconciled in a common impulse of love and moral generosity. The moment is a touching one, and the more so for not being dwelt on for our edification. The scene enlarges both characters in it (as the comparable one in *Doctor Thorne* does not) not only because it is so naturally the product of what has gone before, but also because as it completes one period of relationship it so clearly inaugurates another.

Indeed, nothing is more characteristic of Trollope than this curious sense at the end of his best novels that the characters can now be delivered from the confines of the book to get on with their lives. Certainly, nothing could be further from the Thackerayean reminder that all the men and women in it are merely puppets and that all is vanity anyway. So that when Trollope returns to a character in a later novel his or her reappearance seems prompted not so much by the author's art of resuscitation but due rather to their own energies. The momentum of their lives is so convincingly established that all the author appears to have to do is to observe them running under their own power. Some characters, of course, reappear mainly as guest artistes. Once *The Warden* has settled his course in life for him, Mr Harding only emerges from retirement to remind us of the man he once was; his touches on the imaginary cello are a nostalgic reminder of what was in its day a treasured performance. Only once does Trollope really add something to what we already know of Mr Harding. His appearance in Chapter XVI of *The Small House at Allington* not only shows him to have become 'a fond garrulous old man', but, by juxtaposing his unworldly human kindness with the uneasy self-interest of Crosbie, creates a scene that paradoxically gives him a bit of new life by showing how much life has now passed him by.[4]

The Small House at Allington

Towards the end of the Barsetshire series, however, Trollope began to develop the reappearing character on a scale which naturally led him on to his second series of interlinked novels – the so-called political or Palliser novels – a body of work which he rightly thought of as containing his finest achievement. The last two Barset novels often refer back to their predecessors and contain a number of reappearances of the kind that Mr Harding makes, but they also deal with characters that show a capacity for an after-life that quite transcends anything hitherto achieved by Trollope in this line. Indeed, the examination of the Lily Dale–John Eames situation in both *The Small House at Allington* and *The Last Chronicle of Barset*, and the prolonged analysis in the latter of the woes of Mr Crawley, already dealt with at some length in *Framley Parsonage*, make up sustained acts of unprecedented novelistic attentiveness.

In *The Small House at Allington* (written 1862–3, published 1864) Lily Dale immediately takes the capacity for emotional intensity in the Trollopian heroine into an entirely new dimension. Mary Thorne and Lucy Robarts have their moments of assertion but they do not – as Lily Dale does – make a career of intransigence. Her energy is initially apparent in the badinage with her sister in the opening chapters of the novel – her chatter about Adolphus Crosbie as an 'Apollo' perhaps betrays more physical attraction to him than she is aware of (phrases like 'an Apollo among men' became for Trollope a kind of shorthand for indicating sexual eligibility). The process leading to their engagement – normally something one might expect to be protracted over most of the novel – is virtually omitted; by Chapter IX Lily is already making avowals of the kind presented in this remarkable scene in which Lily and Crosbie are walking in the moonlight in the Allington garden:

> 'Don't you like the moon?' she said, as she took his arm, to which she was now so accustomed that she hardly thought of it as she took it.
>
> 'Like the moon – well; I fancy I like the sun better. I don't quite believe in moonlight. I think it does best to talk about when one wants to be sentimental.'
>
> 'Ah; that is just what I fear. That is what I say to Bell when I tell her that her romance will fade as the roses do. And then I shall have to learn that prose is more serviceable than poetry, and that the mind is better than the heart, and – and that money is better than love. It's all coming, I know; and yet I do like the moonlight.'
>
> 'And the poetry – and the love?'

'Yes. The poetry much, and the love more. To be loved by you is sweeter even than any of my dreams – is better than all the poetry I have read.'

'Dearest Lily,' and his unchecked arm stole round her waist.

'It is the meaning of the moonlight, and the essence of the poetry,' continued the impassioned girl. 'I did not know then why I liked such things, but now I know. It was because I longed to be loved.'

'And to love.'

'Oh, yes. I would be nothing without that. But that, you know, is your delight – or should be. The other is mine. And yet it is a delight to love you; to know that I may love you.'

'You mean that this is the realisation of your romance.'

'Yes; but it must not be the end of it, Adolphus. You must like the soft twilight, and the long evenings when we shall be alone; and you must read to me the books I love, and you must not teach me to think that the world is hard, and dry, and cruel – not yet. I tell Bell so very often; but you must not say so to me.'

'It shall not be dry and cruel, if I can prevent it.'

'You understand what I mean, dearest. I will not think it dry and cruel, even though sorrow should come upon us, if you – I think you know what I mean.'

'If I am good to you.'

'I am not afraid of that; – I am not the least afraid of that. You do not think that I could ever distrust you? But you must not be ashamed to look at the moonlight, and to read poetry, and to –'

'To talk nonsense, you mean.'

But as he said it, he pressed her closer to his side, and his tone was pleasant to her.

'I suppose I'm talking nonsense now?' she said, pouting. 'You liked me better when I was talking about the pigs; didn't you?'

'No; I like you best now.'

'And why didn't you like me then? Did I say anything to offend you?'

'I like you best now, because –'

They were standing in the narrow pathway of the gate

leading from the bridge into the gardens of the Great House, and the shadow of the thick-spreading laurels was around them. But the moonlight still pierced brightly through the little avenue, and she looked up to him, could see the form of his face and the loving softness of his eye.

'Because —' said he; and then he stooped over her and pressed her closely, while she put up her lips to his, standing on tip-toe that she might reach to his face.

'Oh, my love!' she said. 'My love! my love!'

Hastily read, the episode might appear conventionally sentimental, — especially since the author himself intrudes so little. In fact, although Trollope never came to have any formal inhibition about direct intervention, he has already greatly modified the tendency to commentary, apostrophe and digression that periodically weighs heavily on the earlier novels, and increasingly trusts the dialogue to convey his apprehension of his characters. Indeed, it is often a sign of his imagination working with peculiar intentness when (as here) a character is first presented in something like his or her full complexity in a dramatic rather than straightforwardly narrative way. The implications of what Lily says in this scene far outstrip any authorial exposition of her personality that has so far been given. The girl already lives in his mind; what the novel has to do is to deduce the novelistic consequences of that life. If Lily's words here are approached as an actor might look at a page of Chekhov, one can see, in the sub-text of this early and tentative essay in the new world of feeling precipitated by her engagement, a capacity for passion, a reckless sincerity and indiscreet fervour that Crosbie will clearly be unable to match, however much he may fitfully respond to it. In the curious anticipation of her 'even though sorrow should come upon us', Lily hints at what later appears as almost a desire for things to go wrong, since they cannot remain at the level of intensity which she feels to be appropriate. The simple words of love at the end of the dialogue (recalled later by both Lily and Crosbie as a crystallizing moment) convey with uncanny economy her abandonment to love. She wants her identity and her love for Crosbie to merge, and the paradoxical result is that although she is jilted by him, she will not give him up because that would be to falsify herself. She becomes therefore a casualty of her own will.

Her talent for the hopeless situation becomes apparent even in these
relatively early pages. At the end of Crosbie's visit, Lily offers to
release him rather than be a tie:

> 'Are you tired of me, Lily?'
>
> 'No. I shall never be tired of you, – never weary with
> loving you. I did not wish to say so now; but I will answer
> your question boldly. Tired of you! I fancy that a girl can
> never grow tired of her lover. But I would sooner die in the
> struggle than be the cause of your ruin. It would be better – in
> every way better.'
>
> 'I have said nothing of being ruined.'
>
> 'But listen to me. I should not die if you left me – not be
> utterly broken-hearted. Nothing on earth can I ever love as I
> have loved you. But I have a God and a Saviour that will be
> enough for me. I can turn to them with content, if it be well
> that you should leave me. I have gone to them, and –' But at
> this moment she could utter no more words. She had broken
> down in her effort, losing her voice through the strength of
> her emotion. As she did not choose that he should see her
> overcome, she turned from him and walked away across the
> grass.
>
> Of course he followed her; but he was not so quick after her
> but that time had been given her to recover herself. 'It is true,'
> she said, 'I have the strength of which I tell you. Though I
> have given myself to you as your wife, I can bear to be
> divorced from you now, – now. And, my love, though it
> may sound heartless, I would sooner be so divorced from
> you, than cling to you as a log that must drag you down
> under the water, and drown you in trouble and care. I would;
> – indeed I would. If you go, of course that kind of thing is
> over for me. But the world has more than that – much more;
> and I would make myself happy; – yes, my love, I would be
> happy. You need not fear that.' (XV)

The conventional Victorian vocabulary which Lily employs (naturally enough) does not disguise the fact that the desire for reciprocated love and the seductivenes of self-sacrifice hang in an
anguished balance, whatever Lily may think she thinks. The effect
is at once to put an intense pressure on Crosbie and to make Lily

oddly self-sufficient; it is as if her love and its object were somehow separable. Not only can the one survive without the other, but the self is vindicated by its so doing. When Crosbie does abandon Lily she is therefore caught in a trap of her own making, or which at least she could not stop herself making; the later stages of *The Small House* and much of *The Last Chronicle* are taken up with Trollope's watching to see whether she will get out.

Certainly, Lily's reception of the news that Crosbie has engaged himself to another soon after leaving Allington is marked by an extreme toughness of will all the more noticeable because of the obvious imminence of physical collapse. Her insistence that she forgives Crosbie and that she still loves him is so spontaneous that it almost seems in some obscure way premeditated. Her quick intuition of the news of Crosbie's defection that her mother brings may indicate some subconscious recognition of how much her own will to love had clouded her judgement of the man's temperament and situation. Lily's policy of compulsory forgiveness of Crosbie means that she has to struggle against the easy gratification of feeling insulted and injured and has, moreover, to try to curb the impulses towards revenge that her family naturally indulge. That she, who has been most hurt by her former lover, should be his defender is the perverse moral heroism of her position. She even has to fight against the conventional fictional fate of taking to her bed in a decline: when she is laid low partly by grief and partly by scarlatina, she is cross with her invalidism and tries hard to alienate sympathy. The fact that her situation is public knowledge is another cross to bear: to be commiserated with is again not to accept the situation as she has resolved to accept it. That such an attitude is only sustained at great emotional cost is indicated by her behaviour on the day (Valentine's Day) on which Crosbie is to be married. The scene – again almost entirely in dialogue – shows an outward overbearingness and even egoism that effectively reveals the agonies within:

> 'Bell,' she said, stopping her other speech suddenly, 'at what o'clock do people get married in London?'
>
> 'Oh, at all manner of hours – any time before twelve. They will be fashionable, and will be married late.'
>
> 'You don't think she's Mrs Crosbie yet, then?'

'Lady Alexandrina Crosbie,' said Bell, shuddering.

'Yes, of course; I forgot. I should so like to see her. I feel such an interest about her. I wonder what coloured hair she has. I suppose she is a sort of Juno of a woman, – very tall and handsome. I'm sure she has not got a pug-nose like me. Do you know what I should really like, only of course it's not possible; – to be godmother to his first child.'

'Oh, Lily!'

'I should. Don't you hear me say that I know it's not possible? I'm not going up to London to ask her. She'll have all manner of grandees for her godfathers and godmothers. I wonder what those grand people are really like.'

'I don't think there's any difference. Look at Lady Julia.'

'Oh, she's not a grand person. It isn't merely having a title. Don't you remember that he told us that Mr Palliser is about the grandest grandee of them all. I suppose people do learn to like them. He always used to say that he had been so long among people of that sort, that it would be very difficult for him to divide himself off from them. I should never have done for that kind of thing; should I?'

'There is nothing I despise so much as what you call that kind of thing.'

'Do you? I don't. After all, think how much work they do. He used to tell me of that. They have all the governing in their hands, and get very little money for doing it.'

'Worse luck for the country.'

'The country seems to do pretty well. But you're a Radical, Bell. My belief is, you wouldn't be a lady if you could help it.'

'I'd sooner be an honest woman.'

'And so you are – my own dear, dearest, honest Bell – and the fairest lady that I know. If I were a man, Bell, you are just the girl that I should worship.'

'But you are not a man; so it's no good.'

'But you mustn't let your foot go astray in that way; you mustn't, indeed. Somebody said, that whatever is, is right, and I declare I believe it.'

'I'm sometimes inclined to think, that whatever is, is wrong.'

'That's because you're a Radical. I think I'll get up now, Bell; only it's so frightfully cold that I'm afraid.'

'There's a beautiful fire,' said Bell.

'Yes; I see. But the fire won't go all around me, like the bed does. I wish I could know the very moment when they're at the altar. It's only half-past ten yet.'

'I shouldn't be at all surprised if it's over.'

'Over! What a word that is! A thing like that is over, and then all the world cannot put it back again. What if he should be unhappy after all?'

'He must take his chance,' said Bell, thinking within her own mind that that chance would be a very bad one.

'Of course he must take his chance. Well – I'll get up now.' And then she took her first step out into the cold world beyond her bed. (XLIV)

How revealing, for instance, and how touching is Lily's momentary relapse into childishness in '"the fire won't go all round me, like the bed does"'. Lily's performance here is brilliantly reported by Trollope, and remains so for the rest of the chapter, during which Lily vainly tries to find a book she can bear to read, or even focus on. It is in such sequences as these that the essential selflessness of his art – so unobtrusive, so completely at his characters' disposal – can be seen. We suffer with those that we see suffer, but not because we are exhorted to do so, or bullied into doing so. At such times Trollope's intense respect for the experience of his characters seems to preclude any thought of its ethical or rhetorical exploitation by the novelist.

As Lily convalesces, her friends and relations begin to want to push her into the always waiting arms of John Eames, her faithful childhood admirer, and indeed this becomes the chief element of suspense in the novel (her sister Bell's eventual capitulation to the indigent but obviously sterling Dr Crofts is soothingly predictable). However, Eames has to realize that at this stage at any rate, Lily means what she says: it is not that she can't get over Crosbie, but that she won't – '"I should be disgraced in my own eyes if I admitted the love of another man, after – after – . . ."' (LIV) As far as she is concerned, she is a widow, as her mother really is – a move which effectively neutralizes her mother's authority over her – she has already said to her mother, in the now strangely innocent language of her period, '"We shall always be together now . . . I must fall in love with you now."' (XXX) There are hints nevertheless that her resolve may not be quite irrevocable. Her language at times suggests instability. After dismissing Eames, she says '"They should not have let him come . . . But they don't understand. They think that I have lost a toy, and they mean to be good-natured, and to give me another."' (LIV) The 'they' here indicates an almost paranoid element in her feeling. Lily also says that if Crosbie's wife were to die in five years' time and Crosbie then came to her again '"I should think myself constrained to take him"' (LVII) – and again the choice of words perhaps indicates how imprisoned she still is in her situation. The remark also provides an option which is taken up in *The Last Chronicle of Barset*.

For neither Eames nor Crosbie does *The Small House at Allington* provide a satisfactory resolution. It is true that Crosbie does get married, but the expected worldly advantages of having an earl's daughter as a wife do not materialize, and by the time the novel ends the couple have tacitly agreed to separate. Although Crosbie is technically the villain of the piece and knows himself to be so, a surprising amount of the first volume is devoted to monitoring his state of mind. Stray hints of the kind that readers of mid-Victorian novels learn to decode indicate that he is a man whose knowledge of women has not remained at the callow stage seen in Eames's boarding-house entanglements. Lily's 'way of flattering her lover without any intention of flattery on her part, had put Crosbie into a seventh heaven. In all his experience he had known nothing like it.' (VI) We are later told that Crosbie 'had been dealing with women for many years'. (XV) The refusal of Lily's uncle to do anything for her financially on her marriage checks Crosbie's sense of gratification, but the force of her passion soon makes him think again of their engagement with the proper commitment. The trouble is that this only lasts while he is actually with her. As the quotation from their early love-scene shows, Lily always has the ascendancy in their conversations; her innocent ardour awes him into temporary solemnity. His words lack energy because of the unspoken reservations underneath them, so that he seems in an odd way to be acting his way, rather carefully, through the scene (a similar lack of authenticity can be felt in his declaration to Lady Alexandrina in

Chapter XXIII). It is only Trollope's reports of his internal debates
that provide a full account of his drift into perfidy. Trollope does
not apologize for Crosbie or disguise his essential weakness, his
dismay at the sacrifice of his little pleasures that marriage would
demand, his inability to resist the temptingly aristocratic air of
Courcy even though he realizes how detestable most of its occup-
ants are, and his moral inferiority not only to Lily but to John
Eames. At the same time Trollope refuses to emulate Eames's
assault on Crosbie (in which the latter gets a humiliating black eye)
by hounding him novelistically. Crosbie appears to be quite as
entitled to Trollope's attention as anyone else, and indeed as a study
of the ways in which a man may persuade himself to revise his
intentions while half-consciously allowing events to push him
towards an objective that he has never quite brought himself
explicitly to envisage – as a study, that is, on the central Trollopian
ground of dilemma and its resolution – the presentation of Crosbie
is more subtle than anything of its kind in the previous Barsetshire
novels. Trollope sometimes intervenes directly to deflect disapproval and inattention – 'I beg that it may be understood that
Crosbie was not altogether a villain' – the strategy being the same
as in 'There are worse men than Sowerby.' More creative, however, is the kind of sensitivity shown in the analysis at the end of
Chapter XVIII of Crosbie's feelings as he finishes writing his first
letter to Lily from Courcy:

> As he had waxed warm with his writing he had forced
> himself to be affectionate, and, as he flattered himself, frank
> and candid. Nevertheless, he was partly conscious that he was
> preparing for himself a mode of escape in those allusions of
> his to his own worldliness; if escape should ultimately be
> necessary. 'I have tried,' he would then say; 'I have struggled
> honestly, with my best efforts for success; but I am not good
> enough for such success.' I do not intend to say that he wrote
> with a premeditated intention of thus using his words; but as
> he wrote them he could not keep himself from reflecting that
> they might be used in that way.
> He read his letter over, felt satisfied with it, and resolved
> that he might now free his mind from that consideration for
> the next forty-eight hours. Whatever might be his sins he had

done his duty by Lily! And with this comfortable reflection he deposited his letter in the Courcy Castle letter-box.

There is a sting in 'comfortable' of course, but Crosbie's half-awareness of his own motives is too recognizable to be easily shrugged off. The whole process by which Crosbie edges towards, or lets himself be edged towards, his proposal to Lady Alexandrina is one that Trollope finds too absorbing to have time for the outrage that other characters feel at his behaviour. The punch that Eames lands gratifies some of them, but it is a boyish gesture which hardly resolves the nice period problem that Crosbie's conduct raises: how can a gentleman who behaves in an ungentlemanly way be punished if he is not legally at fault, now that duels are out? No doubt he could have been sued for breach of promise, but Lily's friends do not want to expose her to that, nor would she consent to it. Trollope sees to it that Crosbie's marriage is a misery, and he is made to think of Lily's attractions even on the train to his Folke-stone honeymoon in a way that is perhaps a little over-retributive, as if Trollope were anxious to assure his audience that Crosbie is truly punished anyway. But he keeps novelistic faith with the man, nevertheless. The dreary lovelessness of his married life is briefly but tellingly sketched (less dazzlingly than Dickens's portrayal of the conjugal infelicity of the Lammles in the nearly contemporary *Our Mutual Friend*, but with at least as much human truth), and his earlier accumulated resentment at the treatment received at the aristocratic hands of his future in-laws is subtly indicated by the bedtime story told with covert malevolence to one of the de Courcy boys:

> 'I wish you would not call the child nicknames, Adolphus. It seems as though you would wish to cast a slur upon the one which he bears.'
> 'I should hardly think that he would feel disposed to do that,' said Mr Gazebee.
> 'Hardly, indeed,' said Crosbie.
> 'It has never yet been disgraced in the annals of our country by being made into a nickname,' said the proud daughter of the house. She was probably unaware that among many of his associates her father had been called Lord De Curse'ye, from the occasional energy of his language. 'And any such attempt

is painful in my ears. I think something of my family, I can assure you, Adolphus, and so does my husband.'

'A very great deal,' said Mr Gazebee.

'So do I of mine,' said Crosbie. 'That's natural to all of us. One of my ancestors came over with William the Conqueror. I think he was one of the assistant cooks in the king's tent.'

'A cook!' said young De Courcy.

'Yes, my boy, a cook. That was the way most of our old families were made noble. They were cooks, or butlers to the kings – or sometimes something worse.'

'But your family isn't noble?'

'No – I'll tell you how it was. The king wanted this cook to poison half-a-dozen of his officers who wished to have a way of their own; but the cook said, "No, my Lord King; I am a cook, not an executioner." So they sent him into the scullery, and when they called all the other servants barons and lords, they only called him Cooky. They've changed the name to Crosbie since that, by degrees.'

Mr Gazebee was awestruck, and the face of the Lady Amelia became very dark. Was it not evident that this snake, when taken into their innermost bosoms that they might there warm him, was becoming an adder, and preparing to sting them? There was very little more conversation that evening, and soon after the story of the cook, Crosbie got up and went away to his own home. (XXXV)

Such a flicker of resilience shows that, for all his disappointments, Crosbie is by no means finished. John Eames is left at the end of the novel clearly on the threshold of greater things, even if they do not seem likely to include the possession of Lily Dale. But although Eames is theoretically the hero of the book, his affairs are curiously parallel to Crosbie's. Crosbie's position in the Civil Service is greatly superior to Eames's, but both are shown responding to promotion with self-assertion rather than servility, based in each case on confidence in the quality of their work. But, much more obviously, both prove disloyal to Lily Dale. Johnny Eames writes an indiscreet note to his landlady's daughter about wanting to call her his own for ever; it is true that he was drunk at the time, and it is also tacitly understood that even though he is only an £80-a-year clerk the idea of such a marriage is too socially inappropriate to be taken very seriously. But even if it is accepted that Eames gets into a scrape where Crosbie commits a sin, Eames's dallyings with Amelia Roper are bound to put his devotion to Lily Dale in an awkward light.

Nevertheless it is clear that Trollope thinks that extenuating factors operate in Johnny's case which do not in Crosbie's. Although Eames declares his love to Lily with a good deal of dignity and straightforwardness, he knows that he cannot, in his position, offer to marry her, and he concedes that she would not in any case have him. Lily's use of the standard formula about loving Johnny as a brother makes it clear that, sexually speaking, he has no chance. Thus disappointed, why shouldn't he flirt with Amelia? After all, he is far less experienced than she is, and has not achieved 'a tithe of that lady's experience in the world' (whatever that may mean). He has not actually made an offer to her in so many words, and perhaps would not have got involved even so far with her if he had had more friends in London to invite him into their houses where he could talk to nice girls rather than common ones.

The strongest factor in Johnny's favour however is simply that he is young – young absolutely speaking, and young for his age. Trollope calls him a hobbledehoy (*OED*: 'a clumsy or awkward youth') but, as he uses the word, he effectively purges it of its patronizing tone. What seems to make Trollope take Johnny and Johnny's time of life seriously – rather than regarding it as simply a tiresome and embarrassing phase that has to be gone through – is not only Johnny's innate decency and generosity of feeling, but also the imaginative life within that nobody else sees.

> The true hobbledehoy is much alone, not being greatly given to social intercourse even with other hobbledehoys – a trait in his character which I think has hardly been sufficiently observed by the world at large. He has probably become a hobbledehoy instead of an Apollo, because circumstances have not afforded him much social intercourse; and, therefore, he wanders about in solitude, taking long walks, in which he dreams of those successes which are so far removed from his powers of achievement. Out in the fields, with his stick in his hand, he is very eloquent, cutting off the heads of

the springing summer weeds, as he practises his oratory with energy. And thus he feeds an imagination for which those who know him give him but scanty credit, and unconsciously prepares himself for that later ripening, if only the ungenial shade will some day cease to interpose itself. (IV)

Trollope stresses later the thoughtfulness of youth:

Men, full fledged and at their work, are, for the most part, too busy for much thought; but lads, on whom the work of the world has not yet fallen with all its pressure – they have time for thinking. (XIV)

By Eames's 'thinking' however Trollope means not just the effects of reading too much Byron and grandiose reflections on great topics, but also an elaborate fantasy life:

For hours upon hours he would fill his mind with castles in the air, dreaming of wonderful successes in the midst of which Lily Dale always reigned as a queen. He would carry on the same story in his imagination from month to month, almost contenting himself with such ideal happiness. Had it not been for the possession of that power, what comfort could there have been to him in his life? (LII)

As Sadleir notes, the phrases irresistibly recall the later words of the *Autobiography*: 'For weeks, for months, if I remember rightly, from year to year, I would carry on the same tale.' (III) Trollope credits Eames with an activity of the imagination like his own, and it is therefore not surprising that his attitude to the character is tolerant.

What is perhaps surprising is that it is not more than that. The tradition that Johnny Eames represents the young Trollope seems sound enough: it is obvious that in such matters as his office career and the general scruffiness of his London life Eames's experience is very close to Trollope's account of his own earlier years. Yet in neither *The Small House* nor in *The Last Chronicle* does one have the sense of any autobiographical pressure; Eames is not given the kind of privileged status that is almost involuntarily accorded to David Copperfield or to Pendennis. Compensatory mechanisms are not at work, bringing not only literary success but also a suitably spiritualized sexual reward. A comparison of Johnny's affair with

Amelia and Pendennis's parallel involvement with the socially inferior Fanny Bolton shows in Trollope a total absence of that fluster and anxiety so painfully and indeed so embarrassingly registered by the older writer. Trollope's admiration for Thackeray was profound though not unqualified. He wrote the *English Men of Letters* volume on him in 1879, and as he rightly said there (although in another context), Thackeray's pen was not always firm. When it comes to the question of sexual attraction jumping the picket lines of class distinction, Trollope is far less agitated than the other major novelists of his period (another comparison would be the tense liaison between Eugene Wrayburn and Lizzie Hexam in *Our Mutual Friend*). Loyal as he is to Eames's immaturity, Trollope does not seem to feel that because of his intimate connection with the author Eames needs special protection – and the girl is robust enough to look after herself.

This relative freedom from autobiographical loading can also be seen in an earlier and much inferior novel which covers some of the same ground as *The Small House at Allington*. *The Three Clerks* (written and published in 1857) immediately followed *Barchester Towers*. It was admired by Thackeray and the Brownings – no doubt, as Sadleir suggests, for that derivativeness which so much weakens it. One of the original reviewers called the writing 'smart', which suggests that it felt up-to-date without being disturbing. It was clearly topical: the Trevelyan–Northcote reforms of the Civil Service and the exposure of fraudulent speculators and jobbing members of Parliament are pointed to by the *Spectator*'s reviewer as 'prominent features of the passing time that admit of pointed satirical embodiment'. The novel now seems more sentimental than sharp; the apostrophes and moralizing digressions are as much of a liability as anywhere in Trollope's early work, and matters are not improved by inserted tales like 'Crinoline and Macassar', a feeble burlesque of the Thackeray–*Punch* type (in which however Mrs Gamp makes a brief but in every sense spirited appearance). But although Trollope has his eye on matters that were in the public domain, the autobiographical elements are considerable. Charley Tudor's unsatisfactory life as a clerk in a minor branch of the public service, his harassment by a money-lender for smallish but nevertheless critical sums, his weakness in allowing a totally unsuitable barmaid to hope for marriage – these are admitted by

Trollope to derive from his own experience. It seems possible that other things in the book came from Trollope's own early life – the mere fact that there are three clerks may relate to the Tramp Society, a group that Trollope formed with two friends for the purpose of larky expeditions in the Home Counties although the actual characters of the fictional and real-life trios do not correspond. The three clerks of the novel visit the Woodward family, the three daughters of which they eventually marry, who live at Hampton in a house with a garden going down to the river Thames – a convenient excursion distance from London (the men can row there up river, as does Ralph the heir, in the novel of that name, whose attentions are also divided between the middle-class girl in the house by the river and a less genteel one, the daughter of his breeches-maker). In *The Three Clerks* Mrs Woodward pleads with Charley to behave steadily and not get into trouble; the *Autobiography* records Trollope's memory of Mrs Clayton Freeling who, hearing that he is liable to be dismissed from his office, 'with tears in her eyes, besought me to think of my mother' (III; she was an admirer and friend of Mrs Trollope, her father-in-law being Secretary to the Post Office). More curiously, Trollope's own illness of 1840 – not mentioned in the *Autobiography*, but apparently serious enough to endanger his life – may perhaps have been transposed into the decline into which Katie Woodward seems almost voluntarily to sink when warned off Charley by her anxious mother. Trollope's comments in the *Autobiography* certainly indicate that this area of the book retained a powerful emotional appeal for him, which may well have been due to its relationship with his own experience: 'The passage in which Kate Woodward, thinking that she will die, tries to take leave of the lad she loves, still brings tears to my eyes when I read it. I had not the heart to kill her. I never could do that. And I do not doubt but they are living happily together to this day.' (VI) Whatever the basis of this episode in fact, the last sentence is perhaps more significant than it may look. Trollope has made over his own life to his characters, sunk his interests in theirs, so that they survive independently rather than as mere portrayers of the artist.

A reader of *The Three Clerks* who did not know of its autobiographical elements would not be likely to suspect them. Charley's experiences are not presented with the kind of intensity which gets

its energies from the traumas of authorial adolescence; his undoubted sensitivity is not so allied with the novel's point of view
that it seems privileged; his sentimental education is not presented
in an easily generalizable form, implying the vanity of assuming
that what happens to him and what happened to his creator is of
special significance. Alaric Tudor, who is led into speculation and
embezzlement by the unscrupulous Undy Scott, brought to trial,
and ends a dazzlingly begun career with the conventional expiation
of emigration, is given as much attention and analysis as Charley is
– though, in Trollope's earlier manner, his greater sins do produce
more head-shaking. His fall calls forth a heroic loyalty from his
wife, clearly meant by Trollope to be illustrative of that innate
moral superiority of women so widely assumed and celebrated in
his time: 'She would not have changed her Alaric, branded with
infamy as he now was, or soon would be, for the proudest he that
carried his head high among the proud ones of the earth. Such is
woman's love; such is the love of which a man's heart is never
capable!' (XXXVIII) Trollope would probably never have repudiated such sentiments, but in his mature work he is no longer in
practice prepared to rest comfortably on such complacent assumptions. Nevertheless the passage indicates – especially when taken
with the dwelt-on pathos of Kate's noble self-denial – that it is the
women of *The Three Clerks* that provide such heroism as it has; the
men, including the author's own representative, are weaker creatures. Such idealization may be related to the longing for refined
feminine company which according to the *Autobiography* Trollope
himself felt during his early London years, and which he recommends in Chapter II of the novel as a protection against dissipation.

The artistic moral of Trollope's treatment of his own life in both
The Three Clerks and in *The Small House* is that, despite his extreme
sensitivity and its related assertiveness, Trollope did not put himself before others. The inherent modesty that made him ascribe his
success as a writer to unremitting industry and early hours rather
than talent, also ensures that his own experience when expressed in
fictional form is not given special protection. He does not use his
fiction as a way of reordering or compensating for his life: one of
the legacies of 'castle-building' was that it enabled Trollope 'to lay
my own identity aside'. His novels are for his characters to live in
rather than himself. Thus when Trollope takes up the later career of

Johnny Eames in *The Last Chronicle of Barset*, he does so on terms suggested by the whole character as developed in *The Small House at Allington*, rather than by any logic deriving from those elements which Trollope's life and Johnny's had in common.

The Last Chronicle of Barset

The action of *The Last Chronicle of Barset* (written 1866, published 1867) takes place three or four years after that of *The Small House*. Eames's situation has markedly improved: he has become private secretary to the self-important Sir Raffle Buffle, and he has come into some money. His delight in puncturing Sir Raffle's overblown vanities is partly due to a boyish love of insubordination (and doubtless draws on Trollope's own recorded irreverencies), but it also rests on a developing sense of his own value as a public servant; a man is entitled to be treated with consideration when he knows his job and does it well. His little fortune has come from the will of Lord de Guest, whom he saved from an angry bull in Chapter XXI of *The Small House at Allington*. That episode, coming as it did immediately after Johnny's rejection by Lily, had a curious air of fantasy about it. It seems the sort of incident that might occur in those solitary imaginings which Trollope tells us Johnny indulged in. Set-back and discomfiture are compensated for by the glamour of heroism and a stroke of luck. At the same time the episode has an element of farce about it – the rescued victim of the bull is not a damsel in distress but a dotty peer – and this touch of bathos is characteristic of Johnny's fictional environment.

In *The Small House* Eames's exalted devotion to Lily Dale was constantly undercut by his embarrassing involvement with Amelia Roper. In *The Last Chronicle* he has access to a more refined type of girl, his improved prospects having given him a certain style, but his emotional life still shows the same pattern. His love for Lily, reiterated in more than one scene with her, shows no sign of diminishing. After yet another rejection he consoles himself with fantasies of a lifetime's devotion to her. (XXXV) At the same time he cannot resist the artful lures of Madalina Demolines since although she is obviously a mantrap her self-dramatizations and bogus intensities are, as Johnny says, 'as good as a play'. The atmosphere of burlesque in which Madalina lives precipitates a final scene in which she tries to compromise him by fainting in his arms so that she can be discovered by her equally stagey mother ('"What is it that I behold?"' etc.; LXXX). Johnny has to get out of it as best as he can, invoking the aid of one of those conveniently passing policemen who, at about this period, begin their patrol of the pages of English fiction with a view to being of respectful service to chaps in little spots of bother. The whole business is nothing more than a scrape, but scrapes are still what Eames tends to get into, and this inhibits us – and Lily – from taking him as seriously as the underlying integrity of his love for her deserves. His constancy lacks the neurotic quality that appears in some of Trollope's other faithful lovers, but in his case, the more balanced nature of his devotion unfairly tells against him. When Lily says, thinking of the Madalina business, that she thinks he is light of heart, she means, perhaps, that his faithfulness is useless to her because it does not override everything else, does not have the kind of intensity she herself has felt and looked for in love.

For all that, Lily and Johnny are two of a kind. His love for her, which she will not accept, and her love for Crosbie, the man who jilted her, have fixed them both in a state of emotional arrest, out of which they seem unable to break. Although he sees at times that to keep putting the question over and over again to Lily is both unmanly and absurd, Johnny cannot get out of his need to do so. Although she sees that her obsessive recall of her love for Crosbie and of the happiness that she might have had cripplingly reduces the possibilities of life for her, she cannot stop this attenuating retrospection:

> 'When I sleep I dream of him. When I am alone I cannot banish him from my thoughts. I cannot define what it is to love him. I want nothing from him, – nothing, nothing. But I move about through my little world thinking of him, and I shall do so to the end. I used to feel proud of my love, though it made me so wretched that I thought it would kill me. I am not proud of it any longer. It is a foolish poor-spirited weakness, – as though my heart has only been half-formed in the making.' (XXXV)

In the face of such desolate eloquence, Johnny ought to despair, but the plangent candour of Lily's confessions only pulls the knot tighter.

Lily's capacity to look her life in the face goes with an inability to do anything more than that; but however trapped she is by what has happened to her, her broodings have at least given her the power of analysing her situation with remarkable insight. Crosbie becomes a widower when his wife dies at Baden-Baden (putting him to the inconvenient expense of having her remains transported back to England in an appropriately aristocratic manner) and he is thus free to attempt to renew the Dale connection by writing to Lily's mother. Lily discusses the question whether she still loves him and might yet marry him with an almost Jamesian subtlety:

'I think so well of myself that, loving him, as I do; – yes, mamma, do not be uneasy; – loving him, as I do, I believe I could be a comfort to him. I think that he might be better with me than without me. That is, he would be so, if he could teach himself to look back upon the past as I can do, and to judge of me as I can judge of him.'

'He has nothing at least, for which to condemn you.'

'But he would have, were I to marry him now. He would condemn me because I had forgiven him. He would condemn me because I had borne what he had done to me, and had still loved him – loved him through it all. He would feel and know the weakness; – and there is weakness. I have been weak in not being able to rid myself of him altogether. He would recognize this after a while, and would despise me for it. But he would not see what there is of devotion to him in my being able to bear the taunts of the world in going back to him, and your taunts, and my own taunts. I should have to bear his also, – not spoken aloud, but to be seen in his face and heard in his voice, – and that I could not endure. If he despised me, and he would, that would make us both unhappy. Therefore, mamma, tell him not to come; tell him that he can never come; but, if it be possible, tell him this tenderly.' (XXIII)

It is clear that she has brought both her intelligence and her will to bear on the matter with great tenacity.

But Lily is living in the past. The passage of time is forcibly brought home to her by her stay in London, which generally unsettles her from the anodyne routine she has established for herself down in Barsetshire, and in particular by her chance encounter with Crosbie in Hyde Park. The incident is delicately handled by Trollope, who drops back unobtrusively into Crosbie's point of view, used extensively in the early parts of *The Small House*. Crosbie does not however see that Lily is stouter than she was. (He himself has visibly aged, as is made clear when he earlier meets Eames at a dinner party, and they shake hands three years after Johnny's assault on Crosbie at the railway station.) Lily's reflections on the meeting in Rotten Row are probed by Trollope with a characteristic tentativeness ('I do not know', 'It is difficult to explain', 'I think') which nevertheless seems to get the logic of Lily's feelings exactly right.

> When she was alone she sat down in her habit, and declared to herself that she certainly would never become the wife of Mr Crosbie. I do not know why she should make such a declaration. She had promised her mother and John Eames that she would not do so, and that promise would certainly have bound her without any further resolutions on her own part. But, to tell the truth, the vision of the man had disenchanted her. When last she had seen him he had been as it were a god to her; and though, since that day, his conduct to her had been as ungodlike as it well might be, still the memory of the outward signs of his divinity had remained with her. It is difficult to explain how it had come to pass that the glimpse which she had had of him should have altered so much within her mind; – why she should so suddenly have come to regard him in an altered light. It was not simply that he looked to be older, and because his face was careworn. It was not only that he had lost that look of an Apollo which Lily had once in her mirth attributed to him. I think it was chiefly that she herself was older, and could no longer see a god in such a man. She had never regarded John Eames as being gifted with divinity, and had therefore always been making comparisons to his discredit. Any such comparison now would tend quite the other way. Nevertheless she would adhere to the two letters in her book. Since she had seen Mr Crosbie she was altogether out of love with the prospect of matrimony. (LIII)

The two letters in her book to which Lily refers are 'Old Maid' (she is, in fact, twenty-four). They are the logical result of her promise to her mother that she will not marry Crosbie, and her promise to Eames that although she cannot marry him she will not marry anyone else. It looks like a decision, an act of will, but in the end, her refusal to marry seems more like a helpless recognition of something in herself that is not amenable to the will. Her response to Johnny's final attempt to claim her shows her exhaustion, and even her vulnerability (her tears when Johnny confesses that he is late because he fell asleep after his gallant journey to Florence on Mr Crawley's behalf say more than any analysis could about her affection for him and her own frustration that it cannot be more than that).

> He took both her hands, and looked into her eyes. 'Lily, will you be mine?'
>
> 'No, dear; it cannot be so.'
>
> 'Why not, Lily?'
>
> 'Because of that other man.'
>
> 'And is that to be a bar for ever?'
>
> 'Yes; for ever.'
>
> 'Do you still love him?'
>
> 'No; no, no!'
>
> 'Then why should this be so?'
>
> 'I cannot tell, dear. It is so. If you take a young tree and split it, it still lives, perhaps. But it isn't a tree. It is only a fragment.'
>
> 'Then be my fragment.'
>
> 'So I will, if it can serve you to give standing ground to such a fragment in some corner of your garden. But I will not have myself planted out in the middle, for people to look at. What there is left would die soon.' He still held her hands, and she did not attempt to draw them away. 'John,' she said, 'next to mamma, I love you better than all the world. Indeed I do. I can't be your wife, but you need never be afraid that I shall be more to another man than I am to you.'
>
> 'That will not serve me,' he said, grasping both her hands till he almost hurt them, but not knowing that he did so. 'That is no good.'
>
> 'It is all the good that I can do you. Indeed I can do you, – can do no one any good. The trees that the storms have splintered are never of use.' (LXXVII)

There can be no appeal against the elegiac cadence of the last sentence. The imagery makes it clear that Lily still in some way wishes to blight herself for having expected too much, that she still clings to the idea that – as she puts it elsewhere – 'things have gone wrong with me', that she still cannot bear any compromise in her private life which would expose her to public note.

Lily's sense that there is something in one's nature that is hopelessly inexplicable, that is unget-at-able but nevertheless determining, is closely related to Trollope's own deepest apprehension of personality. Instantly recognizable, she remains a mystery. The idiom of her speech – its brisk defensive ironies and underlying morbidity of self-consciousness can be studied at length in the scene in Allington church in Chapter XVI of *The Last Chronicle* – is beautifully heard by Trollope and is demonstrably consistent with her tone in *The Small House*; her visit to London disturbs her mind but not Trollope's secure command of her manner. Indeed, her appearance in two separate novels seems to give her an additional dimension of experience – the initial development and subsequent recapitulation of her essentially static situation lending her particularly the air of having lived through it – a natural if perhaps illogical result of her status as a reappearing character. And yet, despite this overwhelming authenticity of presence, there seems curiously little that we, or Trollope, can say about her in summary terms. There does not seem to be any category to which she can be usefully referred. Perverse as she is, to label her as a masochist, as some modern critics have done, is to substitute clinical diagnosis for creative sympathy.[5] The more we look at her apparently simple little story, the more we see how much she is unlike anyone else. However absorbing and affecting, her history teaches no lessons. Her reappearance in a second novel only shows – and shows far more by dramatization than by authorial analysis – that Trollope's apprehension of her in the first book was essentially correct. He has so conveyed the sense of her identity that we would know her anywhere. But that is not to say that we fully understand her, any more than she does herself. Lily annoys other characters in Barsetshire, just as she annoyed readers in the real world, by insisting on being a law to herself. Her success, as a presented character in fiction, depends – as Trollope must have seen – on her autonomy being respected. When the narrator takes his leave of her, he says, thinking no doubt of all those who, for whatever reasons of their own, wanted Lily eventually to give in to Johnny, 'I can only ask the reader to believe that she was in earnest, and express my own opinion, in this last word, that I shall ever write respecting her, that she will live and die as Lily Dale.' (LXXVII) The fact that we so easily accept that Trollope – Lily's creator, after all – should limit himself to a mere 'opinion' as to her future life is a reminder of how completely she has swum free of him. To admit that, in the end, there is nothing you can do about other people, that you can only let them be, may sound inert, but when such an attitude is combined with as close an attention to what it is that they are as Trollope at his best shows, the results can be as humane and as generous as anything fiction has to show.

The other character to receive, in *The Last Chronicle*, such a peculiar intensity of authorial concentration is of course Mr Crawley, the novel's dominant figure and generally acknowledged as one of the triumphs of Trollope's art. In *Framley Parsonage* he was described as 'morose, silent, dogged'; now, he is not only 'moody, unhappy, and disappointed', but 'morose, sometimes almost to insanity'. The element of mental imbalance is what Trollope has come to see in Mr Crawley since his earlier appearances, and it now becomes the central factor in his situation and in his presentation. The tendency to think of Trollope as the chronicler of the placid continuities of English life can easily lead one to underestimate the amount of abnormality and stress in his pages, but one is encouraged to do so by the total absence on Trollope's part of any factitious excitement. Mr Crawley is not a certifiable lunatic who is given an appropriately bedlamite idiom of incoherence. For most of the time he must be regarded as normal, and from this comes his difficulty. He is accused of stealing £20 because he is unable to give a convincing account of how the cheque for that amount came into his possession (it is clearly a tempting sum for a man trying to support a family respectably on £130 a year – Johnny Eames gets into difficulties as a single clerk on £80). He simply cannot remember how he got the cheque, and he cannot remember because he is subject to periods of intense depression during which he is not fully in command of himself. In the early chapters Mrs Crawley will not admit that her husband may be mad or partly mad, but his condition is as exactly known to her as to the novelist:

That he was not a thief was as clear to her as the sun at noonday.
Could she have lain on the man's bosom for twenty years, and
not yet have learned the secrets of the heart beneath? The whole
mind of the man was, as she told herself, within her grasp. He
might have taken the twenty pounds; he might have taken it
and spent it, though it was not his own; but yet he was no thief.
Nor was he a madman. No man more sane in preaching the
gospel of his Lord, in making intelligible to the ignorant the
promises of his Saviour, ever got into a parish pulpit, or taught
in a parish school. The intellect of the man was as clear as
running water in all things not appertaining to his daily life and
its difficulties. He could be logical with a vengeance, – so
logical as to cause infinite trouble to his wife, who, with all her
good sense, was not logical. And he had Greek at his fingers'
ends, – as his daughter knew very well. And even to this day he
would sometimes recite to them English poetry, lines after
lines, stanzas upon stanzas, in a sweet low melancholy voice,
on long winter evenings when occasionally the burden of his
troubles would be lighter to him than was usual. Books in
Latin and in French he read with as much ease as in English, and
took delight in such as came to him, when he would condescend to accept such loans from the deanery. And there was at
times a lightness of heart about the man. In the course of the
last winter he had translated into Greek irregular verse the very
noble ballad of Lord Bateman, maintaining the rhythm and the
rhyme, and had repeated it with uncouth glee till his daughter
knew it all by heart. And when there had come to him a
five-pound note from some admiring magazine editor as the
price of the same, – still through the dean's hands, – he had
brightened up his heart and had thought for an hour or two that
even yet the world would smile upon him. His wife knew well
that he was not mad; but yet she knew that there were dark
moments with him, in which his mind was so much astray that
he could not justly be called to account as to what he might
remember and what he might forget. (IV)

Everything in this account is borne out convincingly by the narrative
at one stage or another. Throughout the novel, but particularly in
the first twenty chapters or so, Trollope elaborates his study of Mr

Crawley's state by registering small details of behaviour such as only the closest watchfulness would have noted. Already, just before the passage just given, the paranoid element in his temperament has emerged in his complaints to his wife that '"Everyone thinks me guilty. I see it in their eyes."' In Chapter VIII, when his wife tries to persuade Mr Crawley to present himself readily before the magistrates, he replies:

> 'Tell them, then, that they must seek me here if they want me.'
>
> 'But, Josiah, think of the parish, – of the people who respect you, – for their sakes let it not be said that you were taken away by policemen.'
>
> 'Was St Paul not bound in prison? Did he think of what the people might see?'
>
> 'If it were necessary, I would encourage you to bear it without a murmur.'
>
> 'It is necessary, whether you murmur, or do not murmur. Murmur, indeed! Why does not your voice ascend to heaven with one loud wail against the cruelty of man?' Then he went forth from the room into an empty chamber on the other side of the passage; and his wife, when she followed him there after a few minutes, found him on his knees, with his forehead against the floor, and with his hands clutching at the scanty hairs of his head. Often before had she seen him so, on the same spot, half grovelling, half prostrate in prayer, reviling in his agony all things around him, – nay, nearly all things above him, – yet striving to reconcile himself to his Creator by the humiliation of confession.

The fact that, taken in context, the sight of Mr Crawley on his knees in agony seems neither melodramatic nor didactic but simply the natural behaviour of a wretched man is a tribute to Trollope's ability to transcend convention by having his gaze so unblinkingly on the human subject. He had had the picture of Mr Crawley's behaviour in acute depression in his mind's eye since Chapter XIV of *Framley Parsonage*, but the later account is more exact and more suggestive. Mr Crawley's reference to St Paul, for instance, is no doubt natural to a clergyman and in a period when scriptural allusion was far more common than it has since become, but it is also a revealing self-identification. It is Mr Crawley's way to exacerbate his own miseries so that he can feel the perverse luxury of martyrdom. His motives for spending so much time with the brickmakers are various, but they include the fact that, as Trollope says with perhaps a barely perceptible irony in the tone, he 'felt himself to be more a St Paul with them than with any other of his neighbours around him'. (XII) But a later visit to the brickmakers is described with the level neutrality of true compassion:

> He went down among the brickmakers on the following morning, leaving the house almost without a morsel of food, and he remained at Hoggle End for the greater part of the day. There were sick persons there with whom he prayed, and then he sat talking with rough men while they ate their dinners, and he read passages from the Bible to women while they washed their husbands' clothes. And for a while he sat with a little girl in his lap teaching the child her alphabet. If it were possible for him he would do his duty. He would spare himself in nothing, though he might suffer even to fainting. And on this occasion he did suffer, – almost to fainting, for as he returned home in the afternoon he was forced to lean from time to time against the banks on the road-side, while the cold sweat of weakness trickled down his face, in order that he might recover strength to go on a few yards. But he would persevere. If God would but leave to him mind enough for his work, he would go on. No personal suffering should deter him. He told himself that there had been men in the world whose sufferings were sharper even than his own. Of what sort had been the life of the man who had stood for years on the top of a pillar? But then the man on the pillar had been honoured by all around him. And thus, though he had thought of the man on the pillar to encourage himself by remembering how lamentable had been that man's sufferings, he came to reflect that after all his own sufferings were per-haps keener than those of the man on the pillar.
>
> When he reached home, he was very ill. There was no doubt about it then. He staggered to his arm-chair, and stared at his wife first, then smiled at her with a ghastly smile. He trembled all over, and when food was brought to him he

could not eat it. Early on the next morning the doctor was by his bedside, and before that evening came he was delirious. (XLI)

The fact that he here compares himself to St Simeon Stylites makes it not surprising that in literature what moves him are figures like 'Polyphemus and Belisarius, and Samson and Milton': ' "The mind of the strong blind creature must be sensible of the injury that has been done to him! The impotency, combined with his strength, or rather the impotency with the memory of former strength and former aspirations, is so essentially tragic!" ' (LXII)

Mr Crawley's tendency to think of himself as a tragic figure does not preclude his being one, despite his weakness and self-pity. It is not just that he has, academically speaking, a better mind than anyone else in the novel and that despite all discouragements he has taught his daughters Greek; it is not just that it might be more appropriately said of him than of Dorothea Brooke that he exhibits 'a certain spiritual grandeur ill-matched with the meanness of opportunity'; it is simply that he has an extraordinary force of personality. The only person who can subdue Mr Crawley is himself. Others who try to reason with him and to persuade him in his own interests to act sensibly – Arabin, Mark Robarts, even his wife – retire overawed, and a weak opponent – such as the hapless Mr Thumble who is sent by Mrs Proudie to supplant Mr Crawley – is totally demoralized. Mr Crawley's power is perhaps demonstrated most forcefully on the occasion of his visit to the Bishop's Palace.

As he walks to Barchester Mr Crawley indulges in fantasies about the coming interview in which a proper humbleness before the Bishop's summons soon gives way to an imaginary triumph over his superior: 'he would take the bishop in his grasp and crush him, – crush him, – crush him!' Such thoughts make him happy, for the moment. But although the fantasy is to some extent an admission of weakness it turns out to be an accurate prediction of what happens. The Proudies are cowed, for a start, by Mr Crawley's appearance:

He was a man who when seen could hardly be forgotten. The deep angry remonstrant eyes, the shaggy eyebrows, telling tales of frequent anger, – of anger frequent but generally silent, – the repressed indignation of the habitual frown, the long nose and large powerful mouth, the deep furrows on the cheek, and the general look of thought and suffering, all combined to make the appearance of the man remarkable, and to describe to the beholders at once his true character. No one ever on seeing Mr. Crawley took him to be a happy man, or a weak man, or an ignorant man, or a wise man. (XVIII)

It is remarkable that this is the most arresting description of Mr Crawley's appearance Trollope has yet given, even though it occurs well into the second novel in which he has appeared. By now Trollope sees him with complete visual clarity, just as he reproduces with what seems total fidelity the grave and pedantic timbre of his speech. The Bishop is not only unable to prevent Mr Crawley from assuming a personal ascendancy, but he cannot match his finesse in argument or his scrupulousness in expression (a high proportion of the chapter is in dialogue). Mrs Proudie, whom the curate has so far studiously ignored, finally goads him into rebuke: '"Peace, woman . . . you should not interfere in these matters. You simply debase your husband's high office. The distaff were more fitting for you."' (XVIII) The quaintness of the last phrase would be absurd but for the fact that it is so consistent with Mr Crawley's habitual mode of expression. It is also the most striking example of the way in which the authorial penchant for self-conscious use of literary diction in the earlier Barset novels has now been completely assimilated into the characterization.

The exhilaration which accompanies the successful contest with authority is something to which Trollope was always intensely sympathetic, but in Mr Crawley's case it cannot last. His triumph is immediately followed – with great psychological plausibility – by a serious relapse of morale: '"The truth is, that there are times when I am not – sane. I am not a thief, – not before God; but I am – mad at times . . . My spirit is broken, and my mind has not been able to keep its even tenour amidst the ruins."' (XIX) He speaks here 'without any excitement, – indeed with a composure which was horrible to witness', and in language of piercing simplicity – though even here the scholarly habits of speech ('even tenour' derives of course from Gray's *Elegy*) are maintained. The integrity of his admission here and the stoicism of the resolve to endure which follows is of a piece with the later resolve that as he is not fully in possession of his faculties and is not thought by others to be so, he ought to resign his living. This stage is not reached without much internal irresolution. By this time even his wife does not fully understand him:

I think that at this time nobody saw clearly the working of his mind, – not even his wife, who studied it very closely, who gave him credit for all his high qualities, and who had gradually learned to acknowledge to herself that she must distrust his judgment in many things. She knew that he was good and yet weak, that he was afflicted by false pride and supported by true pride, that his intellect was still very bright, yet so dismally obscured on many sides as almost to justify people in saying that he was mad. She knew that he was almost a saint, and yet almost a castaway through vanity and hatred of those above him. But she did not know that he knew all this of himself also. She did not comprehend that he should be hourly telling himself that people were calling him mad and were so calling him with truth. It did not occur to her that he could see her insight into him. She doubted as to the way in which he had got the cheque, – never imagining, however, that he had wilfully stolen it; – thinking that his mind had been so much astray as to admit of his finding it and using it without wilful guilt, – thinking also, alas, that a man who could so act was hardly fit for such duties as those which were entrusted to him. But she did not dream that this was precisely his own idea of his own state and of his own position; – that he was always inquiring of himself whether he was not mad; whether, if mad, he was not bound to lay down his office; that he was ever taxing himself with improper hostility to the bishop, – never forgetting for a moment his wrath against the bishop and the bishop's wife, still comforting himself with his triumph over the bishop and the bishop's wife, – but, for all that, accusing himself of a heavy sin and proposing to himself to go to the palace and there humbly to relinquish his clerical authority. Such a course of action he was proposing to himself, but not with any realized idea that he would so act. He was as a man who walks along a river's bank thinking of suicide, calculating how best he might kill himself, – whether the river does not offer an opportunity too good to be neglected, telling himself that for many reasons he had better do so, suggesting to himself that the water is pleasant and cool, and that his ears would soon be deaf to the harsh noises of the world, – but yet knowing, or thinking that he knows, that he never will kill himself. So it was with Mr. Crawley. (XLI)

Although Trollope's account of the conflicting motives and self-deceptive subterfuges within Crawley is masterly it has no air of priding itself on its penetration, and in no way insists that we derive any moral benefit from it. Its transparent and almost rapt concentration on the experience of a fictive person, with no apparent thought of the literary gratification of author and reader, enhances the extraordinary impression of the character's reality that Trollope has by now created.

The truth is that for Trollope Mr Crawley was more of a fact than a fabrication. It is as if the real life of Mr Crawley was the one he led in Trollope's imagination; *The Last Chronicle* gives us some access to it, but in a way that only seems to underline the character's autonomy. One consequence of this is that it allows for a striking flexibility of treatment: for all the tragic intensity of the clergyman's sufferings, he also appears at times in a light that is almost comic. He is not a prisoner of genre. These possibilities particularly emerge in Mr Crawley's encounters with the lawyer Mr Toogood. The exchange of pleasantries between them at the beginning of their first interview indicates the discontinuities of tone characteristic of their relationship. Mr Toogood, to make his wife's relative feel at home, chatters on about his family with a protractedness that taxes Mr Crawley's stiff courtesy: '"Sir, . . . the picture of your home is very pleasant, and I presume that plenty abounds there." "Well, you know, pretty toll-loll for that. With twelve of 'em, Mr Crawley, I needn't tell you they are not all going to have castles and parks of their own, unless they can get 'em off their own bats."' (XXXII) The contrast between Mr Crawley's 'old-fashioned gravity' and Mr Toogood's easy, slangy, familiarity is touchingly recalled when the lawyer brings the curate the news that his trial will not now be necessary because evidence which clears him has now emerged: "'It's all right, old fellow . . . We've got the right sow by the ear at last. We know all about it.'" Mr Crawley's response is characteristically biblical and sonorous: "'I do not as yet fully understand you, sir . . . being perhaps in such matters somewhat dull of intellect, but it seemeth to me that you are a messenger of glad tidings, whose feet are beautiful upon the mountains." "Beautiful!" said Toogood, "By George, I should think they are beautiful! Don't you hear me tell you that we have found out all about the cheque, and that you're as right as a trivet?"' (LXXIV) However, the comic effect is not at the characters' expense: Mr Toogood's eyes are streaming with sympathetic tears, and his joy at Crawley's release is one that cannot but be shared. But in the happiness that follows (which includes Major Grantly's engagement to Grace Crawley) there is no slackening of authorial attention in the emotion of the moment. For Mrs Crawley, the relief is too much: 'She could only sink on the sofa, and hide her face, while she strove in vain to repress her sobs . . . but the endurance of so many troubles, and the great overwhelming sorrow at last, had so nearly over-powered her, that she could not sustain the shock of this turn in their fortunes. "She was never like this, sirs, when ill news came to us," said Mr Crawley, standing somewhat apart from her.' The last detail, properly visualized, implies and catches up more than can be easily stated: Crawley's pride, his egotism, his reticence and sense of decorum, his perverse hostility to good fortune and nostalgia for bad are certainly involved. But we know from the many opportunities we have had in the course of the novel to observe the extraordinary solidity of their relationship, that this standing apart implies no fundamental criticism of his wife – indeed, his remark is a kind of boast.

Mr Crawley's subsequent rehabilitation – he is given Mr Harding's old parish which he makes typically heavy weather of accepting – puts him in contexts where his prickliness is emphasized; he finds Archdeacon Grantly's secular talk about foxes over his port not only hard to tolerate but barely credible in a man of the cloth. Mr Crawley is never going to be an easy man to assimilate, socially speaking. But the return to something like normality is an important part of the human truth of Trollope's portrayal, and it is Trollope's understanding of the whole nature of Mr Crawley that allows him to take the man out of tragedy and return him to social comedy so convincingly that the changes of literary gear are hardly perceptible.

Just as the Crawley of *The Last Chronicle* is more profoundly known than the Crawley of *Framley Parsonage*, and just as the Lily Dale of the later novel is the result of an even deeper apprehension of her than was apparent in *The Small House*, so do some of the smaller characters benefit from the increased intimacy that reappearance allows for. Mrs Proudie has been the resident monster of the series since *Barchester Towers*. Trollope's immediate reason for killing her off and her after-life in his imagination have been referred to above. She had already proved to be more resilient than her origins in something not far short of caricature might have led one to expect, but it is not until this last Barset novel that her inner nature becomes fully perceived. In fact, touches of the earlier literary mode of presentation remain – Mrs Proudie dresses for Sunday evening service in the following way:

> She was gorgeous in a dark brown silk dress of awful stiffness and terrible dimensions; and on her shoulders she wore a short cloak of velvet and fur, very handsome withal, but so swelling in its proportions on all sides as necessarily to create more of dismay than of admiration in the mind of any ordinary man. And her bonnet was a monstrous helmet with the beaver up, displaying the awful face of the warrior, always ready for combat, and careless to guard itself from attack. The large contorted bows which she bore were as a grisly crest upon her casque, beautiful, doubtless, but majestic and fear-compelling. In her hand she carried her armour all complete, a prayer-book, a bible, and a book of hymns. (XVII)

But Trollope has already given signs of a less external interest in the Bishop's wife. In Chapter XI he distinguishes between the natural hostility felt by a man for someone on the other side, and a more fanatical partisanship.

> The archdeacon had called Mrs Proudie a she-Beelzebub; but that was a simple ebullition of mortal hatred. He believed her to be simply a vulgar, interfering, brazen-faced virago. Mrs Proudie in truth believed that the archdeacon was an actual

emanation from Satan, sent to those parts to devour souls, – as she would call it, – and that she herself was an emanation of another sort, sent from another source expressly to Barchester, to prevent such devouring, as far as it might possibly be prevented by a mortal agency.

A manly oppugnancy is clearly something to which Trollope was always ready to give explicit approval, but irrational and extreme combatants also attract a significant amount of his attention, and the fact that he relates Mrs Proudie to this group indicates that he now realizes that there is more to her than had previously met his authorial eye. After her humiliation of her husband in front of Dr Tempest (she refuses to leave the room while they consider what is to be done about Mr Crawley as a matter of official business), she shows a failure of nerve and even a twinge of remorse – something which, on previous evidence, we should hardly expect her to be capable of. Trollope fears 'that it may be too late for me to excite much sympathy in the mind of any reader on behalf of Mrs Proudie. I shall never be able to make her virtues popular. But she had virtues, and their existence made her unhappy.' (XLVII) Trollope's candid admission that he has miscalculated is less damaging than it might be because it so evidently springs from a generous impulse towards a character to whom full justice has not been done.

In fact, both the Proudies begin to benefit from a quite new kind of scrutiny from Trollope. The Bishop, previously seen simply as the henpecked husband, is so demoralized by his wife's domination, that he retires to his study in a state of passive indecision and querulous misery. His broodings allow Trollope to explore his mind so that we see and suffer his situation with him; in an odd way, his paralysis and isolation have something in common with Mr Crawley's sufferings. Among the thoughts that now emerge are dreams of freedom: he even wonders 'would she ever die?'. The fictional moment is so unobtrusive that it is easy to miss the little shock of psychological truth while the unthinkable surfaces. When Mrs Proudie, allowing her anger with the Bishop's inertia to get the better of her, says '"I suppose, then, you wish that I were dead?"', she speaks more truly than she knows. Her last moments reveal an intimate knowledge of her on Trollope's part which helps to explain his remarks in the *Autobiography* about living in her posthumous company. Trollope's summing-up of her not only characteristically refuses to acquiesce in the conventional verdict, but also shows how the unprecedented turn in her life only underlined the old habits of mind:

> It cannot be said that she was a bad woman, though she had in her time done an indescribable amount of evil. She had endeavoured to do good, failing partly by ignorance and partly from the effects of an unbridled, ambitious temper. And now, even amidst her keenest sufferings, her ambition was by no means dead. She still longed to rule the diocese by means of her husband, but was made to pause and hesitate by the unwonted mood that had fallen upon him. (LXVI)

One of the effects of Trollope's account of Mrs Proudie's last days is to make one wonder whether, as between her and her arch-opponent the Archdeacon, there is after all that much to choose.

Bishop Proudie's reactions immediately before and after his wife's death bring to mind the much earlier demise, in the same palace, of the Archdeacon's father, the previous bishop. Striking as Trollope's handling of the occasion was in *Barchester Towers*, the gains by the time of *The Last Chronicle* in both insight and novelistic tact are evident. The moment of shock is closely observed: '. . . there was no sound; not a word, nor a moan, nor a sob. It was as though he also were dead, but that a slight irregular movement of his fingers on the top of his bald head, told her that his mind and body were still active.' His first reactions are convincingly mixed, but tellingly expressed: 'He was now his own master, and there was a feeling, – I may not call it of relief, for as yet there was more of pain in it than satisfaction, – a feeling as though he had escaped from an old trouble at a terrible cost of which he could not as yet calculate the amount.' The later chapters of the novel show the correctness of the Bishop's intuition. He has had a blessed relief, and become a broken man in consequence. As Trollope guardedly points out, it was probably the case that, without his wife, Dr Proudie would never have become a bishop in the first place:

She had been very careful of his children. She had never been idle. She had never been fond of pleasure. She had neglected no acknowledged duty. He did not doubt that she was now on her way to heaven. He took his hands from his head, and clasping them together, said a little prayer. It may be doubted whether he quite knew for what he was praying. The idea of praying for her soul, now that she was dead, would have scandalized him. He certainly was not praying for his own soul. I think he was praying that God might save him from being glad that his wife was dead. (LXVII)

Trollope's tentative 'I think' seems to suggest a level in the Bishop's consciousness which can neither be denied nor admitted to. At any rate the idea of faking the bereaved man's responses does not cross Trollope's mind; the moral honesty of his reports of such moments is one of the ways in which he earns the reader's trust.

It must be admitted, however, that Trollope's account of Mr Harding's death – the other casualty among the novel's principals – is less satisfactory. It is partly because it happens in the natural course of things: Mr Harding dies full of years, in the bosom of his family, loved by all, and makes a good end – what can one, novelistically speaking, say? The onset of senility and his totterings round the house after he has to give up his daily visits to the cathedral are described delicately enough, although the dirge-like notes of his cello are again allowed – even in their discontinuance – to contribute their overtones of sentiment. His games of cat's-cradle with his grandchild hover perilously near some scene in a genre picture, and his angelic smile as he murmurs to himself 'Lord now lettest Thou Thy servant depart in peace' strike a liturgical note that is rare in Trollope's work because it touches an area of experience which was not of great practical use to him. Belief only becomes important in Trollope's characters when energized by temperament. Trollope's final tribute to Mr Harding – Barchester 'never knew a sweeter gentleman or a better Christian' – is as a tribute truer of his later appearances than of his earlier. The hypersensitivity, the mixture of principle and weakness which were discovered in *The Warden*, have long been allowed to recede, but we are at least spared any excess of pathos at the old man's passing.

One of Mr Harding's last wishes is that Mr Crawley should have his living, and his request provides a pleasant formal connection between the first Barsetshire novel and the last. Both novels concern clergymen whose difficulties become *causes célèbres*, but the briefest of comparisons between the two novels (even when allowance is made for their relative lengths) will show how greatly Trollope's fictive world has expanded, and how skilfully its interconnected nature has been elaborated. Mr Crawley's case concerns not only himself but the whole country, and its outcome affects the lives (and in Mrs Proudie's case hastens the death) of others in a critical way. This seems to happen, however, much more according to the natural connections within a community and the contingencies of everyday contact than according to some thematically conceived model of society. According to Trollope's first biographer T. H. S. Escott, George Eliot once confessed that but for the example of Trollope she would hardly have had the courage to plan *Middlemarch* on 'so extensive a scale' or 'have persevered with it to the close'. But the patterns of social relationships in *Middlemarch* are clearly meant among other things to be generally illustrative of the way provincial society worked at a specific point in historical time. Barsetshire is not offered as a model of this kind, the author being preoccupied with persons studied for the sake of their individuality rather than because of their function in a unified scheme.[6] The last paragraph of *The Last Chronicle* is an assertion that Barset has been so 'real' and 'familiar' to its creator that the imagined world has become virtually self-sufficient. Its importance lies not in its significance as a society in which abstract values can be dramatized, but as an environment which can be actually lived in. Trollope has wandered there so long because of his love of 'old friendships' and 'old faces'. Barset has given him the opportunity to dwell with and on his characters in a peculiarly protracted and therefore particularly valuable way.

As it is the last chronicle of Barset, Trollope naturally wants to revisit as many friends as possible, and familiar names slip into the novel's exposition with the unobtrusive ease of old acquaintance. The early chapters are densely allusive – Luftons, Arabins, Grantlys, and others either appear directly or are referred to without much introduction. An already elaborate set of established relationships is further complicated by the affairs of members of the second generation. The tension between the Archdeacon and his son Major

Grantly, over the latter's proposed marriage to Grace Crawley, provides yet another version of the misalliance situation already used in previous Barsetshire novels. With one daughter married to a marquis, the Grantlys are dismayed by their son's obstinacy in standing by his pledge to the daughter of what appears to be a disgraced and certainly a poverty-stricken man. The question becomes the ground of a quarrel between father and son, the progress of which is chronicled by Trollope with an attention to the conflicting feelings of family obligation and self-assertion that is psychologically more penetrating than anything comparable in the Barset series (though it can be paralleled in many places in Trollope's work outside it).

The parallel between Grace Crawley's situation and Lucy Robarts's, in *Framley Parsonage*, is explicitly recalled when the Archdeacon goes to see Lady Lufton (Chapter LVI), but it is Lady Lufton rather than the narrator who does the recalling. Looking back over the episode in her own life, she admits that the young people had been right and that she had been wrong, but she is bound to understand how the Archdeacon feels now because that is how she felt then. Because the situation is approached dramatically in this way, we do not have the impression of the novelist repeating himself but rather that life is doing so. And the scene that follows (LVII) between Grace and the Archdeacon differs from its predecessor involving Lady Lufton and Lucy Robarts because, although broadly comparable in that the prudential older person is outmanoeuvred by the principled independence of the younger, it concerns two individuals who are different. Grace is much more timid than Lucy was but – as the Archdeacon who is sensitive to such things sees – potentially noble. Indeed, his susceptibility to the combined appeal of Grace's emergent beauty and her moral generosity (in renouncing any claim to Major Grantly should her father be pronounced guilty), is such that he becomes doubly the victim of his innately soft heart and his unwillingness ever to be outdone. The scene therefore ends in a completely opposite way to which he had intended, but the emotional logic of it remains impeccable. The mild teasing of the Archdeacon by his wife for being so susceptible is one of Trollope's nicely engineered returns from unusually strong emotion to the predictably comforting responses of everyday.

Grace's happiness, like so much else in *The Last Chronicle*, is dependent on Mr Crawley's fate, and it is a further measure of the completeness of Trollope's vision of him that his appearances in a paternal capacity are so consistent with the rest of his portraiture. When Major Grantly formally asks for Grace's hand, Mr Crawley's reply under pressure of emotion is at first couched in what is almost a parody of his habitual syntax, only to collapse into words of broken simplicity:

> 'I am sorry that I have not been explicit,' said Mr Crawley, 'but I will endeavour to make myself more plainly intelligible. My daughter, sir, is so circumstanced in reference to her father, that I, as her father and as a gentleman, cannot encourage any man to make a tender to her of his hand.'
>
> 'But I have made up my mind about all that.'
>
> 'And I, sir, have made up mine. I dare not tell my girl that I think she will do well to place her hand in yours. A lady, when she does that, should feel at least that her hand is clean.'
>
> 'It is the cleanest and the sweetest and the fairest hand in Barsetshire,' said the major. Mrs Crawley could not restrain herself, but running up to him, took his hand in hers and kissed it.
>
> 'There is unfortunately a stain, which is vicarial,' began Mr Crawley, sustaining up to that point his voice with Roman fortitude, – with a fortitude which would have been Roman had it not at that moment broken down under the pressure of human feeling. He could keep it up no longer, but continued his speech with broken sobs, and with a voice altogether changed in its tone, – rapid now, whereas it had before been slow, – natural, whereas it had hitherto been affected, – human, whereas it had hitherto been Roman. 'Major Grantly,' he said, 'I am sore beset; but what can I say to you? My darling is as pure as the light of day, – only that she is soiled with my impurity. She is fit to grace the house of the best gentleman in England, had I not made her unfit.' (LXIII)

The moment would be almost Micawberishly unstable, were it not for the security of our knowledge of the psychological processes behind it.

The continuity of personnel in the Barsetshire series enabled

Trollope to establish by its later stages a peculiarly convincing balance between the privacy of interior experience and the social self. Early in *The Last Chronicle* Grace Crawley pays a visit to Allington, and is taken to dine with Lily's uncle, Mr Dale of the Great House at Allington:

> 'My uncle didn't bite you after all, Grace,' said Lily to her friend as they were going home at night, by the pathway which led from the garden of one house to the garden of the other.
>
> 'I like Mr Dale very much,' said Grace. 'He was very kind to me.'
>
> 'There is some queer-looking animal of whom they say that he is better than he looks, and I always think of that saying when I think of my uncle.'
>
> 'For shame, Lily,' said her mother. 'Your uncle, for his age, is as good a looking man as I know. And he always looks like just what he is, – an English gentleman.'
>
> 'I didn't mean to say a word against his dear old face and figure, mamma; but his heart, and mind, and general disposition, as they come out in experience and days of trial, are so much better than the samples of them which he puts out on the counter for men and women to judge by. He wears well, and he washes well, – if you know what I mean, Grace.'
>
> 'Yes; I think I know what you mean.'
>
> 'The Apollos of the world, – I don't mean in outward looks, mamma, – but the Apollos in heart, the men, – and the women too, – who are so full of feeling, so soft-natured, so kind, who never say a cross word, who never get out of bed on the wrong side in the morning, – it so often turns out that they won't wash.'
>
> Such was the expression of Miss Lily Dale's experience. (XVI)

Readers who live with Trollope's characters as he would have wished may recall at such a moment, among other things, Mr Dale's own frustration at the bearish unlovableness of his nature which leads people to reject his schemes for their welfare (see for instance his bitter thoughts as given at the end of Chapter XXXVIII of *The Small House*); they may recollect that the pathway which leads from one house to another was also the scene, at night, of Lily's impassioned exchanges with Adolphus Crosbie. They will not be surprised therefore – since they will remember with Lily her playful attaching of 'Apollo' to Crosbie – when she uses the name in a way that has an obvious general meaning to Grace, but a painful private significance to herself – a significance that Trollope laconically hints at in the last sentence. The art of imagining and transcribing such moments – apparently inconsequential, but deeply freighted with experience – was only fully mastered by Trollope in the last two Barsetshire novels, but their achievement rests on the prolonged communion made possible by characters that reappear.

The Pallisers and Reappearance

Can You Forgive Her?

Trollope embarked upon his second sequence of novels before he had finished the first. *Can You Forgive Her?* (published 1864–5), the first of the series known as the Palliser or the Political Novels, was begun six months after *The Small House at Allington* was completed in February 1863. *The Last Chronicle of Barset* was finished in September 1866; *Phineas Finn*, the second Palliser novel, was begun two months later. The two series, taken together, span twenty-four out of the thirty-nine years of Trollope's writing life. It seems clear that by the end of the Barsetshire chronicles Trollope had come to realize how deep was the affinity between the novel series and the habits of his imagination. The Palliser novels, however, benefit greatly from the fact that they were begun by Trollope in mid-career and at the height of his powers. By the early 1860s he had discovered his true strengths as a novelist, and the unevennesses and inadequacies of the earlier Barset books are thus avoided. His confidence was also increased, no doubt, by the reputation which he had by then achieved. According to the *National Review* for January 1863, Trollope had become 'almost a national institution . . . So great is his popularity, so wide-spread is the interest felt about his tales, that they necessarily form part of the common stock-in-trade with which the social commerce of the day is carried on.' In going on to stress that 'the characters are public property', the writer underlines the extent to which Trollope's own preoccupation in his novels was reciprocated by his first readers. It is also an indication of his position that he sold *Can You Forgive Her?* for £3,525 – the largest sum he ever received for a novel.

The story of the Pallisers begins in the later chapters of *The Small House at Allington*, and there is thus a natural transition from the first of Trollope's novel series to the second. At this stage, however, Lady Glencora is merely sketched in a couple of pages which simply report her still almost childish charm, her wilfulness and energy, and the fact that she is dangerously interested in the dashing but depraved Burgo Fitzgerald – not a suitable match for an inexperienced girl due to inherit large tracts of Scotland. When he took up Lady Glencora again Trollope's imagination had clearly developed in the intervening months a much fuller knowledge of her personality. With Plantagenet Palliser, Trollope had given himself more to go on, but there is a certain ambivalence in his treatment of the character in *The Small House* which presumably indicates Trollope's uncertainty as to which fictive option to take up. It is not really apparent here that the character would turn out to be capable of the extension he ultimately received – that he would prove to have so much blood in him. It is always important to remember that, in Trollope, character is something that is progressively discovered as well as continuously demonstrated.

Plantagenet's first reported remark (in Chapter XXIII of *The Small House*) is 'I don't see anything to laugh at'. His humourlessness is part of an introductory description which stresses his application to politics to the exclusion of everything else: 'He was a thin-minded, plodding, respectable man, willing to devote all his youth to work, in order that in old age he might be allowed to sit among the Councillors of the State.' The fact that he speaks from time to time to the inordinately beautiful Lady Dumbello 'almost with an air of interest' is quickly assumed by others – given the frigidity of his nature – to be evidence of a grand if improper passion. The gossip that Lady Dumbello is about to place herself 'under the protection' (as the phrase then was) of Mr Palliser alarms Plantagenet's uncle, the old Duke of Omnium, on whose wealth Palliser's political ambitions depend. Palliser is aggrieved by the Duke's interference which has the unintended effect of encouraging him to go in for an affair more energetically, wondering whether it might not 'become him as a gentleman to fall in love'. Apart from the fact that Palliser's idea of what is gentlemanly, as later developed, would never have included the conduct he is now contemplating, his whole situation is treated by Trollope in a mode which has an ironic element of mockery. Part of Plantagenet's difficulty is that he has not the faintest idea of how to talk to a pretty woman in public. The scene when (having earlier paved the way with some tender exchanges about sugar duties) he finally brings himself to whisper ' "Griselda" ' to Lady Dumbello is robbed of any romantic effect or sense of narrative danger by the little comedy of his being unable to sit beside her because of the width of her highly fashionable dress. The moment briefly recalls the art of sofa management as understood and practised by La Signora Vesey Neroni. Plantagenet's erotic inhibition and social incompetence place him at a kind of disadvantage which he never has to struggle against in the later novels, even at those moments which are not entirely to his credit. The artistic security with which Lady Dumbello herself is presented in this matter is a notable contrast. When her mother, the Archdeacon's wife, hears dreadful rumours down in Barsetshire and writes to Griselda to recall her to her sense of marital duty, Griselda simply turns the letter over to her disgruntled husband, demolishing any possible case against her and effectively drawing his fire. 'Lady Dumbello was well aware that she had triumphed, and that her mother's letter had been invaluable to her. But it had been used, and therefore she did not read it again. She ate her breakfast in quiet comfort, looking over a milliner's French circular as she did so.' (LV) Her 'quiet comfort' is a lethal touch: Trollope had in the interval between *Framley Parsonage* and *The Small House* confirmed his sense of Griselda's imperturbable egotism, and his treatment of her at this juncture has the serene and severe ease of old acquaintance. His handling of Palliser's reactions, on the other hand, seems tentative, unsure of the weight of what he has in the hand.

When Plantagenet is reintroduced in *Can You Forgive Her?*, the accents are notably more respectful.

> Mr Palliser was one of those politicians in possessing whom England has perhaps more reason to be proud than of any other of her resources, and who, as a body, give to her that exquisite combination of conservatism and progress which is her present strength and best security for the future. He could afford to learn to be a statesman, and had the industry wanted for such training. He was born in the purple, noble himself, and heir to the highest rank as well as one of the greatest fortunes of the country, already very rich, surrounded by all the temptations of luxury and pleasure; and yet

he devoted himself to work with the grinding energy of a young penniless barrister labouring for a penniless wife, and did so without any motive more selfish than that of being counted in the roll of the public servants of England. He was not a brilliant man, and understood well that such was the case. He was now listened to in the House, as the phrase goes; but he was listened to as a laborious man, who was in earnest in what he did, who got up his facts with accuracy, and who, dull though he be, was worthy of confidence. And he was very dull. He rather prided himself on being dull, and on conquering in spite of his dulness. He never allowed himself a joke in his speeches, nor attempted even the smallest flourish of rhetoric. He was very careful in his language, labouring night and day to learn to express himself with accuracy, with no needless repetition of words, perspicuously with regard to the special object he might have in view. He had taught himself to believe that oratory, as oratory, was a sin against that honesty in politics by which he strove to guide himself. He desired to use words for the purpose of teaching things which he knew and which others did not know; and he desired also to be honoured for his knowledge. But he had no desire to be honoured for the language in which his knowledge was conveyed. He was an upright, thin, laborious man; who by his parts alone could have served no political party materially, but whose parts were sufficient to make his education, integrity, and industry useful in the highest degree. It is the trust which such men inspire which makes them so serviceable; – trust not only in their labour, – for any man rising from the mass of the people may be equally laborious; nor yet simply in their honesty and patriotism. The confidence is given to their labour, honesty, and patriotism joined to such a personal stake in the country as gives them a weight and ballast which no politician in England can possess without it. (XXIV)

Palliser is now placed in a context in which his qualities are seen as a national asset, however much (as Trollope goes on to say) they may have their disadvantages in private life. The modification of 'a thin-minded, plodding, respectable man' (in *The Small House*) to, here, 'an upright, thin, laborious man' is subtle but significantly less pejorative. Palliser's care over his language is a new note, and has suggestive affinities with Trollope's own prescriptions on style as outlined in the *Autobiography*. The stress on honesty and integrity in the public interest reflects Trollope's own conception of the ideal civil servant in whom probity, perseverance, and an element of the patrician all combine. Palliser's past feelings about Lady Dumbello are relegated to the status of a 'little threatened mischance' which 'had hardly polluted his natural character'. In asserting that his 'desire had been of a kind which was almost more gratified in its disappointment than it would have been in its fruition', Trollope dextrously extricates Palliser from a compromising situation – almost, one might say, from a false start. Trollope immediately makes it clear however that Palliser has everything to learn about his wife's needs and the nature of marriage, and a major part of *Can You Forgive Her?* is taken up with the process through which this enlightenment comes.

Tipped as a future Chancellor of the Exchequer, Palliser is on the verge of achieving the high political office for which he has so selflessly and yet egocentrically prepared himself. His devotion to his work, as Lady Glencora complains, means late hours: '"He seldom gives over work till after one, and sometimes goes on till three. It's the only thing he likes, I believe."' (XXIII) She misses 'the little daily assurance of her supremacy in the man's feelings, the constant touch of love' (XXIV), and with such a demonstrative nature as hers, it is not surprising that she still pines for the physically glamorous Burgo Fitzgerald. At this stage, Plantagenet is complacent about the situation; the imminent prospect of sitting in the Cabinet is so alluring that 'he could thus afford to put up with the small everyday calamity of having a wife who loved another man better than she loved him'. (XXIV) Trollope's dry, laconic tone anticipates the ironic development of the story. In the event, that 'calamity' not only deprives Palliser of the high office he craves but it also precipitates an emotional commitment to his wife of a depth nowhere previously hinted at.

It must be said that Glencora is not easy to deal with at the best of times. Trollope's evolution of her personality from the few hints dropped in *The Small House* is remarkable. By the time she has finished driving her cousin Alice Vavasor to Matching from the station (XXII), Glencora's incessant and volatile chatter has already revealed many of the main elements in the character that Trollope was to develop with such love and understanding in later novels. As Glencora says, she is a talker (as opposed to the Pallisers, who are speakers), and her talk reveals the inherent contradictoriness of her nature: her childishness and her wisdom, her vivacity and underlying melancholy, her awareness of propriety and her incurable irreverence. Above all, it conveys candour, spontaneity and energy. Her language owes nothing to idiosyncrasy – she is not tagged by tricks of repeated phrase – and yet her dialogue is instantly recognizable. (When Glencora makes a brief appearance in *Miss Mackenzie*, which Trollope began less than a month after finishing *Can You Forgive Her?*, her utterances are immediately characteristic and identifiable.) There can be no doubt that Glencora is now a thoroughly dramatized and familiar presence in Trollope's mind.

One result of this is that (apart from a few embarrassing lines in Chapter XLIII – 'Poor, wretched, overburthened child', etc.) the presentation of Glencora is remarkably free from the kind of apologetic accompanying commentary which, in a novel of this period, one might have expected (and which admittedly one does get with its other heroine, Alice Vavasor). In fact, Glencora's judgements on herself pre-empt criticism, just as a certain ruthlessness in her exploitation of others provokes it. She fastens on Alice because she needs a friend to help keep her straight and she needs someone who will be loving to her because her husband isn't. Her affection for Alice has an element of unscrupulousness: she loves her for her own purposes. When she says to Alice, at the end of Chapter XXV, '"Someone's love I must have found, – or I could not have remained here,"' it is a tribute both to Alice's friendship, and an indication that another equally sympathetic person might have done equally well. Glencora's vulnerability and her resentment at having been bullied into what she thinks of as a mockery of a marriage appear with particular intensity in the scene in the ruins at Matching. She talks of the way '"They told me he would spend my money . . . They told me that he would ill-use me, and desert me, – and perhaps beat me"' with a touch of that paranoid sense of injury that Lily Dale felt at having her private life made the subject of public comment. The 'he' is of course Burgo, although a few

sentences later, in '"I never loved him"', the 'him' is clearly
Plantagenet – the unexpressed antecedents are a tiny but significant
sign of the way Glencora has been brooding on her wrongs. When
she says of Burgo that '"I could stoop at his feet and clean his shoes
for him, and think it no disgrace!"', Glencora is expressing, in a
kind of shorthand of the period, a feeling of abject physical attraction that is not the less powerful for the fact that Glencora has
probably never cleaned a pair of shoes in her life. Nevertheless, the
judgements she passes on herself are harsh:

> 'Alice, look here. I know what I am, and what I am like to
> become. I loathe myself, and I loathe the thing that I am
> thinking of. I could have clung to the outside of a man's
> body, to his very trappings, and loved him ten times better
> than myself! – ay, even though he had ill-treated me, – if I had
> been allowed to choose a husband for myself. Burgo would
> have spent my money, – all that it would have been possible
> for me to give him. But there would have been something
> left, and I think that by that time I could have won even him
> to care for me. But with that man – !' (XXVII)

It is hard not to sympathize with Glencora's feeling (never subsequently fully overcome) that an irreparable wrong has been done
to her when it is accompanied by such a shrewd assessment of
Burgo's character and by such economic realism.

Her sense of injury and her fantasies about having Burgo at her
feet on vine-shaded marble balconies in Italy sharpen Glencora's
wish to have her own way where she can, and Palliser begins to
wonder, after a series of petty squabbles which really signify a
profound struggle of wills, whether he knows how to manage his
wife. Scrupulous – as she is always to remain – about not exploiting
the fact that she has brought Palliser a reputed £50,000 a year,
Glencora proves deeply refractory in minor matters. Things are not
going well physically either: Palliser's embraces are fraternal rather
than conjugal and 'Lady Glencora, with her full woman's nature,
understood this thoroughly, and appreciated by instinct the true
bearing of every touch from his hand'. (XLII) So that when she and
Burgo finally meet at Lady Monk's party (observed by a telling
conjunction and with glacial propriety by Lady Dumbello, now the
Marchioness of Hartletop), there is some reason to suppose that

Burgo's proposal to elope there and then will be favourably received. In his review, written when the book first came out, the young Henry James was frustrated by what he thought of as Trollope's timidity and would clearly have been happier if the *Bovaryisme* of Glencora's private dreams had been followed through into plot fact. James did not fully reckon with Glencora's sense of things as they really are, with the courage that comes from her sense of what is due to herself. 'She had recovered her presence of mind, and understood what was going on. She was no longer in a dream, but words and things bore to her again their proper meaning. "I will not have it, Mr Fitzgerald," she answered, speaking almost passionately.' When Palliser reappears – as Burgo successfully pleads for at least one more meeting – Glencora (still at this stage under twenty-one) displays that temperament which convincingly foreshadows the *grande dame* of the later novels:

> Looking up again towards the doorway, in fear of Mr Bott's eyes, she saw the face of Mr Palliser as he entered the room. Mr Bott had also seen him, and had tried to clutch him by the arm; but Mr Palliser had shaken him off, apparently with indifference, – had got rid of him, as it were, without noticing him. Lady Glencora, when she saw her husband, immediately recovered her courage. She would not cower before him, or show herself ashamed of what she had done. For the matter of that, if he pressed her on the subject, she could bring herself to tell him that she loved Burgo Fitzgerald much more easily than she could whisper such a word to Burgo himself. Mr Bott's eyes were odious to her as they watched her; but her husband's glance she could meet without quailing before it. 'Here is Mr Palliser,' said she, speaking again in her ordinary clear-toned voice. Burgo immediately rose from his seat with a start, and turned quickly towards the door; but Lady Glencora kept her chair.
>
> Mr Palliser made his way as best he could through the crowd up to his wife. He, too, kept his countenance without betraying his secret. There was neither anger nor dismay in his face, nor was there any untoward hurry in his movement. Burgo stood aside as he came up, and Lady Glencora was the first to speak. 'I thought you were gone home hours ago,' she said.

'I did go home,' he answered, 'but I thought I might as well come back for you.'

'What a model of a husband! Well; I am ready. Only, what shall we do about Jane? Mr Fitzgerald, I left a scarf in your aunt's room, – a little black and yellow scarf, – would you mind getting it for me?'

'I will fetch it,' said Mr Palliser; 'and I will tell your cousin that the carriage shall come back for her.'

'If you will allow me – ' said Burgo.

'I will do it,' said Mr Palliser; and away he went, making his slow progress up through the crowd, ordering his carriage as he passed through the hall, and leaving Mr Bott still watching at the door. (L)

The poised dignity of Glencora's '"Here is Mr Palliser"' is answered by the absence of anger or dismay in his face and of 'any untoward hurry in his movement', and also by his chivalry in leaving her with Burgo while he goes to fetch her scarf. Nothing in the novel shows more convincingly how well matched they are than this joint ability to rise with apparent effortlessness to the demands of the public occasion.

The masterly chapter dealing with the aftermath of Lady Monk's party, 'The Pallisers at Breakfast', is a striking indication of the flexibility of manner and method which Trollope's by now secure understanding of his characters permits. Returned home, Glencora sits up late in front of the dying fire analysing her situation in a way that seems to anticipate Isabel Archer's midnight musings in *Portrait of a Lady*. She still does not know how she will react to her husband's words in the morning. At breakfast, Palliser has finally to be flushed out from behind his newspaper – a newspaper which contains political reports of the greatest significance for his career and which makes him feel more than ever 'full of politics' – by direct attack from Glencora. However, during the scene the balance of power slowly changes, as it passes from the almost comic tiff with which it begins into the impassioned confession of feelings by both characters – feelings that Plantagenet at least seems to discover for the first time as he expresses them. Plantagenet decisively gains the initiative when he forces Glencora to admit that her sense of being watched by Mrs

Marsham and Mr Bott does not mean that they were commissioned by Palliser to do so.

'Then it is ignoble in you to talk to me of spies. I have employed no spies. If it were ever to come to that, that I thought spies necessary, it would be all over with me.'

There was something of feeling in his voice as he said this, – something that almost approached to passion which touched his wife's heart. Whether or not spies would be of any avail, she knew that she had in truth done that of which he had declared that he had never suspected her. She had listened to words of love from her former lover. She had received, and now carried about with her a letter from this man, in which he asked her to elope with him. She had by no means resolved that she would not do this thing. She had been false to her husband; and as her husband spoke of his confidence in her, her own spirit rebelled against the deceit which she herself was practising.

'I know that I have never made you happy,' she said. 'I know that I never can make you happy.'

He looked at her, struck by her altered tone, and saw that her whole manner and demeanour were changed. 'I do not understand what you mean,' he said. 'I have never complained. You have not made me unhappy.' He was one of those men to whom this was enough. If his wife caused him no uneasiness, what more was he to expect from her? No doubt she might have done much more for him. She might have given him an heir. But he was a just man, and knew that the blank he had drawn was his misfortune, and not her fault.

Trollope's attentiveness to what each character is thinking and how each strikes the other is wonderfully unobtrusive, not least in the registration of small but intensely suggestive details of gesture and movement:

'Plantagenet, I do not love you; – not as women love their husbands when they do love them. But, before God, my first wish is to free you from the misfortune that I have brought on you.' As she made this attestation she started up from her chair, and coming close to him, took him by the coat. He was startled, and stepped back a pace, but did not speak; and then stood looking at her as she went on:

'What matters is whether I drown myself, or throw myself away by going with such a one as him, so that you might marry again, and have a child? I'd die; – I'd die willingly. How I wish I could die! Plantagenet, I would kill myself if I dared.'

He was a tall man and she was short of stature, so that he stood over her and looked upon her, and now she was looking up into his face with all her eyes. 'I would,' she said. 'I would – I would! What is there left for me that I should wish to live?'

Softly, slowly, very gradually, as though he were afraid of what he was doing, he put his arm round her waist. 'You are wrong in one thing,' he said. 'I do love you.'

She shook her head, touching his breast with her hair as she did so.

'I do love you,' he repeated. 'If you mean that I am not apt at telling you so, it is true, I know. My mind is running on other things.'

'Yes,' she said; 'your mind is running on other things.'

'But I do love you. If you cannot love me, it is a great misfortune to us both. But we need not therefore be disgraced. As for that other thing of which you spoke, – of our having, as yet, no child' – and in saying this he pressed her somewhat closer with his arm – 'you allow yourself to think too much of it; – much more of it than I do. I have made no complaints on that head, even within my own breast.'

'I know what your thoughts are, Plantagenet.'

'Believe me that you wrong my thoughts. Of course I have been anxious, and have, perhaps, shown my anxiety by the struggle I have made to hide it. I have never told you what is false, Glencora.'

'No; you are not false!'

'I would rather have you for my wife, childless, – if you will try to love me, – than any other woman, though another might give me an heir. Will you try to love me?'

She was silent. At this moment, after the confession that she had made, she could not bring herself to say that she would even try. Had she said so, she would have seemed to have accepted his forgiveness too easily.

'I think, dear,' he said, still holding her by her waist, 'that we had better leave England for a while. I will give up politics for this season. Should you like to go to Switzerland for the summer, or perhaps to some of the German baths, and then on to Italy when the weather is cold enough?' Still she was silent. 'Perhaps your friend, Miss Vavasor, would go with us?'

He was killing her by his goodness. She could not speak to him yet; but now, as he mentioned Alice's name, she gently put up her hand and rested it on the back of his.

At that moment there came a knock at the door; – a sharp knock, which was quickly repeated.

'Come in,' said Mr Palliser, dropping his arm from his wife's waist, and standing away from her a few yards. (LVIII)

The concluding knock – it is the butler – provides the little moment of embarrassment that allows an excellently judged return to normality.

At the end of this scene it is clear that the terrain of the Palliser marriage has been irrevocably altered by a kind of conjugal landslide – and it could hardly have been more economically and on the narrator's part more self-effacingly done. At its beginning Palliser can have had no intention of declaring his love for Glencora in the way that her desperation surprises him into; his decision to give up the imminent chance of political office in order to take his wife abroad is taken with an entirely convincing lack of premeditation. He seems to arrive at it by finding that he has already done so – nothing could be truer to life. Only the consequences of it need to be explained. Glencora's response to the springs of generosity that she has so surprisingly tapped finds her unprecedentedly inarticulate, but the little touch of her hand on his is deeply affecting. It marks the real beginning of the Palliser marriage: we know now that for all its superficial instabilities and incompatibilities its durability will not be seriously threatened because it is underpinned by a strength of feeling in Palliser that is the more powerful for being so deeply recessed and so rarely voiced.

The extraordinary quality of dramatic concentration in this

chapter is an indication and a consequence of the way in which Trollope refines his understanding of his characters by allowing them to discover themselves. The sense of identity thus achieved is secure enough to permit the author a wide range of tone (as we saw in the case of Mr Crawley). Here, it is significant that the authorial explanation of Glencora's conduct in the ball-scene comes after its dramatic presentation. After Palliser leaves her Glencora takes out Burgo's letter and tears it up: 'As she did so, her mind seemed to be fixed, at any rate, to one thing, – that she would think no more of Burgo Fitzgerald as her future master. I think, however, that she had arrived at so much certainty as this, at that moment in which she had been parting with Burgo Fitzgerald, in Lady Monk's dining-room.' (LIX) Trollope's 'I think' here is both deliberate and deferential, interpreting the moment firmly, but allowing that there might be other ways of accounting for it, including the character's. Glencora says to herself at this point that Palliser still 'does not know what love means', but she is wrong. The complex of feelings she has provoked is retrospectively analysed by Palliser with a degree of self-accusation that is characteristic of both his generosity and his self-consciousness:

> But of this he was aware, – that he had forgiven his wife; that he had put his arm round her and embraced her after the hearing of her confession, – and that she, mutely, with her eyes, had promised him that she would do her best for him. Then something of an idea of love came across his heart, and he acknowledged to himself that he had married without loving or without requiring love. Much of all this had been his own fault. Indeed, had not the whole of it come from his own wrong-doing? He acknowledged that it was so. But now, – now he loved her. He felt that he could not bear to part with her, even if there were no question of public scandal, or of disgrace. He had been torn inwardly by that assertion that she loved another man. She had got at his heart-strings at last. There are men who may love their wives, though they never can have been in love before their marriage. (LIX)

The laconic irony of Trollope's last sentence here is the sort of thing he permits himself when he feels artistically secure.

The first practical consequences of the trip abroad are related by Glencora to Alice Vavasor in her most volatile vein:

> 'But no; that was the first plan, and Mr Palliser altered it. He spent a whole day up here with maps and Bradshaws and Murray's guide-books, and he scolded me so because I didn't care whether we went first to Baden or to some other place. How could I care? I told him I would go anywhere he chose to take me. Then he told me I was heartless; – and I acknowledged that I was heartless. "I am heartless," I said. "Tell me something I don't know."'
>
> 'Oh, Cora, why did you say that?'
>
> 'I didn't choose to contradict my husband. Besides, it's true. Then he threw the Bradshaw away, and all the maps flew about. So I picked them up again, and said we'd go to Switzerland first. I knew that would settle it, and of course he decided on stopping at Baden. If he had said Jericho, it would have been the same thing to me.' (LXII)

There is no contradiction between this little piece of domestic comedy and the serious presentation of the deepest levels of the Palliser marriage because the characters remain so recognizably themselves in both modes. Palliser's new realization of the intensity of his feelings for Glencora does not alter the fact that her exclusive company, down at Matching, bores him to stupefaction: '"I saw him yawning sometimes," Lady Glencora said afterwards, "as though he would fall in pieces."' (LXII)

In the later chapters of *Can You Forgive Her?* the stabilizing of the marriage is shown by Trollope with great sureness of touch. Glencora remains quite as capricious and unreasonable as before – her delight in maddening Palliser is, if anything, increased. She teases him about statistics, proposes absurd itineraries, and is animatedly difficult without ever becoming absolutely impossible. Palliser's noble sacrifice seems to be poorly rewarded by Glencora's scatty recalcitrance, which is partly prompted by her new sense of that nobility. He has given up the despatch-box for packing-cases and the measured dignities of the House of Commons for Glencora's impulsive chatter, and it is not until his wife has at last some happy news to give him that Palliser can feel that virtue has brought more than its own reward. Glencora's pregnancy resolves the unspoken but apparent tension between them; superficially it gives rise to yet more bickering – Palliser's concern for Glencora's condition being positively old-womanish – but the tetchy idiom of their exchanges begins to settle into a pattern that is at bottom relaxed and reassuring. Indeed, the whole style of their marriage is to rest on a kind of institutionalizing of their incompatibility. The absorbing feature of their relationship, as Trollope now begins to sense it and as he will develop it in later novels, is that they constantly irritate each other because their temperaments are so opposed but they become ever more necessary to each other for that very reason.

A final appearance by Burgo Fitzgerald reveals the degree of marital confidence that has now been established. The Palliser party look in at the gambling rooms at Baden as many travellers then did and discover Burgo staking his last napoleon at the tables. Glencora has had a little flutter herself, and is fluttered at herself for so doing, but Burgo's plight is obviously desperate.

> Lady Glencora immediately ran up to her husband, and took him away from Mr Grey. Rapidly she told her story, – with such rapidity that Mr Palliser could hardly get in a word. 'Do something for him; – do, do. Unless I know that something is done, I shall die. You needn't be afraid.'
>
> 'I'm not afraid,' said Mr Palliser.
>
> Lady Glencora, as she went on quickly, got hold of her husband's hand, and caressed it. 'You are so good,' said she. 'Don't let him out of your sight. There; he is going. I will go home with Mr Grey. I will be ever so good; I will, indeed. You know what he'll want, and for my sake you'll let him have it. But don't let him gamble. If you could only get him home to England, and then do something. You owe him something, Plantagenet; do you not?'
>
> 'If money can do anything, he shall have it.'
>
> 'God bless you, dearest! I shall never see him again; but if you could save him! There; – he is going now. Go; – go.' She pushed him forward, and then retreating, put her arm within Mr Grey's, still keeping her eye upon her husband. (LXXV)

Palliser behaves very decently towards Burgo, acknowledges the curious bond between them, and even concedes a kind of responsibility for him. But what is striking is the degree to which husband's and wife's attitudes fall naturally together with an instinctive common concern and candour. The easy spontaneity of their words and thoughts unobtrusively measures the marital distance travelled between this last encounter with Glencora's lover and the earlier scene at Lady Monk's ball (a gamble too in its way). Moreover, one has only to imagine how other Victorian novelists might have dealt with the occasion – strong scenes of self-sacrifice involving the rejected and accepted claimants of a woman's hand are a feature of the period (as in Mrs Gaskell's *Sylvia's Lovers*) – to realize how completely Trollope has avoided any taint of the conventional Cartonesque melodrama that Dickens would have brought to it. What strikes Burgo about the whole business is its ironic absurdity. Palliser diffidently says that he could offer to accommodate Burgo to the tune of £800 as he happened to have that amount with him –

> There was something pleasant in this, which made Burgo Fitzgerald laugh. Mr Palliser, the husband of Lady Glencora M'Cluskie, and the heir of the Duke of Omnium happening to have money with him! As if Mr Palliser could not bring down showers of money in any quarter of the globe by simply holding up his hand. And then to talk of accommodating him, – him, Burgo Fitzgerald, as though it were simply a little matter of convenience, – as though Mr Palliser would of course find the money at his bankers' when he next examined his book! Burgo could not but laugh.
> 'I was not in the least doubting your ability to raise the money,' said he; 'but how would you propose to get it back again?'
> 'That would be at your convenience,' said Mr Palliser, who hardly knew how to put himself on a proper footing with his companion, so that he might offer to do something effectual for the man's aid. (LXXVI)

The author hardly intrudes during the whole chapter: what point would there be in moralizing over poor Burgo? He would not thank you for it, and Trollope refuses to insult him by doing so.

Nor are we left with a didactic picture of Palliser striking an attitude of magnanimity. He behaves well over Burgo, but then he can in every sense afford to. Not long before, Palliser's reception of

Glencora's intimation that he may expect an heir has shown him in a more mixed light. His exaltation – 'He went out by the lake side, and walked there alone for ten minutes . . . He did not quite remember where he was, or what he was doing' (LXXIII) – is appealingly normal for a man usually so inhibited in acknowledging his feelings even to himself. On the other hand, for all his unassumingness, Palliser has not escaped the arrogance of aristocracy, however much he may wish to deny it: '"I don't think I'm proud because chance has made me my uncle's heir . . . But I do feel that a son to me is of more importance than it is to most men. A strong anxiety on the subject is, I think, more excusable in me than it might be in another."' As Trollope says earlier in the novel, 'Every man to himself is the centre of the whole world' (XXIX), and Palliser's sense of the uniqueness of his situation is sympathetic enough, but there would be something objectionable too in his overweening were it not also presented as faintly absurd. These delicate balances of empathy and mockery are typical of Trollope at his most engaged. He was of course aware of the wider issue involved, as an embarrassing paragraph on the birth of the heir shows. Falling regrettably back on old habits of sub-Carlylean apostrophe, Trollope addresses the 'wondrous little baby, – purpureo-genitus': 'All that the world can give thee will be thine; and yet when we talk of thee religiously, philosophically, or politico-economically, we are wont to declare that thy chances of happiness are no better, – no better, if they be no worse, – than are those of thine infant neighbour just born, in that farmyard cradle. Who shall say that they are better or that they are worse? Or if they be better, or if they be worse, how shall we reconcile ourselves to that seeming injustice?' (LXXX) Not Trollope, clearly, – at this stage of the novel, at any rate.

Trollope has been accused at various times of being a snob because his personnel are so often recruited from what he calls (probably using a then current phrase) 'the Upper Ten Thousand of this our English world'.(I) T.H.S. Escott, who knew Trollope personally, defended him on the grounds that as in life he belonged to the governing classes it was natural for him to write about them. But, as *Can You Forgive Her?* itself shows, Trollope's attention is quite as available to the non-genteel as to the polite. It is true that Mrs Greenow's attempts to decide between the stolid Mr

Cheesacre, the prosperous farmer from Oileymead, and the specious sold-out Captain Bellfield are presented in a genial and often
comic light, but this is partly to do with the novel's overall design.
Mrs Greenow's difficulties in making up her mind between the two
are a near-burlesque version of the indecisions which trouble Glencora and Alice Vavasor, the difference of mode maintaining the
novel's thematic consistency but preventing it from becoming formally overbearing. Although he used them for comic purposes,
Trollope certainly did not think that the un- or the half-educated
were inherently funny. He respects Mrs Greenow as a well-
endowed widow who can afford to please herself and intends to
enjoy doing so. As a practical woman she realizes that life rarely
begins at forty, and she might as well secure a bit of dash while she
can. Unlike Alice and Glencora, she therefore prefers the more
unsound of her two suitors. 'The charm of the woman was in this'
Trollope says, '–that she was not in the least ashamed of anything
that she did.' (VII) Consequently her patent enjoyment of the status
her money gives her, her ridiculous invocations to her departed
lord, and the general vulgarity of her style give her an uncompli-
cated vitality that Trollope is perfectly happy to tolerate for more
pages than many modern readers may feel is necessary. But in
absurdity there is nothing to choose between Mrs Greenow's vulgar manipulation of her widow's weepers and, say, the Duchess of
St Bungay's whinnying complaints about the 'pipes' at Longroys-
ton, a country house with a primitive form of central heating.
Glencora's mockery of the latter's aristocratic inanity, or of the
ancien régime hauteur of the Duke of Omnium, is transcribed by
Trollope with obvious relish. It is always the truth of the individual
situation that absorbs Trollope, at whatever point on the social
scale it is found, and he distrusted writing in which that fidelity was
compromised. In his study of Thackeray he found fault with the
Book of Snobs because it showed more satirical zeal than human
discrimination: 'Thackeray was carried beyond the truth by his
intense desire to put down what is mean.' (II)

A snob is a type, but our constant sense of recognition while
reading Trollope has nothing to do with thinking about people as
examples of categories or classes and everything to do with our
apprehension of the individual case. The future actions of a fictional
type cannot but be largely predetermined; the future of a major

Trollope character is more one of open possibility. At the end of *Can You Forgive Her?* Palliser is again on the threshold of political office. Grey says to him '"To you the British House of Commons is everything." "Yes; – everything," replies Palliser, with unwonted enthusiasm ... "That and the Constitution are everything."' But these undoubtedly disinterested sentiments are coupled with a more personal admission: '"The man who is counted by his colleagues as number one of the Treasury Bench in the English House of Commons is the first of living men. That's my opinion."' (LXXX) It is an early hint of that susceptibility to others' opinion which goes with Palliser's selflessness in the public service – a combination that is subsequently analysed fully in *The Prime Minister*. Some hint too of Glencora's future energies is to be derived from her scornful remarks about the grandiose scale of Gatherum Castle and her resilient feeling that, now she has redeemed herself by giving the Pallisers an heir, she is not going to be pushed around any more: '"I shall dare to assert myself, now."' Both characters seem entirely ready for another three-volume novel straightaway. Our sense that their life will continue is as strong as our uncertainty as to how, exactly, it will work out.

The other principal situation with which *Can You Forgive Her?* is concerned does reach a more natural point of rest by the novel's end. However, Alice Vavasor – to whom the novel's title explicitly refers although it is also to be applied to Glencora – had been in Trollope's mind for many years (as he confesses in Chapter XXXVII), and she is also in a sense a reappearing character. Trollope's first attempt to present her situation had been in a play written in 1850, called *The Noble Jilt*. (There is an arch private joke about this in *The Eustace Diamonds* in which a performance of a play with this title is seen but not well received.) *The Noble Jilt* was written in the wake of *La Vendée* and is similarly set in the 1790s and concerned with the after-effects of the French revolution. Trollope sent the play, written partly in prose and partly in verse, to an actor-friend of his mother's whose reasoned rejection of the piece was felt by Trollope as 'a blow in the face', even though he accepted the verdict. The fact that despite this he did not abandon the material of the play is a good illustration of the remarkable tenacity of Trollope's imagination, once it had dwelt on a situation that seemed to him to be true. The correspondences between play

113

and novel are considerable: the play's heroine jilts her impeccable lover (as Alice Vavasor does) because she feels he will be too contemplative for her active spirit; she is encouraged to renew her friendship with an old lover, more engaged in public life, by his sister (as Alice is); he lets her down and the heroine after much self-criticism returns to what in *Can You Forgive Here?* is called the worthy (as opposed to the wild) man. There is also a comic sub-plot about a widowed aunt's hesitations between a substantial burgomaster and a swaggering captain – an anticipation of Mrs Greenow that extends to quite minor details of characterization.

Trollope's gifts were essentially for the modern and the familiar, and the historical setting of *The Noble Jilt* cuts him off from his natural command of the contemporary. His dialogue normally seems close to the natural speaking voice of his time but this facility and felicity in reproducing the accents of everyday is denied him by his choice of blank verse, as disastrous here as it so often is in nineteenth-century plays. Any psychological truth Trollope may have perceived in the heroine's situation is unable to get past the obstructions which the derivative diction puts in its way:

MARGARET: Sir, I know I've wronged you much,
deceived you past all pardon, injured you
most foully. 'Twas in loving you I did so;
'twas when I took the hand you proffered me,
and made the promise which I now must break.
(*Exit* MARGARET.)
UPSEL: I am amazed, and beyond my wont
put past all sober thinking. What, not mine!
Not to be my wife, my friend, my soul, my all!
Hearts then are naught, and nothing can be trusted.
The earth is all one hell, peopled with angels;
the fairest are the furthest fallen from heaven.
Why, she has sworn she loved me, till her vows
were countless as the stars; has hung on me
as tho' she drew her life from out mine eyes;
has clung around me with such pretty love;
as well becomes a maiden bride betrothed,
but else were lewdness and rank harlotry.
(Act II, scene ii)

114

Not much can be meaningfully conveyed in this idiom of indiscriminate Shakespearean reminiscence in which the general effect is of Hamlet understudied by Ancient Pistol.

But by the time he came to write *Can You Forgive Her?* Trollope had a decade of literary recognition behind him and had gained a corresponding degree of literary assurance. The title itself is in an odd way an indication of this confidence. It is as if Trollope felt he could ask the question because he had himself become clear about the answer.

> But can you forgive her, delicate reader? Or am I asking the question too early in my story? For myself, I have forgiven her and I have learned to think that even this offence against womanhood may, with deep repentance, be forgiven. And you must also forgive her before we close the book, or else my story will have been told amiss. (XXXVII)

At such moments, Trollope appears to be thinking of Alice's situation both as a hypothetical demonstration of a problem in sexual ethics and as a personal dilemma with which he has been long familiar – but it is at the second level that the story was most important to him. Trollope's kind of narratives were bound to bring him up against nice points of Victorian conduct if only because of the insistence in his period on subjecting sexual behaviour to fierce moral scrutiny and a severity of censure that he was instinctively too tolerant and too fair-minded to share. It is clear that Alice has made two bad mistakes – breaking off her engagement to John Grey, and re-engaging herself to her cousin George Vavasor – but to a present-day audience this is hardly likely to seem the 'offence against womanhood' at which Trollope appears – or affects – to be aghast. Alice, he says earlier in the chapter, 'had sinned with that sin which specially disgraces a woman . . . She had thrown off from her that wondrous aroma of precious delicacy, which is the greatest treasure of womanhood'. The idea that a girl's first duty is to preserve her virginal bouquet seems not only to indicate mid-Victorian erotic sentimentalism of the worst sort, but also looks as if it would preclude any real feeling for the agonies of the individual case. However, it is precisely because Trollope is so concerned that we shall sympathize with the individual case that he is driven to these rather unwise appeals. The tactic certainly provoked the young Henry James into a formidable attack:

> The question is, Can we forgive Miss Vavasor? Of course we can, and forget her, too, for that matter. What does Mr Trollope mean by this question? It is a good instance of the superficial character of his work that he has been asking it once a month for so long a time without being struck by its flagrant impertinence. What are we to forgive? Alice Vavasor's ultimate acceptance of John Grey makes her temporary ill-treatment of him, viewed as a moral question, a subject for mere drawing-room gossip. There are few of Mr Trollope's readers who will not resent being summoned to pass judgment on such a sin as the one here presented, to establish by precedent the criminality of the conscientious flutterings of an excellent young lady. Charming women, thanks to the talent of their biographers, have been forgiven much greater improprieties. Since forgiveness was to be brought into the question, why did not Mr Trollope show us an error that we might really forgive – an error that would move us to indignation? It is too much to be called upon to take cognizance in novels of sins against convention, of improprieties; we have enough of these in life. We can have charity and pity only for real sin and real misery. We trust to novels to maintain us in the practice of great indignations and great generosities. Miss Vavasor's dilemma is doubtless considerable enough in itself, but by the time it is completely unfolded by Mr Trollope it has become so trivial, it is associated with so much that is of a merely accidental interest, it is so deflowered of the bloom of a serious experience, that when we are asked to enter into it judicially, we feel almost tempted to say that really it is Miss Vavasor's own exclusive business.

In the same review James also complained that Trollope did not go far enough with Lady Glencora either: he approaches a situation with distinct tragic possibilities, only to back away from them – a clear case of English timidity substituted for Balzacian logic and rigour.

Nevertheless, Trollope's portrayal of Alice does show some

artistic courage, partly because of his refusal to let her situation perish along with its original format, and partly because it did elevate to heroinehood a character who would certainly have appeared perverse to the more *bien-pensant* of his readers, even if some of Trollope's reviewers thought he was being over-protective. No doubt Alice had to encounter the condemnation of Lady Midlothians in life as well as in the book. To be called a jilt does seem to have been a hard thing for a proper-minded mid-Victorian woman to take, and the title 'The Noble Jilt' was clearly meant to be challengingly paradoxical. All the same, there is no suggestion that Alice's behaviour is recommended – only, that in this case it should be excused.

Alice's worries about marriage do not spring from feminist sources. Trollope brings up the question of women's rights only to put it on one side: a 'flock of learned ladies' who ask what a woman should do with her life are thoroughly put down: 'Fall in love, marry the man, have two children, and live happy ever afterwards. I maintain that answer has as much wisdom in it as any other that can be given; – or perhaps more.' (XI) In the previous paragraph Trollope has explained that it is a mistake to think about marriage too much: 'I am inclined to believe that most men and women take their lots as they find them, marrying as the birds do by force of nature.' No doubt Trollope believed that he believed this sort of thing, but the inherent complacency of such generalizations (as so often in his novels) is oddly discontinuous with the sensitivity and subtlety of what he actually shows. It is typical of Trollope authorially to subscribe to a theory of which his novelistic practice then shows the superficiality.[7] The novelist himself, he is anxious to reassure us, is perfectly right-thinking: it is only the character who insists on being difficult – but, of course, for Trollope, and for us, the character is the point. And once Alice's temperament is considered closely, as Trollope gives us ample opportunity to do, the absorption in the particular drives away the claim of the general like the sun dispersing mist.

Alice Vavasor belongs to that large class of Trollopian characters (of whom more below) who are interesting because they vacillate. It becomes plain early on that as soon as Alice makes a decision she feels trapped by it. Her engagement to John Grey is so eminently satisfactory – not least because she really is attracted by him – that she feels a perverse necessity to resist it. The factors involved in this recalcitrance are various and – as is so often the case in Trollope's most sensitive portrayals – the motives behind it are not only mixed but inconsistent. One source of resentment against the admirable Grey is the feeling that he is too admirable. His reply to her letter announcing her proposed trip to Switzerland in the company of her cousin and former fiancé George could not be more proper: 'she knew that he was noble and a gentleman to the last drop of his blood', but in Alice 'there was almost a feeling of disappointment' that he has behaved so correctly. (III) During the scene between them in Chapter XI, which takes place after she asked to be released from her engagement, Alice wishes that Grey's self-control were not so great; she is equally infuriated and mortified by his composure in Chapter LXIII. All the same, his assumption of mastery and even his imperturbability also attract her, and eventually, on her second Swiss trip, she has to give in to their sustained pressure. The physical detail registered in the scene when she finally does give in is significant:

> Of course she had no choice but to yield. He, possessed of power and force infinitely greater than hers, had left her no alternative but to be happy. But there still clung to her what I fear we must call a perverseness of obstinacy, a desire to maintain the resolution she had made, – a wish that she might be allowed to undergo the punishment she had deserved. She was as a prisoner who would fain cling to his prison after pardon has reached him, because he is conscious that the pardon is undeserved. And it may be that there was still left within her bosom some remnant of that feeling of rebellion which his masterful spirit had ever produced in her. He was so imperious in his tranquillity, he argued his question of love with such a manifest preponderance of right on his side, that she had always felt that to yield to him would be to confess the omnipotence of his power. She knew now that she must yield to him, – that his power over her was omnipotent. She was pressed by him as in some countries the prisoner is pressed by the judge, – so pressed that she acknowledged to herself silently that any further antagonism to him was impossible. Nevertheless, the word which she had to speak

still remained unspoken, and he stood over her, waiting for
her answer. Then slowly he sat down beside her, and gradually he put his arm round her waist. She shrank from him,
back against the stonework of the embrasure, but she could
not shrink away from his grasp. She put up her hand to
impede his, but his hand, like his character and his words,
was full of power. It would not be impeded. 'Alice,' he said,
as he pressed her close with his arm, 'the battle is over now,
and I have won it.'

'You win everything, – always,' she said, whispering to
him, as she still shrank from his embrace. (LXXIV)

As so often, Alice's will here is almost paralysed by the conflicting
impulses within. Her troubles often seem attributable to sexual
timidity and an instinct for self-preservation at war with physical
attraction: 'It was the beauty of his mouth, beauty which com-
prised firmness within itself, that made Alice afraid of him.' (XI)
Her other lover George is violent where Grey is controlled (a
violence of which George's facial scar is the rather obvious signifi-
cation). Alice is encouraged by George's sister Kate to see this as
part of his heroic struggle to make his way in the world against
unfair odds, and this appeals to her own restlessness and frustration. But when George, not unreasonably, wants from Alice some
sign that her renewal of their engagement means a revival of her
physical feelings towards him, he is refused it. When she contemplates the real nature of the relationship with George she is again
committed to, the result is something like panic:

Was she to give herself bodily, – body and soul, as she said
aloud in her solitary agony, – to a man whom she did not
love? Must she submit to his caresses, – lie on his bosom, –
turn herself warmly to his kisses? 'No,' she said, 'no,' –
speaking audibly, as she walked about the room; 'no; – it was
not in my bargain; I never meant it.' (XXXVII)

She is perfectly prepared to let George have her money as long as he
doesn't touch her, as indeed a substitute for touching her. (The
reality of George's sexual nature is emphasized by the brief appearance of his cast-off mistress in Chapter LXXI.)

Alice's tendency to shrink from experience is partly rationalized (as we should now say) by her tendency to self-punishment. It is as if she 'pays' for her independence by self-accusation. The initial argument that she was not fit for Grey must apply even more when she has added to the injury of jilting him the insult of her re-engagement to George. She therefore feels that 'She had no right to such happiness after the evil she had done. She had been driven by a frenzy to do that which she herself could not pardon; and having done it, she could not bring herself to accept the position which should have been the reward of good conduct.' (LXX) Even in the end, she regards her happiness as an 'enforced necessity'. However, Trollope makes it clear that 'She could not analyse the causes which made her feel that she must still refuse the love that was proffered her; she could not clearly read her own thoughts', adding that 'the causes were as I have said, and such was the true reading of her thoughts'. (LXX) He is by this late stage of the novel more confident than in the earlier chapter (XXXVII) where he asks 'How am I to analyse her mind, and make her thoughts and feelings intelligible to those who may care to trouble themselves with the study?', as if he felt he lacked a vocabulary adequate to describe the internal conflict he envisages so clearly. However, his anxiety is needless, since it is throughout clear from many small actions and reactions that Alice's internal immobilization is fully conveyed. This is partly done by showing her feelings in parallel with Glencora's. Alice shivers, looking down at the river in Basle with her cousin George, and explains that it is not just the cold night air that makes her do so: '"Little bits of things make me do it, – perhaps a word that I said and ought not to have said ten years ago."' (VI) It is not surprising that the word 'jilt' makes her physically wince. Glencora shivers when she and Alice are in the Matching Priory ruins by moonlight because she remembers the occasion when she saw Burgo in the moonlight and it was only Alice who prevented her from running off with him there and then. (XXVII) Glencora accuses Alice of prudery and '"stony propriety"'. Certainly, Glencora's general spontaneity (as she rightly says, '"nobody can say I am not candid"' contrasts throughout with Alice's inhibition. Glencora's sexual realism shocks Alice (although Alice is considerably the older woman), as in this revealing conversation:

'Ah! how well I remember the first time I danced with him, – at his aunt's house in Cavendish Square. They had only just brought me out in London then, and I thought that he was a god.'

'Cora! I cannot bear to hear you talk like that.'

'I know well enough that he is no god now; some people say that he is a devil, but he was like Apollo to me then. Did you ever see any one so beautiful as he is?'

'I never saw him at all.'

'I wish you could have seen him; but you will some day. I don't know whether you care for men being handsome.' Alice thought of John Grey, who was the handsomest man that she knew, but she made no answer. 'I do; or, rather, I used to do,' continued Lady Glencora. 'I don't think I care much about anything now; but I don't see why handsome men should not be run after as much as handsome women.'

'But you wouldn't have a girl run after any man, would you; whether handsome or ugly?'

'But they do, you know. When I saw him the other night he was just as handsome as ever; – the same look, half wild and half tame, like an animal you cannot catch, but which you think would love you so if you could catch him. In a little while it was just like the old time, and I had made up my mind to care nothing for the people looking at me.'

'And you think that was right?'

'No, I don't. Yes, I do; that is. It wasn't right to care about dancing with him, but it was right to disregard all the people gaping round. What was it to them? Why should they care who I danced with?'

'That is nonsense, dear, and you must know that it is so. If you were to see a woman misbehaving herself in public, would not you look on and make your comments? Could you help doing so if you were to try?'

'You are very severe, Alice. Misbehaving in public!'

'Yes, Cora. I am only taking your own story. According to that, you were misbehaving in public.'

Lady Glencora got up from her chair near the window, on which she had been crouching close to Alice's knees, and walked away towards the fire-place. 'What am I to say to you, or how am I to talk to you?' said Alice. 'You would not have me tell you a lie?'

'Of all things in the world, I hate a prude the most,' said Lady Glencora. (LXII)

Glencora's '"But they do, you know"' reveals a shrewd acceptance of the power of sexual attraction. Alice knows what it is to feel like that – 'Then that other one [Grey] had come and touched her hand, and the fibres of her body had seemed to melt within her at the touch, so that she could have fallen at his feet' (XXXVII) – but, unlike Glencora, cannot openly admit it.

Alice's inconsistencies also manifest themselves in her attitude to politics. She shares Trollope's own conviction that 'It is the highest and most legitimate pride of an Englishman to have the letters M.P. written after his name.' (XLV) In her letter to George Vavasor consenting to the renewal of her engagement, she makes it clear that her interest in his political career is the main motive: '"Dear George, let me have the honour and glory of marrying a man who has gained a seat in the Parliament of Great Britain! Of all positions which a man may attain that, to me, is the grandest."' (XXXII) But, apart from a general inclination towards Radicalism, Alice does not seem to spend her abundant leisure in the serious study of public issues: it is more characteristically given over to morbid self-analysis. When she is introduced to the world of wealth and political power at Matching Priory, she is too socially reserved to make much of an opportunity which a more committed woman would surely have grasped (although she stands up to Palliser vigorously enough when her personal integrity seems at stake). Her life in London, with a father who takes little interest in and spends little time with her, is secluded, and it is perhaps natural that she should not look forward to sharing the noiseless tenor of Grey's retired country life near Cambridge. (Chapter X makes clear Trollope's roundly-expressed view that Cambridgeshire possessed fewer 'rural beauties' than any other county.) Her final submission to Grey is significantly set in romantic Swiss scenery. She dislikes Grey's assumption that the quasi-academic quietism of his existence will suit her, just as she resents the conventional social assumption that it ought to suit her. George Vavasor's connections with the wild fells near the Lake District underline the contrasting sense of energy and excitement that accompanies his restlessness and ambition. But when it comes to the point, Alice cannot bring herself to accept George either, even though he offers the active political life that she says she wants to be connected with.

She has good reason to be cautious: Vavasor's potential for violence is real, and is underlined by the way he knocks his sister about and by the pot-shot he takes at Grey. He can no more be the hero of *Can You Forgive Her?* than Burgo Fitzgerald, but the obvious parallels between their two situations reveal differences as well as likenesses. They share an almost total lack of scruple and an egotism that is either ruthlessly or carelessly prepared to gamble almost everything on a single cast (George leaves the decision to send his letter of proposal to Alice to pure chance – it expresses his contempt for women). However, George's treatment of his former mistress is characteristically cruel; Burgo's kindness to the prostitute whom he treats to a meal when his own fortunes are at their lowest ebb may be offhand, but it has a residual generosity that makes Glencora's love for him more understandable. (XXIX) Both men finally have to leave the country for the outer darkness of abroad.

The remarkable thing, however, is that although Grey is finally brought round by Palliser to thinking that a career in politics might after all be tolerable (so that Alice has her wish at last), it is Vavasor who briefly achieves the ambition which Trollope himself admits to nurturing. In a candid passage at the beginning of Chapter XLV, Trollope confesses that the entrance to the House of Commons which only Members may use 'is the only gate before which I have ever stood filled with envy, – sorrowing to think that my steps might never pass under it . . . I have told myself, in anger and in grief, that to die and not to have won that right of way, though but for a session . . . is to die and not to have done that which it most becomes an Englishman to have achieved.' Trollope's romantic feelings about Parliament are given with a quite Tennysonian enthusiasm: 'from thence flow the waters of the world's progress, – the fullest fountain of advancing civilisation'. Nevertheless, the details of political life, as given in *Can You Forgive Her?*, are thoroughly realistic: elections are crooked affairs in which bribery and a 'cry' are the efficient factors; in the House, debates are bogus in their animosity and speeches boring in their delivery. Trollope's ability to register both the elevated heights to which political life aspires and the shabby underside of its actual practice goes with his admission that Parliament contains men who do not live up to the honour that being a Member of it brings. Like all Trollope's societies, it is inherently mixed: it must be so, since the men who make it up are so. For all Vavasor's villainy, Trollope readily concedes that had he not 'educated himself to badness with his eyes open' George 'might have been a good, and perhaps a great man'. (XLV) As with Sowerby and Crosbie in the Barsetshire novels, Trollope sees that worldliness may bring out the worst in men by no means devoid of good qualities, but he will not unequivocally condemn either them or worldliness for that. The interaction between ambition, circumstance, and individual personality provided Trollope with an inexhaustibly interesting field, and the continuation of the Palliser series was essentially a means of allowing this study to proceed under the kind of conditions most favourable to the nature of his imagination.

Phineas Finn

Phineas Finn is clearly meant to be a hero in a way that George Vavasor's temperament precluded him from being, but the two men not only share the feeling that to get into the House of Commons is to achieve the most worthwhile of all ambitions: they are both prepared to gamble with their lives in order to realize their hopes. It is immediately clear that Phineas is much the nicer man and would no sooner raise his hand to a woman than hurt a fly, but he begins his political career, as George does, without any secure economic base. Phineas Finn is, in the words of Trollope's subtitle, 'the Irish Member', and for most of the first of the two long novels devoted to him he has the luck of the Irish. He needs it because his father, a doctor in County Clare who has made his own way without inherited capital, can only subsidize Phineas's career on a scale that may be handsome enough in Irish terms but which looks a bit pinched in the face of London levels of expense. (At this period, of course, Members of Parliament were not paid.) Phineas is lucky to get elected for the Irish seat of Loughshane without much outlay, and thus begins his Parliamentary career at an unusually early age but without any other professional skill which might tide him over in lean times. This impetuosity is regarded by

Mr Low, the barrister whose pupil Phineas has half-heartedly been, as imprudent and even 'unmanly'. Phineas will be bound to sacrifice his independence and integrity (fundamental qualities of 'manliness' for Trollope) because he will have to accept the constraints of office, since he will be dependent on the salary which goes with it: '"You are to make your way up the ladder by pretending to agree whenever agreement is demanded from you, and by voting whether you agree or do not. And what is to be your reward? Some few precarious hundreds a year, lasting just so long as a party may remain in power and you can retain a seat in Parliament!"' (V) When Phineas replies that Low has Parliamentary ambitions himself, the lawyer points out that if and when he sits on the Treasury bench, it will be by invitation and because he has been successful in his profession. He will be in on his own terms.

Trollope wrote *Phineas Finn* in the winter of 1866–7 (it was serialized from 1867 to 1869 and published in book form in 1869); in 1868 he stood for Parliament himself at Beverley. As a senior official of unquestionable if rather individual standing and as one of the most successful authors of the day, Trollope might be expected to lean to the Low side of the argument. On the other hand, he resigned, prematurely, from the Post Office in 1867 – a step which as he says in the *Autobiography* 'was not unattended with peril, which many would call rash'. Trollope would not, at such a time, have been unsympathetic to the taking of risks. He may also have been distantly expressing, through Phineas's London début, a fantasy version of his own, ultimately successful, return from Ireland (although the *Autobiography* says that Phineas's nationality was due to the fact that 'the scheme of the book' was created during a visit to Ireland). However, the *Autobiography* also shows that Trollope saw his life as essentially divided between its first phase of unhappy and unproductive early years followed by a second phase in which his careers, professional and authorial, brought him satisfaction and recognition. The watershed was his posting to Ireland. On his return Trollope made his way in English society as he had showed no sign of doing before. Moving in from the same quarter, Phineas's fortunes also look like turning out well, and he has the added freedom of being young and unattached. He has the luck Trollope felt he did not have at Finn's age, even as he also perhaps reflects Trollope's sense of his good fortune in middle life. Phineas also has a quality which the *Autobiography* reveals Trollope himself craved – the gift of being popular, of exciting affection. Early on in the novel Trollope notes that 'Everybody who knew our hero, or nearly everybody, called him by his Christian name' (V) – a more telling fact in the formalities of Victorian society than it might be now. The charms that Phineas is shown to have for quite different sorts of people is a natural asset which anyone might envy, and indeed some other characters do. But it is made acceptable by the fact that Phineas seems hardly to realize that he has it, and certainly he makes no conscious effort to exploit it. His attractiveness to women owes nothing to sexual vanity. Who would not wish to see himself in such terms?

But whatever secret sharings Trollope may have had with Phineas, they in no way distort the logic of the character's development, and indeed it seems unlikely that Trollope was consciously aware of them. The case of Johnny Eames has already made it clear that characters who in one way or another might be thought to be specially close to Trollope are not to expect preferential treatment. (Phineas shares with Eames Trollope's own embarrassment at being pestered by a debt-collector.) Phineas Finn's career is not a consoling and self-gratifying rearrangement, in a superior milieu, of furniture from Trollope's own life.

Nor is he the personal bearer of tidings which the political Trollope wanted his prospective constituents to listen to, despite the remarks in the *Autobiography* about the 'semi-political tales' being a vehicle for his opinions. For all its absorption in political life, and for all its allusions to the real state of politics at the period of its writing, *Phineas Finn* is not really a tract for its times. There are no Disraelian interludes which are pamphlets in disguise (like the essay on the Venetian constitution in *Coningsby*), no rhetorically presented episodes (such as the 'Two Nations' scene in *Sybil*) which end in slogans or speeches and which are transparently a way of carrying on politics by novelistic means. Trollope's scorn for Disraeli's fiction (his critique in Chapter XIII of the *Autobiography* has the energy of real antipathy) indicates how little he would be tempted to emulate such procedures. Even though some characters vigorously express Trollope's known opinions, he was not prepared to subordinate their rights as characters by reducing them to authorial mouthpieces. Indeed, the strength of the Palliser series as a whole is that its imaginative activity is not finally dependent on – however much it may take advantage of – political circumstances.

The opening pages of *Phineas Finn* establish with an easy economy far from the earnest field-work of Trollope's early Irish novels the deep provincialism of its hero's original environment. In the next few chapters Phineas's inexperience and immaturity are much stressed. This does him no harm, partly because, as Lady Laura Standish remarks, he is ' "naive without being awkward" '. (XII) As Trollope himself notes, it was simply Phineas's nature to be pleasant, and this, coupled with his patent honesty, apparent cleverness, and undoubted gentlemanliness, more than offsets the fact that he is still only in his mid-twenties and without important connections. In fact, his Irishness (never reflected in his speech, as it is in his compatriot Laurence Fitzgibbon's) gives him a certain social mobility: since he cannot quickly be 'placed' in English terms, the tendency is to take him more at face value (and the face, when Trollope gets round to describing it in Chapter VI, is 'very handsome', as Millais' illustrations also make clear). When he arrives at Westminster Phineas is rather mortified to discover that Irish MPs do not enjoy much prestige, but this again works to his advantage: his own eagerness to put his shoulder to the wheel and his enthusiasm for the Liberal cause are qualities which a party manager like Barrington Erle can use, however much he may wince at Phineas's callow priggishness about political principle. Phineas strikes people as an intriguing exception to the predictable Irish rule, and they are not put off by his Roman Catholicism – certainly Phineas himself makes little of it. At the country houses where he stays, others go off to church on Sundays, but we never see Phineas worrying about finding somewhere where he can go to Mass.

Without much effort on his part, therefore – it is part of his luck – Phineas gets taken up, and chiefly by Lady Laura, who adopts him as a kind of political pupil. She thinks that ' "it is a man's duty to make his way into the House" ' (IV) and later admits that for her ' "a woman's life is only half a life, as she cannot have a seat in Parliament" '. (VI) Lady Laura seems at this stage a figure of power and authority, partly because she is entrenched in the world of high Whiggism and partly because she has the air of a woman of action: 'she would lean forward when sitting, as a man does, and would use her arms in talking, and would put her hand over her face, and pass her fingers through her hair, – after the fashion of men rather than of women; – and she seemed to despise that soft quintessence of her sex in which are generally found so many charms'. (IV) Nevertheless, Phineas is sufficiently impressed to ask 'why should he not now tell himself that he was in love with her?' (V) – a line of thought which two pages later has developed into the idea that 'as an introduction into official life nothing could be more conducive to chances of success than a matrimonial alliance with Lady Laura', with the further self-justification that he would not have thought of such a thing on that account: 'No; – he thought of it because he loved her; honestly because he loved her.' The language indicates the facile nature of Phineas's feelings clearly enough; that they are to bring Lady Laura to personal tragedy there seems not the slightest reason at this stage to anticipate.

Perhaps the chief need of Phineas's nature is for a sympathetic woman to talk to – something he shares with other young men in London lodgings in the novels, and probably with the young Trollope himself. It is not that he is ill at ease in male society or incapable of strong masculine friendship (he eventually develops warm relationships with Lady Laura's brother Lord Chiltern and with Mr Monk, his political mentor), but rather that he has the characteristic Trollopian thin-skinnedness that needs the balm of feminine consolation. Laura provides the necessary comfort and counsel in his early days in Parliament. During his first day in the House, 'he was confused, half elated, half disappointed, and had not his wits about him', and finally decides not to dine there because 'to tell the truth, he was afraid to order his dinner'. (III) New-boy nerves also affect his attempts to make his first speech. He funks one opportunity and only performs moderately when, in Chapter XXVI, he finally gets on his legs. But however much he may blame himself, the sense of physical vertigo, of the 'blood beating hard at his heart' when the Speaker calls his name is not only sympathetic in itself – it is also a testimony to Phineas's lack of self-importance. It is therefore not surprising that he is glad of the support Lady Laura gives. Beneath the perfect manners that Violet Effingham credits him with – his ability 'to live easily with men of all ranks, without any appearance of claiming a special status for himself' (XXVII) – there lies the deep diffidence that is the ultimate source of his appeal.

It is true that as he gets on Phineas does develop a slightly thicker skin. When first attacked by the poisonous pen of Quintus Slide in the *People's Banner*, Phineas shows all the tender vulnerability to press censure of a Mr Harding or a Dr Wortle (in *Dr Wortle's School*); later on, he is prepared to let Slide do his Grub Street worst. Learning such a sense of proportion is an important part of the social and political education that Phineas goes through. Adjusting the sensitivity of the self to the claims of others has a particular importance in politics – at least in politics as Trollope describes them – because men must compromise if they are to be effective and they must act from conviction if they are to remain honest.

To begin with Phineas sees Parliamentary life in very simple terms. He tells Barrington Erle that he intends to sit '"as a sound Liberal, – not to support a party, but to do the best I can for the country"'. (II) To Erle, who sees politics entirely in terms of personal allegiance to Mr Mildmay, the Liberal leader, such high-minded language is 'simply disgusting'. He regards MPs as voting machines and loyalty to your own side as the chief political virtue. This had a particular importance at a time when Parliamentary alliances were relatively unstable and in a period when administrations did not necessarily last long. However, Phineas has no difficulty in supporting Mr Mildmay's administration, and so has no reason not to take a minor office under it when, through another stroke of luck, it is offered to him. He also has before him the example of the politician who most influences his thought. Mr Monk is an 'advanced Liberal' who thinks that although people are frightened of the word equality it should nevertheless be the wish of every honest man '"to assist in lifting up those below him, till they be something nearer his own level than he finds them"' (XIV) – a tenet reiterated with much feeling by Plantagenet Palliser in *The Prime Minister*, and clearly endorsed by the author. Mr Monk is also opposed to secret ballot, as Trollope was, on the grounds that a man should not be afraid to stand up openly for his opinion. Mr Monk's reputation as not only a Radical but, more alarmingly, a Democrat has made his decision to join the Cabinet surprising, but he explains to Phineas that a man is not entitled to refuse to work with those who (broadly speaking) share his principles when they are in power, although he still feels that '"the delight of political life is altogether in opposition"' and to some extent chafes in harness. He defends himself too against the populist Turnbull on the grounds that his presence in the Liberal Cabinet may '"leaven the batch of bread which we have to bake"' so that it has '"more of the flavour of reform"'. The only allegiance Turnbull recognizes, however, is to his constituents and his supporters in the country; he is presented as a powerful figure, but too uncompromising. This intransigence is revealingly connected with his insensitivity in private life: he does not know the difference between a dinner party and a public meeting, and addresses both in the same way. He lacks any element of the self-doubt which Monk has, which Phineas has, and which is so important an element in many of those that Trollope finds sympathetic. Moreover, the work of Turnbull's political life, in Trollope's view, is 'not difficult. Having nothing to construct, he could always deal with generalities. Being free from responsibility, he was not called on either to study details or to master even great facts.' (XVIII)

It is an objection which has a natural appeal to the Civil Service mind, and such a mind is what Phineas increasingly discovers he has. He is not only ambitious of making the House listen to him on large questions of constitutional principle such as the extension of the franchise, but is quite prepared to beaver away in committee on such minor questions as whether the armed services should rely on potted peas grown in Holstein. The advocates of the peas argue that they would 'save the whole army and navy from the scourges of scurvy, dyspepsia, and rheumatism' and that their use was unreasonably opposed by officials 'actuated by some fiendish desire to deprive their men of salutary fresh vegetables, simply because they were of foreign growth'. (XXI) Trollope's little scenes of bureaucratic comedy have the light touch of the insider: he understands that circumlocution is an organic part of public administration rather than a barnacle-like excrescence. Later on, when Phineas has become Under-Secretary at the Colonial Office, he quite loses himself in his zeal for the subject of the projected trans-Canadian railway. He enjoys the comforts of his Whitehall office, but it is made clear that (unlike Fitzgibbon) he earns them by application. Indeed, in the later stages of the novel it is one of Phineas's worries that 'his life was becoming that of a parliamentary official rather than that of a politician'. (LVI) However, there are other signs throughout that he is not likely to become subdued to the medium in which he works, despite his need of the income which his place provides.

The central problem of Phineas's political life – which is that he can only carry it on by becoming a member of a government that he may not always be able to support with a clear conscience – remains. There is thus an inherent tension between his scruples and his survival, and one that is made the greater by Phineas's Trollopian hypersensitivity to the false position. There is, for instance, the tricky question of whether to accept the offer of the constituency of Loughton. It is perfectly clear that Loughton is still in effect a rotten borough of the kind that was supposed to have come to an end with the first Reform Bill. Lady Laura's father, the Earl of Brentford, is careful not to say anything too compromising, but, as he explains to Phineas, '"I do like the people round me to be of the same way of thinking as myself about politics."' (XXXIII) All the houses in the town are on short leases, and farmers on the property have no leases at all. '"They know they're safe"', says the Earl benevolently, but the implication that they are only safe if they vote as he wishes is clear. The whole situation is a working model of the politics of deference, and as a reformer Phineas is in principle bound to disapprove. All the same, while this abuse remained, 'it was better that the thing should contribute to the liberal than to the conservative strength of the House, – and if to the liberal, how was this to be achieved but by the acceptance of such influence by some liberal candidate? And if it were right that it should be accepted by any liberal candidate, – then, why not by him? The logic of this argument seemed to him to be perfect.' (XXXI) The mere fact that Phineas needs to justify his decision to allow himself to benefit from a state of affairs that is accepted in practice even though objectionable in theory illustrates his constant need to reason himself into the worldliness that his ambition makes advisable. And when, seeking re-election at Loughton, Finn is challenged by Quintus Slide and abused by the *People's Banner* as the Earl's lackey, he uncomfortably concedes that although Slide is personally absurd, his attack on the borough's corruption is well founded. Moreover, Phineas cannot but secretly agree with his Trade Unionist landlord Bunce that there is something wrong with a system which obliges '"a young man as has liberal feelings"' to

131

take to '"the governing business just because he's poor and wants a salary"'. (XLIV)

Mr Monk proves a dangerous mentor for a man as vulnerable to scruple as Phineas is; independence is something he has the means to afford, and Phineas has not. Matters come to a head on the issue of Irish tenant-right. Monk has been moving towards the view that Irish tenants ought to be given the same rights as those enjoyed in England, and he is strengthened in this by a visit to Phineas's home. But he warns Phineas more than once that the younger man should not try to follow him, as it is likely to be a policy unacceptable to the Cabinet from which Monk has become ready to resign. For Phineas, the question cannot but raise again his anxieties about honesty and independence, – and in an acute form, since it touches his own country and identity. It is in this context – in one of those tentative generalizations which have the air of an aside but which go to the heart of his concerns – that Trollope says, 'Perhaps there is no question more difficult to a man's mind than that of the expediency or inexpediency of scruples in political life.' (LVIII) The latter part of Finn's parliamentary career is largely given over to weighing scruple against expediency, but Monk himself warns Finn against over-dramatizing and over-simplifying the conflict. When Finn complains that '"a man in office must be a slave, and that slavery is distasteful"', Monk replies, '"There I think you are wrong. If you mean that you cannot do joint work with other men altogether after your own fashion the same may be said of all work."' (LXV) His own resignation is due to his belated feeling that accepting office has been a mistake: it has not benefited the country as he had hoped, and it has been against the grain of his own nature and previous experience. But, he adds, '"Could I begin again, I would willingly begin as you began."'

Phineas is also uneasy about the fact that he feels both Irish and English: 'He felt that he had two identities, – that he was, as it were, two separate persons.' (XXXV) The discontinuity of his two lives troubles him in a way that parallels the conflict between his careerism and his longing for independence. His decision publicly to support Monk on tenant-right is made in Ireland and in defending it he recovers the old joy of student debate which first turned his mind to politics. Although under intense pressure from his English friends and allies, Phineas sticks to his principles not only because he knows they are right but also because in doing so he finds at last a kind of release, however painful, from a long-endured dilemma. His final Commons speech is clearly a great personal success, even though while Phineas is making it 'he knew nothing about himself, whether he was doing it ill or well'. As a Parliamentarian he has travelled a long way since his first mediocre effort: 'He knew that words would come readily enough to him, and that he had learned the task of turning his thoughts quickly into language while standing with a crowd of listeners round him, – as a practised writer does when seated in his chair.' (LXXV) (The last phrase hints clearly enough at the affinity between author and character: Phineas has acquired that facility of expression which Trollope recommends in the *Autobiography* and of which he was himself so clearly a master.) But, having established the significance of the speech for Phineas personally, Trollope declines to discuss its substance, claiming that 'on that terribly unintelligible subject, a tenant-right proposed for Irish farmers, no English reader will desire to know much'. It is a clear demonstration of the greater importance to Trollope as a novelist of the person and the lesser interest of the idea. The heads of Phineas's argument are not even summarized. (In fact, Trollope was writing articles on Irish affairs for the *St Paul's Magazine* while *Phineas Finn* was being serialized in it.)

Phineas finally concedes that Mr Low was right: he '"began at the wrong end"', and now, at thirty, '"I have not a shilling in the world, and I do not know how to earn one."' (LXXV) His luck holds, however, to the extent that he is offered an official job back in Ireland – although a number of his friends clearly expect to see him back. A point of rest has been reached: Phineas has managed (for the moment at least) to maintain his integrity and resolve the divisions within his identity, although the worldly cost has been high.

The threats to that integrity have operated even more powerfully in the emotional life with which his political life is so entangled and which is presented with even more subtlety and force by the novelist in this remarkably rich work. Before he leaves Ireland, in the glory of his first election for Loughshane (actually made possible by the local earl's quarrel with his brother, the previous Member), Phineas has some tender exchanges with Mary Flood

Jones. As Trollope explains, Mary 'was one of those girls, so common in Ireland, whom men, with tastes that way given, feel inclined to take up and devour on the spur of the moment'. (II) Nothing sinister is implied – a snatched kiss, the rape of a ringlet (did Victorian bachelors carry convenient scissors around with them?) – and nothing happens which, according to the sexual protocol of the day, would indicate that Phineas ought to feel irrevocably bound to Mary. However, it is already clear that she will wait for him almost indefinitely. Lady Laura Standish's interest in Phineas's career is so flattering that he can hardly be blamed for construing it as, if not an invitation, at least a permission to think of her in romantic terms. The opportunity to declare himself comes at Loughlinter, the Scottish estate of Mr Kennedy to which Phineas has been invited through Lady Laura's influence. He attempts to propose by the brook of Linter where it is crossed by little bridges – a romantic scene, often to be recalled by both parties – but is stopped in mid-flight by Laura's revelation that she has just accepted an offer from Mr Kennedy. She sees this as a rational decision: '"For me, – like so many other girls, it was necessary that I should stay at home or marry some one rich enough to dispense with fortune in a wife. The man whom in all the world I think the best has asked me to share everything with him; – and I have thought it wise to accept his offer."' (XV) Lady Laura has spent her own fortune in paying her brother Lord Chiltern's debts; moreover, Mr Kennedy is thought of as a rising man in the Liberal party, and through him she can reasonably hope to play the backstage part in high politics that she craves. But it is equally intimated, had prudential considerations not prevailed, she would have accepted Phineas happily – Phineas succeeds in obtaining a kiss '"to treasure in my memory"', after which 'they walked on in silence together, – and in peace, towards the house'.

Phineas's life is full of activity, and he gets over his disappointment quickly enough, but Lady Laura never recovers from her disastrous marriage. Throughout the rest of *Phineas Finn*, and throughout its sequel *Phineas Redux*, the consequences of her mistake gradually wreck her life and tragically distort her personality. Such remorselessness of marital decline (paralleled by the case of the Trevelyans in *He Knew He Was Right*, considered below) reveals a new dimension in Trollope's fiction. Its treatment is marked by Trollope's tenacious grip on the emotional logic of the character's development. It is shown partly by a number of recapitulatory passages of authorial analysis, such as the account in Chapter XVII of Laura's emotions, now she is back in London, married to Kennedy (whom Phineas has recently rescued from a street assault):

I must beg my readers not to be carried away by those last words into any erroneous conclusion. They must not suppose that Lady Laura Kennedy, the lately married bride, indulged a guilty passion for the young man who had loved her. Though she had probably thought often of Phineas Finn since her marriage, her thoughts had never been of a nature to disturb her rest. It had never occurred to her even to think that she regarded him with any feeling that was an offence to her husband. She would have hated herself had any such idea presented itself to her mind. She prided herself on being a pure high-principled woman, who had kept so strong a guard upon herself as to be nearly free from the dangers of those rocks upon which other women made shipwreck of their happiness. She took pride in this, and would then blame herself for her own pride. But though she so blamed herself, it never occurred to her to think that to her there might be danger of such shipwreck. She had put away from herself the idea of love when she had first perceived that Phineas had regarded her with more than friendship, and had accepted Mr Kennedy's offer with an assured conviction that by doing so she was acting best for her own happiness and for that of all those concerned. She had felt the romance of the position to be sweet when Phineas had stood with her at the top of the falls of the Linter, and had told her of the hopes which he had dared to indulge. And when at the bottom of the falls he had presumed to take her in his arms, she had forgiven him without difficulty to herself, telling herself that that would be the alpha and the omega of the romance of her life. She had not felt herself bound to tell Mr Kennedy of what had occurred, – but she had felt that he could hardly have been angry even had he been told. And she had often thought of her lover since, and of his love, – telling herself that she too had once

135

had a lover, never regarding her husband in that light; but her thoughts had not frightened her as guilty thoughts will do. There had come a romance which had been pleasant, and it was gone. It had been soon banished, – but it had left to her a sweet flavour, of which she loved to taste the sweetness though she knew that it was gone. And the man should be her friend, but especially her husband's friend. It should be her care to see that his life was successful, – and especially her husband's care. It was a great delight to her to know that her husband liked the man. And the man would marry, and the man's wife should be her friend. All this had been very pure and very pleasant. Now an idea had flitted across her brain that the man was in love with some one else, – and she did not like it!

Such passages are often lengthy because of Trollope's extreme interest in the exact sequence of feelings and the way they are accommodated, rationalized, indulged, or suppressed. Laura suspects that Phineas is turning his thoughts to Violet Effingham, who has long been sought by her brother Lord Chiltern, but she is in advance of the facts. Her instinct, however, is right: Violet is not only charming in herself but also wealthy, and Phineas does not find it difficult to begin thinking of her in matrimonial terms. His need to confide his problems – even problems involving other women – to a feminine confidante makes him want to ask Laura's advice, when on another visit to Loughlinter. They are at the same spot, above the Linter falls. Phineas hints that he understands that Laura's marriage has not altogether worked out well. '"The truth is, my friend,"' she replies, '"that I have made a mistake."' She finds the contrast between the husband she has and the one she might have had intolerable.

'Phineas,' she said, slowly, 'I have in you such perfect confidence that I will tell you the truth; – as one man may tell it to another. I wish you would go from here.'

'What, at once?'

'Not to-day, or to-morrow. Stay here now till the election; but do not return. He will ask you to come, and press you hard, and will he hurt; – for, strange to say, with all his coldness, he really likes you. He has a pleasure in seeing you here. But he must not have that pleasure at the expense of trouble to me.'

'And why is it a trouble to you?' he asked. Men are such fools; – so awkward, so unready, with their wits ever behind the occasion by a dozen seconds or so! As soon as the words were uttered, he knew that they should not have been spoken.

'Because I am a fool,' she said. 'Why else? Is not that enough for you?'

'Laura – ,' he said.

'No, – no; I will have none of that. I am a fool, but not such a fool as to suppose that any cure is to be found there.'

'Only say what I can do for you, though it be with my entire life, and I will do it.'

'You can do nothing, – except to keep away from me.'

'Are you earnest in telling me that?' Now at last he had turned himself round and was looking at her, and as he looked he saw the hat of a man appearing up the path, and immediately afterwards the face. It was the hat and face of the laird of Loughlinter. 'Here is Mr Kennedy,' said Phineas, in a tone of voice not devoid of dismay and trouble.

'So I perceive,' said Lady Laura. But there was no dismay or trouble in the tone of her voice. (XXXII)

(Phineas's '"Here is Mr Kennedy"' shows considerably less poise than Glencora's '"Here is Mr Palliser"'.) Apart from the momentary clumsiness of Trollope's intrusion at 'Men are such fools', the desolate truth of Laura's feelings is here conveyed entirely and with revealing subtlety by the dialogue. But the dialogue is not just illustrative of the previous analyses: it expresses a new development in Laura's struggle with her love for Phineas, a new link in what is becoming a long chain of events that are not the less affecting for being largely interior. She now tries a new course, hoping that she can get Phineas out of her head by getting him out of her life. This, however, is bound sooner or later to mean resigning him to another woman, a thought that is hard to bear. Her relations with Violet, therefore, become edgy; the dialogues between them, as in Chapters XIX and XXVII, are full of undercurrents. Laura's suppressed feelings about Phineas are also bound to affect adversely her already deteriorating marriage. Kennedy is so taciturn and correct a man that it would have been hard for Laura to have anticipated the domestic tyranny to which she is subjected. However, she had negligently assumed that she could simply carry on her life much as before; Kennedy's sabbatarian strictness, for instance, is a shock for someone used to lounging about with a novel if she felt like it. He refuses to accept her pleas of a headache as a domestic shorthand for a desire to be left alone for a bit, and insists on sending for the dreaded Dr Macnuthrie. Trollope shows with great skill how such hairline cracks are the first signs of what are to become crevasses of incompatibility.

Lady Laura is not capable of maintaining her resolve to see nothing of Finn, and the long interview between them in Chapter XXXIX sets the terms of their later relationship. Phineas foolishly assumes that his former feeling for her is now as distant in her mind as it is in his, and tries again to get her to help his suit to Violet Effingham. At first Laura is able to mask her sense of injury as indignation on behalf of her brother, but Phineas's transparent honesty, if not his tact, deprive her of easy scorn. Trollope makes it beautifully clear that a critical and determining stage has been reached: 'Neither of them knew what was taking place between them; but she was, in truth, gradually submitting herself again to this man's influence. Though she rebuked him at every turn for what he said, for what he had done, for what he proposed to do, still she could not teach herself to despise him, or even cease to love him for any part of it.' After Phineas has left, she bursts into a flood of tears, humiliated that she should not have been able to crush her love 'into nothing and have done with it', in the way that a man would have done, she who from her earliest years 'had resolved that she would use the world as men use it, and not as women do'. She then asks herself why shouldn't Phineas have Violet after all: he is a better man than her brother. So at the end of the chapter her position is the opposite of what it was at the beginning, but the emotional logic of the reversal is impeccable.

When, back at Loughlinter, Lady Laura gets a telegram with the news of Finn's re-election, she reacts with an enthusiasm which Kennedy is not being altogether unreasonable in regarding as excessive. It is clear that her frustration and misery is pushing Laura towards a marital crisis, and her best defence against the suspicion of a guilty passion for Phineas is as brazen a denial of it as possible.

For the first time she issues a kind of ultimatum to her husband: '"If you say another word in any way suggesting the possibility of improper relations between me and Mr Finn, either as to deeds or thoughts, as God is above me, I will write to both my father and my brother, and desire them to take me from your house."' Trollope understands what is going on perfectly: 'She had been cool till the word insult, used by herself, had conveyed back to her a strong impression of her own wrong, – or perhaps I should say a strong feeling for the necessity of being indignant.' (LI) Laura works herself up in her own defence because she knows that in fact she is guilty: she cannot possibly claim that there has been nothing improper in her relationship with Phineas *as to thoughts*. The scene – and the treatment of Lady Laura's situation in general – is remarkably free from accompanying homily. No doubt Trollope felt that the wages of sinful thoughts were apparent enough in Lady Laura's misery, but Trollope's concentration on psychological truth and his restraint in drawing explicit morals from it is typical of the degree to which in his best work the demand of the character to be understood prevails over any ulterior didactic purpose.

When Finn sees Laura again, back in London, he is struck by the fact that she seems old, worn, and wretched. Phineas would like to be consoled for the fact that Violet has now committed herself to Chiltern, but instead Laura reproaches him with gossip about his supposed attachment to Madame Goesler. Her sense of her own suffering, as a woman, has banished her old thoughts of living as a man: '"When men tell me of the cruelty of women, I think that no woman can be really cruel because no man is capable of suffering. A woman, if she is thrown aside, does suffer."' (LVI) She knows which side she is condemned to now. The fact that Phineas's affections have changed and hers have not makes her lose control: '"And whose thoughts did you speak when you and I were on the braes of Loughlinter? Am I wrong in saying that change is easy to you, or have I grown so old that you can talk to me as though those far away follies ought to be forgotten? . . . your heart is one in which love can have no durable hold."' Phineas sees that, in reproaching him for looking elsewhere after she herself had rejected him, Laura is hardly being just, but he cannot but pity her suffering.

'I wish it were possible for me to do something,' he said, drawing near to her.

'There is nothing to be done,' she said, clasping her hands together. 'For me nothing. I have before me no escape, no hope, no prospect of relief, no place of consolation. You have everything before you. You complain of a wound! You have at least shown that such wounds with you are capable of cure.' (LVI)

In the face of such accents of despair, it is not surprising that as Phineas walks back to his office 'so intent was he on that which had just passed that he hardly saw the people as he met them, or was aware of the streets through which his way led him . . . what was his plight as compared with hers?' Again, the moment's intensity and power is not advertised by an author intent on making sure that we do not miss its moral significance. But a reading that allows the scene full weight as the latest and inevitable stage in a long accumulation of emotion will naturally dwell on the way Phineas's moral world is suddenly and movingly enlarged by the intensity of another's pain.

When Laura does separate herself from her husband, it is Phineas who, by a grotesque logic, becomes the messenger between them: Kennedy knows he can get through to Laura that way, and that using Phineas will be some sort of sign that he is not jealous (although, of course, he is). But when Finn passes on Kennedy's plea that the couple should live together again, '"It can never be," said Lady Laura, shuddering; – "never, never, never!"' (LXVIII) The shudder may well be an oblique way of indicating that there were other things wrong with the marriage, apart from the question of Phineas. Laura resolves to go and live abroad, in Dresden, with her father, leaving Kennedy to talk to his lawyer about the restoration of conjugal rights. She now urges Phineas to marry Madame Goesler, as the means by which he can continue his political life; since she is rich, he would not be dependent on holding office. In other words, Laura wants him to make the same move that she made in marrying Kennedy – to make a marriage of political convenience. Again, there is an emotional logic in what she says, since such a course would put the two of them on a level and link them that way, now that no other link is possible. Laura will then be able to feel, through Finn's political life, an involvement by proxy in that world to which she first introduced him and from which she is now exiled. She constructs a version of their past relationship which, without exactly being inaccurate, nevertheless amounts to the consoling myth which she desperately needs if her life is now to have any sense of purpose:

> 'You have had your romance and must now put up with reality. Why should I so advise you but for the interest that I have in you? Your prosperity will do me no good. I shall not even be here to see it. I shall hear of it only as so many a woman banished out of England hears a distant misunderstood report of what is going on in the country she has left. But I still have regard enough, – I will be bold, and, knowing that you will not take it amiss, will say love enough for you, – to feel a desire that you should not be shipwrecked. Since we first took you in hand between us, Barrington and I, I have never swerved in my anxiety on your behalf. When I resolved that it would be better for us both that we should be only friends, I did not swerve. When you would talk to me so cruelly of your love for Violet, I did not swerve. When I warned you from Loughlinter because I thought there was danger, I did not swerve. When I bade you not to come to me in London because of my husband, I did not swerve. When my father was hard upon you, I did not swerve then. I would not leave him till he was softened. When you tried to rob Oswald of his love, and I thought you would succeed, – for I did think so, – I did not swerve. I have ever been true to you. And now that I must hide myself and go away, and be seen no more, I am true still.' (LXIX)

At their final parting, after Phineas has decided to give up Parliament, Laura still insists on seeing Phineas as having a future denied to her: '"you have many years before you will begin to be growing old. I am growing old already. Yes, I am. I feel it, and know it, and see it. A woman has a fine game to play; but then she is so easily bowled out, and the term allowed to her is so short."' (LXXV) What can Phineas say? Such desolate, elegiac little sentences are unanswerable.

Lady Laura's love for Phineas assumes an obsessional note gradually; the passion of her brother Lord Chiltern for Violet Effingham is obsessive from the start. Phineas's first impression of him is of 'something approaching to ferocity'. (IV) His history is bad and his reputation worse. He has contracted enormous racing debts, was expelled from Oxford for being drunk, and has actually – though not culpably – killed 'a ruffian' in a fight at Newmarket. Although he has loved Violet since childhood, it is natural that she should be wary of the idea of marrying him. It's not that she dislikes Chiltern's way of life altogether. As she says, with that deceptive insouciance that is her particular note, '"I like a roué myself; – and a prig who sits all night in the House, and talks about nothing but church-rates and suffrage, is to me intolerable. I prefer men who are improper, and all that sort of thing. If I were a man I should go in for everything I ought to leave alone . . . I like a fast man, but I know that I must not dare to marry the sort of man that I like."' (X) Her style, like her situation, has analogies with Glencora's when tempted by Burgo – an heiress with a suitor to whom she is attracted, but of whom almost everyone disapproves and who, as a husband, is bound to be a risk, to say the least. The problem is, how much of a risk? Chiltern's energy, even in the small exchanges of life, often seems to verge on the uncontrollable. He channels it into hunting most of the time (so that Trollope's personal love of hunting scenes is on this occasion functional rather than gratuitous), but even his horses reflect his temperament: they '"all pull like the mischief, and rush like devils, and want a deal of riding . . . I prefer to have something to do on horseback. When a man tells me a horse is an armchair, I always tell him to put the brute into his bedroom."' (XIX) Phineas has the Irishman's natural management of horses, and copes with Chiltern's appropriately named mount Bonebreaker well enough. But when his thoughts turn to Violet, Chiltern insists on a duel – in which Phineas is slightly wounded and which he afterwards concedes is absurd – on the Belgian sands across the Channel. It is therefore perfectly reasonable of Violet to fear that marriage might not tame Chiltern, might mean that she herself would become subject to his characteristic violence – the sort of violence that breaks out of George Vavasor, for instance. Her difficulty is that she has no reliable means of estimating the risk: as she says to Phineas, '"How can any girl . . . say that she knows the disposition of any man? You can live with Lord Chiltern, and see what he is made of, and know his thoughts, and learn what is good in him, and also what is bad. After all, how is any girl really to know anything of a man's life?"' (XXII) Violet's question is one that resonates throughout Trollope's work, and indicates how clearly he saw that for a woman choosing a man might well mean making a decision about her life without adequate evidence.

What she can trust, of course, is her sexual instinct, and – as the case of Lady Laura shows – she puts it aside at her peril. At a common-sense level, there is much to be said in favour of Phineas, and almost everything to be said against Chiltern. But when Phineas proposes to Violet, her reaction – given entirely in dialogue, without authorial gloss – is swiftly and instinctively negative: '"I do not think I shall ever wish you to be my husband."' (XLVI) She knows that, at the deepest level, Phineas's heart is not in it: '"There be cats that eat their mice without playing, – and cats that play with their mice, and then eat them; and cats again which only play with their mice, and don't care to eat them. Mr Finn is a cat of the latter kind . . ."' The metaphor is playful, but also significantly predatory. When it comes to it, she needs to feel the feeling of being absolutely needed. Chiltern's proposal has none of the decorous, sensitive tentativeness of Phineas's. If he is refused again, he '"will go to some distant part of the world, where I may be killed or live a life of adventure"'. This is not the conventional Victorian reaction to disappointment: '"I shall do so simply in despair."' What is so revealing, and so convincing in the scene as it develops, is its intense physicality:

'You will acknowledge, Violet, that I have never lied to you. I am thinking of you day and night. The more indifferent you show yourself to me, the more I love you. Violet, try to love me.' He came up to her, and took her by both her hands, and tears were in his eyes. 'Say you will try to love me.'

'It is not that,' said Violet, looking away, but still leaving her hands with him.

'It is not what, dear?'

'What you call, – trying.'

'It is that you do not wish to try?'

'Oswald, you are so violent, so headstrong. I am afraid of

you, – as is everybody. Why have you not written to your
father, as we have asked you?'

'I will write to him instantly, now, before I leave the room,
and you shall dictate the letter to him. By heavens, you shall!'
He had dropped her hands when she called him violent; but
now he took them again, and still she permitted it. 'I have
postponed it only till I had spoken to you once again.'

'No, Lord Chiltern, I will not dictate to you.'

'But will you love me?' She paused and looked down,
having even now not withdrawn her hands from him. But I
do not think he knew how much he had gained. 'You used to
love me, – a little,' he said.

'Indeed, – indeed, I did.'

'And now? Is it all changed now?'

'No,' she said, retreating from him.

'How is it, then? Violet, speak to me honestly. Will you be
my wife?' She did not answer him, and he stood for a
moment looking at her. Then he rushed at her, and, seizing
her in his arms, kissed her all over, – her forehead, her lips,
her cheeks, then both her hands, and then her lips again. 'By
G—, she is my own!' he said. Then he went back to the rug
before the fire, and stood there with his back turned to her.
Violet, when she found herself thus deserted, retreated to a
sofa, and sat herself down. She had no negative to produce
now in answer to the violent assertion which he had pronounced as to his own success. It was true. She had doubted,
and doubted, – and still doubted. But she must doubt no
longer. Of one thing she was quite sure. She could love him.
(LII)

It is, perhaps, Chiltern's entirely unexpected tears, accompanied
with the physical contact of hands, that convince Violet of the truth
of their sexual compatibility, so astonishingly mimicked by his
passionate assault and the ensuing separateness. Afterwards, he is
unable to write to his father because his hand shakes too much. 'She
could love him' means that, physically, it is all right – it is going to
be all right. Problems remain – Chiltern cannot change his habitual
recalcitrance overnight – but the essential sexual bond has been
acknowledged and established.

As *Phineas Redux* goes on to show, the violence in Chiltern turns out to be tameable, or at least containable, for all his feral qualities, and by *The Duke's Children* he is almost domesticated. He has explained earlier in the novel that he hates going to the Zoo because '"people would look at me as if I were the wildest beast in the whole collection"'. (XI) Chapter V offers a strikingly suggestive scene actually set in the London Zoo; Phineas is prowling round there on Sunday afternoon, and is introduced to Mr Kennedy. After the barest possible acknowledgement, Kennedy 'stood perfectly still, with his two hands fixed on the top of his umbrella, and gazed at the great monkeys' cage. But it was clear that he was not looking at any special monkey, for his eyes never wandered.' One cannot but wonder how much Kennedy's later development was deduced by Trollope from this vivid, momentary apprehension. Miss Fitzgibbon contrasts the monkey's chatter with Kennedy's taciturnity, but there is a fleeting suggestion of a deeper level of affinity between the man and the isolation of the caged beast. Again, the full consequences of Kennedy's latent violence do not fully emerge until *Phineas Redux*. In a work as densely populated as *Phineas Finn*, with so many characters to engross Trollope's attention, it is not surprising that he should need more than one novel to understand them fully.

Miss Fitzgibbon also roguishly compares the monkey to Phineas himself – they have the same aptitude for climbing – and the third woman whom Phineas comes to know well in England offers him his greatest opportunity to do so.

It is a striking example of Trollope's formal insouciance that he should not introduce one of *Phineas Finn*'s major characters until half-way through the novel. It would be interesting to know whether her belated appearance was planned from the start or whether it was something that came to Trollope in the course of composition. Madame Max Goesler is very fully described at her first appearance, when introduced by Lady Glencora to Phineas (Chapter XL), but this confident portrait is entirely external. In fact, Trollope seems to spend much of the second half of the book wondering what, exactly, Madame Max was like, and finding this out experimentally.[8] In Trollope, a character's nature often seems to be inferred from his or her actions – actions which are not necessarily demonstrations of a personality with already analysed and therefore predictable qualities. What is clearly seen in the mind's eye may take the mind itself time to understand. Like La Signora Vesey Neroni, Madame Goesler is known by her foreign husband's name, but we are now far from any suggestion of provincial burlesque. She is received by Lady Glencora, and although as a hostess Glencora is said to be 'advanced', that is passport enough. Her background is filled in by fits and starts and always remains shrouded in a certain obscurity. At her first appearance, her individual style of dress is noted, and her conversation (she sits at dinner between Phineas and Mr Grey, although what she says to the hero of *Can You Forgive Her?* we are not told) combines easy references to English politics with a certain air of detachment from them. It is as if she had decided to adopt the world of the English ruling class rather than being naturally born to it or desperately aspiring to it. The sprightly unorthodoxy which is always within the bounds of the acceptable she may have picked up from Glencora, but it goes with an apparently complete self-possession. Her general style is a mixture of the cosmopolitan and the exotic, coupled with a seemly deference for the English establishment. She is rumoured to be the widow of a wealthy Austrian banker and the daughter of a German Jew – her father is later said to have been a small country attorney. Violet Effingham says that Madame Max told her 'ever so much' about Mr Goesler, but these details never reach the reader. She has spent much of her life abroad and still has business interests in Vienna; she has a faint foreign accent. Her social behaviour is very correct, but she is exclusive, and this, combined with her money, general mysteriousness and personal attraction, make her exciting.

Phineas quickly senses her appeal and, in his usual way, begins to confide in her. It is not long before Madame Max is sufficiently taken with him to offer him money to help with his political expenses, although she is sufficiently aware of the un-Englishness of what she is doing to do so in French. As a gentleman Phineas of course cannot accept. He tells her of his disappointment over Violet Effingham, and she consoles him very prettily by singing the Scotch song of young Lochinvar – her musicality is another sign of her resources as a *femme du monde*. Her social gifts and the hints they seem to imply of yet more intriguingly personal ones attract the attention of the old Duke of Omnium, and allow him to display at last the fading vestiges of Regency gallantry that had seemed to hang about him in his Barsetshire appearances. Such a conquest would satisfy any ambition, but the question is, as Trollope now warms to his investigation of Madame Goesler's personality, is the game worth the candle? That she is ambitious, she admits freely, but 'with all her ambition, there was a something of genuine humility about her'. (LVII) She has been successful because of her intelligent exploitation of her assets – her money, her wit, and 'a something in her personal appearance which, as she plainly told herself, she might perhaps palm off on the world as beauty' – and such realism is perhaps the greatest of her advantages. Nevertheless, 'she was a woman who did not flatter herself, who did not strongly believe in herself, who could even bring herself to wonder that men and women in high position should condescend to notice such a one as her'. Trollope has now located in Madame Max the element of self-doubt so recurrent in his major characters and which so often seems to function as the guarantee of their authenticity.

By skilful manoeuvre Madame Max – her own name is Marie, as we belatedly learn – brings the old Duke actually to propose, having fended off compromising offers of hospitality in his Italian villa. Any suspicion that the liaison of Becky Sharp and Lord Steyne was one of Trollope's points of departure (Madame Max's house is in Park Lane, Becky's was in Curzon Street – a turning off Park Lane) is deflected by the fact that the relationship is now developed in a thoroughly unThackerayean way. The Duke's offer presents Madame Max with a dilemma of a classically Trollopean kind. In resolving a dilemma one is deciding what person to be, and it is a heavy burden as well as a searching process: 'There is nothing in the world so difficult as that task of making up one's mind. Who is there that has not longed that the power and privilege of selection among alternatives should be taken away from him in some important crisis of his life, and that his conduct should be arranged for him, either this way or that, by some divine power if it were possible, – by some patriarchal power in the absence of divinity, – or by chance even, if nothing better than chance could be found to do it?' (LX) The weight of indecision and the fatigue of the will in trying to make such decisions are felt by Trollope to be so great that he is profoundly tolerant (although not necessarily approving) of the various and sometimes fatalistic ways in which characters allow their dilemmas to be decided. As he wrote in his article 'A Walk in a Wood', 'The most difficult thing that a man has to do is think.' Here, Marie Goesler is wise enough to know that it is impulse, not analysis or calculation, that will clinch matters in the end.

For Madame Max, to become Duchess of Omnium would not only be a social triumph but a means of revenge on those from whom she had received 'scorn ... rejected overtures ... deep social injury' (presumably because of her suspected Jewishness). On the other hand, she is not going to get much out of 'acting the raptures of love on behalf of a worn-out duke who at the best would scarce believe in her acting'. 'The pleasure of love' is something that she has never known, and although there is a hint that she might experience it with Finn, she won't get it from a man in his seventies, however well preserved by nature and his tailor. Moreover, she would make an enemy of Lady Glencora, worried not for herself or Plantagenet as the Duke's heir, but for her children. Glencora's impulsiveness and candour result in a direct if rather flustered appeal to Madame Max to turn the Duke down, and the action is neatly and convincingly related to Glencora's earlier experiences: 'She had wished to be imprudent when she was young; but her friends had been too strong for her. She had been reduced, and kept in order, and made to run in a groove, – and was now, when she sat looking at her little boy with his bold face, almost inclined to think that the world was right, and that grooves were best. But if she had been controlled when she was young, so ought the Duke to be controlled now he was old.' (LXII) It is normal enough to generalize from one's own experience, and the process of Glencora's reasoning here will seem understandable to those who have read *Can You Forgive Her?*.

Madame Max finally rejects the Duke on the ground that by birth and position she is not fit for him, even though she at first objects to Lady Glencora's implying as much. (Her decision is conveyed in two transcribed letters which show that Trollope is now sufficiently intimate with her to act as her amanuensis.) Her proper destiny ought to be with someone like Phineas Finn, who like her has made himself acceptable and valued through his personal qualities and is also in some sense an outsider. Like him, she has a world elsewhere – not Ireland, but Vienna: '"I am there for a couple of months every year, minding my business . . . I dress so differently at such times, and talk so differently, and look so much older, that I almost fancy myself to be another person . . . I rather like it. It makes me feel that I do something in the world."' (LXIV) Like Phineas, Madame Max does not mind getting down to it (Lady Laura, in her eagerness for high politics, had hated constituency chores).

The appropriate convergence of Phineas and Marie Goesler is frustrated by Phineas's precipitate proposal to Mary Flood Jones – an action of his Irish self, and the equivalent in personal terms of his political commitment to the cause of tenant-right. The logic of the engagement is clear, even if Trollope's handling of the matter verges on the perfunctory. Perhaps he was saving his powers for the final scene between Phineas and Madame Max in Chapter LXXII, one of the finest in the novel. It takes place in her drawing-room, described with unusual explicitness by Trollope, although hardly with Jamesian finesse (there are 'two or three gems of English art' on the walls); the point is simply that Madame Max understands the art of living and has the means for it. She inquires about Phineas's future plans with 'that look of true interest which the countenance of a real friend will bear when the welfare of his friend is in question'. When she again offers him money, she seems to him to gain in presence: 'she was stronger, larger, more robust physically than he had hitherto conceived'. When she finally offers herself too, the temptation is made to seem almost overpowering: 'The very air of the room in which she dwelt was sweet in his nostrils, and there hovered around her an halo of grace and beauty which greeted all his senses.' Trollope's customary *tu quoque* to the reader seems to be more than usually fierce: 'What man will say that he would not have been tempted? And what woman will declare that such temptation should have had no force?'

With a letter from dear little Mary in his pocket Phineas just has the power to reject Marie, but the cost of doing so is made brilliantly clear by his immediate reactions after she has left the room:

He never afterwards knew how he escaped out of that room and found his way into Park Lane. In after days he had some memory that he remained there, he knew not how long, standing on the very spot on which she had left him; and that at last there grew upon him almost a fear of moving, a dread lest he should be heard, an inordinate desire to escape without the sound of a footfall, without the clicking of a lock. Everything in that house had been offered to him. He had refused it all, and then felt that of all human beings under the sun none had so little right to be standing there as he. His very presence in that drawing-room was an insult to the woman whom he had driven from it.

Phineas's feelings of guilt in relation to Marie Goesler are the necessary foundation for the relationship that is yet to develop between them, in *Phineas Redux*. There is no immediately compensatory feeling for having been virtuous: 'His first feeling, I think, was one of pure and unmixed disappointment.' Trollope refuses to fake things in the interests of something that may be exemplary but not true to life: 'He had refused it all, because he was bound to the girl at Floodborough. My readers will probably say that he was not a true man unless he could do this without regret. When Phineas thought of it all, there were many regrets.' (LXXIV) He resolves, however, that Mary shall not know of them.

Phineas thus survives the kind of test of integrity that Crosbie, in *The Small House at Allington*, failed to do. In both cases the promise of a worldly alliance – immensely more tempting in Phineas's case since the lady has so much more to offer – is counterpoised with a pre-existing provincial attachment. In one case, honour is sacrificed in the interests of ambition; in the other, fidelity prevails over ambition. But both Crosbie and Finn have the second chance, as Eames does too for that matter, which their status as reappearing characters in a novel sequence allows them. As usual, any analogies in the characters' situations only serve to sharpen our sense of their individuality.

Phineas Redux

Phineas Finn and *Phineas Redux* are, according to Trollope, 'but one novel', even though the latter was written in the winter of 1870–1 – four years after the composition of the former – and not published until 1874. His account of the Phineas books in the *Autobiography* not only provides further evidence of what he meant by living with his characters but also shows him in a rare moment of novelistic pretension. Trollope hoped that Plantagenet Palliser, Lady Glencora, and Mr Crawley would survive the passage of time to become members of the permanent repertory of English fictional characters – significantly all three are reappearing characters – but the degree to which his work is still current would have surprised as much as it would have gratified him. But in his remarks about *Phineas Finn* and its sequel he claims a degree of originality for his design in relation to English fictional tradition which indicates the seriousness of his artistic purpose:

In writing *Phineas Finn* I had constantly before me the necessity of progression in character, – of marking the changes in men and women which would naturally be produced by the lapse of years. In most novels the writer can have no such duty, as the period occupied is not long enough to allow of the change of which I speak ... Novelists who have undertaken to write the life of a hero or heroine have generally considered their work completed at the interesting period of marriage, and have contented themselves with the advance in taste and manners which are common to all boys and girls as they become men and women ... But I do not think that novelists have often set before themselves the state of progressive change, – nor should I have done it, had I not found myself so frequently allured back to my old friends. So much of my inner life was passed in their company, that I was continually asking myself how this woman would act when this or that event had passed over her head, or how that man would carry himself when his youth had become manhood, or his manhood declined to old age. It was in regard to the old Duke of Omnium, of his nephew and heir, and of the heir's wife, Lady Glencora, that I was anxious to carry out this idea; but others added themselves to my mind as I went on, and I got round me a circle of persons as to all of whom I knew not only their present characters, but how those characters were to be affected by years and circumstances. (XVII)

It is clear that formal innovation is the logical consequence of that continuous communion with his characters which, as we have seen, Trollope felt was the only secure basis for fiction. It was because 'so much of my inner life was passed in their company' that characters could be so effortlessly carried forward from one book to the next. Trollope was the first English novelist to do this as a matter of major artistic principle, but his practice seems so natural and inevitable that he has hardly received the credit he deserves as the founder of the sequence novel proper in England. It is deeply characteristic that Trollope was tempted into this course by the felt claims of his 'old friends' rather than by any merely aesthetic or theoretical ambition.

The Eustace Diamonds is one of the eight other novels written between the two Phineas stories, and although here the Palliser circle act more as chorus than principals, Trollope makes a point of keeping an eye on them. The house party down at Matching (which includes the Greys, the Chilterns, and Madame Max) follows the affair of the diamonds with keen interest; indeed, in giving the now declining Duke a topic of interest, it proves to be 'a godsend'. The party insist on being kept in touch 'by the wires' (Trollope must be one of the first novelists in whose work telegrams feature with some regularity). Lady Glencora takes up Lizzie Eustace's cause with the same impulsiveness that later leads her to champion Phineas Finn's. The fact that the one deserves her support and the other does not is typical of a certain indiscriminateness in her energies. In the last chapter of *The Eustace Diamonds* all the people at Matching who comment on the affair are reappearing characters, and their comments are in character. Trollope feels obliged to give the reader who has not read the earlier novels some minimal information, and perhaps gets some amusement (considering what has passed) from such dry introductions as 'Madame Max Goesler was also at Matching, a lady whose society always gave gratification to the Duke'. When bringing Lizzie into *Phineas Redux* Trollope concedes that he 'is not allowed to imagine that any of his readers have read the wonderful and vexatious adventures of Lady Eustace' (XLV); however, the further development of her story had also been promised at the end of the earlier novel. But although Trollope feels driven into such awkwardnesses of presentation by the novelty of his procedure, they only serve to emphasize his commitment to the principle of reappearance.

In the two books bearing his name, Phineas's story is presented chronologically – as is usual in Trollope's work: the novelist seems to have felt the need to inch his way forward along the characters' line of psychological development too strongly to flirt with major dislocations of time-scheme (although sometimes his different plots do get slightly out of phase). Nevertheless, there is a high degree of recapitulation in the two narratives; they are to some extent parallel in structure. In both novels Phineas comes to England with political aspirations; gets into Parliament after an election with some dubious aspects (Tankerville proves to be as corrupt a constituency as Loughton was deferential); has a relationship with Lady Laura Kennedy which has important political consequences, and is also involved with Madame Max Goesler; and is finally caught up in a situation which leads to a disaffection with political life and his temporary retirement from it. In *Phineas Finn*, however, the issue which took our hero back to Ireland was one of political principle and personal integrity; in *Phineas Redux* a more sensational element is introduced by the trial of Phineas for the murder of his political enemy Mr Bonteen. This becomes a *cause célèbre* in the way that the robbery of the Eustace Diamonds had been (some of the same personnel – Mr Camperdown the lawyer, Major Mackintosh the policeman – are active on both cases). Both novels have dramatic court scenes. However, the most important structural analogue for the two Phineas novels is the double-digging method of *The Small House at Allington* and *The Last Chronicle of Barset*, whereby characters are allowed a second chance only to find that they cannot have their time over again. It is the way in which comparable situations and moments of choice recur that allows Trollope to mark so acutely that 'progression of character' to which he wanted to do artistic justice. Of course, there is no reason why characters should not change and age convincingly between one pair of covers – *Phineas Finn* itself covers a period of six years – but, as we saw in the cases of Lily Dale and Crosbie, the simple fact of returning to the same characters after an interval in what is physically a different book adds a curious if illogical credibility to the whole process.

In *Phineas Finn*, Phineas thought of his two lives as being Irish and English; in the sequel he thinks of his career in the first novel as his first life, and of his present concerns as his second. Nevertheless he is to some extent going through the same motions again, so that the old days seem familiar as well as remote. Staying in Dublin is now out of the question. His wife has died in pregnancy, and his father has also died, so that he has no pressing ties. Trollope regretted what he later regarded as his lack of forethought in marrying Phineas to Mary Flood Jones, thus obliging himself to kill her off in this abrupt way. Perhaps he felt that he had behaved churlishly towards Mary in making a novelistic convenience of her; his judgements of his work often seem coloured by his sense of loyalty towards the character, so that a novel's success or failure is partly a matter of whether it has or has not let the character down.

Back in England, Phineas has again that 'feverish' thirst for political life that first seduced him into it, and he takes the same kind of calculated risk in re-entering it. He has means for a year or two, and if he fails, he can always commit suicide or emigrate (as George Vavasor did). He returns to his old lodgings with the Bunces. As his landlord says, he's 'at the old game', or, as Lady Baldock later puts it, 'here he is beginning all over again'. The threads are deftly picked up by Trollope. Phineas's first visit to the Chilterns finds the former Violet Effingham deep in what is obviously a demanding but satisfying domesticity. She has been through 'the great change which turns a girl into a mother' (II), but her dialogue still has the same sprightly independence of mind and sympathy of tone that it used to have. Chiltern's energy and ferocity are now usefully canalized into his work as a Master of Hounds. Phineas's relaxation in the new life of old friends is caught with a skill on the author's part that is so effortless as to be almost unnoticeable. The characters have maintained so intense a reality in Trollope's mind that there is none of the rather pedestrian exposition that he often seems to need to warm up. He drops into and out of passages of dialogue with such seamless ease because he hears so exactly the tones of each personage and recalls so completely what lies behind them.

Phineas's resumption of his relationship with Lady Laura is a much more fraught affair. Early in the novel, as in its predecessor, Phineas makes a visit to Kennedy's Scottish estate Lough Linter (as it is now spelt). The contrast between the great political house party of former days and the gloomy and inhospitable regime that now obtains is an index of the disaster that has overtaken the

Kennedy marriage and the mental imbalance that increasingly takes control of Kennedy himself. Trollope had written *He Knew He Was Right* directly after *Phineas Finn,* and the experience of dealing with madness following marital dispute there may well have contributed to the artistic confidence with which he now presents the deranged Kennedy. Apologizing for the poor cheer, Kennedy says '"How can a man, whose wife has deserted him, entertain his guests? I am ashamed even to look a friend in the face, Mr Finn." As he said this he stretched forth his open hand as though to hide his countenance, and Phineas hardly knew whether the absurdity of the movement or the tragedy of the feeling struck him the more forcibly.' (X) Trollope had known since Mr Crawley that mental imbalance has its comic aspect, and here the point is made with graphic economy. Trollope, and Phineas, are both so absorbed in the man's case that there is no room for and no need to exploit any literary convention of madness. Indeed, Trollope is able to write a lengthy letter in Kennedy's own person, so complete is his understanding of the man's distorted mind – even though its Calvinistic turn was anti-pathetic to him.

Kennedy makes Phineas a go-between, as he had done in the previous book, but still regards him as the destroyer of his marriage and as what he quaintly calls his wife's 'paramour'. Their last meeting is in a seedy London hotel where Kennedy fires at Phineas with a pistol, much as George Vavasor had taken a shot at John Grey. In this case, however, Kennedy is hardly to be thought responsible; he throws Phineas's hat out of the door after him and is clearly 'so mad as to be not even aware of the act he had perpetrated'. (XXIII) Kennedy is taken back to Scotland and subsequently dies. His homicidal attempt is not brought to the law's attention and, as is the case with the murder of Bonteen later, there is no punishment to fit the crime. Trollope generally shows singularly little interest in hounding the authors of the considerable number of misdemeanours which his pages contain, partly perhaps because, as we shall see, his sensitivity to the guilty person's mind in effect makes criminality its own sentence.

In between these two encounters Phineas has been to see Lady Laura in Dresden and the course of his stay here is presented by Trollope with that dramatic objectivity which is the condition of his most moving scenes. Laura's fussing about Phineas's breakfast and whether he wants a wash – he has been travelling all night – as she attempts to conceal her tears at seeing him again is deeply touching, and he feels that he is only now beginning to understand her. The rapidity with which she has lost her former looks fills him 'with ineffable regret'. Her resignation – or apparent resignation – to the fact that she can no longer expect Phineas to return her love has a tragic dignity, for all its ordinariness of expression, that moves us as well as him:

> 'I must insist upon it,' she continued, 'that you shall take me now as I really am, – as your dearest friend, your sister, your mother, if you will. I know what I am. Were my husband not still living it would be the same. I should never under any circumstances marry again. I have passed the period of a woman's life when as a woman she is loved; but I have not outlived the power of loving. I shall fret about you, Phineas, like an old hen after her one chick; and though you turn out to be a duck, and get away into waters where I cannot follow you, I shall go cackling round the pond, and always have my eye upon you.' He was holding her now by the hand, but he could not speak for the tears were trickling down his cheeks. 'When I was young,' she continued, 'I did not credit myself with capacity for so much passion. I told myself that love after all should be a servant and not a master, and I married my husband fully intending to do my duty to him. Now we see what has come of it.' (XII)

The Victorian formula of 'let me be your sister' is entirely redeemed from cliché by the authenticity of Laura's suffering. She has here the power which comes from being able to look one's life in the face, and, it seems, the detachment: '"You will love again, of course . . I tried to blaze into power by a marriage, and I failed, – because I was a woman. A woman should marry only for love. You will do it yet, and will not fail. You may remember this too, – that I shall never be jealous again."'

It is part of Trollope's artistic honesty and of his moral generosity that Laura should turn out to be right about Phineas but wrong about herself. The scene at Königstein – set strikingly on the ramparts of the old Saxon fortress as their first moment of intimacy was picturesquely placed by the falls of Linter – represents an elevation of tone and mood which life (as opposed to conventional literature) could hardly have sustained. Trollope does not make a sermon out of the fact that none of us live up to our best moments, and when Laura does decline into jealousy as it becomes clear that Finn is becoming more closely linked with Madame Goesler, this only provokes him into renewed acuteness of attention. Phineas himself hardly knows what to think about the continued passion for him which Laura cannot disguise, even in her letters:

> He knew now, or thought that he knew, – that the continued indulgence of a hopeless passion was a folly opposed to the very instincts of man and woman, – a weakness showing want of fibre and of muscle in the character. But here was a woman who could calmly conceal her passion in its early days and marry a man whom she did not love in spite of it, who could make her heart, her feelings, and all her feminine delicacy subordinate to material considerations, and nevertheless could not rid herself of her passion in the course of years, although she felt its existence to be an intolerable burden on her conscience. On which side lay strength of character and on which side weakness? Was he strong or was she? (XX)

Phineas's question is left to hang in the air.

When Lady Laura returns to England – Kennedy being by now so manifestly insane that he represents no threat – her resolutions prove hard to keep, and she has the added mortification of finding that she no longer has the political influence which might help Phineas to get a post in the new Liberal administration and which was formerly so valuable to him. When Kennedy dies, leaving Laura the wealthy owner of his estate, she cannot stop herself wondering whether she might not yet 'stand once more beside the falls of Linter, contented, hopeful, nay, almost glorious, with her hand in his to whom she had once refused her own on that very spot'. (LII) Such fantasies grow harder to indulge as Madame Goesler goes off to the continent to obtain evidence which will help to clear the imprisoned Phineas – a mission which must bring the two of them closer – and Laura's frustration expresses itself in a violent hatred for 'this half-foreigner, this German Jewess' (LXV) whose sexual appeal has lasted so much better than her own. Laura has the humiliation of realizing that promises of restraint and

157

self-sacrifice are one thing to make and another to keep. Unhappiness has made her capable of a cheapness of which she would never formerly have been guilty, but Trollope is too understanding to be severe.

After his release from prison Phineas pays his last visit to Laura at Saulsby. He feels obliged to appear to consult her over the offer of a government job which he has in fact already decided to turn down. He has to turn down too her offer of funds (oddly parallel to Madame Goesler's in the previous novel), of an income which would make him politically independent. And he has to tell her that he intends to ask the other woman to marry him. Her reaction is sadly, and very movingly, consistent with her continued inability to sustain the generosity of her love without any hope of possession:

> 'Phineas, you have killed me at last.' Why could he not tell her that it was she who had done the wrong when she gave her hand to Robert Kennedy? But he could not tell her, and he was dumb. 'And so it's settled!'
>
> 'No; not settled.'
>
> 'Psha! I hate your mock modesty! It is settled. You have become far too cautious to risk fortune in such an adventure. Practice has taught you to be perfect. It was to tell me this that you came down here.'
>
> 'Partly so.'
>
> 'It would have been more generous of you, sir, to have remained away.'
>
> 'I did not mean to be ungenerous.'
>
> Then she suddenly turned upon him, throwing her arms round his neck, and burying her face upon his bosom. They were at the moment in the centre of the park, on the grass beneath the trees, and the moon was bright over their heads. He held her to his breast while she sobbed, and then relaxed his hold as she raised herself to look into his face. After a moment she took his hat from his head with one hand, and with the other swept the hair back from his brow. 'Oh, Phineas,' she said, 'Oh, my darling! My idol that I have worshipped when I should have worshipped my God!'

After that they roamed for nearly an hour backwards and

forwards beneath the trees, till at last she became calm and almost reasonable. She acknowledged that she had long expected such a marriage, looking forward to it as a great sorrow. She repeated over and over again her assertion that she could not 'know' Madame Goesler as the wife of Phineas, but abstained from further evil words respecting the lady. 'It is better that we should be apart,' she said at last. 'I feel that it is better. When we are both old, if I should live, we may meet again. I knew that it was coming, and we had better part.' And yet they remained out there, wandering about the park for a long portion of the summer night. She did not reproach him again, nor did she speak much of the future; but she alluded to all the incidents in their past life, showing him that nothing which he had done, no words which he had spoken, had been forgotten by her. 'Of course it has been my fault,' she said, as at last she parted with him in the drawing-room. 'When I was younger I did not understand how strong the heart can be. I should have known it, and I pay for my ignorance with the penalty of my whole life.' Then he left her, kissing her on both cheeks and on her brow, and went to his bedroom with the understanding that he would start for London on the following morning before she was up. (LXXVIII)

Laura's surprising but wonderfully telling gesture with Phineas's hat and his hair convey in the manner of Trollope's best moments all that the character and indeed the novelist cannot say. At such times no novelist of the period has a more complete command of the expressiveness of physical contact. The moonlight scene recalls a not dissimilar setting with Crosbie and the impassioned Lily Dale in *The Small House at Allington*, but the pain brought by such unreserved passion has here already been lived through, and the intensity of feeling has therefore a tragic legitimacy. Laura's cry about Phineas as an idol keeping her from God is for her a novel note and Trollope does not gloss it: perhaps he senses that in her despair she will become a true Kennedy at last, using for the first time the idiom of the husband with whom she never previously had anything in common.

Lady Laura's spiteful comments on Madame Max Goesler might

have seemed more justifiable half-way through *Phineas Finn*, when she was still something of an unknown quantity. In *Phineas Redux* she continues to become more sympathetic, as Trollope's understanding of her situation increases. After what has passed at the end of *Phineas Finn*, the reintroduction of Marie and Phineas is bound to be a delicate matter, especially as only they know about her offer and his rejection of it. When they do meet, down at Matching, it is a contingency which she has clearly been pondering: '"I shall be very glad to see him,' said Madame Goesler, slowly: 'I heard about his success at that town, and I knew that I should meet him somewhere."' (XIV) That 'slowly' carries a wealth of implication about her inner life. Their first meeting is one of excessive nervousness on both sides. As often in Trollope, hunting provides an occasion when people can talk intimately and privately (in the previous novel Phineas had had a romantic conversation with Violet Effingham while riding at Saulsby), and Madame Goesler has a chance to give Finn a candid account of her recent life with the old Duke of Omnium. Her rejection of the Duke's offer of marriage, over which she was so much exercised, has paradoxically led to a feeling for him which she does not hesitate to call love and which she has allowed to remodel '"the whole fashion of my life"'. It is a matter of great surprise to her that she '"should have become as it were engulfed in this new life; almost without will of my own"', and she concedes that as a young man Phineas cannot be expected to understand '"how natural it is that a young woman . . . should minister to an old man"'. (XVII) Phineas, forgetting no doubt that Madame Goesler is after all the widow of another elderly man, does find it hard to see what she gets out of it, and there may be in his incomprehension a touch of that antagonism towards the Duke, born of sexual rivalry, which surfaced briefly in the previous novel. Marie is performing the same services for the Duke that would have been her duty had she actually accepted his proposal, even though she will now have little reward for them when he dies (and she refuses to accept the legacy she is entitled to when he does die). Her disinterestedness gives her a new dimension of moral dignity; we feel a respect for her understanding of the odd ways in which life develops. It seems too that her devotion goes some way towards meeting her own emotional needs. Under her care, the old Duke himself visibly mellows, even as he lies on his death-bed holding Marie's hand. His last days are presented with that lack of fluster which makes Trollope's treatment of approaching death so unlike what we normally think of as Victorian. He can modulate without difficulty from the comic attempts to intrude by the now grotesque Lady Hartletop, for many years the Duke's 'intimate friend', to the low-keyed understatement of the old man's last moments:

> 'It is nearly done now, Marie,' he said to Madame Goesler one evening. She only pressed his hand in answer. His condition was too well understood between them to allow of her speaking to him of any possible recovery. 'It has been a great comfort to me that I have known you,' he said.
> 'Oh no!'
> 'A great comfort; – only I wish it had been sooner. I could have talked to you about things which I never did talk about to any one. I wonder why I should have been a duke, and another man a servant.'
> 'God Almighty ordained such difference.'
> 'I'm afraid I have not done it well; – but I have tried; indeed I have tried.' Then she told him he had ever lived as a great nobleman ought to live. And, after a fashion, she herself believed what she was saying. Nevertheless, her nature was much nobler than his; and she knew that no man should dare to live idly as the Duke had lived. (XXV).

Madame Goesler's sense of retrospect is one that the Duke's intermittent appearances in both of Trollope's novel sequences (from *Doctor Thorne* onwards) allow the reader to share, and certainly it is only by virtue of his reappearances that Trollope has finally achieved an inner understanding of what was at first a very externally perceived presence.

Madame Goesler's persistence in refusing to accept the Duke's legacy of extremely valuable diamonds is a further indication of her integrity (and is the exact opposite of what Lady Eustace did), just as it is also a product of a typically Trollopian obstinacy. Nor is she blind to the fact that, like her refusal of the Duke himself, it places her in a strong moral position, with its accompanying tactical advantages. Her tenacity is again displayed by her activity when

Phineas is in prison. Phineas's perennial need for a female confidante has already drawn them closer together again, and the atmosphere of attraction between them is palpable. Although she attempts to play it down, Marie's journey to the continent to seek out the vital evidence which suggests that Emilius and not Finn is the murderer of Bonteen is obviously due to her renewed love for him. (A comparable journey was made by John Eames, to get at the truth about Crawley's cheque, but for him virtue had to be its own reward.) The reunion of the released Phineas and Marie is arranged by Lady Glencora, who perceives perfectly well how matters stand:

> 'Yes, there she is,' said the Duchess, laughing. She had already told him that he was welcome to Matching, and had spoken some short of word of congratulation at his safe deliverance from his troubles. 'If ever one friend was grateful to another, you should be grateful to her, Mr. Finn.' He did not speak, but walking across the room to the window by which Marie Goesler stood, took her right hand in his, and passing his left arm round her waist, kissed her first on one cheek and then on the other. The blood flew to her face and suffused her forehead, but she did not speak or resist him or make any efforts to escape from his embrace. As for him, he had no thought of it at all. He had made no plan. No idea of kissing her when they should meet had occurred to him till the moment came. 'Excellently well done,' said the Duchess, still laughing with silent pleasant laughter. 'And now tell us how you are, after all your troubles.' (LXXIV)

Phineas's spontaneity has always been one of the sources of his charm: he has the knack of doing the right thing, simply, and without physical inhibition and awkwardness. So that when, finally, he makes his declaration to Marie, it is done with the manly directness that Trollope admires and is presented with an appropriate simplicity:

> At a little before noon the next morning he knocked at her door, and was told to enter. 'I didn't go out after all,' she said, 'I hadn't courage to face the sun.'
> 'I saw that you were not in the garden.'
> 'If I could have found you I would have told you that I

should be here all the morning. I might have sent you a message, only – only I didn't.'

'I have come –'

'I know why you have come.'

'I doubt that. I have come to tell you that I love you.'

'Oh Phineas; – at last, at last!' And in a moment she was in his arms. (LXXIX)

Marie's 'at last, at last' implies with affecting economy her own sense that Phineas's love was what everything in her life had led her to need. Our understanding of the evolution of that life, as Trollope has gradually unravelled it through the two novels, is now sufficiently full for us intuitively to supply the weight of emotion that the trivial words (also used as the chapter's title) carry. This ability to make ordinary language tell so powerfully is one of the great rewards of Trollope's patient accumulative methods.

After his trial, and contrary to Madame Goesler's advice, Phineas withdraws from public life, but – although both parties justifiably assure themselves that he has not married her for her money – it is clear that the fundamental problem of Phineas's career has now been solved. Throughout *Phineas Redux* itself however, the necessity of making his political way on the proceeds of office presses on our hero as much as it did in *Phineas Finn*. This time, however, he is no longer the 'child of fortune'; doors do not open magically at his touch. His luck no longer holds. The association with Lady Laura, formerly so beneficial, is now compromising. Although he acts throughout with the strongest sense of a need to maintain his and her reputations, his pity for Laura and his sense of what he owes her mean that he cannot desert her or refuse to concern himself with her situation. Others besides the deranged husband find it easy to be suspicious of the continued association, and Finn's name becomes tarnished. Like so many of Trollope's principal characters, Phineas is extremely sensitive to what other people say and think, and many small but deft touches demonstrate the way Phineas's stock slides. The renewed efforts of the *People's Banner* are an important factor in this decline. Grand people like the Liberal leader Mr Gresham do not concern themselves with a scandal sheet, but nevertheless they get wind of what it contains through others. Mr Bonteen – Phineas's enemy since the first Loughlinter house party in *Phineas Finn* – is happy enough to intimate that smoke must imply fire. Hence, indeed, the quarrel between them at the Universe Club, which leads so naturally to the arrest of Phineas as a suspect when Bonteen is murdered in the street shortly afterwards. The episode loosely parallels while greatly developing the garrotters' attack on Kennedy in *Phineas Finn* (which Trollope reminds us of just before the crime is committed).

Trollope's return to the question of newspaper persecution has, in this case, a certain complexity. Quintus Slide proves on reappearance to be a more interesting person than his rather burlesque treatment in *Phineas Finn* would lead one to expect. He is in his way a true professional. When Kennedy sends him an account of his wrongs for publication, Slide is thoroughly alive to the sales advantage of being seen as the guardian of purity of morals in the aristocracy. When Phineas and his old tutor Mr Low obtain an injunction stopping publication of Kennedy's letter, he feels 'done – sold' and 'treacherously misused'. This may seem a proper reward for the newspaper's arrogant assumption of power over private individuals and on previous evidence from *The Warden* onwards one would expect Trollope to take some pleasure in Slide's being worsted. In fact, the novelist cannot help seeing the matter from the character's position too: 'It must be acknowledged on behalf of this editor that he did in truth believe that he had been hindered from doing good.' (XXVII) Trollope spends some time putting Slide's case: 'If there be fault in high places it is proper that it be exposed'; 'That such details will make a paper "pay" Mr Slide knew . . . [but] an unprofitable newspaper cannot long continue its existence, and, while existing, cannot be widely beneficial. It is . . . the profitable circulation . . . which is beneficent.' The self-justifying alignment of ends and means recalls such arguments as Finn used to himself in accepting Lord Brentford's borough. Moreover, Slide's feeling that the Vice-Chancellor's injunction would not have been so readily granted in favour of someone without establishment connections has an already demonstrated validity. The full texts of Slide's editorial thunderbolts against Finn are quoted, and one cannot but feel that Slide's 'delight' in them was shared by Trollope who himself so intensely enjoyed writing strongly worded official memoranda. He quickly reminds the reader that the article is 'full of lies', but 'Mr Slide did not know that he was lying, and did not know that he was malicious.' (XXVIII) Trollope's transition from a hostile external view of an abuse to a not unsympathetic inquiry into the psychology of the person guilty of it reminds us again of the way in which his fiction veers away from the abstract principle and towards the particular case.

This tendency is written large in the development of *Phineas Redux* as a political novel. Here, as in its predecessor, Trollope dramatizes the political conflict between Conservatives and Liberals by focusing on a major constitutional issue. In *Phineas Redux*, which was written at the time of the second Reform Bill, the question of the extension of the franchise lay to hand. In *Phineas Redux* the battle is fought on the highly hypothetical ground of the proposed disestablishment of the Church of England. (The Irish Church had been disestablished in 1869.) The party responsible for such a change ought in the nature of things to be the Liberals, the party of reform. In the novel it is brought forward, with characteristic audacity, by the Conservative leader Mr Daubeny, who thus attempts to steal the Liberals' clothes, as Disraeli had done in reality over the franchise in 1867. The question whether Daubeny is a portrait of Disraeli has been much discussed, as has the problem of other identifications of characters in the Palliser novels with historically real analogues or originals. Trollope's intense interest in the politics of his day, not to mention his own parliamentary aspirations, must have meant that his conceptions of political life were much influenced by the dominant figures of the time. Personalities as powerful as Disraeli, Gladstone and Palmerston (whose life Trollope was later to write) were bound to have some degree of defining effect. Trollope would naturally form part of his ideas about political types and behaviour from those he observed, but it would be against everything in his practice as a novelist to force the character as it took shape in his imagination to imitate slavishly the historical person who may have contributed to that character's genesis.[9] That Daubeny and Gresham have much in common with Disraeli and Gladstone is obvious enough and admitted by Trollope in a letter of 15 June 1876, but 'it has only been as to their political tenets. There is nothing of personal characteristic here.' In the political novels Daubeny is repeatedly presented as a conjuror, 'a political Cagliostro'; in the *Autobiography*, Trollope

165

holds it against Disraeli's novels that 'an audacious conjuror has generally been his hero'. (XIII) The autobiographer, however, is much more scathing than the novelist, and Daubeny is treated with altogether more respect and patience, if also, in the end, with as much disapproval. For all his courage, Daubeny personifies for Trollope the betrayal of that probity which may be difficult to maintain when political and personal advantage beckon but which is the foundation of the integrity that a statesman ought to have. Daubeny's appropriation of measures which are the natural property of the party of reform means the sacrifice of principle in the interests of some cheap legerdemain. Daubeny's argument that 'audacity in Reform was the very backbone of Conservatism' (XXXIII) is fundamentally perverse. What is the point of Conservatism if it does not conserve? Trollope understands very well the unease of stolid Tories from the shires who disapprove of Daubeny's policies and distrust his manoeuvres but who are bound to follow the leader of the party they love. Their dilemma is typical of the sort of mixed feelings which most interested Trollope in political as in other forms of life. Trollope's political world exists in the same mode as his clerical world or his Irish world: it is in parallel with historical reality rather than a series of clues to it.

Although Phineas commits himself to disestablishment on the hustings, it is not a question on which he seems deeply engaged; as a Catholic it is not of intimate concern to him. For a time it looks as if he might get out of step with his party on the question (as he did about Irish tenant-right, on which the party has now caught up with him). Nothing comes of this, however, because it is super-seded by the much more personal question of the way in which, despite Lady Glencora's backstairs support, Phineas's career is checked by the antagonism of Bonteen. After Bonteen's murder, which immediately follows their public quarrel, and Phineas's incarceration as a suspect, political life seems virtually suspended until the question of Finn's guilt or innocence is decided, and opinion on that question is not necessarily on party lines.

Phineas is far from being the first Trollopean character to find himself either in court or with the prospect of being so. Apart from the proceedings against Mr Crawley, there has been a series of trial scenes going right back to *The MacDermots of Ballycloran* and including *Orley Farm* in which Lady Mason was defended – as

Phineas is – by the celebrated barrister Chaffanbrass. Such reliance on a relatively sensational procedure might seem foreign to what Trollope calls his 'spirit of calm recital', but the *Autobiography* points out that sensationalism only seems so when imperfectly harmonized with realism; as long as a novel is truthful – 'truth of description, truth of character, human truth as to men and women' (XII) – it can hardly be too sensational. But Trollope would have been drawn to trial scenes for something more than mere narrative excitement; any dividend from suspense is as usual ostentatiously refused in *Phineas Redux* when Trollope makes Emilius's guilt clear early on. A trial is a highly dramatized and formalized confrontation between the self and the world. Like many of Trollope's characters, Phineas's sensitivity to the world's opinion becomes so extreme under pressure as almost to seem morbid. Whatever appearances may suggest, Phineas is not only innocent of murder: he knows that he would never be guilty of murder, and what he finds hardest to bear is that anyone else should for a moment think him capable of murder. In prison, he develops an almost extra-sensory perception of the true feelings of his visitors – when Barrington Erle escorts Lady Laura to visit Phineas 'He spoke cordially to his old friend, and grasped the prisoner's hand cordially, – but not the less did he believe that there was blood on it, and Phineas knew that such was his belief.' (LV) Phineas is especially mortified by the doubts of Mr Monk even though Monk himself 'was made miserable even by his doubts'; Monk, like Palliser, believes that a man is not prosecuted in England without good cause, and 'if the evidence against his friend was strong enough to send his friend for trial, how should he dare to discredit the evidence because the man was his friend?' (LXI) Their confidence in judicial process is sharply offset by Glencora's pragmatic insistence that Finn should have the best legal advice money can buy, because '"twenty thousand pounds spent among the lawyers would get him off"'. (LIV) Her impetuous readiness to buy up the Home Secretary himself if necessary can be put down to her usual exaggeration of manner, but what she says about the relation of money to legal proceedings would raise some uncomfortable questions if pursued (questions also raised from a different angle by Mr Crawley, who refuses legal aid because, knowing his innocence, he will not depend on hiring someone to lie on his behalf).

Phineas is relieved in prison by his rich friends as far as physical wants are concerned, but his anguish of mind finds little respite.

> 'They can't believe it,' he said aloud. 'It is impossible. Why should I have murdered him?' And then he remembered an example in Latin from some rule of grammar, and repeated it to himself over and over again. – 'No one at an instant, – of a sudden, – becomes most base.' It seemed to him that there was such a want of knowledge of human nature in the supposition that it was possible that he should have committed such a crime. (LV)

The boyhood memory of the Latin tag is tellingly used as a touch of free association (as Bill Overton notes, it had already been applied by Mr Harding to Mr Crawley in *The Last Chronicle*). Phineas's assumption that anyone who understood what people are like would naturally think him innocent is also revealing. It is always puzzling when the world does not take the favourable view of the self that the self knows it deserves if it were truly known. The point is wittily decorated when at the trial Chaffanbrass cross-examines Mr Bouncer, a well-known novelist, and manoeuvres him into saying that murders as unpremeditated as the one Phineas is accused of would not be admitted in literature because it would not be in accord with human nature as Shakespeare, Scott, and for that matter Mr Bouncer, understand it.

Phineas's long spell in solitary confinement demoralizes him badly; he keeps a diary in which he endlessly expatiates on the injustice of his position, but he cannot read. He fears the loss of reputation more than of life; 'the sorrow that broke him down' (LX) was the fear that those with whom he had aspired to live and work should think that 'after all he had been a base adventurer', unworthy of them. (In other words, he fears that he will be thought of as a Vavasor, or as someone like Ferdinand Lopez, soon to arrive on the Palliser scene in *The Prime Minister*.) When Phineas declares he would sooner hang than be acquitted on technicalities and afterwards still looked on as the murderer, even the hardened Chaffanbrass (privately convinced of his client's guilt as usual) is impressed by his eloquence and grace. In court Phineas similarly bears himself well even though, to his almost paranoid sense of things, its whole proceeding seems loaded against him. When

Madame Goesler returns with the vital evidence which makes Emilius a suspect too and the climate of opinion changes dramatically in Phineas's favour, his reaction is of the querulous Crawley kind; he should not have had to depend on his friends to clear him from a charge which should never have been brought and a crime of which he should never have been suspected. All the same, the testimony in court as to Finn's character from the Chilterns, from Lord Cantrip, and from Mr Monk is deeply consoling because it transcends the reticence normal in Trollope's society, being 'words such as neither men nor women can say to each other in the ordinary intercourse of life, much as they may wish that their purport should be understood'. (LXIV)

When Phineas leaves the court without a stain on his character, he is in a state of profound shock as the result of his ordeal. Physically, he tends to be tearful and shivers and shakes 'like one struck by palsy'. Despite offers of convalescence in country houses, he prefers to creep back to his own humble lodgings *chez* Bunce in Great Marlborough Street. On the first night of his freedom he puts on the grey coat which had been so damning a part of the evidence against him and retraverses the route he took on the night of the murder, so as to pass the spot on which it had been committed. It is a way of challenging those who believed that he might have done it. This brings him to the club where he had quarrelled with Bonteen, but he cannot face going in. Trollope's characters walk about the London streets and parks a good deal, but one does not get the strong physical impression of the city that Dickens provides. This may be partly because Trollope's people patrol the more respectable and less picturesque areas, but it also illustrates how Dickens's omnivorous eye for the external is replaced in Trollope by a preoccupation with what lies within. When Phineas goes through the mews off Clarges Street from which the murderer was seen to hurry away, there is no attempt to evoke a Dickensian *frisson* at the renewed sight of the fatal venue. Trollope is entirely concerned with Phineas's thoughts, relying on the reader to supply the sense of location from his assumed knowledge of the West End. (The *Autobiography* states that the Phineas books were written for the class of readers who would have known Phineas, Lady Laura, and so on, in life, and who would naturally know their way about the best parts of the capital.)

Phineas is also in a state of shock mentally. His first thought is that the resumption of his Parliamentary career is out of the question. 'He had been so hacked and hewed about, so exposed to the gaze of the vulgar, so mauled by the public . . . He could never more enjoy that freedom from self-consciousness, that inner tranquillity of spirit, which are essential to public utility.' (LXVII) He explains his decision to give up his seat to Mr Monk by saying that '"there is an offensiveness in murder which degrades a man even by the accusation"'. (LXVIII) In all this Phineas is, as his friends point out, behaving irrationally. Trollope, however, is intensely sympathetic to his state of mind, even though he sees, and Phineas more or less admits, that in due course it will pass. Phineas has generally struck people as composed and at ease with himself, but the trial has revealed a fundamental vulnerability due to his hypersensitivity to public opinion and his deep need to be in good standing with the world: 'Had his imagination been less alert in looking into the minds of men, and in picturing to himself the thoughts of others in reference to the crime with which he had been charged, he would not now have shrunk from contact with his fellow-creatures as he did.' When Mrs Low accuses Phineas of an insufficiently stiff upper lip, Trollope disagrees roundly, and his accompanying comments on manliness are an important elaboration of that stress on personal integrity to which he so often recurs. Manliness is not a matter of being lofty about the small things of life and cultivating 'a certain outward magnificence of demeanour'. For Trollope the essential point is that 'Manliness is not compatible with affectation.' It cannot be put on as a manner; any self-conscious assumption of style is fatal to it. It is immediately recognizable: 'Let a man put his hat down, and you shall say whether he has deposited it with affectation or true nature'. Such instant detection is perhaps more Trollope's gift as an artist than ours as common readers – and the comment, made so casually, is a telling example of the way Trollope makes deductions from what is imaginatively *seen*. The moral truth is inferred from the everyday gesture: the gesture is not made allegorically so as to dramatize the abstract truth. Phineas would certainly pass the hat test – we have already seen his natural power of acting simply and directly at crucial moments. In admitting that he has been broken up by what he has gone through, he may be weak and womanly – as Lord

Chiltern accuses him of being – but paradoxically his manliness is not thereby compromised, because 'He could not pretend to be other than he was.' Transparency is the corollary of integrity.

Phineas resigns his seat, as he did at the end of *Phineas Finn*, but the action, for which there is no necessity and no real justification, only serves to increase his popularity. In spite of his wishes, his constituents re-elect him with enthusiasm. Discontented with political life as he now is, Phineas is reluctant to reappear in the House; his hesitation is called cowardly by Mr Low, but as Phineas explains to Mr Monk: '"I don't think . . . that Low quite understands my position when he calls me a coward . . . I think he mistakes the matter. When a man becomes crooked from age it is no good telling him to be straight. He'd be straight if he could. A man can't eat his dinner with a diseased liver as he could when he was well . . . Low seems to think the disease shouldn't be there. The disease is there, and I can't banish it by simply saying that it is not there."' (LXXIII) As so often in Trollope, the easy, colloquial and almost dateless English makes the character's point with modest but unanswerable force. However, Phineas's morale is beginning to pick up. When he grumbles about the graciously turned welcome Daubeny gives him when Phineas does take his seat in the Commons again, complaining that he would have done it just as well in an appropriately funereal tone if Phineas had been hung, Monk replies that '"It is rather a grim matter for joking."' Phineas explains that '"The grimness and the jokes are always running through my mind together. I used to spend hours in thinking what my dear friends would say about it when they found that I had been hung in mistake."' The ability to extract this degree of mordant humour from the situation indicates a reviving buoyancy, and immediately afterwards, Phineas does the expected manly thing and resolves that nothing will make him talk about the matter any more. But it has been characteristic of Trollope's novelistic interests that as much attention should have been given to the psychological trauma left by the trial as to the strong effects offered by the trial itself. By the end of *Phineas Redux*, with Phineas married to Marie Goesler and off on his second honeymoon abroad, his famous luck seems to have returned. Trollope comments dourly that his hero will not be truly fortunate unless he gets down to some work (which in the later Palliser novels he indeed proceeds to do).

Phineas's essential industriousness is implicitly contrasted with the constitutional inertia of Gerald Maule, whose problems in marrying Adelaide Palliser make up the novel's sub-plot. This area of the book is treated with some perfunctoriness by Trollope and is relatively thin; it also involves a hunting rival for Adelaide's hand straight out of Surtees. Gerald's difficulties arise from the fact that he cannot see much point in getting out of bed in the morning. As he says, '"What's the use of it?"' He would have sympathized with Dickens's Eugene Wrayburn, with his complaint that '"idiots talk of Energy"'. It is a type that Trollope does more with in characters like Dolly Longstaffe (in *The Way We Live Now* and *The Duke's Children*). Here the whole situation – with Chiltern sternly asking Maule what he means to do about that girl, and Lady Glencora finally engineering the lovers' reconciliation and finding the funds for them to live on – seems at times to tremble on the brink of the Wodehouse world. However, it has hardly more than a contingent connection with Phineas's, and is something of a distraction from it.

There are other liabilities in *Phineas Redux*, compared with its better-integrated predecessor. One of the rewards of reappearance is that Trollope can by now call on a considerable number of familiar figures to respond to the progress of Phineas's trial in various characteristic ways, but the trial itself is a distraction from the political material. The two are connected by the political rivalry between Phineas and Bonteen, but there is little significant development of Trollope's treatment of the tensions between political principle, party conflict and personal temperament. The sensational aspects of the case, and Chaffanbrass's virtuoso display of forensic brilliance, upstage the political concerns of the novel's first half. This imbalance, combined with the arbitrariness of the Maule plot, means that there are no scenes which have the formal elegance of the sequence in *Phineas Finn* (LXIII, LXIV) describing Phineas's successive meetings (at Lady Glencora's great party at her riverside house The Horns) of the three women in his life, Violet Effingham, Lady Laura, and Madame Max – a brilliantly devised retrospect of the whole progress of his amatory relationships in that novel. Again Trollope's drafting of Emilius from *The Eustace Diamonds* to murder Bonteen gives the oleaginous preacher a function which is hardly compatible with a character who has always had one foot in burlesque. Mr Emilius's line in high-flown biblical gush has not previously seemed to imply that he could be capable of dispatching the President of the Board of Trade with his own bare hands. His bigamy – he is ultimately proved to have an existing wife in Bohemia – is much more plausible, and has the useful result of getting Lizzie Eustace out of her absurd marriage. Emilius's career is in a way weirdly similar to Madame Goesler's – they are both central European adventurers trying to establish themselves in English high society – but a truer and much more fully studied analogue was to follow in the person of Melmotte, in *The Way We Live Now*. As far as *Phineas Redux* is concerned, it is hard not to feel that Emilius has to some extent been taken advantage of by the author – perhaps that is why he is never actually convicted of murder: Trollope's guilty subconscious has let him off.

But there is one area in *Phineas Redux* where Trollope is consistently in the fullest communion with his material, and that is the continuing life of the Pallisers. Lady Glencora seems to increase in vigour with every line she speaks, and her deployment of her energies in the Maule business and on behalf of Finn – and against the disliked Bonteen – prepare us for the vigour of her performance in *The Prime Minister*. Plantagenet is so preoccupied with politics and the problems of decimal coinage that she is left with great freedom of action. Madame Goesler's wise handling of the old Duke's affection has made Glencora her firm friend, and with Glencora loyalty to her friends takes the form of bustling activity on their behalf. She perceives clearly enough the nature of Marie's feelings for Phineas during the long periods they spend together as joint nurses of the old man, and this would be enough in itself for Glencora to bestir herself in Phineas's cause. Her request to Plantagenet that he should ensure a place for Finn in Mr Gresham's administration is met as usual by the straight bat of political propriety: 'I never interfere.' All the same, as what Trollope calls 'an affectionate man, and an indulgent husband' (XXXVII), he does his best. Glencora's persistent refusal to accept Establishment evasion constantly recalls Palliser and ourselves to the realities of political life, despite her reckless enthusiasms and her sometimes erratic command of fact. Palliser has become wise enough to realize that attempts to control Glencora are even less likely to succeed now than they were in the days of *Can You Forgive Her?*. When he complains that her public display of interest in Phineas's trial makes people talk, she replies '"They have been doing that ever since we were married; – but I do not know that they have made out much against me. We must go after our nature, Plantagenet. Your nature is decimals. I run after units."' (LVIII) Palliser lets the matter drop, realizing perhaps that the differences between them could hardly be more succinctly put.

When the old Duke dies, Palliser to his chagrin succeeds to the title. This means that, as a member of the House of Lords, he cannot any longer expect to be Chancellor of the Exchequer, and he is cut off from the House of Commons: '"My whole life was there,"' he says, simply. (LVIII) There is no question for Plantagenet of inheriting his uncle's *ancien régime* grandeur with his rank. For someone as addicted to work in the public service as Palliser, the old Duke's inactivity is inexplicable: '"My Uncle's life to me was always a problem which I could not understand."' Palliser insists on taking the now vacant Presidency of the Board of Trade, despite the fact that its lower status implies a degrading demotion, because he cannot bear to be without the work which gives meaning to his life. In some ways his indifference to what people think and say is quite as great as Glencora's, despite his lack of pretension. Indeed, as Trollope says, 'There was such an absence about him of all self-consciousness, he was so little given to think of his own personal demeanour and outward trappings' that he 'hardly knew insolence when he met it'. (XLIII) Glencora complains that '"Plantagenet considers himself inferior to a sweeper while on the crossing"'. (XXVI) When she twits him about his drop in salary she observes sarcastically that her husband is '"above all such sublunary ideas"' as rank, influence, prestige, and the general fitness of things. Plantagenet '"would clean Mr Gresham's shoes for him, if – the service of your country required it" . . . These last words added in a tone of voice very similar to that which her husband himself used on occasions.' But the new Duke refuses to rise to his wife's mockery of his own manner. '"I would even allow you to clean them, – if the service of the country required it."' (LVIII) His commitment to what the phrase implies is too serene to be eroded by ironic imitation. The little scene – like so many in *Phineas Redux* – shows Trollope in effortless command of that atmosphere of combined affection and irritability which is so characteristic of their marriage, so that when the relationship is put under greater strain in the next novel in the series Trollope's understanding of it – and his fascination with it – never falters. In the *Autobiography*, Trollope explicitly connects this exchange with another in *The Prime Minister* as an example of a progression of effect which he aims at but which he fears readers will miss because of the unfamiliar format of the novel sequence. (XX) He might have added that Glencora's remarks also recall her earlier assertion in *Can You Forgive Her?* that she would have thought it no disgrace to clean the shoes of Burgo Fitzgerald.

At first, Glencora seems to be quite as much put out by becoming a duchess as Plantagenet is by his elevation. She fears that it will restrict her freedom and curb her irresponsibility: 'She must lay down her mischief, and abandon her eccentricity, and in some degree act like other duchesses.' (XXVI) But there is no real prospect of her dwindling into conformity. She has become too used to what Trollope calls 'all the disturbing excitements of life' to be in any danger of becoming ornamental and inactive. The last words of *Phineas Redux* are 'Nothing will ever change the Duchess'; the next novel in the sequence shows how rewardingly true that is.

The Prime Minister

Exactly three years after finishing *Phineas Redux* – and ten after completing *Can You Forgive Her?* – Trollope returned to the Pallisers 'with a full heart'. His account in the *Autobiography* of *The Prime Minister* published 1876 makes it clear that the phrase means what it says. His aim was to draw 'the completed picture of such a Statesman as my imagination had conceived . . . of whom I had long thought'. (XX) It is in relation to this novel that Trollope laments that correlations of detail between one book in the series and another (such as the exchange between Plantagenet and Glencora just mentioned) will be missed by the inadvertent reader, even though he has been manufacturing such details 'for many years past'. It is at this point too that Trollope prophesies that in the unlikely event of his still being read in the next century, his claim to permanence will 'probably rest on the characters of Plantagenet Palliser, Lady Glencora, and the Rev. Mr Crawley'. A yet more personal commitment is illustrated by the touching footnote added three years later in which Trollope records his pain at an adverse review of the novel by a normally fair critic: 'in this case I could not agree with him, so much do I love the man whose character I had endeavoured to portray'. Trollope speaks as if an injustice has been done to a living person, rather than as an author whose text has been found wanting.

In the same passage Trollope roundly states that 'I think Plantagenet Palliser, Duke of Omnium, is a perfect gentleman. If he be not, then I am unable to describe a gentleman.' There is no question, however, of Palliser's being offered as a Grandisonian exemplar. Indeed, the main result of his period as Prime Minister, inevitably the summit of his political career, is that it brings out to an unprecedented degree the inadequacies in his character and even to some degree corrupts it. But since the qualities which make the Duke unhappy in his office are also qualities which deeply engage Trollope's sympathy, the phrase 'a perfect gentleman' seems rather an intense intimation of personal support than a judicial summing-up or didactic recommendation.

Although it is clear that the main motive for writing *The Prime Minister* was Trollope's desire to explore further the exact working-out of the inner contradictions and external idiosyncrasies of Palliser's personality – a nature too unusual and even eccentric to be adequately described by any simple label – the novel follows the by now well-established procedure of dealing with the Pallisers in the context of a parallel and connected plot.

In fact, the first five chapters of *The Prime Minister* are exclusively concerned with the prospects of Ferdinand Lopez, who aspires to the hand of Emily Wharton, the daughter of a wealthy and conservative-minded lawyer. We are thus well into the Lopez situation before the Pallisers are introduced, or reintroduced, in Chapter VI (with a characteristic line of *badinage* from Glencora). Is Lopez a gentleman? The question is so frequently asked, both by the author and by many of the characters, that though it is often raised elsewhere in Trollope's work, it is bound to seem thematic here, especially when Lopez's career is patently counterpointed with Palliser's. It is not quite a question of snobbery, in the Thackerayean sense. The general increase in prosperity since *The Book of Snobs* (1847) meant that a great many more men had the means to support a social position to which their birth alone would in no way have entitled them. City merchants who dream of estates and titles are familiar enough – Jacobean drama in which Trollope was well read is full of them – but the growth of the stock market and the increase in speculation characteristic of the mid-Victorian period (and especially in the boom years of the early 1870s) clearly gave a topical impetus to an immemorial process. Trollope had finished *The Way We Live Now* shortly before beginning work on *The Prime Minister*, and the earlier novel (discussed below) specifically addresses itself to the rise and fall of the great speculator Melmotte. Lopez is much younger and never achieves the same temporary degree of social or political success, but they are both adventurers whose dexterity and deviousness in financial transactions is conventionally to be expected from Jews of unspecified continental origin; they both aim to establish themselves in English society through their financial acumen, or at least their reputation for it; when they fail to do so they both commit suicide. However, Madame Max Goesler was also the widow of a continental Jew of uncertain provenance, and in *The Prime Minister* she is established more securely than ever as the wife of Phineas Finn and the closest confidante of the Duchess of Omnium. As usual in Trollope, a character is not to be restricted to his type: the type is rather a point of departure for the gradually discovered individual.

Although 'it was admitted on all sides that Ferdinand Lopez was a "gentleman"' (I), no one knows anything about him. His reserve carries with it a latent imperiousness, so that when it comes to the point even close friends like Emily's brother Everett don't quite like to ask about his background. Indeed, Lopez seems 'created self-sufficient, independent of mother's milk or father's money'. (II) He is always impeccably dressed, and has the manners of a gentleman, even though he went to a German university and has business in the City, the nature of which is obscure. Trollope's introductory account stresses his inherent pugnacity, but then Lord Chiltern, who is certainly a gentleman, is pugnacious and so was George Vavasor. Lopez is shown manoeuvring his partner Sexty Parker into signing a bill, but then gentlemen are always asking their friends to accommodate them in this way in Trollope's pages (Finn feels obliged to do so for Fitzgibbon, and, further back, Mark Robarts gives Sowerby his name, not without anxiety in both cases, but relying on their honour as gentlemen). But although external appearances are in Lopez's favour, he is unlike Finn or Vavasor in his inability to produce any respectable relatives and also, revealingly, in his opinion that a seat in Parliament would be a waste of time except for the fact that being an MP can be useful in business. Such an attitude to an ambition so close to Trollope's patriotic heart is certainly ominous. Moreover, Lopez's love for Emily, although genuine and even reverential, is not allowed its head until he has established that her father really is well-off. All the same, Mr Wharton's objections to Lopez are, as he himself is obliged to concede, pure chauvinism: '"He is not an English gentleman. What was his father?"' Lopez does not have much difficulty in deflecting such Podsnappery, especially since he has been careful to observe the strictest protocol in asking Mr Wharton for Emily's hand before actually proposing to her. Old Mr Wharton is so upset by the whole business that he is unable to prevent a marriage which his determined daughter has decided she wants; he fails too to make sufficiently searching inquiries about Lopez's means, which would have been within his rights.

A further cause of distress to Mr Wharton is that his daughter's inexplicable partiality for the objectionable Lopez necessarily means the rejection of the admirable Arthur Fletcher. Mr Wharton likes Fletcher '"because he is a gentleman of the class to which I belong myself; because he works; because I know all about him so that I can be sure of him; because he had a decent father and mother; because I am safe with him."' (X) Not that Emily isn't also deeply fond of Arthur – an affection based on childhood memories of the close association of the Whartons and the Fletchers down in Herefordshire – but she has 'taught herself to understand by some confused and perplexed lesson that she did not love him as men and women love'. (XVII) It is not very clear what this means, and it is a weakness of the novel that the inner motives for Emily's preference are insufficiently explored and too belatedly supplied. Lopez is attractive in a romantic sort of way, and has a good voice which is useful in his discussions of literature with Emily before, though not after, their marriage. Arthur on the other hand, is essentially English, with his light wavy hair and frank eye. Presumably Emily finds Lopez's appeal more exotic and sexually more promising, although she does not seem to be the sort of girl who will admit to having such thoughts even to herself. When Arthur resigns all claims to her, Emily is disappointed not to get a valedictory kiss; she is sad that Arthur is sad, and 'for a moment the idea of a comparison between the two men forced itself upon her, – but she drove it from her, as she hurried back to the house'. Her susceptibility to Arthur remains, and gradually becomes one of several causes of marital dissension. When Arthur writes to Emily to explain how he has come to stand as a candidate for the same Parliamentary seat that Lopez seeks, Lopez begins to mutter about horsewhips, and Emily is obliged to revise what Trollope now explains was her original theory of the desirable man. She had once thought to reject her father's ideas of gentlemanliness, as something that 'could exist without intellect, without heart, and with very moderate culture'. There was no reason why her hero should not be the offspring of working mechanics, and foreigners at that. However, her husband's behaviour is bringing her round to her father's views about the benefits of 'living with gentlemen'. The introduction of these ideas as late as Chapter XXXI looks too much like an afterthought on Trollope's part – as if the real reasons behind Emily's choice of Lopez had just occurred to him. It is sometimes a disadvantage of his exploratory method that analysis comes too far after the event to seem organically connected with it. Here, his imagination has not sufficiently dwelt on Emily's premarital state; it is inadequately dramatized, and so the explanation of her feelings now supplied does not convincingly account for what we have already been shown.

Lopez becomes Fletcher's electoral rival because the Duchess of Omnium indiscreetly encourages him to stand for Silverbridge, traditionally regarded as the Palliser family borough. Glencora takes Lopez up more or less out of caprice; she simply likes the look of him – perhaps there is something Burgo-ish about him (although, in a novel which several times recalls the days of *Can You Forgive Her?*, Trollope doesn't actually say this). Given his poor opinion of political life, Lopez's candidacy is, to say the least, opportunist. Even when he does act well, he is always giving himself away. When Lopez rescues Everett from some muggers in St James's Park much as Finn saves Kennedy from a similarly nocturnal garrotting, his first thought is how to 'turn the events of the evening to his own use' (XXII) – something which would not even have crossed Finn's mind. The early days of marriage are spent on a continental tour (it says something for the then strength of sterling that even someone in as financially precarious a position as Lopez can afford some months abroad) during which he begins to try to indoctrinate Emily with his own belief that the acquiring of money is 'the most important pursuit in the world'. (XXV) He wants to get at what will in due course be Emily's inheritance so as to use it as working capital – capital that as a speculator on the commodity market he badly needs. He certainly needs more than can be supplied by his 'partner' Sexty Parker, a decent enough man with a family out at Ponders End to support (Trollope is quick to reflect the expanded range of commuting made possible by better communications). Lopez cannot see that his wish to exploit his father-in-law's funds is improper or even insensitive, much as Emily is revolted by the idea. According to his set of values 'what we call cheating was not dishonesty'. He is animated by the idea of a battle with the world that is 'bold, grand, picturesque, and almost beautiful' (XXIV); his conduct may not be gentlemanly and he may simply not understand what gentlemanly standards of honesty are, but he does have a perverse value-system of his own. As Trollope reminds us more than once, Lopez does not know that he is a villain. His accounts of Lopez's inner thoughts and calculations gain in impartiality as the novel proceeds.

It is characteristic of such thoughts that they should be pre-occupied with that self-justification in which Trollope's characters of whatever hue so often find themselves engaged. And since Lopez is an intelligent man, he is often able to present events to himself in such a way as to put the blame on others. He spends £500 on the Silverbridge election before having to withdraw prematurely, and induces Mr Wharton to reimburse him on the grounds that he was lured into the contest by the Duchess, which is not altogether untrue. When Lopez subsequently succeeds in getting the Duke of Omnium to give him another cheque for the same amount on the same grounds, he persuades himself that the two sums are quite distinct so that the receipt of one need not involve the return of the other: 'Was it not spoil got from the enemy by his own courage and cleverness?' Mr Wharton's refusal to give Lopez any more of his money is construed by Lopez as a robbery of which he is the victim – the sort of self-interested distortion of the facts which Trollope reminds us is common enough. Lopez, therefore, is not a half-foreign fiend, but an understandable man made dishonest by his constitutional inability to comprehend what honesty is. It is not that he is given over to enthusiastic depravity (there is no hint of Vavasor's sexual irregularity), but that the moral sense – at least as understood among English gentlemen – is simply missing.

Lopez's ethical instability is matched by his increasing lack of that self-possession which was at first so striking. The marriage by which he had hoped to get so much turns out to be a fatal miscalculation: it burdens him with responsibilities he cannot afford and limits his freedom of manoeuvre, without providing any compensating inflow of those funds he needs to continue trading. Although he resolves that on his honeymoon, at least, he will not even think about money, he cannot prevent himself from raising the question of his new father-in-law's financial intentions as soon as he and Emily are on the train to Dover. (The scene is not so fully or subtly developed as a similar one in *The Small House at Allington* where Crosbie, *en route* for Folkestone with Lady Alexandrina, cannot help wondering whether he has made the right marital bargain; on that occasion the bride's tetchiness – ' "Take care of my bonnet" ', ' "I do so hate tunnels" ' – is not encouraging.) Emily is made to write to Mr Wharton from Italy asking for £3,000 as a marriage portion, and is puzzled by Lopez's unnatural elation when the old man pays up. She dislikes being told that her father has 'answered to the whip' (XXVI), and is progressively dismayed, disgusted, and distressed by Lopez's efforts to get her to extort further sums. It is not long before she 'reads' her husband's moods and motives with an appalled clarity; she thus sees perfectly well what is behind Lopez's attempts to ingratiate himself with her father.

Lopez's attempts at manipulation become cruder as his affairs become more critical. There is a significant loss of control when he has a public row with his wife about her relationship with Arthur Fletcher when they are guests of Lady Glencora's reception at The Horns (a scene which echoes another with the same venue in *Phineas Finn*, in which Lady Laura tells Phineas that her husband's insinuations about their friendship have made her decide to leave him). Lopez has already threatened Fletcher violently during the abortive Silverbridge campaign, and has been ignominiously bound over to keep the peace. He becomes more tyrannical in his behaviour both to his wife and to Sexty Parker as things grow financially more desperate. His last throw is an attempt to become the manager of a mine in Guatemala. Emily feels that it is her duty to accompany him even though all wifely affection has now disappeared. The woman who is actually invited by Lopez to go with him, however, is a new acquaintance, although an old friend of the author's: Lizzie Eustace. In her presence Lopez's language takes on an Emilius-like tinge of absurdity:

> 'I certainly will fly from such a country to those golden shores on which man may be free and unshackled.'
> 'And your wife?'
> 'Oh, Lizzie!' It was the first time that he had called her Lizzie, and she was apparently neither shocked nor abashed. Perhaps he thought too much of this, not knowing how many men had called her Lizzie in her time. 'Do not you at least understand that a man or a woman may undergo that tie, and yet be justified in disregarding it altogether?'
> 'Oh, yes; – if there has been bigamy, or divorce, or anything of that kind.' Now Lizzie had convicted her second husband of bigamy, and had freed herself after that fashion.
> 'To h— with their prurient laws,' said Lopez, rising suddenly from his chair. 'I will neither appeal to them nor will I obey them. And I expect from you as little subservience as I myself am prepared to pay. Lizzie Eustace, will you go with me, to that land of the sun,
>
> "Where the rage of the vulture, the love of the turtle,
> Now melt into sorrow, now madden to crime?"
>
> Will you dare to escape with me from the cold conventionalities, from the miserable thraldom of this country bound in swaddling clothes? Lizzie Eustace, if you will say the word I will take you to that land of glorious happiness.'
> But Lizzie Eustace had £4000 a year and a balance at her banker's. 'Mr Lopez,' she said.
> 'What answer have you to make me?'
> 'Mr Lopez, I think you must be a fool.'
> He did at last succeed in getting himself into the street, and at any rate she had not eaten him. (LIV)

Lopez has here suffered the humiliation of becoming a momentarily comic figure. It is a bold stroke on Trollope's part, and as far as Lizzie Eustace is concerned entirely credible: her perennial gift for flirting with romance while remaining firmly committed to number one is simply strengthening with the years. But we have not actually heard Lopez in this literary vein before, and the scene is therefore under-prepared.

Lopez's paranoid sense of a general conspiracy to defraud him of the rewards that should have been his, and his gambler's temperament which tells him when he has nothing left to play with, finally drive him to suicide; he walks in front of a train at a busy junction Trollope calls Tenway, on the northern outskirts of London. The obvious precedent for this is Dickens's excited and even gloating description of Carker's death in *Dombey and Son*. That forms the climax of the long diorama of the journeyings of Carker's last days which could hardly be more unlike Trollope's measured though still intent account. Trollope calls the tangle of railway lines at Tenway 'unintelligible' rather than crediting it with the sort of intoxicated insanity that Dickens relishes in his Christmas story 'Mugby Junction', but it is not really so because there are 'pundits of the place' (LX) that understand the shriek of every train. The patronizing facetiousness of calling porters pundits ominously signals a hundred years of pseudo-pedantic railway humour of the *Punch* variety – but it also indicates the daringly relaxed calmness with which Trollope approaches the final moment. Despite the watchfulness of one of the pundits, Lopez walks on to the track 'with gentle and apparently unhurried steps' and in a moment is 'knocked into bloody atoms'. Although it comes round the curve 'at a thousand miles an hour' the train is perfectly normal, and certainly not the demonic monster of Dickens's imagination: it is the morning express from Euston to Inverness.[10]

The same tethering references to the real world of the contemporary reader occur in Trollope's careful narrative of Lopez's movements immediately before his end. He braves the disapproval of other members of the Progress Club (much as Melmotte on his last night shows himself in the House of Commons out of bravado), and then walks home by a circuitous route through named streets so that anyone who knows central London can easily see how aimless his itinerary is. Next morning, saying he has to go to Birmingham on business, Lopez leaves the house, has his breakfast at Euston Station and exchanges pleasantries with the waitress (compare Burgo Fitzgerald's casual encounters on the night of his failure to get Glencora to elope), and then takes a ticket for Tenway. The fact that it is a first-class ticket is tellingly in character. The extreme watchfulness of Trollope's presentation of this episode not only illustrates his typically level approach to sensational material, but is also related to his recurring interest in this particular situation. Lopez's last hours and self-destruction are anticipated not just by the parallel case of Melmotte in *The Way We Live Now*, but much earlier in the suicide of Sir Henry Harcourt in *The Bertrams* (1859). This was the novel Trollope began the day after he had finished *Doctor Thorne* and came to regard as a failure because none of its characters had 'dwelt in the minds of novel-readers'. What clearly had dwelt in Trollope's mind was the situation of a man whose luck runs out after a run of worldly success, so that suicide is simply the alternative to ruin and disgrace. Harcourt has become Solicitor-General, but – out of office, with his wife having left him and his debts mounting – he knows, when his grandfather-in-law's will is read and contains nothing for him, that the game is up. Like Lopez, he has banked on his wife's inheritance. After showing himself at the House he goes home and shoots himself in his dressing-room (Melmotte swallows prussic acid in his sitting-room). Writing of Harcourt Trollope says, in the course of an obtrusive commentary on the episode, 'How impossible it is to describe the workings of a mind in such a state of misery as he then endured!' In the later treatments of the situation, Trollope has lost the apologetic nervousness of his earlier technique and moves towards an increasingly objective mode. After Lopez's farewell to his wife, the treatment becomes entirely external; we are given his last actions, but not his last thoughts. The paradoxical result is a great gain in fictional authority, but naturally that in turn rests on the way we have been taken through all the characteristic workings of Lopez's mind throughout the novel. Our intimacy with him allows us to 'read' him from external signs, just as his wife had learned to do.

The only question to be decided as far as Lopez's widow is concerned is how long it will be before she sinks into the waiting arms of Arthur Fletcher. To the intense irritation of the families involved, it takes longer than might have been expected and, although Trollope goes through the motions of explaining the feelings which inhibit Emily from capitulating sooner, the reader is likely to suspect Trollope of prolonging things artificially. Emily is too proud to be forgiven quickly; she feels that a woman has 'no right to a second chance in life, after having made such a shipwreck of herself in the first'. (LXXI) In this case such a state of mind is not likely to prevail against the physical attraction for Arthur that she has clearly felt all along, nor has it been shown to have its roots deep in the personality, as was the case with Lily Dale or in a different way with Alice Vavasor. The self-punishment that goes with their perverse kinds of integrity may have different final results – Alice gets over it while Lily obstinately remains an 'old maid' – but in both cases it is seen to be part of the very ground of their natures. Emily is not given, from the start, the kind of full and patient analysis from which her predecessors benefit and her ultimate fate is therefore the less involving. It is a disadvantage of Trollope's repetitive methods that the later presentation of a certain state of mind previously dealt with may sometimes be skimped because the novelist has already investigated it fully elsewhere.

It is easy to feel similar reservations about Trollope's treatment of Arthur Fletcher. From John Eames onwards, Trollope shows a recurrent interest in a kind of constancy which is almost pathological. The man who refuses to get over it is the natural counterpart to the woman who, having made her choice, feels permanently bound by it. In both cases, to admit any change of affection would involve an unacceptable compromise of their integrity. When Arthur Fletcher sends Emily a note on her marriage to Lopez which simply says '"I am as I always have been"' (XXIV), he is showing the kind of determined devotion in the face of the marital facts which is shared by a number of Trollope's unsuccessful suitors. The Lopez-Emily-Fletcher situation is yet another instance of Trollope's 'inveterate system', but it is not the best example of it, partly because of the thinnesses already noted in the presentation of Emily, and partly because Arthur himself does not develop the individuality which would make his behaviour more than merely an example of Trollope's general interest in the state he is shown to be in. His thorough gentlemanliness, which shows Lopez to such disadvantage, is accompanied by an immaturity which makes him seem light-weight. When Emily's father tells Arthur he has no hope, the disconsolate lover tries to resign himself to his disappointment, but can only feel that he is crippled for life. The scene is placed on the banks of the Wye – another case, like Phineas's, of romantic riverside rejection – and as Arthur tearfully throws stones into the water 'he told himself that it must be so with him always'. (XV) Although he resolves to bear his pain manfully, he still indulges fantasies about being able to serve Emily in the future and prove his love; his brother has to lecture him on the need to pull himself together. Arthur's moping seems rather adolescent for someone about to be elected as the Member for Silverbridge. He stands up well enough to Lopez's physical threats during the election campaign (advised by Frank Gresham, who, as Trollope himself recalls, thrashed a man in the streets 'twenty years ago' – i.e. Mr Moffat, in *Doctor Thorne*). But the price Trollope pays for engineering this somewhat facile contest between the two rivals is to deprive it of political seriousness. Arthur's enthusiastic chat to Mr Wharton later on about a bill to drain common land is hardly enough to give him much credibility as a legislator. Although a supporter of the Duke of Omnium's coalition government, his contact with the Pallisers is purely nominal, and he does not therefore gain political stature through that association. And although Arthur's later scenes with Emily show a more assertive manner, the quality of their dialogue is poor. When he throws himself on his knees and twines his arms around her, Emily replies, '"I have lain among the pots till I am foul and blackened. Take your arms away. They shall not be defiled."' (LXXIV) Such language does not add to the dignity of either party.

But the overwhelming reason for the relatively thin quality of Emily and Arthur Fletcher is probably to be found in Trollope's preoccupation with the Pallisers. The 'full heart' with which he returned to them pre-empted most of his imaginative energy. The non-Palliser areas of *The Prime Minister* deal with material that was familiar enough to Trollope to allow him to rely on reflexes that were, if not automatic, at least well developed. However, the events in the novel involving Plantagenet Palliser and Lady

Glencora are not only unprecedented for them but new to Trollope, although the persons themselves are by this time deeply familiar. Nowhere perhaps in Trollope's work are the benefits of living with his characters 'in the full reality of established intimacy' more fully felt. One can hardly doubt that the characters were with him as he lay down to sleep and as he woke from his dreams, as Trollope recommends they should be. Nowhere, too, is one more aware of Trollope's remarkable understanding of the effects of the passage of time on the individual nature. Glencora and Plantagenet are not the less recognizably themselves for the changes which life has inevitably produced in them. To aim to present such a balance between the essential continuity of the individual personality and the ways in which it is modified by the contingencies of experience may not seem particularly ambitious, but who among Trollope's contempories managed it more successfully? Trollope's deference to the long-term demands of his characters implies a sustained selflessness that is at the heart of his greatness. The results of that long and attentive communion could only be fully conveyed if the characters were to reappear in novels that were themselves spread over a considerable period of time, and the maintenance of the imaginative world which makes this possible was a large artistic enterprise that could only have been accomplished by a major act of creative will. The modesty of Trollope's novelistic demeanour – his gentle reminders of 'former chronicles' about the Pallisers, for instance – should not blind us to the scale of his achievement.

One implication of Trollope's design is that once again fidelity to individuals and their relationships takes precedence over abstract considerations. The repeated doubts as to whether Lopez is or is not a gentleman can be easily related to the *Autobiography*'s assertion that Plantagenet is 'a perfect gentleman', but to resolve the novel into thesis and antithesis would both insensitively attenuate its human appeal and ignore the ways in which it resists simple-minded oppositions. As we have seen, Lopez's lack of gentility does not deprive him of a legitimate claim on our interest. Palliser's gentlemanliness is unquestionable, but it takes such a pronounced tincture from his idiosyncratic nature that it can seem positively outlandish. At all events, gentlemanliness, as refracted through his individuality, proves to be as much of a hindrance as a help in the discharging of that office which Trollope certainly felt to be the natural object of an English gentleman's ambition.

The Prime Minister is sometimes said to offer Trollope's portrait of the ideal gentleman, but it is in fact one of the grand ironies of the book that the very virtues which have made Palliser so widely respected and thus peculiarly acceptable as the head of a coalition government should turn into handicaps and liabilities under the stress of office. Palliser has devoted himself with exceptional diligence and austerity to the service of his country, and it is a further irony that the job of leading it should be a task for which his sometimes irresponsible and often ignorant wife is in some ways better suited. Palliser's term of office both brings them closer together than ever and underlines the fundamental differences between them. And it is characteristic of the bias of Trollope's novelistic nature that the most valuable parts of a book ostensibly given over to political matters should turn out to be the further development and deeper understanding of the marriage between the two fictional individuals that in his later creative life he most cared about.

The relative lack of emphasis on matters of political principle in *The Prime Minister* is symbolized by the Parliamentary impasse with which the novel begins. Neither Mr Daubeny nor Mr Gresham can command a workable majority, and a coalition seems the only practical answer for the time being. No one thinks that it can last long because politically speaking it is against the nature of things, and of course such an administration can hardly put forward much in the way of a programme. But it can ensure the voting of supplies and generally carry on the business of government. Fortunately the country is prosperous, and large-scale measures seem neither called for nor necessary. We hear nothing for instance of the populist agitation formerly so vigorously supported by Mr Turnbull. The question of Disestablishment, so deviously mooted by Mr Daubeny, appears to have faded away. Towards the end of the coalition's life – which to general surprise prolongs itself for three years – some reform of county suffrage is proposed; Phineas Finn, who returns as the minister responsible for Irish affairs, tinkers with the Home Rule problem but hardly hopes to solve it – and in any case is moved to the Admiralty before he can get very far with it. Palliser does make a speech or two about his old love decimal coinage, but makes no serious effort to introduce it. When Sir

Orlando Drought argues (for personal reasons, it is true) that the government ought to have 'something of a policy', he gets nowhere, and later resigns out of pique. In fact, the politics of *The Prime Minister* are the politics of *laissez-faire*.

Plantagenet and Lady Glencora, now Duke and Duchess of Omnium, are reintroduced by Glencora's abrupt and sarcastic question '"And what are they going to make you now?"' Palliser's readiness to serve in a humbler capacity after his elevation to the Lords has made him ineligible for the Exchequer has not been taken in good part by his wife, and she suspects him of yet further self-abasement. When the Duke tells her that he is to see the Queen with a view to forming his own cabinet, her reaction is transformed:

> 'You are going to be Prime Minister!' she exclaimed. As she spoke she threw her arms up, and then rushed into his embrace. Never since their first union had she been so demonstrative either of love or admiration. 'Oh, Plantagenet,' she said, 'if I can only do anything I will slave for you.' As he put his arm round her waist he already felt the pleasantness of her altered way to him. She had never worshipped him yet, and therefore her worship when it did come had all the delight to him which it ordinarily has to the newly married hero. (VI)

The little comment about Glencora's 'worship' can easily pass unnoticed, but it implies much. For all the solidity of the Palliser marriage as presented in the Phineas books, it has not seemed to have included the kind of emotional abandonment that Glencora here shows. It is as if, for a moment at least, she is in love with him at last. Although she does many things in this novel which annoy Plantagenet and even estrange him, there is throughout a perceptible deepening of her understanding of his nature and his needs and a capacity to respond to his love for her which is the more moving for having taken so long to develop. We are reminded of the beginnings of their marriage in this very passage, when the Duke recalls his decision not to accept office in *Can You Forgive Her?* because 'of a domestic circumstance'. As he says this 'he again put his arm round her waist'. '"I remember that too,"' she replies, 'speaking very gently and looking up at him.' The arm round the waist and the looking-up indicate a closeness that began with the same gestures in the breakfast scene in *Can You Forgive Her?* and which often recurs at such moments of mutual tenderness: the Pallisers, like other married couples, develop their own habitual code of physical contact. Such moments are not the less significant because they are invariably evanescent. In the present instance, any gratification Plantagenet feels is offset by his prescient anxiety that he may not be the man for the job: '"But for this attempt I have no belief in myself. I doubt whether I have any gift for governing men."'

The Duke of Omnium accepts the burden of being Prime Minister with a noble reluctance that indicates both his high sense of duty and his scruples about his capacity. The Duchess greets the prospect with much more enthusiasm, although her own motives are also mixed. She certainly believes that because Plantagenet is '"so much honester than other people"', he must be the best man for the place. But she is totally unconcerned about any party political principles that Palliser's assumption of office must presumably involve – as she says to Mrs Finn, '"The country goes on its own way, either for better or for worse, whichever of them are in."' Her sense that society is impervious to politics and unaffected by legislation expresses in a more reckless way a scepticism that Trollope keeps coming back to, and which clearly had its attractions for him. Glencora's ambitions are highly personal. It is partly a matter of honours and high positions for '"our set"', and it is also a question of developing yet further the distinctive position in society that she has already made for herself. She is extremely miffed when Palliser refuses to make her Mistress of the Robes (this is the episode referred to in the *Autobiography* as an illustration of the interconnections between the Palliser novels). She admits privately to Mrs Finn that she would '"like to put the Queen down . . . I should like to make Buckingham Palace second-rate."' (VI) It is still possible to feel a sense of shock at Glencora's extraordinary lese-majesty: who else in Victorian fiction has the candour to admit such an ambition or even the courage to entertain it? (It also contrasts refreshingly with the male politicians' use of the conventional formula 'the Queen's comfort' during their own manoeuvres.) But perhaps the fundamental reason for the Duchess's excitement at the Duke's elevation is that it gives her at last a field of action commensurate to her formidable energies and her social ambitions. As she says, '"I like to be busy."'

Glencora realizes in her pragmatic way that a government put together on a basis of expediency rather than principle needs extra-political means of creating a sense of unity. She therefore embarks on a grandiose campaign of lavish entertainment which her pro-digious wealth enables her to fund. The scale of her entertainments is something that Palliser finds it hard to accept; his deep aversion to anything that might appear ostentatious is part of his gentleman-liness. When Glencora proposes – for the good of the ministry – a massively extended house party which will test even the palatial accommodation of Gatherum Castle, the Duke at first objects to the expense: '"No man is ever rich enough to squander."' The remark precipitates one of those telepathic moments of marital negotiation where little is said but much is understood, which are so characteristic of their relationship:

> Though they were to squander her fortune, – the money which she had brought, – for the next ten years at a much greater rate than she contemplated, they might do so without touching the Palliser property. Of that she was quite sure. And the squandering was to be all for his glory, – so that he might retain his position as a popular Prime Minister. For an instant it occurred to her that she would tell him all this. But she checked herself, and the idea of what she had been about to say brought blood into her face. Never yet had she in talking to him alluded to her own wealth. 'Of course we are spending money,' she said. 'If you give me a hint to hold my hand, I will hold it.'
>
> He had looked at her, and read it all in her face. 'God knows,' he said, 'you've a right to do it if it pleases you.'
>
> 'For your sake!' Then he stooped down and kissed her twice, and left her to arrange her parties as she pleased. After that she congratulated herself that she had not made the direct proposition, knowing that she might now do pretty much what she pleased. (XI)

Glencora's receptions and house parties give Trollope no technical trouble: since the early days of Barsetshire he has been able to handle such occasions with an ease that comes ultimately from having such a large and interrelated repertory of characters in permanent suspension in his imagination. We are not surprised to find among her guests in London, 'Mr Broune, of the "Breakfast Table" ... his wife Lady Carbury, and poor old Booker of the "Literary Chronicle"' – all of whom had recently appeared in *The Way We Live Now* (though Trollope does not explicitly remind us of this, nor does he explain why Booker should be referred to so patronizingly). But the Duchess's hospitality is so inclusive as to become indiscriminate; men such as Ferdinand Lopez are favoured, drones like Captain Gunner and Major Pountney – 'two middle-aged young men' – are drafted into service 'as being useful in their way'. The stream of guests – never less than forty for two months on end, with an average bed-occupancy of two nights, as Lady Glencora's discussions with the housekeeper reveal – means that the Castle really does become the place for the *omnium gatherum* from which it must have derived its name (it is first described in *Doctor Thorne*).

Palliser views all this with distaste and an increasing sense of personal injury. It exposes him to impertinences such as a request for an invitation from Finn's journalist enemy Quintus Slide, of the *People's Banner*. As Plantagenet explains to his old friend the Duke of St Bungay, '"The idea of conquering people ... by feeding them, is to me abominable. If it goes on it will drive me mad. I shall have to give up everything, because I cannot bear the burden."' (XVIII) This outburst is one of a number of signs of strain which begin as soon as the Duke of Omnium takes office. The senior Duke has already had to help him through the task of making up the Cabinet because the younger Duke feels he cannot do it 'with fitting judgment', and has indeed had to speak severely about such a disabling fineness of conscience. Palliser's hypersensitivity prompts much the same charge of 'unmanliness' as did Phineas Finn's when he was in prison. Palliser's extreme vulnerability to Slide's attacks later in the novel also echoes Finn's acute sense of outrage earlier on. The increasing intimacy of Finn and the Duke as *The Prime Minister* proceeds has a political logic, but at a more fundamental level it indicates the profound affinity between the exacerbated self-consciousness that both men reveal when pilloried by the press and subjected to certain kinds of exposure.

Before the Duke and Duchess go down to Gatherum, Plantagenet tries to be gracious about Glencora's plans:

> 'But don't let us misunderstand each other. You are doing the best you can to further what you think to be my interests.'
> 'I am,' said the Duchess.
> 'I love you the better for it, day by day.' This so surprised her, that as she took him by the arm, her eyes were filled with tears. (XVIII)

Glencora thinks of herself as such a different type of person from her husband and is so conscious of the need to tread carefully where he is concerned that she still hardly knows how to respond to such sudden avowals. Nothing illustrates so well the extraordinarily living quality of their relationship as Trollope imagines it than their mutual capacity to be momentarily amazed by the person who is more familiar than any other. This declaration is one of several that Palliser makes during the course of the novel, and they have their common source in his need for Glencora's support in his difficulties. His emotional dependence on her increases the more he becomes angered and humiliated by his inability to relate successfully to others in the way that his office makes desirable. Even so, Palliser's more tender exchanges with his wife (often indicated by his use of 'Cora' rather than of the full name) alternate with periods of stand-offishness which can be prolonged on both sides. Shortly after the passage quoted above, Palliser again complains that the preparations and alterations at Gatherum – he thinks they have 'an assumed and preposterous grandeur that was as much within the reach of some rich swindler or of some prosperous haberdasher as of himself' (XIX) – show distressing signs of vulgarity. The word is a hard one for Glencora to stomach, and it rankles. In the end, however, she comes to the conclusion that even if she is being vulgar it is all for Palliser's good, although he won't see it. Glencora's determination both to have her own way and the profound loyalty of her better nature are here in convincing equipoise.

Being a hostess on the Duchess's scale is extremely hard work, especially when the Duke himself will do nothing to help. Even Phineas complains that he is 'neither gregarious nor communicative'. (XXVII) He cannot reconcile himself to seeing 'that grand idea of public work' (XVIII) which has always animated him being reduced to what seems an increasingly nominal activity. Keeping a government together is no substitute for having a department to run, like the Exchequer or even the Board of Trade, or a specific project to advance, like decimal coinage. Although there is a layer of political passion in him, Palliser is essentially a civil servant, though of the noblest sort. He begins to suspect that his usefulness is thought by others to lie in his wealth, rank, and the 'power of cohesion' exerted by his wife's gift for 'social arrangements' (XVIII), and not through his own Parliamentary capacity. It is typical of his inherent generosity of spirit that he should not be jealous at Glencora's success, and typical too of his Trollopian gift for self-accusation that he should feel it as shameful to owe the survival of his administration to anything other than lofty principle. He envies the activities of his ministers with budgets to prepare or colonies to control, and is mortified to have to occupy himself over trivial matters like the patronage in which Glencora takes so active an interest. Like Trollope himself, he seems to think of unremitting industry as necessary to well-being. Having to be agreeable to house guests is a humiliating reminder that he is a fainéant. The only visitor at Gatherum whose company he finds tolerable is the unlikely Lady Rosina De Courcy (brought forward from *The Small House at Allington*). Glencora can hardly believe it. '"Perhaps there is nothing so sad in the world as the female scions of a noble but impoverished stock,"' says Plantagenet sententiously, to which Glencora briskly replies, '"Nothing so dull certainly."' Palliser's next remark is unassuming enough, but it might serve as a simple expression of his creator's fundamental artistic principle and as an epigraph to his *oeuvre*: '"People are not dull to me, if they are real."' (XXI) Such an attitude is certainly appropriate to a novelist with what Henry James called a complete appreciation of the usual, but it comes a little oddly from Palliser. Human nature is more his wife's province than his, as she often reminds him. What Palliser seems to indicate by 'real' here is almost an envy of Lady Rosina's ability to live on good terms with her situation: '"She is proud of her blood and yet not ashamed of her poverty."' Her self-absorption spares him from feeling that he is being got at. Palliser takes to walking with Lady Rosina in the park, even in inclement weather:

'Weather never frightens me, your Grace. I always have

thick boots; – I am very particular about that, – and cork soles.'

'Cork soles are admirable.'

'I think I owe my life to cork soles,' said Lady Rosina
enthusiastically. 'There is a man named Sprout in Silverbridge
who makes them. Did your Grace ever try him for boots?'

'I don't think I ever did,' said the Prime Minister.

'Then you had better. He's very good and very cheap too.
Those London tradesmen never think they can charge you
enough. I find I can wear Sprout's boots the whole winter
through and then have them resoled. I don't suppose you ever
think of such things?'

'I like to have my feet dry.'

'I have got to calculate what they cost.' (XXVII)

That the Prime Minister should enjoy discussing cork soles with this
'tall, thin, shrivelled-up old woman' is both absurd and touching.
Lady Rosina is obviously tiresome, but her untroubled sense of her
own authenticity consoles the self-conscious Palliser. It is a relief to
simplify life to a question of boots – and of finding a bootmaker who
can supply an honest product. Glencora told Alice Vavasor as long
ago as the early days of *Can You Forgive Her?* that Plantagenet was
particular about his shoes. It will be remembered that in the *Autobiography* Trollope recommends the shoemaker's disciplined industry
as a model for novelists to follow. Just before the Prime Minister's
walk with Lady Rosina the Duke of St Bungay, in one of several
attempts to stiffen his political sinews, put the same example before
him: '"A certain nervous sensitiveness, from which you should free
yourself as from a disease, is your only source of weakness. Think
about your business as a shoemaker thinks of his. Do your best, and
then let your customers judge for themselves."' Tranquillity is to be
found in application, and with application comes release from the
burden of self-consciousness. One cannot but suspect that Trollope
insists on this lesson because he had found it so true in his own case –
and the novel-making work that brought him such alleviation could
hardly, with consistency, be thought of as an expression of the self
but rather as a way of losing it, in the face of claims not the less felt
because they are fictional.

Palliser, however, cannot get out of his difficulties by becoming a
novelist, but at least Lady Rosina's company takes him out of

himself. 'She was natural, and she wanted nothing from him.
When she talked about cork soles, she meant cork soles.' Palliser
has more time for her than for Sir Orlando Drought, who is put
down very ducally, or Major Pountney, whose presumptuous
request for support in the Silverbridge by-election is met with
summary ejection. Palliser's high-handed expulsion of the unfortunate Major is a further sign of his general frustration and unease.

This unhappy state of mind is compounded by the way in which
the affair of the Silverbridge election develops (it is caused by the
fact that Mr Grey, pursuing the career in public life he embraced at
the end of *Can You Forgive Her?*, has been sent on a mission to
Persia, and has therefore, with characteristic scruple, resigned his
seat). The Duchess has indiscreetly hinted to Lopez that the Castle
will support his candidature (much as Lord Brentford once supported Finn's). The Duke's annoyance at Pountney's request drives
him to announce publicly that he will not seek to influence his
tenantry in any way whatever, and Glencora is thus unable to
deliver. When Lopez later applies to the Duke for the reimburse-
ment of his expenses, Palliser over-reacts with such a tragic air that
Glencora cannot mock or mimic her way out of trouble as she so
often does during their differences. Palliser's attempts to think the
problem through and Glencora's responses indicate again his
extreme concern for principle and her robust practicality:

'I shall know why I pay this £500. Because she who of all the
world is the nearest and the dearest to me,' – she looked up
into his face with amazement, as he stood stretching out both
his arms in his energy, – 'has in her impetuous folly committed a grievous blunder, from which she would not allow her
husband to save her, this sum must be paid to the wretched
craven. But I cannot tell the world that. I cannot say abroad
that this small sacrifice of money was the justest means of
retrieving the injury which you had done.'

'Say it abroad. Say it everywhere.'

'No, Glencora.'

'Do you think that I would have you spare me if it was my
fault? And how would it hurt me? Will it be new to any one
that I have done a foolish thing? Will the newspapers disturb
my peace? I sometimes think, Plantagenet, that I should have

been the man, my skin is so thick; and that you should have
been the woman, yours is so tender.' (XLII)

The scene develops into another declaration by Palliser of the
supreme value to him of his marriage; since he could not say a word
against her even to a friend, how can he possibly blame her in
public? Moreover, '"A man and his wife are one. For what she
does he is responsible."' Much of the scene is in dialogue – though,
as before, the *rapprochement* between husband and wife is signalled
by his gradual putting of his arm round her waist. It reflects
Trollope's sense, apparent throughout his treatment of the Palliser
marriage, of how much there is to be said on both sides.
Plantagenet's chivalric defence of his wife's honour has to be put
against Glencora's telling point that being thick- rather than thin-
skinned is '"the only way to decently comfortable in such a coarse,
rough-and-tumble world as this is."'

The consequences of the cheque the Duke feels bound to send
Lopez do not become acute for him until after a relatively pleasant
autumn spent at Matching. Palliser has forbidden any more guests
(except for Lady Rosina) and Glencora has mischievously taken
him at his word. This, however, suits Palliser, who often now talks
of retiring into rural quiet with his children and his books, but
Glencora is soon weary of it. Their attitudes to life at Matching
have ironically become the opposite of what they were in the early
days of their marriage, as presented in *Can You Forgive Her?*. After
returning to London when Parliament resumes, however, the
Prime Minister is assailed by bitter editorials in the *People's Banner*
written by Slide, who has got hold of the Lopez story from Lady
Eustace. Palliser broods obsessively on the matter until he begins to
feel he ought to resign. The Duke of St Bungay is again disappointed not to find his noble friend more manly, and it becomes
understood among the Prime Minister's staff that in his nervous
and sensitive state he has to be 'coddled'. Palliser admits to Glencora that he '"cannot endure to have my character impugned"'
even by a man like Slide whom Glencora energetically dismisses as
'"a reptile"'. (LI) She regards Palliser's refusal to acknowledge her
participation in the Silverbridge affair – on the grounds that '"A
man's wife should be talked about by no one"' – as merely '"high-
foluting"' (a typically Glencora-ish use of what was then modern

197

slang). She will have nothing to do with Palliser's theory that wives should not interfere with politics: '"That's all you know about it, Plantagenet. Doesn't everybody know that Mrs Daubeny got Dr MacFuzlem made a bishop, and that Mrs Gresham got her husband to make that hazy speech about women's rights, so that nobody should know which way he meant to go? There are others just as bad as me."' Her appeal to things as they are reminds one of her early conversation with Alice Vavasor about the way girls actually behave. (That their relationship is still active in Trollope's mind, although unexploited novelistically, is indicated in passing in Chapter XLII by Glencora's complaint that Mrs Grey '"always lectured me, and she does it still"'.) Thus Glencora's instinct for the real continues to complement Plantagenet's hankering after the ideal, so that each needs but conflicts with the other.

As the strain increasingly tells on the Duke, however, the Duchess becomes softer and more considerate towards him, as she also becomes more disillusioned with her own part in the business. In a long conversation with Mrs Finn, Glencora sums up with all the accuracy that her intuitive penetration gives her the nature of her marriage and the way in which Palliser's Premiership has affected it:

'Though in manner he is as dry as a stick, though all his pursuits are opposite to the very idea of romance, though he passes his days and nights in thinking how he may take a halfpenny in the pound off the taxes of the people without robbing the revenue, there is a dash of chivalry about him worthy of the old poets. To him a woman, particularly his own woman, is a thing so fine and so precious that the winds of heaven should hardly be allowed to blow upon her. He cannot bear to think that people should even talk of his wife. And yet, Heaven knows, poor fellow, I have given people occasion enough to talk of me. And he has a much higher chivalry than that of the old poets. They, or their heroes, watched their women because they did not want to have trouble about them, – shut them up in castles, kept them in ignorance, and held them as far as they could out of harm's way.'

'I hardly think they succeeded,' said Mrs. Finn.

'But in pure selfishness they tried all they could. But he is too proud to watch. If you and I were hatching treason against him in the dark, and chance had brought him there, he would stop his ears with his fingers. He is all trust, even when he knows that he is being deceived. He is honour complete from head to foot. Ah, it was before you knew me when I tried him the hardest. I never could quite tell you that story, and I won't try it now; but he behaved like a god. I could never tell him what I felt, – but I felt it.'

'You ought to love him.'

'I do; – but what's the use of it? He is a god, but I am not a goddess; – and then, though he is a god, he is a dry, silent, uncongenial and uncomfortable god. It would have suited me much better to have married a sinner. But then the sinner that I would have married was so irredeemable a scapegrace. . .

'. . . They should have made me Prime Minister, and have let him be Chancellor of the Exchequer. I begin to see the ways of Government now. I could have done all the dirty work. I could have given away garters and ribbons, and made my bargains while giving them. I could select sleek, easy bishops who wouldn't be troublesome. I could give pensions or withhold them, and make the stupid men peers. I could have the big noblemen at my feet, praying to be Lieutenants of Counties. I could dole out secretaryships and lordships, and never a one without getting something in return. I could brazen out a job and let the "People's Banners" and the Slides make their worst of it. And I think I could make myself popular with my party, and do the high-flowing patriotic talk for the benefit of the Provinces. A man at a regular office has to work. That's what Plantagenet is fit for. He wants always to be doing something that shall be really useful, and a man has to toil at that and really to know things. But a Prime Minister should never go beyond generalities about commerce, agriculture, peace, and general philanthropy. Of course he should have the gift of the gab, and that Plantagenet hasn't got. He never wants to say anything unless he has got something to say. I could do a Mansion House dinner to a marvel!' (LVI)

199

This conveys, with a kind of poignant vivacity, Glencora's appreciation of her husband's nobility as it has accumulated over the years. The reference to the period 'before you knew me' – the time of *Can You Forgive Her?*, before Madame Max Goesler had entered on Trollope's scene – gives the reader an odd sense of having known Glencora longer than Mrs Finn, who is now her closest friend, and encourages us to feel a special kind of intimacy with her. The novelist does not explain what Glencora refers to but her allusion can only make its full point if the events of the earlier novel are as present in the reader's memory as they are in Glencora's. What she says indicates too the deep inhibitions and inarticulacies of her marriage – '"I could never tell him what I felt"' – just as it also demonstrates her exact understanding of Plantagenet's state of mind, even though the matter '"has gone beyond speaking"'. There is now a remarkable clarity in her view of the respective virtues and weakness of both herself and her husband which we assent to because it so clearly agrees with our own long experience of them. Palliser's complete honour may make him 'a god', but the justice of the epithets 'dry, silent, uncongenial and uncomfortable' is hard to deny. It is hard to resist too Glencora's claim that she could have done 'the dirty work' of politics much better than Palliser has. An 'ideal statesman' would need her pragmatism as well as his principle. After Phineas Finn has made a gracious and adroit speech in the House (reported verbatim in a way that his purely political utterances have never been) exculpating the Duke from any impropriety in the matter of the Lopez cheque and without mentioning the Duchess's name, he is thanked by the Duke in a manner which is actually full of gratitude but which 'Phineas felt . . . to be cold'. (LVII) He would not have felt it so had the thanks been given by Glencora, the cause of all the trouble.

Glencora's concern for the physical as well as the mental strain of his office on Palliser increasingly preoccupies her, to the exclusion of her old social ambitions. As she says to the Duke of St Bungay, '"He does not eat and does not sleep. Of course I watch him."' She speaks to the old Duke with a special confidence and anxiety because he is one of the only two people in the world '"besides Plantagenet and the children . . . whom I really love"'. (LXIII) The other is Mrs Finn, and again it is only the reappearance of Marie in successive novels allows us to appreciate the irony of the fact. In view of the initial uncertainty that Trollope seems to have felt about Madame Max it is remarkable that things should have turned out as they have but presumably that is the way the character seemed to want to go. The complex of motives which made Marie Goesler refuse the old Duke of Omnium's offer has ensured Glencora's loyalty, which as Trollope remarks is one of her chief qualities. The practical result is the female friendship which, as with Alice Vavasor in the early days, Glencora cannot do without – and which, with so uncommunicative a husband, is natural enough. Glencora not only worries that Palliser is ill, but that his office is having a deleterious effect on his moral nature. When asked by Mrs Finn if she is really sorry that Palliser became Prime Minister, she replies

> 'I should have thought him a poltroon if he had declined. It is to be the greatest man in the greatest country in the world. Do ever so little and the men who write history must write about you. And no man has ever tried to be nobler than he till, – till – '.
>
> 'Make no exception. If he be careworn and ill and weary his manners cannot be the same as they were, but his purity is the same as ever.'
>
> 'I don't know that it would remain so. I believe in him, Marie, more than in any man, – but I believe in none thoroughly. There is a devil creeps in upon them when their hands are strengthened. I do not know what I would have wished. Whenever I do wish, I always wish wrong. Ah, me; when I think of all those people I had down at Gatherum, – of the trouble I took, and of the glorious anticipations in which I revelled, I do feel ashamed of myself.' (LXXII)

Glencora's subsequent expression of weariness – '"Oh, dear, I wish I knew something that was really pleasant to do. I have never really enjoyed anything since I was in love, and I only liked that because it was wicked"' – is characteristically provocative and is not meant to be more than half-true, but it registers the disillusion that fills her as well as her husband during the later pages of the novel. The Duke adds to his woes by making a quixotic decision when a vacancy occurs among Knights of the Garter. He appoints Lord Earlybird in recognition of his good works, but as this philanthropic peer is totally unparliamentary, the honour is not well received by party men who expect one of their number to be preferred. However, as soon as the letter to Lord Earlybird is on its way the Duke sees the absurdity of his action (an absurdity which the facetious name serves to underline). 'Who was he that he should venture to set aside all the traditions of office?' (LXVI) As Trollope explains, it is 'the chief torment of a person constituted as he was' that although he may be determined on an action, convinced of its rightness, the objections to it suddenly acquire truth and force once it is too late to revoke. Palliser's mind is by now almost monopolized by such vacillation and with the self-accusation that goes with it.

Before the Duke's ministry finally comes to an end, after too narrow a majority on the County Suffrage Bill, he recovers his mental tone sufficiently to state the fundamentals of his political creed to Phineas Finn during a walk at Matching. He sees it as a weakness in his own career that, having a seat in Parliament ready-made for him at an early age, he did not sufficiently inquire what Liberalism means. The demands of particular offices have kept him, as they have many, from becoming '"real politicians"' in the sense of considering first principles: the performance of depart-mental duties has seemed a sufficiently responsible activity. Although he dismisses as '"mischievous and absurd"' the idea that political virtue is all on one side, he expresses with unwonted energy his commitment to the fundamental tenet of Liberalism, which he defines as the lessening of social distances between man and man. '"Equality would be a heaven, if we could attain it."' Palliser concedes that the word itself has been tarnished for right-thinking Englishmen by attempts elsewhere to proclaim it as an achieved fact (in France and the United States, presumably), but claims that the idea itself must be the natural correlative of sym-pathy for our fellows: '"How can you look at the bowed back and bent legs and abject face of that poor ploughman, who winter and summer has to drag his rheumatic limbs to his work, while you go a-hunting or sit in pride of place among the foremost few of your country, and say that it all is as it ought to be?"' (LXVIII) The Duke's credo is memorable because of its unexpectedness. It seems to be the result of a long process of thought which has gradually gathered to a head, so that it becomes suddenly clear to him what it is that he really thinks. Although what Palliser says corresponds exactly with Trollope's own opinions (as stated, for instance, in the *Autobiography*) there is no question of the fictional character being merely the author's mouthpiece. Our physical view of him at this juncture is minutely detailed:

> The Duke in his enthusiasm had thrown off his hat, and was sitting on a wooden seat which they had reached, looking up among the clouds. His left hand was clenched, and from time to time with his right he rubbed the thin hairs on his brow. He had begun in a low voice, with a somewhat slipshod enunciation of his words, but had gradually become clear, resonant, and even eloquent. Phineas knew that there were stories told of certain bursts of words which had come from him in former days in the House of Commons. These had occasionally surprised men and induced them to declare that Planty Pall, – as he was then often called, – was a dark horse. But they had been few and far between, and Phineas had never heard them. Now he gazed at his companion in silence, wondering whether the speaker would go on with his speech. But the face changed on a sudden, and the Duke with an awkward motion snatched up his hat. 'I hope you ain't cold,' he said.
>
> 'Not at all,' said Phineas.
>
> 'I came here because of that bend of the river. I am always very fond of that bend. We don't go over the river. That is Mr Upjohn's property.' (LXVIII)

Palliser's embarrassed return to normality is both slightly comic and curiously touching in a way that reminds one of the end of the breakfast scene between him and Glencora in *Can You Forgive Her?* – and his aristocratic but untypical use of 'ain't' after his passionately egalitarian idealism adds a tiny but sympathetic irony.

After this episode Palliser's morale seems to improve, so that in office nothing becomes him more than the leaving of it. However bitterly he may regret what he thinks of as his failure, and however gloomily he contemplates the emptiness of his future (he is still only forty-seven, but what is there for an ex-Prime Minister to do?), he is fundamentally relieved at getting out of a false position. His discussion with his wife of their thoughts at this terminal point is perhaps the most moving of all their conversations, in its simplicity, in its details of physical expression, and in the mutual love and understanding of each other's natures which so patently shines through it:

'Will it make you unhappy, Cora?'

'What; – your going?'

'Yes; – the change altogether.'

She looked him in the face for a moment before she answered, with a peculiar smile in her eyes to which he was well used, – a smile half ludicrous and half pathetic, – having in it also a dash of sarcasm. 'I can dare to tell the truth,' she said, 'which you can't. I can be honest and straightforward. Yes, it will make me unhappy. And you?'

'Do you think that I cannot be honest too, – at any rate to you? It does fret me. I do not like to think that I shall be without work.'

'Yes; – Othello's occupation will be gone, – for awhile; for awhile.' Then she came up to him and put both her hands on his breast. 'But yet, Othello, I shall not be all unhappy.'

'Where will be your contentment?'

'In you. It was making you ill. Rough people, whom the tenderness of your nature could not well endure, trod upon you, and worried you with their teeth and wounded you everywhere. I could have turned at them again with my teeth, and given them worry for worry; – but you could not. Now you will be saved from them, and so I shall not be discontented.' All this she said looking up into his face, still with that smile which was half pathetic and half ludicrous.

'Then I will be contented too,' he said as he kissed her. (LXXII)

The tact and delicacy with which the novelist leaves the characters alone at such a point is not the least part of the scene's penetrative appeal. But, as we have by now come to expect, the harmony and repose of such moments are quickly destabilized by a resumption of the more usual style of marital dialogue. Relieved of office and a little consoled to be offered an honourable position in Gresham's new Cabinet (which he refuses), Palliser proposes to go abroad but Glencora is just as irritating about travelling as she once was in the early days of their marriage. When Plantagenet suggests 'some months in Italy', Glencora ironically welcomes the prospect of Rome in July, and suggests following it up with a winter in Norway. In some ways at least it certainly looks as if the last words of *Phineas Redux* have been proved true enough: nothing will change the Duchess – not even being the Prime Minister's wife for three years.

The last words of this novel also promise that, after all, Palliser will '"endeavour to look forward to a time when I may again perhaps be of some humble use"'. The formal modesty of his tone underlines again his lack of personal grandeur, and they follow a conversation in which Mr Monk tries to persuade the Duke that his term of office was valuable, honourable, and such as probably only he could have sustained. After all, the Prime Minister's chief duty is to look after the prosperity of the nation: '"It is not often that we want great measures, or new arrangements that shall be vital to the country."' (LXXX) It is odd to hear the radical Monk of former years argue that '"Politicians now look for grievances, not because the grievances are heavy, but trusting that the honour of abolishing them may be great."' Monk seems to accept the practical limitations that the Duke had earlier acknowledged in his conversation with Finn: '"we can only do a little"' to hasten the arrival of the heaven of equality; Matching will not be at risk during his lifetime. The 'little' that immediately concerns Monk and Palliser is such legislation as the County Suffrage Bill – one of those Trollopian measures as to whose inevitability everyone is agreed, the only questions being whether it will be enacted sooner rather than later, and by whom.

There is thus a kind of passivity at the heart of Trollope's idea of political life; at the deepest level, those involved in it respond rather than initiate. They canalize and rationalize change rather than foster or foment it. It is understandable that Trollope should have called himself a 'Conservative Liberal', even if an 'advanced' one. Resistance to change is an instinct for which he had a profound sympathy. Despite his restlessness and outspokenness as an official himself, he understood the bureaucrat's natural reverence for established custom and practice. An intense feeling for continuity was also of fundamental importance to his imaginative life, and it is not surprising therefore that in *The Prime Minister*, as in the other

Palliser novels, the personal claims of the reappearing character proved stronger than the local demands of political argument. The discussion of political ideas for their own sake is accommodated and where necessary gives way to the further study of the individual temperament. It is characteristic of this bias that a novel with such a title should turn out to be – in its imaginatively most intense pages – not material in the public domain but the continuing private history of a marriage whose development had already been in Trollope's mind for over a decade.

The Duke's Children

Trollope finished the *Autobiography* on 30 April 1876 (according to Sadleir's Calendar). A few pages before its end, and following his discussion of *The Prime Minister* and the characters of the Pallisers, he adds that he has 'an idea that I shall even yet once more have recourse to my political hero as the mainstay of another story'. That story, *The Duke's Children*, was begun almost immediately, on 2 May, although not published in volume form until 1880. One effect of Trollope's habit of living with his characters is the absence of any need for the prolonged gestation of a new work. His refusal to adopt a policy of elaborate plot-making in advance meant that, once the main lines of a character's nature and circumstances had been established, events could virtually be left to look after themselves. The introductory chapters of many of his novels are really exploratory elaborations of the dramatis personae. Trollope's facility in assembling his characters is partly a matter of his use of reappearance (as his development of the novel sequence has shown), assisted by his interest in recurring situations (in ways that later chapters in this book will hope to indicate), but it comes above all from the incessant activity of his imaginative life, as he went about his normal business.

In the case of *The Duke's Children*, the character of Palliser himself was by now so intimately known to Trollope that there must have seemed even less reason for delay. The new novel, however, puts the Duke into two situations which he has not had to face before: he is deprived of his wife by her premature death, and consequently he has to bear alone the unfamiliar burden of children who refuse to act as he wishes. These concerns distract him almost completely from political activity, of which there is relatively little in this final novel of the series. The *Autobiography* refers to Trollope's 'hero' only, and it would be interesting to know how long the idea of Glencora's death had been in his mind. *The Duke's Children* pays a certain price for being deprived of her vitality, but her absence means that Palliser's reappearance here does not involve the wrong sort of repetition which would merely duplicate previous dilemmas. He has not had to face the world alone since his tepid attempts to interest Lady Dumbello in *The Small House at Allington* – aspirations quite uncharacteristic of the character as Trollope came later to understand him. In the twenty years and more since *Can You Forgive Her?* closed with the birth of a son and heir, the Palliser children have naturally grown up to marriageable age. Lord Silverbridge, the eldest son, has been mentioned occasionally in intervening novels, but the Duke's mind, like the novelist's, has been on other matters. It is a shock, therefore, for Palliser to find that he has suddenly to deal with grown-up individuals with wills of their own, and to have to do it without the vital if unreliable help of their mother who, unlike himself, was close to them and in their confidence.

There are a number of lonely widowers in Trollope's later work – Mr Wharton in *The Prime Minister* and Sir Thomas Underwood in *Ralph the Heir*, for instance, sit disconsolately in their chambers in a solitude that their children cannot really alleviate – but the immediate experience of conjugal loss as Palliser feels it is presented with a closeness of attention unique in Trollope's fiction. There are certain kinds of extreme emotion which Trollope's delicacy and stoicism usually combine to avoid, and the onset of Palliser's grief may only escape this embargo because of the long-established intimacy between character and author. Not that there is any dwelling on death-bed detail, even to the degree of precedent set by Trollope himself on the occasion of the old Bishop's demise, long ago, in *Barchester Towers*. Some touching details emerge (such as the description in Chapter II of the Duke sitting by her bedside holding his wife's hand, 'dumb, because at such a moment he knew not how to express the tenderness of his heart'), but the initial stress is on the seismic effect on the Duke's life. The novel's first sentence makes the point with unusual emphasis: 'No one, probably, ever felt himself to be more alone in the world than our old friend, the Duke of Omnium, when the Duchess died.' Nothing, certainly, illustrates more poignantly the degree to which Palliser's marriage had become the largely unacknowledged precondition of his life than this sudden sense of total alienation:

> It was not only that his heart was torn to pieces, but that he did not know how to look out into the world. It was as though a man should be suddenly called upon to live without hands or even arms. He was helpless, and knew himself to be helpless. Hitherto he had never specially acknowledged to himself that his wife was necessary to him as a component part of his life. Though he had loved her dearly, and had in all things consulted her welfare and happiness, he had at times been inclined to think that in the exuberance of her spirits she had been a trouble rather than a support to him. But now it was as though all outside appliances were taken away from him. There was no one of whom he could ask a question. (I)

On the day of the funeral, Mrs Finn thinks that Plantagenet has suddenly become an old man; although never young-looking, 'he who was not yet fifty might have been taken to be over sixty'. He has always lacked his wife's resilience, and is now barely able to cope with the problem of his children's welfare. What is to be done, for instance, with Lady Mary? Mrs Finn will not accept the charge, although there was no one closer to the dead Duchess; her sense of her unsuitability – her argument that Mary should have as a companion '"those who are more naturally connected to her"' – is hardly explicable to the new reader although understandable to those who recall the full history of her relationship with the house of Omnium. Moreover, she has come to know that Mary has already entered into an engagement of which the Duke is quite unaware. Mary's attachment to Francis Tregear, formed while the family were on their travels after the Duke's resignation from office, was encouraged by her mother for reasons that have more to do with her own past than the young man's qualities, unexceptionable as these seem to be: '"Not but that Plantagenet has been to me all that a husband should be. Only if she can be spared what I suffered, let her be spared."' (II) The Duchess had counted on being able to bring the Duke round to Tregear in time; although

not rich, he is indisputably a gentleman even if he is a Conservative, and has long been Silverbridge's best friend.

It is not surprising that when Tregear formally asks for Mary's
hand and has to reveal the Duchess's complicity, the Duke should
be 'almost beside himself with rage and grief'. (V) Palliser recognizes immediately, with a kind of posthumous telepathy, that she
permitted what he regards as 'this most pernicious courtship'
because of 'that romantic folly by which she had so nearly brought
herself to shipwreck in her own early life'. In attempting to provide
Mary with an alternative suitor in the form of the vacuous if
inoffensive Lord Popplecourt, the Duke vainly hopes to repeat 'the
past success of a similar transaction', exactly recalling his own first
words to Glencora and her reaction, in *The Small House at Allington.* (XLVI) In seeing the Mary–Tregear situation as essentially a
repetition of the Glencora–Burgo situation both Duke and Duchess
distort the present facts under the pressure of their own past experience, as people do. Thus, although Glencora can no longer be
active in the novel, her presence is still felt because of her role in
precipitating part of its action. Palliser's frustration because Glencora can no longer be got at and made to see reason agonizingly
compounds his sorrow. The past lives again too in the way in
which Palliser wants his child to have the one happiness which he
feels has eluded him:

> He had never spoken of his hopes about her even to his wife,
> but in the silence of his very silent life he had thought much of
> the day when he would give her to some noble youth, – noble
> with all gifts of nobility, including rank and wealth, – who
> might be fit to receive her. Now, even though no one else
> should know it, – and all would know it, – she would be the
> girl who had condescended to love young Tregear.
>
> His own Duchess, she whose loss to him now was as
> though he had lost half his limbs, – had not she in the same
> way loved a Tregear, or worse than a Tregear, in her early
> days? Ah yes! And though his Cora had been so much to him,
> had he not often felt, had he not been feeling all his days, that
> Fate had robbed him of the sweetest joy that is given to
> man, in that she had not come to him loving him with her
> early spring of love, as she had loved that poor ne'er-do-well?

How infinite had been his regrets. How often had he told himself that, with all that Fortune had given him, still Fortune had been unjust to him because he had been robbed of that. Not to save his life could he have whispered a word of this to anyone, but he had felt it. He had felt it for years. Dear as she had been, she had not been quite what she should have been but for that. And now this girl of his, who was so much dearer to him than anything else left to him, was doing exactly as her mother had done. (VII)

What neither Duke nor Duchess grasp is the central Trollopian truth that although things may appear to repeat themselves, they will not do so exactly because the people involved are never quite the same. It is, of course, an inevitable disadvantage of the way the Palliser series was written and published, that a reader new to its personnel would react to this passage as if it were merely outlining the novel's point of departure. Only those who have followed closely the history of the relationship between Plantagenet and Glencora will be able to sense the full weight of lived experience behind the simple dignity of Trollope's language at this moment. The profound isolation of Palliser's personality, which meant that 'there had been no other human soul to whom he could open himself' (I), is something that we have had ample opportunity to observe. The Duke's dependence on his wife was never greater than when, during his Prime Ministership, they were often at cross purposes. If her waywardness and lack of support – or, rather, her provision of the wrong sort of support – caused him such anguish then, how much more will he now be demoralized by her final withdrawal? Trollope sums up the complementariness of their natures in two sentences of magisterial authority and tone. 'He had so habituated himself to devote his mind and his heart to the service of his country, that he had almost risen above or sunk below humanity. But she, who had been essentially human, had been a link between him and the world.' (I) (Trollope's prose in general reads so effortlessly that it is easy not to dwell on the resonance of such passages.) As for living, in other words, Plantagenet had come to count on his wife to do that for him. Now that she is gone, he has painfully to relearn how to do it on his own. This process – the novel's essential subject – is not offered in a didactic spirit; there is no attempt to emulate those passages in George Eliot (noble as they are) in which characters are shown to accept their tragedy and the burden of going on with life in an exemplary way. Trollope does not appeal to the reader to correlate his own life with that common lot which the persons in the novel vicariously live out. His mind is too much on the particular agonies of the fictive individual for that – although that empathy indeed demonstrates in practice the kind of charity of imagination which George Eliot recommends.

The Duchess is buried amidst the remains of the old Priory at Matching. Trollope does not explicitly remind us of her imprudent wanderings there in the cold moonlight when newly married, confessing her continuing love for Burgo to Alice Vavasor, and finding in the ruins the romance for which her chilly husband has no feeling. (*Can You Forgive Her?*, Chapter XXVII.) It is, however, the sort of connection that is characteristic of Trollope's creative method and which helps to give to his most prominent reappearing characters such an appearance of accumulated experience. The irony of this association is not advertised – we remark it, if at all, as the sort of odd conjunction that is more typical of life's contingencies than the product of art's purposes. Similarly, the little love scene between Glencora's son and the girl he has chosen which takes place in the ruins later in the novel also connects with but is not made specifically to recall our first introduction to the Priory.

It is soon clear that although Lady Mary has many of her mother's physical features, her nature is quite different. She already has a 'personal dignity of manner which had never been within her mother's reach'. (II) But what she lacks in volatile energy, she makes up in a tremulous but stubborn tenacity characteristic of many of Trollope's girls. She regards her engagement as 'a bond almost as holy as matrimony itself' (V), and it is easy to predict that she will wear down paternal opposition much as Emily Wharton did in *The Prime Minister*. The difference is that Tregear is not another Lopez, even though Palliser would like to think so. As the younger son of an antique Cornish family, he is not a man no one knows anything about. He has a small income, so that he can just about live like a gentleman. Even so, he is not in debt. He starts with more advantages than Phineas Finn, although as a Conservative, his politics are of less interest to Trollope and inevitably antipathetic to Palliser. It is clear that although he is worldly enough 'to feel the advantage' of marrying a duke's daughter, his love for Mary is genuine and honourable. He has taken a good degree at Oxford, has tried to dissuade Silverbridge from wasting money on racehorses, and has sufficient influence over his friend to make him stand for Parliament as a Conservative in defiance of all the Omnium traditions. Unlike Burgo, therefore, except in his good looks, and unlike Lopez, Tregear is a serious if somewhat starchy young man whom the Duke finds he cannot easily overawe or dismiss. Even when most incensed against him, Palliser is secretly impressed by the man's composure and courage. The Duke's concession, in his conversation with Finn at the end of *The Prime Minister*, that neither political side can have a monopoly of virtue, is now taken up with a distressingly personal application. In the long run, however, the fairness of Palliser's mind prevails over prejudice, as it always does, and he submits to having his principles put to this familial test. Much of the psychological interest of *The Duke's Children* lies in the internal struggles by which Trollope's hero finally brings himself round – without Glencora's help – to magnanimity.

There is much to distress him, too, in the conduct of his eldest son. Here there is a similar gap between his secret hopes and the mortifying reality. The relationship between father and son was one of profound and perennial interest to Trollope (the Palliser series has already dealt at some length with the impasse between the Earl of Brentford and his son Lord Chiltern, who is now seen again at full stretch as the Master of a Hunt which not only provides sport for Tregear, but involves the latter in an accident very like Chiltern's own in an earlier novel). Trollope's interest in primogeniture and inheritance (of which more below) was not merely legalistic; the fathers in his fiction often look forward to their eldest son's taking over with eagerness rather than resentment, anxious to assist that human continuity in the world which seems of so much more importance to them than any posthumous consolation in an extra-terrestrial after-life. There are indeed some Calvinistic mothers (Mrs Bolton in *John Caldigate*, for instance) who insist on the importance of laying up treasure in heaven rather than transmitting it on an earth not yet subject to death duties, but it is clear that Trollope regards such attitudes as deeply damaging, both to others and to the self. The fathers' wish to see their own lives and work extended through time by their sons' continuation of them is not deprecated as materialist but regarded as a normal human emotion that it is natural to feel with some intensity. It will be recalled that at the end of *Can You Forgive Her?* the prospect of a son and heir roused Palliser to peculiar enthusiasm; his hope – his expectation, even – that Silverbridge will carry on not only his line but also his ideals and habits of public service receives therefore a deeply unwelcome shock when the boy has to leave Oxford prematurely after a spectacular prank. Nor does the Duke much care for his son's association in racing matters with a Major Tifto, and in particular for their common interest in a Derby favourite, a horse named (through a touch of Trollopian irony) The Prime Minister. The subsequent loss of £70,000 on the St Leger (through Tifto's treachery) cannot but look disgraceful, even though the sum is trifling in relation to the ducal resources. The chief matter for regret, however, is Silverbridge's Conservatism, adopted under Tregear's tutelage but maintained without his intellectual sophistication. Silverbridge's decision to stand as a Conservative (when the constituency whose name he bears again becomes vacant with that opportuneness we have come to expect) cannot be welcome to the head of a family which has given such distinguished service to the Liberal cause for so long. Silverbridge argues that '"We've got to protect our position as well as we can against the Radicals and Communists"' (VII) – a point his father brushes aside by remarking that neither Communism nor revolution has the support of a major party. The young man's politics are based on class self-interest rather than on the more altruistic principles of his father, but serious discussion between them is hardly possible partly because Palliser is so upset by his son's defection and partly because Silverbridge's ideas are so callow. Indeed, his political behaviour throughout the novel is so juvenile that his desertion of the family tradition looks more like a matter of a conventional rebellion against paternal principles than a question of serious political conviction. It is no surprise when he finally returns to the Liberal fold.

In fact, Silverbridge's little essays in independence are hardly more than token demonstrations. His worried sense, even as he throws off the reins, that his father will be disappointed and hurt, and the degree to which Palliser's lectures mortify him (and even reduce him to tears), clearly show the underlying strength of the filial bond. When the younger brother gets into trouble at Cambridge in his turn, Silverbridge goes to great lengths to try and smooth the matter over because he is so acutely conscious of the distress that his father will feel. The Duke himself has even more reserves of tenderness which he longs to be able to show. He is immensely gratified, in his simple way, by Silverbridge's spur-of-the-moment invitation to dine at the Beargarden Club. Readers of *The Way We Live Now* will not need to be reminded that the Beargarden is a free-and-easy place, but the Duke likes his dinner – 'or rather he liked the feeling that he was dining with his son'. Nevertheless, the inherently selfish mode of life that such clubs encourage is not something that the Duke approves of, and he recommends marriage, even early marriage, as the antidote. Indeed, he looks forward to Silverbridge's with an almost luxurious sense of self-abnegation:

> 'Though as yet you are only the heir to the property and honours of our family, still, were you married, almost everything would be at your disposal. There is so much which I should only be too ready to give up to you!'
> 'I can't bear to hear you talking of giving up anything,' said Silverbridge energetically.
> Then the father looked round the room furtively, and seeing that the door was shut, and that they were assuredly alone, he put out his hand and gently stroked the young man's hair. It was almost a caress, – as though he would have said to himself, 'Were he my daughter, I would kiss him.' 'There is much I would fain give up,' he said. 'If you were a married man the house in Carlton Terrace would be fitter for you than for me. I have disqualified myself for taking that part in society which should be filled by the head of our family. You who have inherited so much from your mother would, if you married pleasantly, do all that right well.'
> (XXVI)

The moment touchingly recalls those similarly furtive demonstrations of affection to Glencora, the tentative gesture again implying reserves of emotion of unsuspected and normally undetectable power and extent. Had his wife still been living, such a display of love would hardly have been needed: she would have acted as the medium of feeling between father and son. *The Duke's Children* thus imposes on Palliser the sad necessity of belatedly learning how to cope at first hand with the emotional demands of family life without that 'link between him and the world' which his wife's humanity had provided.

The Duke's unwonted gentleness at this point prompts Silverbridge to confess that he does have a prospective bride in mind. As the daughter of an earl, Lady Mabel Grex is a satisfactory choice for one who despite his egalitarian ideals thinks as much of the maintenance of the aristocracy as the Duke does, even if her gambling father is not much of an ornament to his order. Lady Mab is in much the same position as Lady Laura, in the Phineas novels, in that she can only continue the life to which her birth has accustomed her by marrying advantageously. The early attachment between her and Frank Tregear has therefore, and at her insistence, been broken off, his means being impossibly slender in relation to her style. She is quite willing to encourage Silverbridge's attentions since he is both eligible and likeable, but she fends off both an unequivocal declaration from him and a binding commitment on her part because of her feeling that he is still only a boy, and also because of her residual attachment to Tregear. When Lady Mary and Tregear meet by chance at Lady Mabel's and a passionate if highly improper embrace follows, Mabel defends Mary's conduct against Silverbridge's censure. (XXIX) Instead of being conventionally if covertly jealous, she is protective about the girl's public display of a love that she herself shares and has had to suppress. (She later remembers it as 'a fine and brave thing to do'.) In fact, Mabel generally finds that, much as she calculates, she cannot keep to her calculations: her true feelings always seem to insist on expression, against self-interest, even against self-respect. In thus going against the grain of her nature, she risks doing the kind of violence to it incurred by Lady Laura. The result is less tragic, partly because Mabel's egocentricity contrasts unfavourably with Laura's hankering after the life of high politics which her mistaken marriage was intended to secure. All the same, Trollope treats Mabel's situation with considerable creative sympathy. Lady Mabel is allowed to express her feminine frustration in a conversation with Tregear in which his genuine if new-found attachment to Lady Mary Palliser is contrasted with her coldly contemplated parallel alliance with Silverbridge:

'Only think how a girl such as I am is placed; or indeed any girl. You, if you see a woman that you fancy, can pursue her, can win her and triumph, or lose her and gnaw your heart; – at any rate you can do something. You can tell her that you love her; can tell her so again and again even though she should scorn you. You can set yourself about the business you have taken in hand and can work hard at it. What can a girl do?'

'Girls work hard too sometimes.'

'Of course they do; – but everybody feels that they are sinning against their sex. Of love, such as a man's is, a woman ought to know nothing. How can she love with passion when she should never give her love till it has been asked, and not then unless her friends tell her that the thing is suitable? Love such as that to me is out of the question. But, as it is fit that I should be married, I wish to be married well.'

'And you will love him after a fashion?'

'Yes; – after a very sterling fashion. I will make his wishes my wishes, his ways my ways, his party my party, his home my home, his ambition my ambition, – his honour my honour.' As she said this she stood up with her hands clenched and head erect, and her eyes flashing.

'Do you not know me well enough to be sure that I should be loyal to him?'

'Yes; – I think that you would be loyal.'

'Whether I loved him or not, he should love me.'

'And you think that Silverbridge would do?'

'Yes, I think that Silverbridge would do.' (X)

It is part of Mabel's frustration that she has more energy than any other woman in the book and no proper object for it, but, as she says, '"What can a girl do?"' Her exposé of the impossible position she is put in by the sexual ethics of her time has a force for which Tregear has noticeably no answer. Trollope's own comforting bulletins about love and marriage elsewhere do not adequately reckon with the case against their complacency which Lady Mabel here puts. Locally, however, no discomfort from authorial

216

intrusion arises because this chapter, like many others in *The Duke's Children*, is almost entirely in dialogue.

Mabel Grex's eventual fate seems the natural result of the inter-action of her circumstances and her conscious or unconscious will rather than the effect of authorial decree. It is true that she comes off worst of the novel's lovers in the end, and might thus be said to be punished for putting worldly considerations before love. She and Tregear could have decided to keep faith despite the economic disadvantages of so doing (as Imogen Docimer and Frank Houston eventually decide to do in a comparable situation in *Ayala's Angel*, considered below), but she could also have succeeded in ensnaring Silverbridge had she brought herself to be a bit more unscrupulous; as she more than once insists, she would have been a good and loyal wife to him. It is her bad luck that there is a kind of honesty about her which will not in the end let her reap the benefits of her worldly calculations. This compulsion to get the truth out into the open frustrates her schemes, but has its admirable aspects. It gives her a dominant role in her dealings with both Tregear and Silverbridge. When the former visits her at her family home at Grex – a crumbling Jacobean house of which she is significantly fond in a melancholy part of the fells on the Westmorland–Yorkshire border – Mabel has little difficulty in exposing his assumptions that they can be just 'friends' after what has happened. She still loves him, while he has taken his love elsewhere: 'friendship' can hardly survive on that basis. Lady Mabel feels at this point the pathos of the woman's lot, rather as Lady Laura had done; time and the old love conspire to make the woman wilt, while the man is revived by the freshness of her rival and supplanter:

'Your bloom is not fading; your charms are not running from you. Have you not a strength which I cannot have? Do you not feel that you are a tree, standing firm in the ground, while I am a bit of ivy that will be trodden in the dirt unless it can be made to cling to something? You should not liken yourself to me, Frank.'

'If I could do you any good!'

'Good! What is the meaning of good? If you love, it is good to be loved again. It is good not to have your heart torn to pieces. You know that I love you.' He was standing close to her, and put out his hand as though he would twine his arm round her waist. 'Not for worlds,' she said. 'It belongs to that Palliser girl. And as I have taught myself to think that what there is left of me may perhaps belong to some other one, worthless as it is, I will keep it for him. I love you, – but there can be none of that softness of love between us.'

Then there was a pause, but as he did not speak she went on. 'But remember, Frank, – our position is not equal. You have got over your little complaint. It probably did not go deep with you, and you have found a cure. Perhaps there is a satisfaction in finding that two young women love you.'

'You are trying to be cruel to me.'

'Why else should you be here? You know I love you, – with all my heart, with all my strength, and that I would give the world to cure myself. Knowing this, you come and talk to me of your passion for this other girl.'

'I had hoped we might both talk rationally as friends.'

'Friends! Frank Tregear, I have been bold enough to tell you I love you; but you are not my friend, and cannot be my friend.' (XXXVII)

Tregear's motives may or may not correspond to Mabel's suspicions – again, the chapter is almost entirely in dialogue and Trollope does not at this point offer any authorial commentary – but the scene leaves him looking by far the flimsier of the two. (The romantic location, with the characters seated on a rock overlooking water and then returning to the house echoes the Laura–Phineas dialogues at Loughlinter, but the similarity only serves to underline Tregear's thinness as a character when compared to Finn.)

Another aspect of Mabel's bad luck is that Silverbridge is so smitten with the overwhelming beauty and charm of the American Isabel Boncassen that the thought of persisting with the difficult and often discouraging Mabel is put aside, despite the awkwardness of having had his father's approval of her. Mabel insists on a similar sort of show-down with Silverbridge as she has had with Tregear. Her counter-attack against Miss Boncassen's charms comes to grief when Silverbridge tells her (in another scene of disappointment in love set on the banks of a stream) that he has proposed to the

American girl. Nevertheless she still hopes, during a long stay with the Duke at Matching, that parental horror at such an incongruous match may work to her advantage. However, after an abortive attempt to shame Silverbridge out of his new love by taunting him with the old, she has to be content with a promise that they will still be 'friends', pleading now for what she had formerly refused Tregear. When Silverbridge will not be moved even by Mabel's simulated admission that she loves him, Mabel knows that she has lost, and cannot bear that he should remain ignorant of the truth. Not only does she insist on revealing that in fact she has never loved him; she also feels compelled to confess her continuing passion for Tregear. She again generalizes her situation in the elegiac tones she has used before:

> 'A man has but one centre, and that is himself. A woman has two. Though the second may never be seen by her, may live in the arms of another, may do all for that other that man can do for woman, – still, still, though he be half the globe asunder from her, still he is to her the half of her existence. If she really love, there is, I fancy, no end of it. To the end of time I shall love Frank Tregear . . . I would give one of my eyes to be able to disregard him.'
>
> 'Time will do it.'
>
> 'Yes; time, – that brings wrinkles and rouge-pots and rheumatism. Though I have so hated those men as to be unable to endure them, still I want some man's house, and his name, – some man's bread and wine, – some man's jewels and titles and woods and parks and gardens, – if I can get them. Time can help a man in his sorrow. If he begins at forty to make speeches, or to win races, or to breed oxen, he can yet live a prosperous life. Time is but a poor consoler for a young woman who has to be married.' (LXXIII)

The desolate perspective offered here is allowed to stand without comment, the last few pages of the chapter being again entirely in dialogue. The idea, in both passages quoted, of woman as parasitic and ivy-like, is reminiscent of the use of the same figure when Mrs Bold unites with Mr Arabin as long ago as *Barchester Towers* – except that here it seems the natural if bitter result of the character's own experience rather than a complacent authorial gloss.

Ironically, although there is not much that Silverbridge can say, his behaviour during this last interview gives Mabel a new respect for him. As she tells Tregear, in their last exchange, his truthfulness reconciles her, in a perverse way, to his fickleness:

> 'But when a man can look a girl in the face with those seemingly soft eyes, and say with that seemingly soft mouth, – "I have changed my mind," – though she would look him dead in return if she could, still she must admire him.'
>
> 'Are you speaking of Silverbridge now?'
>
> 'Of course I am speaking of Silverbridge. I suppose I ought to hide it all and not to tell you. But as you are the only person I do tell, you must put up with me. Yes; – when I taxed him with his falsehood, – for he had been false, – he answered me with those very words! "I have changed my mind." He could not lie. To speak the truth was a necessity to him, even at the expense of his gallantry, almost of his humanity.'
>
> 'Has he been false to you, Mabel?'
>
> 'Of course he has. But there is nothing to quarrel about, if you mean that. People do not quarrel now about such things. A girl has to fight her own battle with her own pluck and her own wits. As with these weapons she is generally stronger than her enemy, she succeeds sometimes although everything else is against her. I think I am courageous, but his courage beat mine. I craned at the first fence. When he was willing to swallow my bait, my hand was not firm enough to strike the hook in his jaws. Had I not quailed then I think I should have – "had him".' (LXXVII)

Her words strike Tregear as 'horrid', but, as she says, she has got to tell the truth to somebody, however 'unfeminine' it may seem. Her love for Tregear, at their final parting, is if anything fiercer than before, and her agony of abandonment is left quite unresolved; she can only look forward, as Lily Dale did, to being an 'old maid'. She is not going to recover from 'the terrible evil' that Tregear has done her by ceasing to love her.

Both Silverbridge and Tregear have thus changed their affections in ways which could be represented as culpable and which are certainly hurtful: can we forgive them? In practice, and as usual in

Trollope, the problem theoretically considered somehow dissolves in the light of the actual circumstances. Silverbridge's change of heart might be made to look like, say, Crosbie's (although there was no formal engagement to break), but his motives and moral character are so obviously superior to Crosbie's that the comparison has no force. Tregear's change of heart duplicates Finn's transfer of affection from Lady Laura to Violet Effingham and later to Madame Goesler, and it is no more his fault that Mabel cannot stop loving him than it was Phineas's that Laura continued to be obsessed with him. Mabel's tragedy remains, however, even if it is presented with much less power than Laura Kennedy's. Such possibilities must always be present in Trollope's fiction, given the fact of his extreme and even-handed interest both in people who change their minds and in those who cannot do so. Those who are constant are sometimes regarded as admirable and sometimes as perverse; those who change can be thought of as manly or as weak. But whatever one may think in advance and in the abstract on such questions, it is so modified in the fictional event by our access to the characters' own view of their particular case, that the drawing up of a moral balance-sheet seems otiose. Whatever Trollope may say, in the *Autobiography* and elsewhere, about the novel's moral teaching, in practice he lets the characters do what they turn out to want to do or what they cannot help doing, being the people they are. Hence the absence in Trollope of those magical transformations in Dickens like Scrooge's where the character divests himself of his own nature and is born again, or even of those inspiring *éclaircissements* in George Eliot where previously egocentric characters are baptized by some event or encounter into a new awareness of altruistic possibility. But if Trollope is more determinist, he is also more profoundly charitable. The impulse to bully one's creations must lie in wait for every novelist; it is an essential part of the sweetness of Trollope's artistic nature that he seems so immune to the temptation.

But if Trollope's novels insist that every person has something to be said for him whatever his fate, it is also true that they minister to the deep desire of most readers to see that at least some people's lives work out happily. The chief beneficiary at the end of *The Duke's Children* is clearly Silverbridge, although Tregear has also done pretty well since he has obtained a seat in Parliament, Lady

Mary Palliser's hand, and the honour of being called by his Christian name by the magnanimous Duke. Silverbridge however has the gratification not only of winning the dazzling Miss Boncassen but of seeing his father's whole-hearted adoption of her; this sets the seal on the full reconciliation of father and son. Miss Boncassen is herself the daughter of a highly civilized American man of letters who is spoken of as a possible future President, but her homely mother is – in terms of English high society – barely presentable, and the family comes from nowhere, or rather from the poorer parts of New York which amounts to the same thing. However, Isabel is a success and even becomes the fashion, because in addition to her beauty she has the physical vitality (she plays tennis with great energy) and the social freedom of manner of an American girl. She is also quick-witted: her early sparring conversations with Silverbridge at her Maidenhead river party show that she is a good deal sharper than he is. *The Duke's Children* was written in the mid-1870s, a time when the American girl was beginning to impinge on readers as an available and interesting subject. Henry James's successful *Daisy Miller*, an influential example of the type, appeared in the *Cornhill Magazine* in 1878. Isabel Boncassen's situation, however, had already been prefigured by Trollope in an earlier novel, *He Knew He Was Right* (considered below). Trollope himself had had considerable first-hand experience of America and Americans, and in *The American Senator* (written in 1875, the year before *The Duke's Children*) had shown the earnest Senator Gotobed's attempts to penetrate the mysteries of English life. Hunting, for instance, perplexes him – ' "A hundred dogs to kill one fox!" ' – but he perseveres in his inquiries, finally attempting to summarize them in a public lecture on 'The Irrationality of Englishmen', which though well meant is not well received. The Senator survives to make a brief appearance in *The Duke's Children* at a lunch given by Mr Boncassen. However, the more absurd aspects of Americans (from an English point of view) are greatly toned down in *The Duke's Children*. The objectionable 'twang' or nasal intonation is quite absent from Isabel Boncassen's diction, and Mr Boncassen himself is clearly a man of distinction; he has after all come to London in order to be able to read in the British Museum. Even the Duke of Omnium says that ' "they seem to be sensible people" ', and adds that ' "I don't know when I have met a man with higher ideas on politics than Mr Boncassen"' (XLVII) – praise indeed. The Duke also finds Isabel 'lady-like' and 'well-educated' and clearly unbends in her company. Approval is one thing, however, and alliance another, as both Silverbridge and Isabel are uncomfortably aware. Palliser may publicly subscribe to theories of an egalitarian tendency, but his private feelings run the other way. Recalling her father's humble origins, Isabel thinks that her father's rise would be impossible in England because so much deference is paid to rank – a position which Palliser vigorously denies: '"Our peerage is being continually recruited from the ranks of the people, and hence it gets its strength . . . There is no greater mistake than to suppose that inferiority of birth is a barrier to success in this country."' As he says this, however, he is unaware that his son has already committed himself to the granddaughter of a New York labourer, and is hardly conscious of the profound inconsistency in his own mind.

> The peer who sat next to him in the House of Lords, whose grandmother had been a washerwoman and whose father an innkeeper, was to him every whit as good a peer as himself. And he would as soon sit in counsel with Mr. Monk, whose father has risen from a mechanic to be a merchant, as with any nobleman who could count ancestors against himself. But there was an inner feeling in his bosom as to his own family, his own name, his own children, and his own personal self, which was kept altogether apart from his grand political theories. It was a subject on which he never spoke; but the feeling had come to him as a part of his birthright. And he conceived that it would pass through him to his children after the same fashion. It was this which made the idea of a marriage between his daughter and Tregear intolerable to him, and which would operate as strongly in regard to any marriage which his son might contemplate. (XLVIII)

In effect, *The Duke's Children* takes Palliser's doctrine of lessening distances between the classes as expounded in *The Prime Minister*, and brings them literally home.

Isabel sees clearly how Silverbridge's proposal is likely to be received. Apart from the fact that the Duke is still under the illusion that Silverbridge favours the blue-blooded Lady Mabel, the idea of an American girl becoming the wife of the heir to the dukedom is bound to strike him as almost unthinkable. She therefore accepts Silverbridge with the proviso that she will marry him only if his father consents. In this she is following not only her American predecessor Caroline Spalding (in *He Knew He Was Right*), but also the earlier Barsetshire heroines Lucy Robarts and Grace Crawley, who will only marry when their lovers' parents give their blessing. In other words, the Silverbridge-Isabel situation is not so much a precursor of the Jamesian International Theme as a new version of an impasse which had long interested Trollope. As before, the problem can only be resolved satisfactorily when the desires of the self are in harmony with and receive the sanction of those with whom the self is inevitably and intimately connected. Happy endings in Trollope characteristically embody this reconciliation of the personal and the familial, the private and the social.

For this to happen in *The Duke's Children* the Duke himself has not merely to accept but to welcome misalliances that at first seem to him intolerably offensive. The first significant victory of his magnanimity over his prejudice is shown by his dealings with his and our old friend Mrs Finn. One of the difficulties of the novel series is obviously that it becomes progressively harder as the series accumulates to cue new readers in. The story of the odd but profound relationship between Madame Max Goesler, as she originally was, and the Omnium family, has been going on since *Phineas Finn*: it can hardly be adequately summarized at this late date, and in the early pages of *The Duke's Children* Trollope can only make slight gestures towards it. 'She knew – the reader may possibly know – that nothing had ever been purer, nothing more disinterested than her friendship' (II): such a reference hardly does justice to the complex mixture of calculation and charity which lay behind Marie's decision to reject the old Duke's offer, but the reader will not fully understand the nature and tone of her present dealings with the present Duke unless he remembers all that has gone before. The early chapters of *The Duke's Children* – and indeed much of the whole novel – may seem thin to new readers at just those points where old Palliser hands find it most resonant.

Mrs Finn finds herself in a situation of peculiar difficulty at Lady Glencora's death. She sees the situation not only from the distraught Duke's point of view but also with the shrewd sense of the world's opinion for which she has always been notable, and which makes her insist that she is not the fitting person to take charge of the Duke's daughter. Lady Mary's confession to Mrs Finn of the clandestine engagement with Tregear means that Marie is torn between her loyalty to the dead Glencora and her duty to the surviving Plantagenet; duty clearly dictates that either the lovers or Mrs Finn herself must reveal the secret and therefore improper attachment. Tregear is summoned to Park Lane and finds himself in the same pretty, flower-filled room in which the old Duke, Phineas, and others in their time had also had crucial conversations; Tregear has heard 'rumours' about such matters. In the present interview Mrs Finn's fine command of tactic and tone easily outflanks Tregear's resentment at her interference, and he is obliged to promise to see the Duke forthwith.

Made more hypersensitive than ever by grief, the Duke is not only outraged by what he sees as Tregear's presumption, but also indignant at what he hastily regards as Mrs Finn's betrayal. He promotes her to the role of an accomplice in a conspiracy to deceive him partly because it is a way of transferring to her the blame which really belongs to the dead wife, who can thus be exculpated. He is trapped between a chivalrous feeling that he should take on himself Glencora's faults, and a wish to find a scapegoat for them. His quarrel with Mrs Finn, the product of confused but understandable motives exacerbated by the intensity of his grief, is in a way a continuation of the kind of disagreements which Palliser used to have with Glencora, and which always resolved themselves in due course so as to stabilize yet further the marriage whose end now so demoralizes him. Such a division is harder to heal without the intimacies of daily contact. Mrs Finn chafes under the accusation that she has done something which is in fact 'repugnant' to her, but her attempts to set herself right with the Duke are fended off with impersonal notes of lethal frigidity. She has to bear in mind the political dangers for her husband of any open quarrel with the Duke, and in fact she understands his state of mind with her usual perspicacity; as Trollope reminds her, 'in all their political troubles, she had understood him better then the Duchess had done'. (XIII) Nevertheless, she finds the present situation so intolerable that in lieu of an interview with Palliser, she decides to defend herself on paper. Nothing releases the full energies of the Trollopian character like a long letter of self-justification, and Mrs Finn's is a notable example of this indignant genre. The Duke's mixture of emotions as he reacts to the letter are sympathetically traced by Trollope to their true cause: the pain caused by Glencora's death coupled with the pain of having to admit that she remained her irresponsible self to the last.

A sense of injury, a burning conviction of wrong sustained, will justify language which otherwise would be unbearable. The Duke felt that, and though his ears were tingling and his brow knitted, he could have forgiven the language, if only he could have admitted the argument. He understood every word of it. When she spoke of tenacity she intended to charge him with obstinacy. Though she had dwelt but lightly on her own services she had made her thoughts on the matter clear enough. 'I, Mrs Finn, who am nobody, have done much to succour and assist you, the Duke of Omnium; and this is the return which I have received!' And then she told him to his face that unless he did something which it would be impossible that he should do, she would revoke her opinion of his honesty! He tried to persuade himself that her opinion about his honesty was nothing to him; – but he failed. Her opinion was very much to him. Though in his anger he had determined to throw her off from him, he knew her to be one whose good opinion was worth having.

Not a word of overt accusation had been made against his wife. Every allusion to her was full of love. But yet how heavy a charge was really made! That such a secret should be kept from him, the father, was acknowledged to be a heinous fault; – but the wife had known the secret and had kept it from him, the father! And then how wretched a thing it was for him that anyone should dare to write to him about the wife that had been taken away from him! In spite of all her faults her name was so holy to him that it had never once passed his lips since her death, except in low whispers to himself, – low whispers made in the perfect, double-guarded seclusion of his own chamber. 'Cora, Cora,' he had murmured, so that the sense of the sound and not the sound itself had come to him from his own lips. And now this woman wrote to him about her freely, as though there were nothing sacred, no religion in the memory of her. (XV)

Plantagenet's silent mouthing of the shortened form of his dead wife's name – associated in previous novels with moments of particular conjugal closeness – deepens with affecting pathos that intimacy with the most private areas of the self that Trollope has established over so long a period. It takes the Duke 'five minutes of perfect stillness . . . five minutes during which great beads of perspiration broke out from him and stood upon his brow' to admit to himself that he has been unjust. Eventually he sends Mrs Finn an unreserved apology, knowing that the tone is ungracious but unable to improve it, so inhibited is he by his sense of her kindness over many years and his inability to discharge that indebtedness. As often before in political matters – it was a major handicap during his period as Prime Minister – Palliser's true feelings are masked rather than revealed by his external behaviour. Nevertheless Mrs Finn understands the true intent behind Palliser's cold words of apology so clearly that 'as she read the few words her eyes became laden with tears'. (XXIII) To the reader who knows only this novel those tears will not seem as touching as they do for those who have lived with Mrs Finn as Trollope would have wished and who therefore understand the accumulated experience behind them. It is characteristic of such moments in Trollope that they seem to owe everything to his sense of human life and nothing to literary art.

In the days of her first introduction in *Phineas Finn* Madame Max Goesler was said to have business interests in Vienna which required her presence once a year; this continental connection proved invaluable in *Phineas Redux* in obtaining the evidence which helped to clear Phineas, and is used again in *The Duke's Children*. Palliser's remedy for domestic trouble is travel, as *Can You Forgive Her?* and *The Prime Minister* have indicated, and he now attempts to distract Lady Mary's mind from its preoccupation with Tregear by taking her to Austria, where they encounter the Finns on their annual visit. The Duke's strategy is similar to that used by Sir Harry Hotspur of Humblethwaite, in the novel of that name. Sir Harry tries to cure his daughter Emily of her love for the disreputable George Hotspur by taking her to Italy, but she refuses to be consoled and dies. The Duke is worried by Lady Mary's headaches and secretly fears that a broken heart would lead, if not to Emily Hotspur's fate, at least to broken health. Mrs Finn bravely tells him that he is bound to give in, if the alternative is to see Mary suffer. The Duke has now sufficiently recovered his sense of balance not only to accept such counsel without offence, but to apologize again, and with patent simplicity and sincerity, for the pain he has given: '"I know how good you are and how reasonable. I know how much you have to forgive."' (XLI) In a later scene, he adds 'almost sternly' that '"I am under a debt of gratitude to you of which I cannot express my sense in words."' (LXVI)

The inherent justice and generosity of Palliser's nature, so evident in his dealings with Mrs Finn, also ensures his final reconciliation with his children. He brings himself to realize and to accept that, like their mother, they have wills of their own but that unlike her, they will not, in the long run, accept his authority or live according to the patterns suggested by his imagination. His only recourse is to give way gracefully; by doing so he not only restores but enhances his moral dignity. His honesty will not allow him to pretend that Isabel is the wife he would have chosen for Silverbridge, but once he has accepted her, he does so with a completeness that, for all the slight quaintness of phrase with which it is expressed, could hardly be more handsome. His words to Isabel are unprecedentedly tender, generous, and – when all that has gone before is kept in mind – moving, despite their economy. When he gives her Glencora's ring his typically brief expression of emotion is marked by the characteristic swerve to normality: '"It was the first present that I gave to my wife, and it is the first that I give to you. You may imagine how sacred it is to me. On no other hand could it be worn without something which to me would be akin to sacrilege. Now I must not keep you longer or Silverbridge will be storming about the house."' (LXXII) Again, the scene between father and prospective daughter-in-law is largely in dialogue, and there is no question of authorial underlining for sentimental effect. Nor is there any pretence that the brave new world exists for the Duke himself. Laying down the burden of the Prime Ministership brought Palliser an odd serenity, and his acceptance of his children's marital choices is similarly accompanied by something unusually buoyant in his manner. But the disappointments and the pain remain:

Perhaps the matter most remarkable in the wedding was the hilarity of the Duke. One who did not know him well might have said that he was a man with very few cares, and who now took special joy in the happiness of his children, – who was thoroughly contented to see them marry after their own hearts. And yet, as he stood there on the altar-steps giving his daughter to that new son and looking first at his girl, and then at his married son, he was reminding himself of all he had suffered. (LXXX)

The fact that Palliser will continue to suffer in private only makes his public 'hilarity' the more noble. Trollope had not written these words when, in the *Autobiography*, he stated that he thought Plantagenet Palliser, Duke of Omnium, 'a perfect gentleman', but they indicate something of what he meant by the phrase. In the character which he regarded more highly than any other, the consciousness of self ineradicably remains, even at the moment in which it most shares in the happiness of others.

III
Recurring Situations

Trollope's two novel series provide the best opportunities for understanding what he meant by living with his characters, although it would need a much fuller account than has been given here to do adequate justice to their novelistic richness and human interest. No English predecessor had used reappearance on the scale and in the manner of the Barsetshire and Palliser sequences. Thackeray's novels have some points of interconnection, but in his hands the technique is more opportunist than habitual and sometimes more arch than serious. Despite Trollope's warm relationship with Thackeray, there seems no evidence that his interest in reappearing characters was the result of the older novelist's influence rather than the logical development of the habits of his own imagination. *The Times'* leader on the death of Trollope (7 December 1882), written by Mrs Humphry Ward, noted that 'In connecting together a number of different novels by means of a common locale and a stock of common characters Mr Trollope was following at least one great precedent, the example of Balzac, who owed a good deal of his peculiar effect to this device.' There is, however, no indication that Trollope understood or wished to emulate Balzac's practice, as Mrs Humphry Ward may seem to imply. Balzac is not mentioned in the *Autobiography*, and the only reference to him in Trollope's surviving letters comes late on, when he acknowledges the gift of a book on the French novelist that he is clearly in no hurry to read. The literary ambitions of the two writers were in fact profoundly dissimilar.

Trollope's work was not animated, as Balzac's came to be, by the desire (in Henry James's phrase) 'simply to do everything that could be done'. Balzac's *Avant-propos* indicates the grandiose scale of his project, explaining and justifying the various divisions and subdivisions of the *Comédie Humaine* – the classification of 'Études de Moeurs', 'Études Philosophiques', 'Études Analytiques', and the subsections of the first category, the Scenes of Private Life, Provincial Life, Parisian Life, Military Life, and so on. The *Avant-propos* also speaks of Balzac's need to 'study the causes or central cause of these social facts, and discover the meaning hidden in that immense assembly of faces, passions, and events'. He was convinced that the laws governing the will, passion, and energy were accessible or could become accessible to be a sufficiently penetrating intelligence. His characters therefore tend to be doubly significant since they are both socially and historically representative and are also individual organisms obeying the laws of human biology. Although Trollope's fiction cannot but betray everywhere the conditions of its historical provenance, it shows not the slightest sign of being underpinned by any comparable infrastructure.

The difference in approach might be illustrated by comparing the careers of Phineas Finn and Eugène de Rastignac. We have already seen that Trollope's interest in Phineas's public career is in practice constantly preoccupied with private consciousness and intimate relationship. Rastignac's value to Balzac seems to have become clear to him during the writing of *Le Père Goriot* (written 1834–5), the first novel in which the idea of reappearing characters is systematically developed. He figures in twenty-one of Balzac's narratives, and his reappearances allow one to trace the stages by which he gradually becomes a pillar of the élite whose lack of feeling so shocked him initially in *Goriot*. Rastignac is not so much a single spy as a battalion; in him is reflected the quest for status and wealth, and the compromises necessary to achieve them, in French society under the July Monarchy. His history thus has a representative dimension of a kind never envisaged for Phineas Finn. Eugène's dubious but profitable involvement in a shady financial manoeuvre by the Baron de Nucingen, for instance, tells us something about the historical operations of international banking which Phineas's connection with Madame Max Goesler, a banker's widow, does not.

The pervasive nature of reappearance in Balzac (some of whose novels contain well over a hundred *personnages reparaissants*) makes Trollope's use of the device look relatively diffident. It was inextricably bound up with his ambition to present a complete model of French life. The fact that, as Henry James put it, 'He proposed to himself to "turn over" the great garden from north to south and from east to west', meant that Balzac hardly had leisure for the kind of repetition involved in Trollope's studies of Mr Crawley or Lily Dale. Indeed, the nature of his scheme required that each piece of fiction in it should contribute something distinct, supplying details which, when correlated with those specified elsewhere, would help to fill in his enormous microcosm. In Balzac any return to former sites is not likely to be the product of a felt authorial loyalty to the character for its own sake or of the sort of artistic nostalgia that drew Trollope back to record, for instance, the death of Mr Harding. Nevertheless, the two novelists were clearly alike in the thronged vigour of their imaginative life, thickly populated with characters kept in temporary reserve but whose careers could be resumed whenever appropriate.

However, Trollope's apparent lack of interest in justifying his use of reappearance as the necessary means towards the realization of a large Balzacian conception has been more than made up for by the claims of modern critics on his behalf. Criticism of Victorian fiction has now been under heavy and sustained inflationary pressure for a generation, and Trollope could hardly be expected to escape. Nevertheless, the terms in which his art has latterly been discussed may come as something of a shock after the homely preoccupations of Trollope's original reviewers with fidelity in portraiture and purity of morals, and after the mellow avuncularities of Michael Sadleir, the doyen of pre-war Trollopiana. Trollope is currently credited with what amounts to a Balzacian breadth of vision almost as a matter of course. The assumption that his fiction functions as a searching critique of his society often seems automatic, even though the exact terms of that critique vary a good deal from one account to another. He is credited not just with that photographic realism which his contemporaries admired, but with that understanding of those hidden meanings and central causes that Balzac sought.

Academic criticism often seeks to justify the status of a major novelist by showing his sense of historical responsibility towards his material, and the more pervasive and profound that particular kind of seriousness can be, the more impregnable the artist's position naturally becomes. The writer is expected to offer a maturely pondered assessment of his age; it is not seriously envisaged that he might take the state of his society as given; it is not thought enough to be interested in people. Individual novels are treated as if the milieux they portray constitute microcosms with certain built-in characteristics which it is the object of the author to evaluate; sentences beginning 'The world of . . .' *The Prime Minister* or *The Eustace Diamonds* or whatever title it may be, are symptomatic of a compulsion to generalize and an inability to let the novels' particulars be. The pressure on the individual fictional character is in consequence greatly increased, even as attention to his peculiarities is reduced; he comes to matter more for what he represents or illustrates than for himself since he is the vehicle for the author's social and moral judgements. Once characters are seen as the necessary instruments of a larger inquiry into Victorian civilization, or the decline of the old values, or the nature of the gentleman, or the triumph of the commercial ethic, they are inevitably nudged away from idiosyncrasy towards allegory. They become expendable foot-soldiers caught up in the Napoleonic strategies of theme.

Trollope's consolidation of Barsetshire through his use of re-appearing characters in a novel sequence has offered critics a temptingly separate and safe-seeming world which, because it is rural and remote, can be played off against metropolitan decadence. James Kincaid goes so far as to claim that what he calls the Barsetshire Chronicle 'deals with an epic theme: the establishment and preservation of a civilization'.[1] The Barset world exhibits traditional values of 'right feeling and basic goodness' which Kincaid calls 'pastoral' – a term which has had a heady effect on some subsequent criticism – and which need defending against the corruptions of the capital. The chief shepherd of this pastoral is Mr Harding; at the end of the series his office is inherited by Mr Crawley, who becomes 'the spiritual centre of the community'. Even quite minor incidents are absorbed into this pattern: Frank Gresham's street assault on Mr Moffat becomes 'a scourge from the pastoral world to punish London'. London, the centre of the Palliser world, is naturally – or rather unnaturally – antithetical to Barsetshire; it is a fallen world in which human beings attempt 'to live in a world without community'. The two series are thus given a quasi-mythic relation to each other. One does not need to engage at close quarters with Professor Kincaid's densely-argued and influential book to see how his kind of interpretation is bound to involve not only continuous negotiation between individual character and abstract implication but also the effective subordination of the former to the latter.

The general level of conceptual activity in recent discussions of Trollope's work is apt to be as high as the pressure of moral earnestness is unremitting. There almost seems at times an atmosphere of pedagogic collusion. Kincaid is typical of the tendency when he defines the subject of *The Prime Minister* as 'the education of the Duke and Duchess'. It is perhaps understandable that those of us who earn our living teaching literature to our students should expect Trollope to teach life to his characters. At any rate, the practical effect of such emphases is again to conscript characters into embodying values, demonstrating ethical truths, and generally behaving like refugees from *The Faerie Queene*. The terror of the modern academic critic in the face of a work which might turn out not to have a unifying concept or thematic pattern often drives him to import and plant one. Again, the cost is borne by the hapless character, made to perform in a masque not of his own devising. If the situations of the principal persons in a given novel are all to be seen as examples of perversity, or variations on the theme of illusion and truth, or whatever the hospitable formula is, the threat to the character's individuality is real because he risks being reduced to the ranks of category. The highest common factor of theoretical abstraction can easily turn out in fictional practice to represent the lowest common denominator of human interest; it locates the least intriguing aspect of the particular case. In the last analysis, the novel of character is bound to value what people do not have in common over what they do.

Although patently well-meant, such attempts to give Trollope's work greater formal respectability go against the grain of his improvisatory creative method. His imaginative priorities as indicated by the *Autobiography* and his unease about the dehumanizing effect of satire – as well as what we have so far seen of his practice – ought to serve as a caution against taking away from his characters that individuality which was always his prime concern. James Kincaid argues that 'Trollope's most serious and pressing claim to be recognized as a major artist rests principally with his subtle and organic use of the dramatized narrator', and the increased finesse which he and others have brought to analysis of the authorial presence is certainly welcome. Nevertheless, the emphasis ought surely to be put the other way round: it is the dramatized *character* that is at the heart of both Trollope's own artistic practice and of his greatness. In any case, how far *is* the narrator dramatized? The question is part of what critics have come to refer to – not without a certain professional relish – as 'the Trollope problem'. Trollope intervenes so readily in his narratives – or at least a device purporting to be him does so – that it is dismaying to find considerable critical disagreement over what he is supposed to think. As we have already seen, the narrator often reminds the reader that the character's way of looking at things has its own legitimacy. Shrewdly observing that it is the general tendency of Trollope's characters to 'seem to take their development out of the writer's hands', Ruth apRoberts argues that such lack of subservience implies a flexible morality on the author's part, a working acceptance of the fact that systems are insufficiently sensitive to local circumstance, and that circumstances alter cases. This relativism gives both novelist and characters the maximum freedom of manoeuvre, and while allowing the fullest human and moral involvement of all parties including the reader, does not predetermine issues in ways which distort Trollope's habits of mind and imagination. The world of Trollope's characters, including those that reappear, is thus acknowledged as being self-governing in a way that Balzac's could never be. As J. Hillis Miller puts it, the general mind in Trollope's novels depends fundamentally on particular minds: 'the individual will . . . is the ground of everything else in society'. As a novelist, Trollope characteristically leans towards devolution; Balzac's instincts are inherently imperialist.

Miss Mackenzie

In Trollope, significance is not demonstrated through the person: it is the person. But how to find out what the person is? One of the main methods by which his characters are discovered is by letting them find their own way through situations that other characters have had to face before them. Trollope's fiction is full of recurring dilemmas, but generally their resolution does not seem fixed in advance because it is the character that seems to decide how things will work out – or, rather, it is the character of the character that so decides. The situations themselves, of course, cannot but be set up by the novelist but – as the following pages hope to show – the degree to which the character is felt to be proceeding under his own steam is closely connected with how much imaginative vitality he seems to have.

These situations invariably include affairs of the heart. Trollope's assumption in the *Autobiography* that 'a novel can hardly be made interesting or successful without love' may appear to be and no doubt partly was a matter of meeting the demands of the market, but he also offers a more dignified defence: 'the passion is one which interests or has interested all. Everyone feels it, has felt it, or expects to feel it.' (XII) In such a matter Trollope, like the rest of his contemporaries, was limited by what his market would stand for. Deeply as Balzac was indebted to Scott, the French novelist had complained (through Daniel d'Arthez in *Illusions Perdues*) that '"Walter Scott est sans passion, il l'ignore, ou peut-être lui était-elle interdite par les moeurs hypocrites de son pays."' In reality, '"la femme porte le désordre dans la société par la passion"', although for Scott and his readers women were the incarnation of duty, little Clarissas. From a Balzacian point of view, if you cannot deal with passion, you cut yourself off from a prime mover in human affairs. Trollope, as we have seen, did not take the obvious Balzacian option in *Can You Forgive Her?* – had Glencora really run away with Burgo, she would certainly have brought some disorder into her society – but in not doing so preserved the character for a more extended if less sensational fictional life. The ever-present love interest is the most repetitive element in Trollope's work, but he does not seem to nag away at it because he wishes he could say more about it than he is allowed to. He accepted the inhibitions and decorums of his period not because he was constrained by the sensitivity of Mudie and the lending libraries on which the mid-Victorian fiction market depended so heavily, but because in practice they did not stop him from writing about love as he wanted to.

In the *Autobiography*, Trollope refers to love as if it were a straightforward state about which there is a consensus (there is a virtually complete black-out as far as any analysis of his own experience is concerned). In the novels authorial statements are likely to end with the assertion that a woman's place is in the home because that is where nature means her to be. He was constant in advising his feminist American friend Kate Field to put matrimony before independence. However, it is easy in practice to detach Trollope's theoretical ideas about love (as about other matters) from the chapter by chapter conduct of the fiction in which it plays such a dominant part – and it is just as well, since those ideas are hardly subtle, complex, or even intelligent enough to sustain him through nearly fifty novels. What sustains us as readers from being numbed by reiteration of the conventional is our sense that in the local event the characters are not merely vehicles of the author's predilections or his period's prejudices. Indeed, Trollope's own orthodoxy – as expressed by the narrator, whether dramatized or not – is so patently solid that it often has the curious but liberating effect of dispensing the character from living up to it.

An intriguing example of a character apparently deciding to take her own emotional life into her own rather unlikely hands is the eponymous heroine of *Miss Mackenzie* (written in 1864 immediately after *Can You Forgive Her?*, published 1865). In *Miss Mackenzie* Trollope states his standard doctrine with a characteristically bluff directness:

> I believe that a desire to get married is the natural state of a woman at the age of – say from twenty-five to thirty-five, and I think also that it is good for the world in general that it should be so ... There is, I know, a feeling abroad among women that this desire is one of which it is expedient that they should become ashamed ... But I confess to an opinion that human nature will be found to be too strong for them. ... A woman's life is not perfect or whole until she has added herself to a husband. (XI)

The next sentence shows a typical blend of fair-mindedness and realism: 'Nor is a man's life perfect or whole till he has added to himself a wife; but the deficiency with the man, though perhaps more injurious to him than its counterpart is to the woman, does not, to the outer eye, so manifestly unfit him for his business in the world.' After this it is disconcerting to find that, according to the *Autobiography*, the book 'was produced with a desire to prove that a novel may be written without any love', even though Trollope adds that the attempt 'breaks down before the conclusion'. (X) In fact, it is difficult to locate any point in the text at which Trollope is clearly altering course. At thirty-six Miss Mackenzie finds herself alone in the world with a legacy of £800 a year from the brother she has long nursed. It is made clear from the beginning that although technically middle-aged she is not really so; her development has been arrested; she is 'still a young woman'. (II) The possibility of her marrying is entertained in the first chapter. She is more than once compared (rather jocosely) with Tennyson's Mariana, but her money effectively emancipates her from any question of a moated grange and subjects her to the attentions of a dealer in oil-cloth with a terrible taste in gloves, a predatory preacher with a frightful squint, and more respectably a genuinely middle-aged widower encumbered with children but with the advantages of being a relative and having a title. The happy ending brought about by her acceptance of the last-named suitor after the gentle gradients of thirty mildly eventful chapters seems an obvious vindication of Trollope's thesis about the natural desirability of marriage.

However, Trollope's assumptions are more in the nature of an underlying premise to the book than a source of such literary interest as it has. What made the book interesting to its first reviewers (including the twenty-two-year-old Henry James who confessed 'we have long entertained for Mr Trollope a partiality of which we have yet been somewhat ashamed') was the novelist's boldness in selecting such unpromising material. James was distressed by Trollope's success in making the dull and disagreeable interesting, but he conceded that the regrettable vulgarity of life had been caught with photographic accuracy. Trollope describes 'those facts which are so close under every one's nose that no one notices them'. The fidelity of Trollope's social observation is naturally less likely to strike us now as remarkable since the manners he here records no longer exist in the same form; when he says of the Reverend Mr Stumfold, a shining light down in Littlebath where Miss Mackenzie tries to start a new life, that 'His friends said that he was evangelical, and his enemies said that he was Low Church' (LII), a nuance is being expressed which more readers would have picked up in Trollope's day than in ours.

Socially speaking Miss Mackenzie hovers on the border between the shabby and the genteel: emotionally speaking, she seems to bear little resemblance to the conventional heroine but they have more in common than might be supposed. What the novel traces is Miss Mackenzie's realization of her own romantic potential, spinster though she may be and pursued for her money. The most touching moment in the story – and, given its prevailing lack of excitement, the most startling – is when, after the first proposal of marriage, she looks at herself in the mirror:

> She moved up her hair from off her ears, knowing where she would find a few that were grey, and shaking her head, as though owning to herself that she was old; but as her fingers ran almost involuntarily across her locks, her touch told her that they were soft and silken; and she looked into her own eyes, and saw that they were bright; and her hand touched the outline of her cheek, and she knew that something of the fresh bloom of youth was still there; and her lips parted, and there were her white teeth; and there came a smile and a dimple, and a slight purpose of laughter in her eye, and then a tear. She pulled her scarf tighter across her bosom, feeling her own form, and then she leaned forward and kissed herself in the glass. (IX)

This little incident can be taken simply as an illustration of Trollope's thesis about a woman's natural destiny, but, in the context of Miss Mackenzie's drab little history, it seems not so much an academic point but a valid moment of individual self-discovery.

Miss Mackenzie – as its reviewers clearly saw – shows in a way that is typical of Trollope's generosity of understanding that people who do not look like creatures of romance to others are so to themselves. When the careworn widower John Ball proposes to Miss Mackenzie for the second time (in the shrubbery on their way back from Twickenham station), they hardly make a glamorous couple, but for her the occasion means that 'romance had turned itself into reality'. (XX) She feels the authentic erotic vertigo – 'Even in the gloom, the trees were going round her, and everything, even her thoughts, were obscure and misty' – and why shouldn't she? The moment seems to belong more to the character than to the author, in that the need of the individual character to find her role has assumed a more urgent fictive interest than the author's conventional definition of that role. Trollope may have begun to write or at least to think about *Miss Mackenzie* as a novel without love, but love was what its heroine turned out to want.

Trollope's original intention to strike out a new path in this book is also undermined by the ghostly presence of motifs found elsewhere in his work. What is Miss Mackenzie's situation but a repetition of Miss Dunstable's, transposed a good way down the social scale? In the Barsetshire novels, Miss Dunstable is courted because she is reputed to be the richest woman in England rather than for her own sake – a fact of which she is well aware; Miss Mackenzie's competence may seem modest by comparison but it is enough to attract attentions which would not otherwise be paid, as the best of her suitors is candid enough to admit. But they are both ladies of a certain age, faced with much the same sort of personal choice between marriage or the kind of spinsterhood represented in *Miss Mackenzie* by Miss Todd, a game old girl with something of Miss Dunstable's vigour of manner brought forward from Trollope's earlier novel *The Bertrams*. The similarity of situation however only emphasizes the dissimilarity of temperament, as the discrepant natures of the middle-aged men that Miss Dunstable and Miss Mackenzie do marry (the proud and self-sufficient Dr Thorne, the unassertive and dejected John Ball) indicates.

Again, the situation as it develops between Miss Mackenzie, her future husband, and Lady Ball, is highly reminiscent of comparable moments of impasse in the Barset chronicles. Lady Ball, regarding an alliance between her son and someone as grotesquely unsuitable as this poor relation as unthinkable, tries to browbeat Miss Mackenzie out of it, rather as Lady De Courcy did with Mary Thorne, or Lady Lufton did with Lucy Robarts, or Archdeacon Grantly did with Grace Crawley. As in those cases, the attempt merely rouses a spirit of self-assertion which ensures its failure. Miss Mackenzie is not, as her predecessors were, in the first flush of youth, but the emotional contour of her resistance to pressure is very similar.

Other connections with other novels by Trollope could be made. The plot of *Miss Mackenzie*, such as it is, turns on a question of inheritance, as is often the case. Owing to some legal twist it appears that the heroine is not entitled to the cash after all. The fictional possibilities offered by an inheritance that is not an inheritance are more elaborately developed in some later novels (to be considered below), but Trollope had already begun to sense what can be done with the basic notion, however sketchily handled in this case. Interconnections of a more obvious kind are provided by brief reappearances in *Miss Mackenzie* of such figures from the great world as Lady Glencora, Lady Hartletop, and the sprightly Mrs Conway Sparkes, not to mention those dilatory solicitors Messrs Slow and Bideawhile, consulted by a wide range of Trollope's characters, from the Greshams in *Doctor Thorne* to the Longstaffes in *The Way We Live Now*.

Miss Mackenzie is not one of Trollope's stronger performances, but it would be a mistake to attribute any weakness of impression to the fact that at certain points the author seems to be going over familiar ground. Whatever sense we may have of the heroine's individuality is enhanced rather than diminished by those aspects of her nature and situation which are directly comparable with those of other people in other novels. The truth is that Trollope's work is often, though not invariably, at its strongest when he is in some way repeating himself. The artistic stature of the two novel sequences is profoundly dependent on the most obvious form of repetition, the use of the reappearing character. In his other novels what recurs is not the person but certain types of predicament, some of which are now to be studied. Parallelism of situation encourages individual personality to emerge since few things serve to define the differences between people more sharply than putting them in the same boat. For Trollope the use of recurrence as a creative method was complementary to that of reappearance; it provided another way of living with his characters 'in the full reality of established intimacy', an intimacy that he rightly saw as the cause of 'whatever success I have obtained'. The formation and development of such relationships was to him sufficiently important to be an artistic end in itself; they did not need to be validated by becoming the means of realizing some Balzacian grand design.

Vacillation and Indecision

In the *Autobiography* Trollope classed himself as a 'realist' rather than as a 'sensationalist' although he did not regard the two terms as mutually exclusive.[2] Violent events certainly occur but they are usually few and far between. But Trollope's refusal to earn the reader's attention through adventitious suspense was offset by his extraordinarily secure command of psychological process. Indeed, the process is the point, rather than the result; that is why discussing Trollope in summary terms tends to be so unsatisfactory. One reads Trollope not to find out simply what happened in the end, but to understand the stages by which it came to happen and was bound to happen, given the individual personalities involved. And even when events of some abruptness do occur, the stress is characteristically on reaction rather than on the action itself. The effect of this emphasis is often to defuse incidents that might in other hands have seemed melodramatic: suicide, attempted murder, assault and battery are easily accommodated within Trollope's 'spirit of calm recital'. Much of the time, however, the recital is calm because nothing sensational takes place.

The Belton Estate

The Belton Estate, for instance, involves a suicide, but it occurs off-stage and merely precipitates the state of affairs with which the novel deals. Considering that the novel (written and published in 1865) originally took up three volumes, it is remarkable how little actually occurs in it. James's review sums up the essential plot not unfairly: 'The lady loves amiss, but discovers it in time, and invests her affections more safely. Such, in strictness, is the substance of the tale; but it is filled out as Mr Trollope alone knows how to fill out the primitive meagreness of his dramatic skeletons.' Nevertheless, Michael Sadleir was right to regard the novel as quintessentially Trollopian.

The thirty-two chapters of *The Belton Estate* concern themselves almost exclusively with the single question of whether Clara Amedroz will marry Captain Aylmer or Will Belton. Aylmer is the MP for her part of Somerset, and the heir of Clara's courtesy 'aunt' who wishes them to marry; he seems to be eminently eligible. Will is her cousin who farms impetuously in Norfolk. When Clara's querulous father dies, Clara is unprovided for, her inheritance having been wasted by her suicidal brother. She could accept from Captain Aylmer the £1,500 that her 'aunt' intended to give her before dying suddenly; or she could collude with Will to evade the entail which makes him the heir of Belton, or at least accept the £800 a year that the lawyers will allow him to make over. The difference in the two amounts of money is a measure of the correct legalism of the one suitor and the reckless generosity of the other. Under the influence of his aunt's death, Aylmer proposes to Clara and is accepted with rather more energy than he had anticipated. Will appears on the scene too late, proposes to Clara too soon, and has to be content with her request that he be a 'brother' to her. It is perfectly clear to the reader early on that Clara has made a mistake; the novel simply charts the stages by which she comes to admit this first to herself and then to others. The various railway journeys made by the characters (to which James refers in his review) have a certain significance in this development: trips from the West Country to London and from London to the Aylmer family seat in Yorkshire were feasible enough by the mid-1860s but still not lightly undertaken (especially by unattached ladies), so that the decision to make them can usefully reveal how far a person was prepared to put himself out. Will thinks nothing of running down to Somerset from East Anglia; Captain Aylmer is a distinctly more reluctant passenger.

If the novel's paucity of incident had been combined with a clearly didactic intention, the result would have been insufferable. Its morality is certainly unexceptionable, but this is because it exists more as a set of agreed premises to the story than as a body of doctrine which the narrative is designed to enforce. A novelist of a more retributory kind would surely have made more fuss over the Askerton business. Mrs Askerton is apparently Clara's only genteel and conversible neighbour, but it turns out that she is also a woman with a past. Now formally married to Colonel Askerton, she left her first husband 'under his protection' (she herself says candidly that she lived with him as his mistress). The circumstances were extenuating: her husband drank intolerably and conveniently confirmed his dipsomania by dying of delirium tremens. Was it proper for Trollope's heroine to associate with someone who had thus strayed beyond the pale, even though she had now strayed back in again? A nice point in mid-Victorian ethics, but Trollope's use of it is essentially pragmatic. Although he goes through the motions of deploring Mrs Askerton's 'sin', he is more interested in reaching a properly balanced assessment of her general character: 'though she was not high-minded, so also was she not ungenerous'. (XXI) Nor does he make any novelistic capital out of an artful delay in the extraction of her 'secret', involving perhaps a battle of wits in the manner of Wilkie Collins. Mrs Askerton's real importance in the book lies in the way in which the moral ambiguity of her situation is exploited by the other characters rather than by the novelist. Captain Aylmer's dragonish mother grasps eagerly at the excuse it provides for rejecting a prospective daughter-in-law of whom she disapproves; Clara stands by her friend partly out of sympathetic loyalty but also because it gives her an issue through which she can assert her independence of Aylmer influence and which allows her to feel less guilty about breaking off her engagement. Any theoretical questions raised by the morality or otherwise of Mrs Askerton's situation are thus shelved in favour of the tactical exploitation of it by her friends and enemies.

Less peripherally, Clara's final preference for Belton rather than Aylmer is a predilection that it would be tempting, but tactless, to over-moralize. It would be easy to construe the novel as recommending the ready expression of strong impulses of feeling. Both hero and heroine are highly emotional and act on impulse. Will's physical urgency and energy is much stressed. His tendency to seize Clara and kiss her passionately is quite unlike Captain Aylmer's chilly physical restraint, and has its analogue more in Clara's enthusiasm of response to Aylmer's initial proposal. There is no doubt that the hearty and honest feelings of Clara and Will are, in Trollope's view, to be preferred to the prudential timidities of the Aylmers, but Aylmer is not therefore to be regarded as the villain of the piece; it is not his fault that he is not warm-blooded. When first introduced, Aylmer is said to be 'member for Perivale on the Low Church interest, and . . . therefore, when at Perivale he was decidedly a Low Churchman'. He goes to church three times on Sundays, and 'could say a sharp word or two in season about vestments' and 'was strong against candles'. Trollope comments drily, 'I am not aware that the peculiarity stuck to him very closely at Aylmer Castle . . . or among his friends in London', but is quick to add 'but there was no hypocrisy in this, as the world goes'. (I) Aylmer's behaviour may not meet the highest standards, but whose does? Trollope's casual wrong-footing of the conventional reader is typical of his general reluctance to expect more from characters in fiction than from people in life. The Aylmer way of life is not admirable – Trollope's sketch of the respectable indigencies of life at Aylmer Park is sharply satirical – but Aylmer is not to be written off:

> What a cold-hearted, ungenerous wretch he must have been! That will be the verdict against him. But the verdict will be untrue. Cold-hearted and ungenerous he was; but he was no wretch, – as men and women are now-a-days called wretches. He was chilly hearted, but yet quite capable of enough love to make him a good son, a good husband, and a good father too. And though he was ungenerous from the nature of his temperament, he was not close-fisted or over covetous. And he was a just man, desirous of obtaining nothing that was not fairly his own. But, in truth, the artists have been so much in the habit of painting for us our friends' faces without any of those flaws and blotches with which work and high living are apt to disfigure us, that we turn in disgust from a portrait in which the roughnesses and pimples are made apparent. (XIX)

Aylmer is a decent enough man, by his own lights, and the fact that he will not do for Clara is not necessarily a serious aspersion of his character. It must be attributed rather to those incompatibilities of personality which appear so clearly in his dealings with her. When Aylmer first proposes, not suspecting the strength of Clara's feeling for him, he is unprepared for the look of triumph which the realization of her wishes brings – 'his eye almost quailed beneath

hers'. But Clara is too preoccupied with her own feelings to consider what may be Aylmer's: 'As regarded herself, she was quite
equal to the occasion; but had she known more of the inner feelings
of men and women in general, she would have been slower to
show her own.' (X) Clara's sincerity has its insensitive side. Will is
guilty of the same impulsiveness when he insists on expressing his
own devotion regardless of Clara's possible reaction. Neither show
that delicacy as regards the claims of others which, say, the
favoured couple of a Jane Austen novel would be expected to
display. Clara is from the first strong-minded, and ironically the
force of her final rejection of Aylmer has the mortifying effect of
arousing the opposite response to the one wished for. As she speaks
of the opposition between herself and his mother, Aylmer

> was seated near her, on a chair from which he was leaning
> over towards her, holding his hat in both hands between his
> legs. Now, as he listened to her, he drew his chair still nearer,
> ridding himself of his hat, which he left upon the carpet, and
> keeping his eyes upon hers as though he were fascinated.
> (XXVIII)

The visualization of the whole scene is very exact:

> He had his hand upon her arm, having attempted to take her
> hand. In preventing that she had succeeded, but she could not
> altogether make herself free from him without rising. For a
> moment she had paused, – paused as though she were about
> to yield. For a moment, as he looked into her eyes, he had
> thought that he would again be victorious. Perhaps there was
> something in his glance, some too visible return of triumph to
> his eyes, which warned her of her danger. 'No!' she said,
> getting up and walking away from him; 'no!' (XXIX)

When he is not thus galvanized by Clara's presence and energy,
Aylmer subsides into his usual tepid calm, but Trollope shows us
enough of their relationship at close quarters (the passage dealing
with their life in their aunt's house together immediately after her
death but before his proposal is also very subtly done) to make clear
both why it began and why it did not continue. We come to
understand their engagement and its collapse not as a quasi-
allegorical encounter of opposed moral qualities, but as a sequence

of individual responses to everyday events, none of them apparently decisive but cumulatively irresistible.

It is Clara's increasing awareness of the laws of her own nature that takes her away from Aylmer and towards Will. In an early rehearsal of their respective virtues, one of the reasons why the former is initially preferred by Clara to the latter is that whereas Will is admittedly more generous, more energetic, and in person 'undoubtedly the superior', Aylmer 'knew everybody, and had read everything' and understood 'the inner world of worlds which governs the world' (VI) – the world, in other words, of the Palliser novels. But her engagement to Aylmer does not expand Clara's provincial horizons; instead, she spends a betrayingly large amount of her time thinking about her farming cousin. Her first feelings about him are that he is 'a dear cousin, and safe against love-making!' Trollope's comment – 'Why that warranty against love-making should be a virtue in her eyes I cannot, perhaps, explain' (IV) – seems disingenuous; the surface reason for Clara's relief is related to her attraction to Aylmer, but Trollope also wishes to suggest that Clara unconsciously uses Aylmer as a protection from what are already felt as the more urgent claims of her cousin. When Will leaves Belton at the end of his first visit, Clara, even though she has rejected him, gets up early in the morning to see him off although 'she hardly understood . . . why she was doing this' (VI); she says goodbye to him with her eyes full of tears.

Clara is suspiciously quick to release Aylmer from his engagement when he rather ineptly gives her grounds for supposing that his proposal was prompted by a promise to his dying aunt; shortly after this she can reflect that 'it seemed but the other day that [Will] had been with her up on the rock in the park; but as she thought of Captain Aylmer, to whom she had become engaged only yesterday, and from whom she had separated herself only that morning, she felt that an eternity of time had passed since she had parted from him'. (XII) Such sensations indicate the emotional undertow of her life clearly enough, and it is unsurprising (and, from a formal point of view, pleasing) to find that, half-way through the novel, she is poised midway between the two men: 'in truth, she hardly knew which was the man she loved!' (XVI)

Will's next passionate embrace so disturbs Clara that she throws herself on the sofa sobbing, 'her whole body . . . shaken as with convulsions'. (XXII) She then preaches him 'a solemn, sweet sermon on the wickedness of yielding to momentary impulses', after which she feels much better, perhaps because it restores some balance of power between them after a moment in which she is forced to realize how vulnerable to Will's passion she really is. The need to seal off the incident in this way is in itself an indication that she is more thrown by it than she cares to acknowledge. After this, and the disastrous visit to Aylmer Park and the accompanying hostilities with Lady Aylmer, it is simply a matter of Clara being brought – both by her friends and by her own increasing self-knowledge – to the point of accepting Will (another passionate scene by the rock in the park) and also of accepting the shame of having publicly changed her mind. Perhaps indeed Clara herself helps unconsciously to precipitate her own capitulation: her later appeals to Will to go on being 'a brother to her' seem almost provocative rather than discouraging. From time to time Clara has bemoaned the dependence of her state in particular and that of the single woman in general; but once she concedes her own dependence on Will, these complaints discontinue. Aylmer would not have been right for her because he was too dependent on her; in all their scenes, she naturally assumes the ascendancy. In Will, Clara has met her match.

No general principles are inevitably implied by this conclusion. One could of course say that Clara has discovered that a warm, energetic humanity is to be preferred to glacial respectability and worldliness, and that the novel therefore records her moral education. But one has only to think for a moment of a novel which really does take its heroine's education seriously and has the vocabulary to do so – Trollope's admired *Pride and Prejudice* perhaps – to see that the experience of reading *The Belton Estate* cannot be usefully discussed in such terms. Clara's happiness as the end of the story belongs to her; it is not prescriptive; if we are glad for her, it is because we have lived with her rather than because we approve of or admire her. The final pages of the novel give by way of a postscript an account of a dinner party at Belton a year or two later with not only Captain Aylmer and his new bride but also the contaminating Askertons as guests. In Thackeray's hands such a conclusion would have been laceratingly or at least uneasily ironic. In fact, it simply bears witness to the undidactic serenity of Trollope's tolerance.

Such complaisance can easily be construed as complacency. What infuriated Henry James was that the novel's very palpable artistic merits should be, as usual, so unaccompanied by artistic intelligence:

> 'The Belton Estate' is a *stupid* book; and in a much deeper sense than that of being simply dull, for a dull book is always a book that might have been lively. A dull book is a failure. Mr Trollope's story is stupid and a success. It is essentially, organically, consistently stupid; stupid in direct proportion to its strength. It is without a single idea. It is utterly incompetent to the primary functions of a book, of whatever nature, namely – to suggest thought.

James's indictment is one from which more recent critics have tried to rescue Trollope by suggesting that his novels, when squeezed by modern methods of analysis, can be made to yield more intellectual substance than was apparent to James at first pressing. All the same, his arguments in this early review have great force. His remark, a little later in his notice, that all Trollope's 'incidents are, if we may so express it, *empirical*', could hardly put the matter more suggestively. The point is tellingly illustrated when *The Belton Estate* is compared with *Can You Forgive Her?*, written in the previous year. Both heroines are compulsive vacillators and both stories have a number of comparable elements, but the way in which Trollope recombines them shows how far he is from relying on stable formulae – and how far the characters are from being victims of fixed authorial ideas. Neither novel can be taken to demonstrate much beyond what obtains in its own particular case. The indecisive careers of Clara Amedroz and Alice Vavasor are intriguingly parallel, but a reader experiencing the books consecutively would not find himself thinking that the girls were closely alike, despite the similarity of their histories and ages. Alice's shivers and shrinkings are a long way from Clara's aggressive forwardness. In the end, Alice gets the world of London politics she says she longs for; Clara gives it up to be the wife of a Somerset squire. In *The Belton Estate* the impulsive man Will Belton is favoured; in *Can You Forgive Her?* George Vavasor, comparably energetic if less benevolent, is rejected. John Grey, Alice's eventual husband, shares with Will an East Anglian address but little else; the one is a Cambridge scholar, the other a farmer fairly described by James as having 'a head large enough for a hundred prejudices, but too small for a single opinion'. Both of them have a constancy that seems at times almost ruthless in its tenacity, and for which they are rewarded by the lady of their choice. There are plenty of other men in Trollope's fiction, however, who exhibit a comparable devotion and get nothing out of it: one has only to recall Johnny Eames's unavailing loyalty (*The Last Chronicle of Barset* was Trollope's next major novel after *The Belton Estate*), or the rejected addresses of another East Anglian squire, Roger Carbury, *The Way We Live Now*. Repetition, in other words, is the means by which human variousness, male and female, is apprehended.

The Claverings

In Trollope's novels, the man who changes his mind is quite as common as the woman who cannot make up hers. However, Trollope was conscious of the fact that forgiving her might be easier than exonerating him; a woman's weakness might be flutteringly feminine where a man's indecision would be spinelessly wet if not downright dishonourable. Trollope shows himself nervously aware of the problem in *The Claverings* (written at the end of 1864 between *Miss Mackenzie* and *The Belton Estate*, published 1867). Harry Clavering is jilted by his cousin Julia Brabazon because, although she loves him, he has no money; she marries instead the rich but debauched Lord Ongar. Harry is naturally cut up but, in what looks like a strong show of manly independence, he gives up his college fellowship, abandons any thought of the Church, and takes the ungentlemanly step of joining a well-known firm of civil engineers. He then becomes attached to the daughter of one of the partners. Lord Ongar has meanwhile drunk himself to death in Italy and his widow returns, secretly hoping to give Harry the benefit of her late husband's funds and looking to him for support. Harry cannot bring himself to tell her of his engagement, and Julia's still formidable sexual appeal makes him pledge himself to her once more. His escape from this impasse owes more to the efforts of his mother and prospective sister-in-law than to any innate strength of character – his resistance being weakened at a critical period (as Thackeray's Pendennis was) by a timely fever. It is not surprising that some reviewers found Harry's career less than dignified: 'one of the most insipid, well-intentioned, and weak-willed young exquisites who ever parted their hair in the middle, and didn't know their own minds', complained the *London Review*. Mrs Oliphant in *Blackwood's*, noting that 'uncomfortable vacilla-tion between two lovers ... has been for some time past [Trol-lope's] favourite topic', felt that Harry's situation was 'not an elevated position for a man'; 'the reader feels slightly ashamed of him'; the blunder he makes 'goes against the very character of a hero'. When a reviewer of Mrs Oliphant's calibre makes this objec-tion, one can see that Trollope had real grounds for apprehension about Harry Clavering's reception. He makes an early attempt to offset the reader's impression that there is not much that is heroic about the novel's hero by arguing that although Harry doubtless had faults and weaknesses, 'there may be a question whether as much evil would not be known of most men, let them be heroes or not heroes, if their characters were, so to say, turned inside out before our eyes'. (X) A more spirited defence appears in Chapter XXVIII, where Trollope complains that 'Perhaps no terms have been so injurious to the profession of the novelist as those two words, hero and heroine. In spite of the latitude which is allowed to the writer in putting his own interpretation upon these words, something heroic is still expected; whereas, if he attempt to paint from nature, how little that is heroic should he describe!' Harry's weakness in regard to Lady Ongar may be unheroic, but it is natural because 'the first love, if that was true, is ever there ... love never dies'. 'But it is not to be thought that I excuse him altogether,' Trollope hastens to add. 'A man, though he may love many, should be devoted only to one.'

Trollope's attitude to Harry Clavering seems throughout the novel to be marked by this rather embarrassed mixture of hesitancy and endorsement. There is not the kind of intimacy between them as there is between the novelist and Johnny Eames or even Crosbie. Perhaps this is partly due to the fact that Harry's commitment to his work is suspect. His decision to resign his fellowship and become an engineer is announced in terms that are suspiciously grandiose: '"I could have no scope in the church for that sort of ambition which would satisfy me. Look at such men as Locke, and Stephenson, and Brassey. They are the men who seem to me to do most in the world."' (II) His praise of such self-made men hardly squares with his (and his father's) class hostility to the pretensions of Mr Saul, a socially inferior curate, to Fanny Clavering's hand, and it is strained when he has actually to buckle down to the narrow discipline his training demands (though we see virtually nothing of him actually at work – Trollope could not command in this field the kind of inside knowledge he had of the public service). Theodore Burton, for whom Harry works in London – a man who feels as Trollope did that '"work never palls on us, whereas pleasure always does"' – thinks that Clavering's fellowship has encouraged him to think that '"the hard work of life is pretty well over with him"'. (VIII) Certainly, the novel itself relieves Harry of the necessity of earning his living by a denouement – ostentatiously prepared for – in which the two obstacles between him and the Clavering estate and title are conveniently drowned in the North Sea. The novelist almost appears to conspire with the womenfolk in the novel to dismiss Harry to happiness. Trollope admits that 'justice was outraged' by the welcome given him by the women in his return to the matrimonially straight and narrow. Any word that would have seemed to imply some fault was avoided by them with a tact that 'excels the skill of men'. (XLI) Trollope seems to mean not just that the women were simply more tactful than men would have been on this occasion but that their tact is inherently superior to what we might expect from the stronger sex. The sort of generalization about men and women that occurs earlier in the chapter – 'To confess, submit, and be accepted as confessing and submitting, comes naturally to the female mind' – carried an implication that was not acceptable to Mrs Oliphant: 'It seems to be Mr Trollope's idea that, so long as he is faithful to her, a woman can see no blemish in a man whom she has once loved. But we fear this is far from being the fact . . . Women are neither so passive nor so grateful as they are made out to be.'

As so often happens in Trollope, the novel itself provides an exception which challenges its ostensible rule. For all its murmurings about what is 'woman-like', the most interesting woman in it is, according to conventional criteria, markedly unfeminine, – the most interesting woman, that is, to Trollope as well as to us. The *Spectator* was driven to concede that 'few readers will fail to find that . . . there is more that is fascinating in Lady Ongar, in spite of

her great, her unwomanly sin in marrying such a man as Lord
Ongar for rank and money, than in Florence Burton'. The security
of Trollope's command of the anti-heroine's mind and manner is
apparent from the first chapter. It is clear that her characteristic tone
is already completely audible to him. It is, in fact, in dialogue that
she generally seems to have most life; her crucial conversations
with Harry (Chapter XXI, Chapter XLIII), as well as her meeting
with Mrs Theodore Burton when she goes to plead on Florence's
behalf (Chapter XXXVII), and her final encounter with Florence
herself (Chapter XLVII), tend to resolve themselves into scenes;
her manner is naturally actressy. She creates round her a field of
emotional intensity and heightened physical awareness:

> 'Does it not seem odd, Harry, that you and I should be
> sitting, talking together in this way?' She was leaning now
> towards him, across the table, and one hand was raised to her
> forehead while her eyes were fixed intently upon his. The
> attitude was one which he felt to express extreme intimacy.
> She would not have sat in that way, pressing back her hair
> from her brow, with all appearance of widowhood banished
> from her face, in the presence of any but a dear and close
> friend. He did not think of this, but he felt that it was so,
> almost by instinct. 'I have such a tale to tell you,' she said;
> 'such a tale!' (VII)

It is not surprising that after this meeting Harry feels that 'a new
form of life had been opened to him'. (VIII) Even if her speeches
about her love and misfortunes have a certain staginess, she makes
the idiom seem spontaneous. Although in the weaker position, she
dictates the actual development and rhythm of each encounter. She
knows when and how to make her exit:

> 'I thought, when I returned, that bad as I had been I might
> still do some good in the world. But it is as they tell us in the
> sermons. One cannot make good come out of evil. I have
> done evil, and nothing but evil has come from the evil which I
> have done. Nothing but evil will come from it. As for being
> useful in the world, – I know of what use I am! When women
> hear how wretched I have been, they will be unwilling to sell
> themselves as I did.' Then she made her way to the door, and

left the room, going out with quiet steps, and closing the lock
behind her without a sound. (XLV)

But, as this last passage suggests, there is nevertheless something
over-schematic in the whole conception of Lady Ongar. When left
to herself, she thinks of her situation (as in Chapter XVI for
instance) in terms of conventional judgements on it ('But her youth
had been stained, her beauty had lost its freshness; and as for her
wealth, had she not stolen it?'), suggesting a more timid temperament than the apparently frank and poised worldliness of the first
chapter leads us to expect. There is too great a collusion between
Julia's harsh judgement of herself and the novel's official programme for the character to seem quite free. At times she sounds as
if she would have been more at home in strong society melodramas
or even in the type of sensation novel from which Trollope
explicitly dissociated himself. The sequence in the Isle of Wight
when she is pursued and surprised on the cliff-top by Count
Pateroff, who tries to exploit his knowledge of her husband's last
days so as to manoeuvre her into marriage, has a distinctly Collinsy
air, as indeed have the comic machinations of the Count's sister,
Sophie Gordeloup. At any rate, the fact that Julia Ongar is a
woman with a past to live down, puts her into a different category
from Alice Vavasor and Clara Amedroz, who also made the wrong
choice initially but were saved, or saved themselves, from living it
out – and whose motives were at least in part more disinterested.
The experience of her marriage is only alluded to in shuddering
innuendo, and a certain amount of vagueness (perhaps Trollope's
own) shrouds what actually happened as Lord Ongar's delirium
tremens finally took its toll. As we have seen, when Trollope came
to deal with another woman who made the wrong choice and lived
to regret it – Lady Laura in the Phineas novels – we are not cut off
in this way from the conjugal life and thus from a fuller understanding of the character's experience.

Of course, in Lady Laura's case we have the advantage of her
reappearance in two successive novels. In the *Autobiography* Trollope notes that in *The Claverings* he denied himself the opportunity
of introducing characters already familiar from other novels
(although he has forgotten that there is a mention of the Proudies in
Chapter II: '"Bishop Proudie was vulgar and obtrusive, such being

the nature of his wife, who instructs him.''') But even if Lady Ongar had had the opportunity of an extended life, it is not at all clear what she, and Trollope, would have done with it. At the end of *The Claverings*, she retires to the remote obscurity of Tenby with her newly widowed sister, having resigned most of her ill-gotten wealth in a burst of expiatory renunciation. She insists that her punishment should fit her original crime in a way which might have indicated a promising morbidity of the kind we have seen suggestions of in Alice Vavasor, were it not for the fact that her acquiescence in her fate seems primarily the result of authorial unease – almost of a failure of nerve.

However, *The Claverings* itself provides at least one instance where the proprieties of the case do strike Trollope as morally outrageous. When Sir Hugh Clavering and his brother are drowned, their passing has to be commemorated in a sermon in the parish church; Trollope remarks that 'It is, perhaps, well that such sermons should be preached.' (XLIV) The trouble is that both men lived lives of total selfishness and, in the case of Sir Hugh, habitual cruelty: 'I doubt whether either of them had ever contributed anything willingly to the comfort or happiness of any human being'. The fact is that the world was well rid of them – but how can you say that in a sermon? Anyway, as Trollope drily observes, 'not so are sermons preached'. Trollope's characteristic impatience with hypocrisy has here led him into a reckless questioning of the proprieties not easily harmonized with what the *Saturday Review* called his 'wonderful faith in respectability', as illustrated by his treatment of Lady Ongar – and by her own belated trust in sermons.

The relative severity of that treatment is also likely to make one wonder why Harry is let off so lightly. It is true that Julia actually went through with her mercenary marriage whereas Harry only temporarily contemplated betraying his fiancée, but to dispatch her to the outer darkness of Tenby while rewarding him with the prospect of a baronetcy hardly seems equitable. The double standards involved are tellingly exposed by Theodore Burton when in his impatience with Harry's conduct he asks his wife

'Can you believe any good of a man who tells you to your face that he is engaged to two women at once?'

258

'I think I can,' said Cecilia, hardly venturing to express so dangerous an opinion above her breath.

'And what would you think of a woman who did so?'

'Ah, that is so different! I cannot explain it, but you know that it is different.'

'I know that you would forgive a man anything, and a woman nothing.' (XXXI)

Mrs Burton's helpless 'It is different' would no doubt have been endorsed by most of Trollope's readers, but it does little to make the morality of *The Claverings* more intelligent or coherent. Trollope's explicit engagement with nice points of social ethics, therefore, can make for inconsistency and insecurity. In his best work, however, the dramatized experience of his characters becomes so much more important than his commentary on it that any inadequacies in the latter are not seriously damaging; it is only when the fictive life is undernourished, as it is in *The Claverings*, that the lack of intellectual rigour becomes compromising.

The Eustace Diamonds

Although particularly addicted to his 'inveterate system' in the mid-1860s, Trollope's interest in the indecisive hero or heroine continued to show itself in later work. *The Eustace Diamonds* (written 1869–70, published 1872) explicitly returns to the question of whether he who hesitates can be heroic. The vacillator in this case is Frank Greystock, a talented young lawyer who already has a seat in Parliament but who hasn't begun to earn the kind of money needed to advance the career so promisingly begun. His clerical father, the Dean of Bobsborough, is not in a position to help much. Like Phineas Finn (although we see hardly anything of Frank's Parliamentary activities), Frank would do well to marry well. The opportunity to do so occurs when his cousin Lady Eustace returns after seeing off a depraved but titled husband to a premature demise in Italy (exactly as Lady Ongar had done in *The Claverings*). As a young widow, she looks to Frank for protection (as Julia Ongar had done to Harry Clavering), and in both cases the relationship is made easier if also more ambiguous by the cousinship involved: it permits a kind of intimacy that would otherwise be improper. But Frank, like Harry, has a prior engagement; he is committed to Lucy Morris, the governess at Lady Fawn's. There is much to be said for Lucy: '"a treasure"' says the author, and even Frank's mother agrees that she is '"a perfect lady"'. (III) But unlike Lizzie Eustace, she has neither birth, beauty, nor cash, and the advantages she can bring Frank in his assault on the world are merely private and domestic. Domestic, moreover, on a modest scale; in Chapter XIII Trollope defines the choice before Frank in allusive, even journalistic terms which must have made it very clear to his first readers exactly what social distinctions were involved. One kind of life before him was 'the Belgrave-cum-Pimlico life, the scene of which might extend itself to South Kensington, enveloping the parks and coming round over Park Lane, and through Grosvenor Square and Berkeley Square back to Piccadilly', in other words, the enclave of the Upper Ten Thousand. Marrying Lucy would mean giving up his clubs, his rooms at the Grosvenor Hotel for 'dim domestic security and the neighbourhood of Regent's Park'. Trollope's characters at this period tend to feel that settling anywhere north of Oxford Street represents an acknowledgement of, if not failure, at least modified ambitions and reduced expectations. By Chapter XVIII Frank's thoughts have become even more gloomily suburban as he contemplates 'a small house somewhere, probably near the Swiss Cottage' from which he would have 'to come up and down to his chambers by the underground railway'. Frank, like Trollope himself, is acutely aware of the difference in status that these residential alternatives indicate. Lizzie Eustace's £4,000 a year, plus a castle in Scotland, would certainly relieve Frank of the indignity of what a writer in 1885 cited by *OED* calls 'the stuffy underground railway journey to Baker Street', which is what Frank would have had to endure on his way home to Swiss Cottage.

For Frank, therefore, as for so many of Trollope's characters, the question of who to marry is an integral part of the larger problem of how to make one's way. As the author says, Frank intends to get on in the world, and believes that happiness is to be achieved by success. It is understandable that, when it comes to implementing his engagement with Lucy – an engagement that was precipitated by genuine love and an impulse from his better side – Frank tends to waver. He is much employed on Lizzie's affairs throughout the novel – defending her retention of the Eustace family diamonds which she claims were given to her outright by her late husband, harassing the unfortunate Lord Fawn who is manoeuvred by her into an engagement from which he understandably wishes to retreat – and it is, moreover, clear that Lizzie herself would be happy to submit entirely to Frank. He comes to see the inherent duplicity of Lizzie's nature eventually, and returns to the loyal Lucy, but it would have been easy for him to have gone the way of Crosbie, in *The Small House at Allington*. The interest, as Trollope explains in a valuably explicit passage, derives from seeing whether he will or won't do so:

> . . . There are human beings who, though of necessity single in body, are dual in character; – in whose breasts not only is evil always fighting against good, – but to whom evil is sometimes horribly, hideously evil, but is sometimes also not hideous at all. Of such men it may be said that, Satan obtains an intermittent grasp, from which, when it is released, the rebound carries them high amidst virtuous resolutions and a thorough love of things good and noble. Such men, – or women, – may hardly, perhaps, debase themselves with the more vulgar vices. They will not be rogues, or thieves, or drunkards, – or, perhaps, liars; but ambition, luxury, self-indulgence, pride, and covetousness will get a hold of them, and in various moods will be to them virtues in lieu of vices. Such a man was Frank Greystock, who could walk along the banks of the quiet, trout-giving Bob, at Bobsborough, whipping the river with his rod, telling himself that the world lost for love would be a bad thing well lost for a fine purpose; and who could also stand, with his hands in his trousers pockets, looking down upon the pavement, in the purlieus of the courts at Westminster, and swear to himself that he would win the game, let the cost to his heart be what it might. (XVIII)

The quality of generalization here is hardly of the calibre that George Eliot would have offered and the momentary touch about Satan is uncharacteristic, but it illustrates, in its plain way, a theory of human nature in which vacillation plays an essential part. But

Trollope's air of stating what we all know to be obvious, his qualifications – the 'rebound' towards virtue which follows a bad patch, the range of possibilities hinted at in 'various moods' – betray his interest in the practice of the matter, the actual mechanics and circumstances of vacillation. It is the interaction between the individual's nature and the particulars of his situation that will decide which element in his dual nature will preponderate, and this involves too many variables for prediction to be easy. Such a dual nature can hardly be heroic in the conventional sense of the term, and it is not surprising that, with the example of Frank's hesitation before us, Trollope should again launch into an attack on art that idealizes, and defends the presentation of things as they really are:

There arose at one time a school of art, which delighted to paint the human face as perfect in beauty; and from that time to this we are discontented unless every woman is drawn for us as a Venus, or, at least, a Madonna. I do not know that we have gained much by this untrue portraiture, either in beauty or in art. There may be made for us a pretty thing to look at, no doubt; – but we know that that pretty thing is not really visaged as the mistress whom we serve, and whose lineaments we desire to perpetuate on the canvas. The winds of heaven, or the fleshpots of Egypt, or the midnight gas, – passions, pains, and, perhaps, rouge and powder, have made her something different. But still there is the fire in her eye, and the eager eloquence of her mouth, and something, too, perhaps, left of the departing innocence of youth, which the painter might give us without the Venus or the Madonna touches. But the painter does not dare to do it. Indeed, he has painted so long after the other fashion that he would hate the canvas before him, were he to give way to the rouge-begotten roughness or to the fleshpots, – or even to the winds. And how, my lord, would you, who are giving hundreds, more than hundreds, for this portrait of your dear one, like to see it in print from the art critic of the day, that she is a brazen-faced hoyden who seems to have had a glass of wine too much, or to have been making hay? (XXXV)

The apostrophe at the end of this passage is too Thackerayean to be comfortable, but the style soon recovers to a more truly Trollopian firmness:

> We cannot have heroes to dine with us. There are none. And were these heroes to be had, we should not like them. But neither are our friends villains, – whose every aspiration is for evil, and whose every moment is a struggle for some achievement worthy of the devil.
>
> The persons whom you cannot care for in a novel, because they are so bad, are the very same that you so dearly love in your life, because they are so good.

The reference back to the reader's own moral world is as natural a reflex in Trollope as are the reminders of other modern facts like underground railways. Trollope's patent eagerness to carry the reader with him is here prompted by his desire to deflect censure from and promote sympathy for Frank Greystock, and such discussions in Trollope generally have the effect of returning us back to the individual case rather than of assimilating that case to what George Eliot calls the 'vast sum of human conditions' available to 'the mind that has a large vision of relations'. (*The Mill on the Floss*, Book Fourth, Ch. I) So that when Trollope returns after his exordium on the heroic to 'our hero, Frank Greystock, falling lamentably short in his heroism' we are in a sufficiently empirical state of mind to enter imaginatively into Frank's self-deceptions. Frank's motive in going home to his constituency and family may have been

> because he felt, that were he to determine to be false to Lucy, he would there receive sympathy in his treachery. His mother would, at any rate, think that it was well, and his father would acknowledge that the fault committed was in the original engagement with poor Lucy, and not in the treachery.

Frank knows that he can rely on his family to bail him out, morally speaking. Or rather, as Trollope's tentative 'may' suggests, he would know it if he allowed his thoughts to surface sufficiently for them to become explicit. It is in such analyses of semiconscious subterfuge that the real subtlety of Trollope's art is often to be found.

The whole character of Lizzie Eustace is riddled with deception; she doesn't oscillate between truth and falsehood as Frank does, but lives permanently in a climate of lies. But lies are so natural to her that in a curious way they cease to be as offensive as one might expect. She is, after all, only being herself. Although Trollope worries in the *Autobiography* that this authenticity will seem compromised by readers who will remember Becky Sharp (Lizzie is actually referred to as 'that opulent and aristocratic Becky Sharp' in Chapter III), Lizzie's origins are more Trollopian than Thacker-ayean. It is revealing that the two titles of the novels in which the two women appear – *Vanity Fair* and *The Eustace Diamonds* – indicate, respectively, the general state of human affairs and a particular famous case. Becky's ruthless exploitation of men is meant to have large moral and social implications; Lizzie has moments when she savours her sexual power, but her energies are essentially directed towards self-preservation and hanging on to what she has already got. Her misbehaviour is not seen by Trollope (as it is by some of his modern critics) as symptomatic of some pervasive social malaise.[3] She derives ultimately from La Signora Madeline Vesey Neroni in *Barchester Towers*, and relates too to Madalina Demolines in *The Last Chronicle*. The type has been crossed, however, with the strain represented by Lady Ongar of *The Claverings*, who shares with La Signora a scandalous Italian provenance, but whose staginess reflects serious emotional distur-bance rather than the frivolous burlesque of Johnny Eames's Madalina. Trollope stresses the histrionic power which Lizzie Eustace shares with Becky, but she puts it to less sinister use. She has a gift for precipitating physical contact so that little tableaux are formed:

> 'I have no brother, Frank; do you ever think of that?' She put out her hand to him, and he clasped it, and held it tight in his own; and then, after a while, he pulled her towards him. In a moment she was on the ground, kneeling at his feet, and his arm was round her shoulder, and his hand was on her back, and he was embracing her. Her face was turned up to him, and he pressed his lips upon her forehead. 'As my brother,'

she said, stretching back her head and looking up into his face.

'Yes; – as your brother.' (XIX)

Both know that the use of the brother formula is entirely specious; the scene is simply a piece of self-indulgent rehearsal, and Trollope's immediate comment – 'They were sitting, or rather acting their little play together, in the back drawing-room . . . ' – only notes what is already apparent. Later, when Frank visits Lizzie at her Scottish castle, 'She was lying back in a low armchair as her cousin entered, and she did not rise to receive him . . . "Well, Frank?" she said, with her sweetest smile, as she gave him her hand. She felt and understood the extreme intimacy which would be implied by her not rising to receive him.' (XXIII) The strategy is comparable with Lady Ongar's, even if the motivation is more calculating. (The moment when Lizzie and Frank are surprised in embrace by the caustic retainer Andy Gowran is virtually a rerun of the scene in which Sophie Gordeloup discovers Lady Ongar in the arms of Harry Clavering; both moments have a distinctly theatrical character.) On Frank's second visit to Portray Lizzie stages a strong scene designed to provoke Frank into some sort of declaration and which she concludes as a last resort with abuse of Lucy Morris:

'I know her for what she is, while your eyes are sealed. She is wise and moral, and decorous and prim; but she is a hypocrite; and has no touch of real heart in her composition. Not abuse her when she has robbed me of all, – all, – all that I have in the world! Go to her. You had better go at once. I did not mean to say all this, but it has been said, and you must leave me. I, at any rate, cannot play the hypocrite; – I wish I could.' He rose and came to her, and attempted to take her hand, but she flung away from him. 'No!' she said, – 'never again; never, unless you will tell me that the promise you made me when we were down on the sea-shore was a true promise. Was that truth, sir, or was it a – lie?'

'Lizzie, do not use such a word as that to me.'

'I cannot stand picking my words when the whole world is going round with me, and my very brain is on fire. What is it to me what my words are? Say one syllable to me, and every word I utter again while breath is mine shall be spoken to do you pleasure. If you cannot say it, it is nothing to me what you or any one may think of my words. You know my secret, and I care not who else knows it. At any rate I can die!' Then she paused a moment, and after that stalked steadily out of the room. (XXXI)

Afterwards Frank cannot but admire 'her courage, her power of language, and her force'. The third-rate theatricality of the language cannot survive a moment's calm scrutiny – the power that Frank acknowledges is the ability of the talented performer to make rubbish sound like the real thing. As her abortive attempts to read Shelley on the sea-shore so charmingly show, Lizzie has no real taste: she uses literature simply as a looking-glass, or (in her wonderings about who is going to be her Byronic 'corsair') as a kind of horoscope.

Lizzie's biggest scene (which she spends a good deal of time looking forward to) is with Lord Fawn. Fawn hasn't a ready wit at the best of times and he is further handicapped by an inhibiting sense of propriety; he is easily worsted by the quicker Frank Greystock in both Parliamentary and personal matters. He is certainly no match for Lizzie in full histrionic cry:

It is hardly too much to say that the man quailed before her. And it certainly is not too much to say that, had Lizzie Eustace been trained as an actress, she would have become a favourite with the town. When there came to her any fair scope for acting, she was perfect. In the ordinary scenes of ordinary life, such as befell her during her visit to Fawn Court, she could not acquit herself well. There was no reality about her, and the want of it was strangely plain to the most observant eyes. But give her a part to play that required exaggerated strong action, and she hardly ever failed. Even in that terrible moment, when, on her return from the theatre, she thought that the police had discovered her secret about the diamonds, though she nearly sank through fear, she still carried on her acting in the presence of Lucinda Roanoke; and when she had found herself constrained to tell the truth to Lord George Carruthers, the power to personify a poor weak, injured creature was not wanting in her. The reader will not think that her position in society at the present moment was very well established, – will feel, probably, that she must still have known herself to be on the brink of social ruin. But she had now fully worked herself up to the necessities of the occasion, and was as able to play her part as any actress that ever walked the boards. (LXI)

Again, it is easy to see through some of her devices – her claim that the Duke of Omnium '"is my friend"' is palpably absurd – but the energy and fluency of her style cannot but overwhelm the stiff and stuffy Fawn. It is not surprising that Frank Greystock, as he looks back over Lady Eustace's career, should think of it in theatrical terms: 'he brought to mind . . . all those scenes which she had so successfully performed in his presence'. (LXXI)

But although Lizzie and Julia Ongar are both actressy, there is a fundamental difference between them. If Lady Ongar has a sense of reality which leads her in the end to accept the judgement of others, Lady Eustace has no such grasp: '. . . the guiding motive of her conduct was the desire to make things seem to be other than they were. To be always acting a part rather than living her own life was to be everything.' (XIX) Her very possession of the Eustace diamonds is founded on a fiction, but her story about her late husband's gift of them to her becomes with repetition indistinguishable from the truth as far as she is concerned. Her ability to rearrange facts in the interests of the self naturally allies her with the bogus, and it is appropriate that her companions should be an aristocrat of obscure origins and a dubious mode of life such as Lord George de Bruce Carruthers and his friend Mrs Carbuncle, 'a wonderful woman . . . the wife of a man with whom she was very rarely seen, whom nobody knew, who was something in the City, but somebody who never succeeded in making money; and yet she went everywhere'. (XXXVI) The two 'were in the habit of seeing a good deal of each other, though, as all the world knew, there was nothing between them but the simplest friendship'. (XXXI) The disingenuously bland tone of Trollope's comment, and such revealing tips as Lord George's casual use of Mrs Carbuncle's Christian name, implies clearly enough what their real relationship is, or, at least, had been. But by the end even Lord George is curiously impressed by Lizzie's ability to impose upon the facts. Lizzie's preference for the false over the real finds what might seem to be its comeuppance in her liaison with the smart but repellent Mr Emilius. Mr Emilius is a fashionable preacher whose oleaginously ecclesiastical manner of flattery can be traced back to the syco-phantically scriptural style of Mr Slope in *Barchester Towers*, com-pounded by the fact that he is both Jewish and foreign. Emilius's pursuit of Lady Eustace is, like Slope's attempt on Mrs Bold, based on her economic attractions as a widow with property, and – at least from his point of view – desirable social advantages. Emilius is rumoured to have a wife already somewhere on the continent, he is 'hookey-nosed', has 'greasy hair' and 'something almost amount-ing to a squint' which, though hardly visible in the pulpit, is disagreeable when seen close to. One way and another, it is clear that the Anglican authorities are not likely to take him seriously and it is hard to see why Lizzie should. But she does so because, as Emilius realizes at the time of his proposal, she has largely run out of friends, and also because he is not, after all, entirely con-temptible. He makes his proposal with courage and even dignity; although greasy, a liar, and an impostor, 'there was a certain manliness in him'. (LXXIII) When Emilius renews the attack his rhetoric becomes yet more flowery and more insincere but Lizzie cannot help succumbing to it, even though 'she knew, or half knew, that the man was a scheming hypocrite'. (LXXIX) As Trollope reminds us, 'she liked lies, thinking them to be more beautiful than truth'.

There is an obvious poetic justice as well as emotional logic in this marital solution to Lizzie's difficulties, but although Lizzie has got what she deserved, that does not quite seem to tie things up in the way that Lady Ongar's self-exile at the end of *The Claverings* did. Trollope begins to sketch the nature of the future Emilius household at the end of Chapter LXXIX, and promises to go further into the matter: 'The writer of the present story, however, may declare that the future fate of this lady shall not be left altogether in obscurity.' Lizzie is here on the verge of becoming a reappearing character because the imaginative apprehension of her personality that Trollope has developed in the course of the novel needs more space to be fully conveyed (hence her revival in *Phineas Redux* and *The Prime Minister*). Lizzie's vitality has enforced a kind of open-endedness. One of the reasons for our sense of that vitality is, perhaps, her unpredictableness. It is true that, when discussing

Frank Greystock's 'dual' character, Trollope contrasted it with the single and consistent natures of Lucy and Lizzie, who can be judged with confidence once one has sufficient knowledge of them. But although there is no change in Lizzie's essential nature, it is by no means clear what she will do, according to that nature, in a given situation. Like Trollope himself, she is an improviser, not a plotter – as Trollope confessed, neither of them knew in advance that she was going to steal her own jewels at Carlisle; she acts on the spur of the moment, and indeed this spontaneity is the cause of many of her difficulties. Although she would think of herself as an intensely sensitive person, she has in fact an extraordinary lack of imagination; she cannot really see herself as others see her, just as she cannot see the world as it really is. As Frank Greystock repeatedly finds when trying to explain points of legal principle to her, impersonal tenets of law are quite meaningless to her except as they impinge on her comfort. She escapes in the end by committing perjury and because she becomes a vital witness for the prosecution of the thieves who really do get away with the diamonds, but she is impervious to the moral squalor of her position, much as she is distressed by its indignity. As Mr Camperdown, the Eustace family lawyer, mournfully concludes, '"There's nothing a pretty woman can't do when she has got rid of all sense of shame."' (LXXII) Her total lack of scruple gives her an odd kind of resilience – simply the thing she is makes her live – and her consequent ability to elude moral and social restraint gives her buoyancy. The effect is attractive, however much one disapproves of the cause. Lizzie herself may briefly realize – under heavy authorial pressure – that Lucy is the 'real stone' and she herself merely paste (LXV), but of the two women she is by far the more interesting to the reader, however reassured we may be by the fact that Frank opts for the genuine article in the end.

The Eustace Diamonds itself is less of a closed system than *The Claverings* because of this spontaneity and freedom in one of its principal agents. Conventional theme – whether in Victorian or modern critical terms – pulls one way, but artistic energy and human vitality exert a stronger appeal in the other direction. Some of the ethical problems raised in the earlier novel recur in the later: the question of how adequately to punish a flagrant case of jilting, for instance – as Lady Fawn's up-to-date daughter says '"There used to be a sort of feeling that if a man behaved badly something would be done to him; but that's all over now."' (LX) Frank may be prepared to write Lord Fawn stiff notes but he is not going to punch him on the Paddington platform, as Eames did Crosbie, much less fight a duel, as Chiltern did with Finn (an incident alluded to in Chapter XLVII). Trollope too evades being embarrassed by the problem, as he had been in *The Claverings*. Indeed he shows unusual aplomb not only in keeping it within dramatized terms rather than confronting it theoretically, but also in connecting it with a private joke. In Chapter LII Mrs Carbuncle is determined to see a new play called *The Noble Jilt* by 'a very eminent author', which is none other than the source (discussed above) of *Can You Forgive Her?*. She concludes that a noble jilt is '"a contradiction in terms . . . The delicacy of the female character should not admit of hesitation between two men. The idea is quite revolting."' Mrs Carbuncle's high moral tone is hardly one which her general conduct entitles her to adopt, as Trollope urbanely refrains from pointing out. (Her attempts to coerce Lucinda Roanoke into marrying a man she finds physically repellent show her in a deeply unattractive light.)

A related problem which is more explicitly debated is the propriety or otherwise of a woman's taking the sexual initiative. As usual Trollope begins to discuss the matter as if it admitted of no argument, only to proceed to a demonstration that actually the thing is not quite so simple:

> The offer of herself by a woman to a man is, to us all, a thing so distasteful that we at once declare that the woman must be abominable. There shall be no whitewashing of Lizzie Eustace. She was abominable. But the man to whom the offer is made hardly sees the thing in the same light. He is disposed to believe that, in his peculiar case, there are circumstances by which the woman is, if not justified, at least excused. (XXXV)

Frank Greystock certainly doesn't find the situation easy to negotiate when he sits by Lizzie's bedside – she has been 'ill' and cousins are allowed to visit – and she again renews her offer.

> 'O Frank, Frank, will you give me back my heart? What was it that you promised me when we sat together upon the rocks at Portray?'

It is inexpressibly difficult for a man to refuse the tender of a woman's love. We may almost say that a man should do so as a matter of course, – that the thing so offered becomes absolutely valueless by the offer, – that the woman who can make it has put herself out of court by her own abandonment of the privileges due to her as a woman, – that stern rebuke and even expressed contempt are justified by such conduct, – and that the fairest beauty and most alluring charms of feminine grace should lose their attraction when thus tendered openly in the market. No doubt such is our theory as to love and love-making. But the action to be taken by us in matters as to which the plainest theory prevails for the guidance of our practice, depends so frequently on accompanying circumstances and correlative issues, that the theory, as often as not, falls to the ground. (LIII)

The 'accompanying circumstances and correlative issues' which make Frank's position here so difficult are also just what make it interesting. Lizzie's attack on Frank is made several times, but in each case the rendering by the novelist of the dialogue and the scene has a strikingly relaxed precision. Artistically, there is a clear improvement on the more self-conscious staging of *The Claverings*, even if the interviews do not have the subtlety, poignancy, and interior life that mark Madame Max Goesler's more oblique proposal to Phineas Finn.

Trollope's phrase about 'accompanying circumstances and correlative issues' indicates how far his practice differed from that of his friend George Eliot. In her eagerness to give her fiction the kind of moral intensity and authority that she thought it was the obligation of the novelist to strive for, she sometimes found it hard to be indulgent towards the individual case. Rosamund Vincy's egotism and Fred Vincy's irresponsibility are almost hounded by George Eliot in a way that contrasts markedly with Trollope's indulgence of Lizzie's self-centredness and Frank's vacillation. George Eliot's characters tend to reach early on the point at which they are not allowed to benefit from the argument that circumstances alter cases; if they were, their fictive lives would be the less exemplary and therefore, from their creator's point of view, the less deserving of art. Trollope's less strenuous and less stringent view of art's moral obligations, and his greater tolerance of the mediocre and the average, allowed him to deal with his morally weaker characters without the rigour George Eliot felt enjoined to show, but also without sacrificing that enlargement of readers' sympathies that she looked for.

The 'accompanying circumstances and correlative issues' clause gives Trollope much freedom of manoeuvre, even as he honours the restrictive Mudie-esque contract that a popular mid-Victorian novelist was obliged to sign. It allows him considerable flexibility of approach to attitudes and situations which may seem similar considered in summary terms, but which, because of the variables and contingencies involved, are in fact *sui generis*. But, of course, however genial Trollope's patience with Lizzie's ways, and however complete his absorption in her shabby machinations, there is bound to be limit to the official sympathy she can expect, as the fact that in the end she is consigned to Emilius rather than Frank shows.

Ayala's Angel

Suppose, however, a comparable addiction to romance and a similar reluctance to see things as they really are were found in a girl who *was* ultimately prepared to reconcile herself to reality? Such a girl is the heroine of *Ayala's Angel* (written 1878, published 1881). The novel indicates that eight years after *The Eustace Diamonds* and thirteen after *The Belton Estate*, Trollope is still strongly attracted both by the idea of a conflict between romance and reality as a way of releasing human possibilities, and by the idea of a change of heart that is really a discovery of where the heart truly lies. It is true that Ayala is essentially a good girl whereas Lizzie Eustace is essentially not, and it is also true that Ayala's *ingénue* bounce is a long way from Clara Amedroz's stately decorum, but the three women have enough in common to illustrate again how, in allowing his imagination repeated play over recurring situations, Trollope was enabled to envisage new characters in their full individuality.

Like these predecessors, Ayala is left alone in the world (apart from her sister Lucy) by the death of her parents. Her father, however, had been an artist, and was sufficiently successful to afford 'the most perfect bijou of a little house in South Kensington'

(I) with a blue set of china, a painted cornice in the studio, satin hangings in the drawing-room, a piano of the best kind, and other facilities for a life too elegant to be Bohemian but free enough to seem romantic. In such an environment, it is natural that Ayala should develop a notion of an ideal lover whom she calls, with a significantly secular and unthinking use of biblical phrase, her 'Angel of Light'. To begin with, this fantasy is a source of strength. This makes her impervious to the adoration of her cousin Tom Tringle, the son and heir of the wealthy Sir Thomas Tringle, who takes Ayala into his house while Lucy goes to the respectable but shabby house of their other uncle who is merely a minor civil servant. Ayala's inherent taste enables her to despise the vulgarity of the *nouveau-riche* Tringles. Tom's little gifts of diamonds can have no effect on her when he himself is loaded with flashy rings and sports a waistcoat which, as Trollope notes, 'would of itself have been suicidal'. (XI) The energy with which she clings to her aesthetic view of things is felt by the Tringles to be, at the least, tactless in her dependent circumstances, and Ayala is swapped for her sister. However, her repeated rejection of Tom as well as of other aspirants is almost as irritating to her poorer relations: '"If there is anything I do hate"', says her aunt, '"it is romance, while bread and meat, and coals, and washing, are so dear."' (XXXIX)

It is romance that makes her first impressions of Colonel Jonathan Stubbs so mixed. Stubbs is ugly, has violent red hair, and tells preposterous stories which fantasticate life with great animation; he is, as Ayala thinks, 'the Genius of Comedy . . . But the Angel of Light must have something tragic in his composition, – must verge, at any rate, on tragedy.' (XVI) It is very soon clear to the reader that Ayala has mistaken her own nature and that she is meant for both Stubbs and comedy, – so clear that one's attention can be freed from any distraction of suspense to concentrate on the process by which self-discovery and external event interact to precipitate this conclusion. As in *The Belton Estate*, where the heroine finally capitulates to a similar urgency of masculine appeal, it is in the way that she gradually accepts the inevitability of what had at first seemed unthinkable that the narrative interest lies; again, it is process, not conclusion, that really matters. In Ayala's case it is a question of adjusting her ideas to her experience.[4] As she finally concedes, she falls in love with Stubbs at first sight, or at any rate at first sound, but she rejects his first proposal because she cannot bring herself to abandon the romantic possibility that the Angel of Light seems to represent. Stubbs's rightness for Ayala is indicated by the quickness with which he understands the grounds of her objection to him:

'Tell me; – why cannot you love me?'

The altered tone of his voice, which now had in it something of severity, seemed to give her more power.

'It is because –' Then she paused.

'Because why? Out with it, whatever it is. If it be something that a man may remedy I will remedy it. Do not fear to hurt me. Is it because I am ugly? That I cannot remedy.' She did not dare to tell him that it was so, but she looked up at him, not dissenting by any motion of her head. 'Then God help me, for ugly I must remain.'

'It is not that only.'

'Is it because my name is Stubbs – Jonathan Stubbs?' Now she did assent, nodding her head at him. He had bade her tell him the truth, and she was so anxious to do as he bade her! 'If it be so, Ayala, I must tell you that you are wrong, – wrong and foolish; that you are carried away by a feeling of romance, which is a false romance. Far be it from me to say that I could make you happy, but I am sure that your happiness cannot be made and cannot be marred by such accidents as that. Do you think that my means are not sufficient?'

'No; – no,' she cried; 'I know nothing of your means. If I could love you I would not condescend to ask, – even to hear.'

'There is no other man, I think?'

'There is no other man.'

'But your imagination has depicted to you something grander than I am,' – then she assented quickly, turning round and nodding her head to him, – 'some one who shall better respond to that spirit of poetry which is within you?' Again she nodded her head approvingly, as though to assure him that now he knew the whole truth. 'Then, Ayala, I must strive to soar till I can approach your dreams. But if you dare to desire things which are really grand, do not allow yourself to be mean at the same time. Do not let the sound of a name move you, or I shall not believe in your aspirations.' (XXV)

Stubbs's intuitive reading of Ayala's immature mind establishes an authority over her which she finds it progressively harder to resist. When they are both staying at Lady Albury's, Trollope suggests with practised skill the increase in intimacy which the round of country-house activities fosters, and Ayala is clearly in a heightened state of consciousness where Stubbs is concerned; when he uses her Christian name, for instance, she cannot help remembering every other occasion on which he has done so. Nevertheless, she still resists his second proposal; even though she now knows that she loves him, her answer is still simply, '"I cannot."' Trollope's explanation at this stage is that the inhibition is caused by 'those dreams' which 'had been so palpable to her and so dear . . . so vast a portion of her young life'. (L) As he says later, 'her dreams had been to her a barrier against love rather than an encouragement'. (LV) Ayala's own subsequent explanation to Stubbs is that '"I knew how to love you, but I did not know how to tell you that I loved you . . . I was ashamed to tell you the truth when I had once refused to do as you would have me."' (LVI) Ayala, in fact, realizes – as Clara Amedroz and Alice Vavasor (in *Can You Forgive Her?*) had done before her – that to accept her lover, in the end, is to accept judgement against herself. Those fantasies which enabled Ayala to feel superior to Tringleism have turned out to be a dangerous indulgence.

For the critic anxiously looking for some thematic lifeline amidst the welter of circumstance, it is tempting to allegorize the situation: Ayala's fantasies could be said, for instance, to show 'the dangers of excessive romanticism' (the phrase used on the dust jacket of the old World's Classics edition). It is true that many of the characters in *Ayala's Angel* consciously consider the question of romance in relation to the realities of life and thus to some extent the various strands of narrative in the novel are combined by a common theme, but the debate is not resolved in so simple-minded a way as the phrase suggests. In Ayala's own case, it is not so much that she abandons her dreams as that her dreams and reality, the ideal hero and the actual man, coalesce. Stubbs becomes the Angel by substitution. And without the dreams, would he ever have been attracted by her? 'That the dreams had all been idle she declared to herself, – not aware that the Ayala whom her lover had loved would not have been an Ayala to be loved by him, but for the dreams.' (LI) Despite his military duties at Aldershot (which seem nominal enough) and his effortless air of practical authority (which has policemen springing to his assistance), Stubbs has his romantic side. His own thoughts about matrimony, which centre on worries about the erosion of the initial rapture by the cares of providing for a family, are reported in the context of his picturesque Highland cottage:

> Pine-trees enveloped the place. Looking at the house from the outside any one would declare it to be wet through. It certainly could not with truth be described as a comfortable family residence. But you might, perhaps, travel through all Scotland without finding a more beautifully romantic spot in which to reside. From that passage, which seemed to totter suspended over the rocks, whence the tumbling rushing waters could always be heard like music close at hand, the view down over the little twisting river was such as filled the mind with a conviction of realised poetry. (XVIII)

The man who chooses such a spot for his holiday can hardly be insensible to the things which charm Ayala so.

Staying with Stubbs in Scotland is Lucy's lover, the sculptor Isadore Hamel, a friend of the girls' artist father. At this stage he has romantic notions about his calling which express themselves in large unsellable works such as 'an allegorical figure of Italia United, and another of a Prostrate Roman Catholic Church'. (XXXIII) When he goes to see Sir Thomas in Lombard Street to announce his intentions towards Lucy, he is deeply affronted by Sir Thomas's philistine suggestion that the thing to do with things you cannot sell is to auction them off, particularly in view of the fact that Hamel is making less than £300 a year. But what looks like a straight confrontation of values is again complicated by the fact that Sir Thomas takes this line partly because he finds Hamel's standing on his artistic dignity priggish, partly because he feels he ought, being *in loco parentis*, to make appropriate noises about prudence, and partly because his wife's violent prejudice against Hamel (who is not only an artist but also illegitimate) puts him in a difficult position. Actually, Sir Thomas is anxious to be good-natured, and part of the comedy of the novel comes from the way in which a giant of the City is unable to control his family. Hamel, who is thoroughly respectable, has had difficulties with his own father, whose behaviour really is Bohemian, so he is not likely to be eager to placate Sir Thomas as a prospective father-in-law. He despises the Tringles on principle anyway, since to make money out of money was 'an employment which he regarded as vile ... To create something beautiful was almost divine. To manipulate millions till they should breed other millions was the meanest occupation for a life's energy.' (XXXIII) By the end of the novel, however, Hamel, faced with the necessity of providing for Lucy as his wife, has become markedly more pragmatic. As far as the grandiose sculptures are concerned, he concedes that Sir Thomas was right: they should have gone under the hammer, except that the auctioneer would have got nothing for them. Not that they were unnecessary at the time: '"They were the lessons which I had to teach myself, and the play which I gave to my imagination."' (LXIII) But for now he is content to work on busts for Jones and his family to stand on their bookshelves; that at least will earn an honest living. The philosophy that Hamel expresses here is close to that of the *Autobiography* – Trollope's 'shoemaker' aesthetic, the industrious production of honest work for which there is a real demand. But although Hamel cannot in the end be held up as an Arnoldian hero enlisted in the struggle for culture against the philistines, his defence of his youthful experiments has a certain dignity and indicates that, although he is now prepared to accommodate himself to the market, he does not feel he has lost his artistic integrity in doing so.

In fact, in *Ayala's Angel* money turns out to be relatively powerless over those who retain some feeling for romance. Both Ayala and Lucy find husbands who are to them romantic and not remarkable for worldly advantages, even though Ayala has to revise her ideas about what romance means. The parallel story of Frank Houston and Imogene Docimer is a further example of worldliness failing to prevail. There has been an understanding between them, broken off when it became clear that they could not expect more than about £600 a year between them. Houston is a dilettante gentleman of leisure and regards earning his own bread as out of the question. With as much energy as the inherent languor of his life-style permits, he therefore pursues Gertrude, the second of Sir Thomas's daughters. (The first has married Mr Traffic, a Parliamentary expert on supply and demand, and the son of Lord Boardotrade – even in this late work Trollope has not entirely given up those facetious habits of nomenclature which understandably made Henry James wince.) Houston's object is the money that will presumably go with Gertrude. When Sir Thomas makes it brutally plain that Houston is welcome to Gertrude but that he will have to take her without the expected £100,000, Houston cries off and returns to the waiting Imogene. She now begins to vacillate and proposes at the most a permanent engagement; Houston, with an unprecedented burst of energy, insists on an early day, and is even, at the book's close, contemplating painting a few portraits for ready cash.

His salvation, however, is a closely run thing: if Gertrude had played her cards better and not rashly proposed a runaway match in Ostend, or if Sir Thomas had not been put out by such irritants as Tom's going to pieces over Ayala or Traffic's refusal to deprive himself of the free board and lodging provided at his father-in-law's various residences, Houston might have allowed himself to be hooked. He several times reiterates his considered preference for the tolerable comfort which Gertrude's presumed money would ensure over the love in a baby-crammed cottage which is all that Imogene can offer, even though Imogene is a woman of refinement and Gertrude is vulgar. It is perhaps significant that Houston's first farewell to Imogene takes place amidst the romantic scenery of the Tyrol, and occurs at much the same time as Stubbs's meditations on matrimony in his Highland retreat. The chapter (XLI) in which Houston decides to return once and for all to Imogene is one of the most interesting in the novel. Houston has three days in which to make up his mind, but he fails to do so; as Trollope notes, 'a man's mind will very generally refuse to make itself up until it be driven and compelled by emergency'. The emergency occurs in a sudden gust of emotion during his conversation with Imogene, an impulse of feeling which he had clearly not foreseen, and which perhaps Trollope himself had not anticipated. The moment comes in a passage of dialogue, in which authorial intrusion is confined to stage directions, very much in the manner of *The Duke's Children*, written two years earlier:

'I got a letter last night from my lady-love, in which she tells me that she is very ill, and that her sickness is working upon her father's bowels.'

'Frank!'

'It is the proper language; – working upon her father's bowels of compassion. Fathers always have bowels of compassion at last.'

'You will return then, of course?'

'What do you say?'

'As for myself, – or as for you?'

'As a discreet and trusty counsellor. To me you have always been a trusty counsellor.'

'Then I should put a few things into a bag, go down to Merle Park, and declare that, in spite of all the edicts that ever came from a father's mouth, you cannot absent yourself while you know that your Gertrude is ill.'

'And so prepare a new cousin for you to press to your bosom.'

'If you can endure her for always, why should not I for an hour or two, now and again?'

'Why not, indeed,? In fact, Imogene, this enduring, and not enduring, – even this living, and not living, – is, after all, but an affair of the imagination. Who can tell but that, as years roll on, she may be better-looking even than you?'

'Certainly.'

'And have as much to say for herself?'

'A great deal more that is worth hearing.'

'And behave herself as a mother of a family with quite as much propriety?'

'In all that I do not doubt that she would be my superior.'

'More obedient I am sure she would be.'

'Or she would be very disobedient.'

'And then she can provide me and my children with ample comforts.'

'Which I take it is the real purpose for which a wife should be married.'

'Therefore,' said he, – and then he stopped.

'And therefore there should be no doubt.'

'Though I hate her,' he said, clenching his fist with violence as he spoke, 'with every fibre of my heart, – still you think there should be no doubt?'

'That, Frank, is violent language, – and foolish.'

'And though I love you so intensely that whenever I see her the memory of you becomes an agony to me.'

'Such language is only more violent and more foolish.'

'Surely not, if I have made up my mind at last, that I never will willingly see Miss Tringle again.' Here he got up, and walking across the rug, stood over her, and waited as though expecting some word from her. But she, putting her two hands up to her head, and brushing her hair away from her forehead, looked up to him for what further words might come to him. (XLI)

As in previous scenes of a comparable kind already discussed, Trollope's extreme attentiveness to physical gesture and position and his abdication of any right of commentary are a sign of the degree to which his imagination has become engrossed in his characters' feelings moment by moment. Houston and Imogene are cousins, as Clavering and Lady Ongar as well as Greystock and Lady Eustace were, and again the situation involves the readiness of the woman to take the man, the worldly consequences of so doing, and the hovering possibility of an alternative union. The scene is not identical to its predecessors, but some of its features repeat elements of a dilemma that had long fascinated Trollope. The immediate consequence here is that Houston is now accused by Imogene's brother of making both himself and her '"wretched for ever just to satisfy the romance of a moment"'. (XLII) '"He always was a hard, unfeeling fellow," said Frank to himself,' on whom the irony of his volte-face seems largely lost.

It is also an irony, although a much larger one, that Tom Tringle, Ayala's rejected suitor, is as much under the sway of romance as she is, although his manner of bearing disappointment sometimes approaches burlesque. Trollope explains early on that 'in spite of his rings and a certain dash of vulgarity, which was, perhaps, not altogether his own fault, [Tom] was not a bad fellow'. (XI) His love for Ayala is 'of a wholesome cleanly kind'. He is driven to despair by Ayala's persistent refusals, the sources of which he is not really able to understand, and is driven to drown his sorrows in dubious champagne. An assault on a policeman is not taken in good part, and Tom has to spend an ignominious Christmas in the lock-up. Attributing his lack of success to Ayala's preference for Stubbs, he meditates vengeance in terms of Dickensian extravagance: 'I'll shoot that fellow down like a dog . . . I should have no more compunction in taking his life than a mere worm. Why should I, when I know that he has sapped the very juice of my existence?'' (XXXV) The result of these dire threats is that he attempts to land a retributory punch on Stubbs as he is going into the Haymarket Theatre. As he is drunk at the time and exhausted by wandering round the streets in the rain, the blow has little effect – and Stubbs magnanimously succeeds in getting the police to drop the matter. The episode is partly absurd, but it is described by Trollope in Chapter XLIV with the intentness that recalls the London ramblings of other characters in disturbed states of mind – characters as far apart in other ways as Septimus Harding and Burgo Fitzgerald. Tom's actual assault is a repetition of Eames's in *The Small House at Allington*, and it is obvious enough that Tom's general situation has its parallels with Johnny's. Both of them are beneficiaries of Trollope's special loyalty to rejected lovers who simply will not or cannot give the girl up. The only thing that Sir Thomas can think of to do with Tom is to dispatch him on a prolonged business trip to America and Japan, but he refuses to go until Ayala is irrevocably beyond his reach. As he puts it in a letter that is both ridiculous and slightly touching, '''I WILL NEVER STIR FROM THESE REALMS TILL I KNOW MY FATE!''' (LIV – his capitals). When his sisters express their conviction that he will soon find another girl abroad, Tom rounds on them: '''I don't believe that either of you know anything about it.''' (LXI). The remark has an unexpected authority. It is not entirely perverse of Trollope, therefore, to argue earlier in the chapter that Tom 'if the matter be looked at aright, should be regarded as the hero of this little history'. Tom was admittedly foolish, vulgar, and ignorant, but he was constant even when he had no grounds for hope, and 'the merit is to despair and yet to be constant'. When the 'hero' of the novel turns out to be as romantic as this, despite the touches of bathos which dog his devotion, it becomes difficult to regard the book as unequivocally critical of romance.

Tom, however, does not receive the sort of rewards given to

Harry Clavering – rewards described in one of Frank Houston's letters to Imogene as '"that fault which is so prevalent in the novels of the present day"', in which the hero, although '"a very namby-mamby sort of fellow . . . comes out right at last . . . Some god comes out of a theatrical cloud and leaves the poor devil ten thousand a year and a title."' (XXXVIII) It is a criticism to which *The Claverings* is vulnerable but which *Ayala's Angel* escapes. It is also a comment on the art of fiction which is not in this case voiced by the intruding author but which – quite appropriately in view of his character and situation – is made over to the dramatized and understood character. Disavowing suspense in *The Eustace Diamonds*, Trollope scorned to keep a secret from the reader; in a similar way he is not one to reserve insights for the novelist's use only, according to some special privilege of authorship.

Cousin Henry

Trollope's interest in vacillation was not confined to its operation in affairs of the heart. Doubt, hesitation and changeableness seemed to Trollope so fundamental to human nature (except where displaced by single-mindedness and obsession in such studies as those to be considered below) that there is hardly a novel in which they do not play a significant part. In the case of *Cousin Henry* (begun a month after *Ayala's Angel* in 1878 but published earlier in 1879), however, the vacillation of the hero constitutes the central and almost exclusive interest, and his fluctuating feelings have to do not with love but with a will.

Trollope found uncertainties over inheritance so suggestive that they became one of the plot motifs on which he most relied. In the case of *Cousin Henry* the uncertainty is initially created by the hero's uncle Indefer Jones, owner of an estate on the coast of Carmarthenshire. The old man cannot finally decide between what he feels (with the passionate attachment to traditional custom shared by many of Trollope's landed gentry) he ought to do, and what he would like to do. Duty suggests that the estate should go to the nearest male heir, his nephew Henry Jones, a clerk in a London office; affection underlines the claims of his niece Isabel Brodrick, who lives with him virtually as his daughter and who has the true interests of the estate and its tenants at heart. The conflict is revealed by the dialogue between uncle and niece which opens the novel with a clarity which suggests that its essential features were thoroughly familiar to Trollope – and indeed the whole story, being concerned with one issue and markedly economical in length, maintains almost to the end (where there is some unnecessary recapitulation) a concentration that gives the book its security if also its narrowness of effect. Indefer has made several wills in the past, and, as his life draws to a close, his testamentary anxiety increases. The will that is found after his death is in favour of cousin Henry, but is it the *last* will? Isabel has heard his dying murmur '"It is all right. It is done,"' and thinks not; moreover there are witnesses that another will was made. But since a search fails to reveal it, Henry is bound to take possession, although he does so in an atmosphere made inimical to him partly by his uncle's wavering intentions. Had Henry been of the sort of calibre to have won Isabel's affection and his uncle's respect, the old man's dilemma could have been resolved by the cousins' marriage. But although Henry goes through the motions of proposing to Isabel, he is rejected with a scorn that Indefer understands and shares. Henry inherits therefore with feelings that are, to say the least, mixed, and understandably so.

By the fifth chapter Henry has taken to spending all his time in a book-room not much otherwise used, and there he remains for most of the rest of the novel. Other characters comment that he does not look well – but the reasons are psychological rather than physical. By accident he has discovered, shut up in a volume of sermons that his uncle was reading on his death-bed, the genuine last will and testament of Indefer Jones, which makes Isabel heir to the estate. Should Henry publish the will and disinherit himself, or should he destroy it and run the risks attaching to such a felony? In strict justice he ought immediately to reveal what he has found; nevertheless, 'there was an idea present to him through it all that abstract justice, if abstract justice could be reached, would declare that the property should be his'. (IX) After all, he had been brought down to Wales to be acknowledged as the heir; that was Indefer's manifest intention. Why should it be frustrated by some last-minute death-bed change of mind, probably due to failing powers? But Henry is not hardened enough to follow through the logic of that argument, which would be to destroy the document. He is terrified at the thought of being found out and put in prison if he did so, and even speculates gloomily about his consequent damnation hereafter. He can be neither criminal nor honest. Much of the rest of the novel traces his deterioration under the weight of this dilemma, and the vacillations of his mind as he tries to commit himself to one course of action or another. He is obsessed with the particular book in which the will is hidden: 'On the back near the bottom was a small speck, a spot on the binding, which had been so far disfigured by some accident in use. This seemed to his eyes to make it marked and separate among a thousand. To him it was almost wonderful that a stain so peculiar should not at once betray the volume to the eyes of all.' (X) He cannot bear to leave it unguarded, even though he knows his conduct is arousing suspicion. When he does walk around the estate, he has fantasies about drowning the book in the sea or even about throwing himself off the cliffs; he has nightmares about it. Dreams are extremely rare in Trollope's work – perhaps because he was so skilled in revealing the operations of the irrational in the ordinary transactions of life that he had little technical need of them. Here – as with Mr Harding's doze in the cigar divan in *The Warden* – the dream is a product of a sense of personal isolation.

When Henry first discovers the will he says to himself with a revealingly paranoid petulance 'Let them find it', and when the will is finally found by the family solicitor Henry is relieved rather than otherwise, since the burden of indecision had become so much greater than the charms of inheritance. These have been blighted anyway by the insinuations of the *Carmarthen Herald* – another Trollopian case of press persecution. The actual discovery in Chapter XXI is very exactly dramatized, the details of the book-room, the shelves, the solicitor's awareness of cousin Henry's involuntary glances all being vividly recorded. The physical struggle over the document – Henry perversely wants to retain it at the last moment – is a satisfying resolution of what has been a drama of inaction. Conscience and calculation have been so equally poised in Henry's mind that vacillation has become paralysis; the conflicting forces balance out so exactly as to produce a state of inertia. One impulse is immediately cancelled by the next: 'No sooner had he resolved to destroy the will than he was unable to destroy it. No sooner had he felt his inability than again he longed to do the deed.' (XV)

Mr Apjohn, the family solicitor who ends this stasis, finds the will more by thinking himself into Henry's situation than by a strict following of a chain of evidence. As he himself says of the reasoning which led him to the final scene in the book-room '"there is more of imagination in it than of true deduction"'. (XIX) Although his professional pleasure in straightening things out recalls Mr Toogood, the solicitor who traced the missing cheque in *The Last Chronicle of Barset*, Apjohn has more in common with the sort of detective who, with Maigret-like empathy, immerses himself in the criminal's – or, here, the potential criminal's – consciousness. It is not surprising therefore that Apjohn should be prepared to let Henry off relatively lightly: he has come to understand him. Trollope too asks the reader for 'some compassion' on the grounds that Henry had been injured by the old squire's change of mind, and that he had not actually destroyed the will. However, the reader's sympathy for Henry has been created not so much by special pleading of this kind, but by sharing the lived experience of Henry's agonies in the book-room. As in earlier instances, it is through closely following the little ebbs and flows of the will, the tacking movements of vacillation, that Trollope shows us how understandable and how forgivable indecision is.

Trollope's lenience towards Henry is thrown into relief by the presence of a heroine who is as strong-minded as Henry is weak. The early pages indicate that Isabel is both forthright and self-sufficient and that she almost likes being a martyr to principle. Although she is obviously in love with William Owen, a minor canon at Hereford cathedral, she accepts her uncle's social prejudice against Owen when she is still the old man's principal legatee; she again refuses to consider Owen when she has lost her expectations on the grounds that she is now too poor. Nevertheless, her physical feelings are clearly of great force: in describing her idea of marriage, she says that '"In marrying a man a woman should be able to love every little trick belonging to him. The parings of his nails should be dear to her . . . It should be pleasant to her to serve him in things most menial."' (I) The sentiment sounds conventional but for the odd detail about the finger-nails which indicates that Isabel knows what she is talking about. There is a latent violence in Isabel's vocabulary which may well be a sign of a suppressed and frustrated capacity for passion. Her language to Henry – she tells him to his face that he is '"odious"' (III) to her and refuses his offer of a legacy because we do not take presents '"from those we despise"' (VIII) – has an almost Brontëish ferocity. Henry's personality may not be attractive but it is unjust of Isabel to turn on him in this way, as she herself comes to realize. The later scenes between Owen and Isabel offer considerable physical tension, but they are brief, and in the end Isabel's temperament is left sketched rather than fully delineated. As Trollope says on the book's last page, 'it has not been, so to say, a love story'. Isabel's vacillations, like her uncle's, are subservient to those of the unfortunate heir, cousin Henry himself. His situation allowed Trollope to study vacillation in a remarkably pure condition – it was not quite the last of such studies, but its late date shows how sustained Trollope's absorption in such states of mind continued to be.

ii
Inheritance and Guilt

Trollope's use of uncertainties over inheritance in *Cousin Henry* was far from being a novelty: 'No subject for a plot', complained *The Examiner*'s reviewer, 'is, we think, so entirely worn-out as the loss of a last will and testament.' The plot of *The Warden* itself had been based on the idea of a testator's wishes being ignored or misinterpreted, even though in that case the benefactor had been defunct for some centuries. More usually, the Trollope inheritance plot revolves round the question of who will get an old or elderly man's estate, the estate being understood in a living sense – house, land, tenants, rents – rather than simply a legal one. Trollope's most significant early success with this motif was *Orley Farm*, which he began to write in 1860, a few days after finishing *Framley Parsonage*, and published in 1861–2; the popularity of the two novels did much to confirm his reputation. As *The Examiner*'s irritation reminds us, wills play a large part in the plots of the period; Dickens relies heavily on them, and *Middlemarch* is not above exploiting their potential. The Trollope family, however, had personal reasons for being conscious of their importance. Anthony's father had expected to inherit the Hertfordshire estate of his uncle Adolphus Meetkerke, and had indeed visited the property as the acknowledged heir. In his sixties, however, Meetkerke unexpectedly married a young wife whose subsequent children put an end to Thomas Trollope's hopes. This disappointment began the decline in the family's fortunes which was only arrested by Mrs Trollope's success as an author whose capacity for early morning literary production regardless of circumstances exceeded even her younger son's. Anthony would not himself have benefited directly had the Meetkerke estate passed into the Trollope family – his older brother Tom would have succeeded – but the episode may have been one of the factors which impressed the question of inheritance on his young imagination. Another important influence on *Orley Farm* is certainly the maturer Trollope's views on lawyers and the conduct of the law.[5]

Orley Farm

One element in *Orley Farm* is indisputably autobiographical. As he reveals in the *Autobiography*, Trollope's account of the property itself is a description of the farmhouse at Harrow to which the Trollopes moved when they could no longer expect the Meetkerke estate to solve their problems. The illustration of it in the novel, drawn to Trollope's great satisfaction by Millais, is from the life. Nevertheless, as we should by now expect, the novel's interest depends on the degree to which the characters grow into autonomy under the author's hand; the original Orley Farm may supply the setting, but the book's energies do not derive from unassuaged memories of the miserable youth Trollope spent there.

It is indicated as early as Chapter II that 'the interest of this tale will be centred in the person of Lady Mason', although she is too old to be technically eligible as the heroine. Lady Mason is the second wife and widow of Sir Joseph Mason, who was elderly when he married him. According to a codicil to his will, Orley Farm itself was settled on their son Lucius, the rest of the considerable estate going to the eldest son of the first marriage. Twenty years on, Lucius has returned from a continental education, and begins to take charge of the farm. A disaffected tenant, an attorney called Dockwrath (the name is presumably not meant to pass unnoticed) suspects the legality of the codicil, and easily persuades the present Sir Joseph Mason, who has always felt outraged by the provisions of the original will, to contest it. Was it forged by Lady Mason? Her conduct throughout her widowhood has been so irreproachably correct that it seems hard to believe, and certainly her principal neighbours, Sir Peregrine Orme and his daughter-in-law Mrs Orme, are profoundly indignant at any such suggestion. Their influential friendship is naturally of great value to Lady Mason as her malignant enemies try to reopen 'The Great Orley Farm Case' (which, Trollope tells us, should have been the novel's title). However, Lady Mason is guilty; when her dying husband would not provide for their son, she did forge the codicil. Trollope does not explicitly admit this until just over half-way through the novel's very considerable length, although by then he seems to hope that the reader will have rumbled Lady Mason early on. This self-inflicted inhibition contravenes his usual practice, and although it creates the conditions for a striking scene of revelation, it also means that for half the book the author is damagingly cut off from full intimacy with its central personality. Commenting in the *Autobiography* on *The Eustace Diamonds* – another novel about a guilty widow who hangs on to what does not belong to her – Trollope disclaims any forethought about her manoeuvres and the minutiae of the plot, but there the effect, as we have seen, is not seriously harmful. He does not, however, reveal what he later admitted in his article 'A Walk in a Wood' (published in *Good Words*, September 1879) – that he did not decide that Lady Mason really had forged the will until the chapter before she confesses. This indecision over the novel's *donnée* rather than its development does have its drawbacks.

As far as Lady Mason is concerned, part of Trollope's problem is that like her near contemporary Lady Audley she has a secret and the main business of her life is simply to keep it. The stresses and strains of conscience struggling with her love for her son (who would be dispossessed if the truth were to come out) have to be taken on trust, since Trollope does not allow himself a full internal account until after Chapter XLIV, in which the crime is confessed. Lady Mason is described initially as having a character 'full of energy' (II) even though her manner shows a habitual sad repose, but the energy is devoted to suppressing the conflicts within, to which we do not at first have full access. In Chapter V we are shown her sitting alone, so that she 'could allow her countenance to be a true index of her mind'; we are told that 'there was sorrow at her heart, and deep thought in her mind', but little more. Normally, when a Trollope character sits 'perfectly still for an hour thinking what she would do', we can expect a full account of what elsewhere in this novel are tellingly described as 'those inward words which a man uses when he assures himself of the result of his own thoughts' (XXXIV); on this occasion no such words are forthcoming. It is a striking admission of the disadvantages of this book's authorial policy that in its later stages Trollope should remind the reader that his illustrator Millais had presented Lady Mason's hour of sorrow and deep thought better than he had:

> In an early part of this story I have endeavoured to describe how this woman sat alone, with deep sorrow in her heart and deep thought in her mind, when she first learned what terrible things were coming on her. The idea, however, which the reader will have conceived of her as she sat there will have come to him from the skill of the artist, and not from the words of the writer. If that drawing is now near him, let him go back to it. Lady Mason was again sitting in the same room – that pleasant room, looking out through the verandah on to the sloping lawn, and in the same chair; one hand again rested open on the arm of the chair, while the other supported her face as she leaned upon her elbow; and the sorrow was still in her heart, and the deep thought in her mind. But the lines of her face were altered, and the spirit expressed by it was changed. There was less of beauty, less of charm, less of softness; but in spite of all that she had gone through there was more of strength, – more of the power to resist all that this world could do to her. (LXIII)

Passages of retrospect, comparing past with present and measuring the changes between the one and the other, are a common as well as a crucial part of the Trollopian method. This graceful but embarrassed tribute to Millais' contribution is probably unique. So much of the action of Trollope's fiction is interior that illustration cannot usually add much; it is a sign of the novelist's uncertainty that in this case he felt it could do so. Trollope's earlier admission in Chapter XX that 'All that passed through her brain on that night I may not now tell', is a further sign of a highly uncharacteristic constraint.

Although forty-seven, Lady Mason is still an attractive woman, despite the studied sobriety of her dress, and it is not altogether clear whether her appeal is something she knowingly exploits. It is certainly powerful enough to secure the professional devotion of her lawyer Mr Furnival, despite his growing private conviction of her guilt. Some familiarity with a female client in distress is not unnatural, but Mr Furnival's holding of Lady Mason's hand is more solicitous than strict professionalism requires: 'Lady Mason let him keep her hand for a minute or so, as though she did not notice it; and yet as she turned her eyes to him it might appear that his tenderness had encouraged her'. (XII) Admittedly, Mr Furnival has become susceptible in his successful middle age: his jealous wife frequently looks back nostalgically to their earlier, struggling days in Keppel Street, Bloomsbury (where Trollope himself was born) before domestic harmony gave way to society and status. But Lady Mason's subtle attractions are not only felt by lawyers with a penchant for pretty women. No one could be more scrupulous and honourable than Sir Peregrine Orme, or more Christian and charitable than Mrs Orme, and from both of them Lady Mason receives a remarkable devotion. Had Trollope's conception of the character before her confession been less 'fluctuating and (what is very rare with Mr Trollope) – indistinct' as the perceptive reviewer in the *Spectator* put it, – we might have been given a more exact idea of how far this high opinion was the effect of the Ormes' own goodness and how far the result of Lady Mason's calculation. In due course the goodness is obviously meant to prevail over the calculation, and the irony of the story is that Sir Peregrine's nobility leads Lady Mason to emulate and thus tragically to disappoint him.

Lady Mason has been careful not to presume on the friendship of the Ormes, so that their support – desperately needed as it becomes clear that she will have to face another trial – seems to them freely given, not angled for. Sir Peregrine is so outraged at the charge of perjury, which arouses to the full the archaic instinct of chivalry for which his character is most notable, that he contemplates offering Lady Mason marriage. He would need the approval of his daughter-in-law and would naturally guarantee the rights of his grandson heir, but Lady Mason's stately femininity would ensure that the gesture would be gratifying as well as altruistic. As Trollope now tells us in Chapter XXXV, Lady Mason has so far used her 'female charms . . . partly with the innocence of the dove, but partly also with the wisdom of the serpent' – though he hastens to add in his extenuating way that in this 'I do not think that she can be regarded as very culpable'. Sir Peregrine's proposal, however, is the one form of succour which she would rather not receive and which, when it comes, she at first reluctantly accepts and then decisively rejects. He makes it with characteristic generosity, indicating that he will stand by her whatever happens, if not as a

husband then as a father. He does not of course know what the
reader has not yet been officially told – that because Lady Mason
is guilty her trial may end in her conviction. When she is debating
internally the pros and cons of the marriage, she asks herself
'would it be well in her to drag him down in his last days from
the noble pedestal on which he stood' (XXXV); the implication
seems to be that she will come to grief because of her guilt, but
she might be thinking simply of the dishonour of having to
appear in court at all. A further cause of anguish for Lady Mason
is the resentment of her son Lucius at her dependence on the
Ormes. Later in the same chapter, Trollope's analysis of the
bitterness of her thoughts – her understandable distress at the
estrangement of the son whose welfare had been her only motive
– is again inhibited by the fact that the essential premise governing
her dilemma has not been formally declared.

As the moment of confession nears, Trollope moves with
increasing confidence to a more inward presentation of Lady Mason's mind. He gives verbatim her letter to Mr Furnival asking for
advice about Sir Peregrine's offer in Chapter XLI – such texts are
nearly always a sign of Trollope's full understanding of the
writer's motives – and the subsequent interview with Mr Furnival
begins to develop with the true Trollopian attentiveness. In this
scene Lady Mason goes through nearly the whole gamut of the
emotions by which she is animated in a way that may come close
to being stagey, but which is registered with sufficient precision
to offset its histrionic tendencies. The heaving bosom and violent
sobs are just rescued from behavioural cliché by other gestures
that are less conventional and more interesting in their implications, so that the resulting intensity is enough to keep the
reader, as well as Mr Furnival, impressed:

'It is of him I am thinking; – of him and Lucius. Mr
Furnival, they might do their worst with me, if it were not
for that thought. My boy!' And then she rose from her
chair, and stood upright before him, as though she were
going to do or say some terrible thing. He still kept his
chair, for he was startled, and hardly knew what he would
be about. That last exclamation had come from her almost
with a shriek, and now her bosom was heaving as though

her heart would burst with the violence of her sobbing . . .

She sat down again, and leaning both her arms upon the table, hid her face within her hands. He was now standing, and for the moment did not speak to her. Indeed he could not bring himself to break the silence, for he saw her tears, and could still hear the violence of her sobs. And then she was the first to speak. 'If it were not for him,' she said, raising her head, 'I could bear it all. What will he do? what will he do?'

'You mean,' said Mr Furnival, speaking very slowly, 'if the – verdict – should go against us.'

'It will go against us,' she said. 'Will it not? – tell me the truth. You are so clever, you must know. Tell me how it will go. Is there anything I can do to save him?' And she took hold of his arm with both her hands, and looked up eagerly – oh, with such terrible eagerness! – into his face . . .

'Mr Furnival,' she said; and as she spoke there was a hardness came over the soft lines of her feminine face; a look of courage which amounted almost to ferocity, a look which at the moment recalled to his mind, as though it were but yesterday, the attitude and countenance she had borne as she stood in the witness-box at that other trial, now so many years since, – that attitude and countenance which had impressed the whole court with so high an idea of her courage. 'Mr Furnival, weak as I am, I could bear to die here on the spot, – now – if I could only save him from this agony. It is not for myself I suffer.' And then the terrible idea occurred to him that she might attempt to compass her escape by death. But he did not know her. That would have been no escape for her son.

'And you too think that I must not marry him?' she said, putting up her hands to her brows as though to collect her thoughts.

'No; certainly not, Lady Mason.'

'No, no. It would be wrong. But, Mr Furnival, I am so driven that I know not how I should act. What if I should lose my mind?' And as she looked at him there was that about her eyes which did tell him that an ending might be possible. (XLI)

Trollope credits Furnival with an understanding of 'the very essence and core of her feelings' since he is at this point acting as a kind of proxy for the reader – the reader whom Trollope no longer wishes to keep in any suspense as to Lady Mason's guilt. The imminent prospect of being able authorially to come clean seems to give him a new freedom of novelistic movement; we can expect Lady Mason's actual confession to be for author as well as for character a kind of release.

When at last the confession is made, it is presented almost entirely in dramatic terms, the novelist intervening only to supply a few stage directions. With Trollope's usual generosity at times of crisis, the scene is completely made over to the characters. The temptation to underline, to supply a background music of authorial comment which would guide the reader's moral response while intensifying his excitement, was a strong one for a mid-Victorian author, and Trollope's resistance of it at this point does him the more credit:

'Sit down, Mary.' And she did sit down, while he stood leaning over her and thus spoke. 'You speak of sacrificing me. I am an old man with not many more years before me. If I did sacrifice what little is left to me of life with the object of befriending one whom I really love, there would be no more in it than what a man might do, and still feel that the balance was on the right side. But here there will be no sacrifice. My life will be happier, and so will Edith's. And so indeed will that boy's, if he did but know it. For the world's talk, which will last some month or two, I care nothing. This I will confess, that if I were prompted to this only by my own inclination, only by love for you –' and as he spoke he held out his hand to her, and she could not refuse him hers – 'in such a case I should doubt and hesitate and probably keep aloof from such a step. But it is not so. In doing this I shall gratify my own heart, and also serve you in your great troubles. Believe me, I have thought of that.'

'I know you have, Sir Peregrine, – and therefore it cannot be.'

'But therefore it shall be. The world knows it now; and were we to be separated after what has past, the world would say that I – I had thought you guilty of this crime.'

'I must bear all that.' And now she stood before him, not looking him in the face, but with her face turned down towards the ground, and speaking hardly above her breath.

'By heavens, no; not whilst I can stand by your side. Not whilst I have strength left to support you and thrust the lie down the throat of such a wretch as Joseph Mason. No, Mary, go back to Edith and tell her that you have tried it, but that there is no escape for you.' And then he smiled at her. His smile at times could be very pleasant!

But she did not smile as she answered him. 'Sir Peregrine,' she said; and she endeavoured to raise her face to his but failed.

'Well, my love.'

'Sir Peregrine, I am guilty.'

'Guilty! Guilty of what!' he said, startled rather than instructed by her words.

'Guilty of all this with which they charge me.' And then she threw herself at his feet, and wound her arms round his knees. (XLIV)

It is true that the tableau with which the chapter ends provides Trollope with a strong curtain (of which Millais' illustration 'Guilty' takes effective advantage) – perhaps too strong, considering that like some other important conversations in his fiction it takes place straight after breakfast – but it was a passage Trollope remained proud of; he mentions it with approval in the *Autobiography*.

The chapter which immediately follows begins with a clumsy apology – 'I venture to think, I may almost say to hope, that Lady Mason's confession at the end of the last chapter will not have taken anybody by surprise. If such surprise be felt I must have told my tale badly' – but, having got that over, Trollope settles to a more leisurely treatment of the states of mind of the two characters at this new juncture. Sir Peregrine has always been an open book, if an old-fashioned one, and he is chiefly taken up with trying to reconcile the admission he has just heard with the woman he loves and thought he knew. It is not easy for an old man incapable of a lie to understand a person who has lived one for twenty years. As for

Lady Mason, what sees her through here, as generally, is what Trollope calls her 'great power of self-sustenance': 'She did not faint, nor gasp as if she were choking nor become hysteric in her agony; but she lay there, huddled up in the corner of the sofa, with her face hidden, and all those feminine graces forgotten which had long stood her in truth so royally. The inner, true, living woman was there at last, – that and nothing else.' (XLV) In other words, Trollope is now able to get at his true subject. The psychological presentation of Lady Mason in the rest of the book consequently gains greatly – if also intermittently – in authority. Immediately after leaving Sir Peregrine, she makes her way back to her room where there is no fire despite the cold. She refuses a servant's offer to light one although her teeth are chattering because she finds the chill more bearable at such a moment than other people. The insight of this episode contrasts markedly with the externality of the earlier solitary hour of 'sorrow in her heart, and deep thought in her mind' already discussed. Even so, Trollope – in this still relatively early work – is not able entirely to resist adding comments of the 'Wretched miserable woman, but yet so worthy of pity!' sort. He is also nervously careful to put it on record that Mrs Orme's practical charity and forgiveness is creditable but misguided: 'she was full of pity for her who had committed the crime. It was twenty years ago, and had not the sinner repented? Besides, was she to be the judge? "Judge not, and ye shall not be judged," she said, . . . altogether misinterpreting the Scripture in her desire to say something in favour of the poor woman.' (XLV) But Trollope's thoughts about conduct were so instinctively secular that his infrequent invitations to view matters from a more spiritual perspective are inherently unwise, since they do not resolve themselves according to strict religious principle. However, Trollope thought of himself as a moral writer, and Lady Mason must be seen to atone for her guilt even though she is finally let off the retributory hook. After the trial (in which she is acquitted), and after a second confession to her hitherto unsuspecting son (another scene where she falls to the ground and clasps the man's knees), the two of them resign Orley Farm to its rightful owner and go into voluntary exile in Germany (though we last hear of Lucius in Australia, a common Victorian refuge of those who emigrate under a cloud).

Lady Mason is thus not allowed to get away with it in the sense that she keeps the proceeds of her crime, even though she is through a travesty of natural justice legally declared to be innocent of it, and so escapes the prison to which seclusion in Germany is no doubt preferable. Nor does she have to compensate Joseph Mason for her twenty years' possession of Orley Farm: his claim for full restitution is not unreasonable from his point of view, but the lawyers refuse to press it. It may partly be Trollope's worry that readers will feel that she is being let off too lightly that accounts for the recurrence, during the novel's second half, of melodramatic moments where the crime is made to seem its own punishment; she has already, it is implied, more than paid the price. The trouble with this emphasis is that it does not altogether square with what it was in Lady Mason that made her commit her felony in the first place. On the one hand, there are passages of near-melodrama:

> It was matter of wonder to her now, as she looked back at her past life, that her guilt had sat so lightly on her shoulders. The black unwelcome guest, the spectre of coming evil, had ever been present to her; but she had seen it indistinctly, and now and then the power had been hers to close her eyes. Never again could she close them. Nearer to her, and still nearer, the spectre came; and now it sat upon her pillow, and put its claws upon her plate; it pressed upon her bosom with its fiendish strength, telling her that all was over for her in this world: – ay, and telling her worse even than that. (LIII)

Lady Mason's anguish is real enough, but the highly un-Trollopian spectre seems entirely factitious. In a later colloquy with Mrs Orme, Lady Mason is shown in an extremity where again the language betrays too great a sense of strain:

> 'But then came my baby, and the world was all altered for me. What could I do for the only thing that I had ever called my own? Money and riches they had told me were everything.'
> 'But they had told you wrong,' said Mrs Orme, as she wiped the tears from her eyes.
> 'They had told me falsely. I had heard nothing but falsehoods from my youth upwards,' she answered fiercely. 'For

myself I had not cared for these things; but why should not he have money and riches and land? His father had them to give over and above what had already made those sons and daughters so rich and proud. Why should not this other child also be his father's heir? Was he not as well born as they? was he not as fair a child? What did Rebekah do, Mrs Orme? Did she not do worse; and did it not all go well with her? Why should my boy be an Ishmael? Why should I be treated as the bondwoman, and see my little one perish of thirst in this world's wilderness?'

'No Saviour had lived and died for the world in those days,' said Mrs Orme.

'And no Saviour had lived and died for me,' said the wretched woman, almost shrieking in her despair. The lines of her face were terrible to be seen as she thus spoke, and an agony of anguish loaded her brow upon which Mrs Orme was frightened to look. (LX)

Trollope adds that Mrs Orme's attempt to administer spiritual consolation is something 'which I may not dare to handle too closely in such pages as these', — perhaps because he felt such religious matters ought not to be treated in fiction, or perhaps because he knew he was getting out of his novelistic depth. The analyses of Lady Mason which stress her endurance and tenacity are couched in far more plausible terms:

There was much that was wonderful about this woman. While she was with those who regarded her with kindness she could be so soft and womanly; and then, when alone, she could be so stern and hard! And it may be said that she felt but little pity for herself. Though she recognized the extent of her misery, she did not complain of it. Even in her inmost thoughts her plaint was this, — that he, her son, should be doomed to suffer so deeply for her sin! Sometimes she would utter to that other mother a word of wailing, in that he would not be soft to her; but even in that she did not mean to complain of him. She knew in her heart of hearts that she had no right to expect such softness . . .

Yes; she would still bear up, as she had borne up at that other trial. She would dress herself with care, and go down into the court with a smooth brow. Men, as they looked at her, should not at once say, 'Behold the face of a guilty woman!' There was still a chance in the battle, though the odds were so tremendously against her. (LXIII)

Here the reasoned tenacity of her will and the consequent rigorous control of her behaviour are explored by Trollope without anything unconvincing in the tone, if also without much distinction in the expression. But even this account modulates into more admonitory accents as Trollope again feels obliged to emphasize the cost of her 'self-sustenance': 'She longed for rest . . . She had never known true rest. She had not once trusted herself to sleep without the feeling that her first waking thought would be one of horror, as the remembrance of her position came upon her.' And yet in the chapter quoted above we were told that 'for years she had slept in that room, if not happily at least tranquilly. It was matter of wonder to her now . . . that her guilt had sat so lightly on her shoulders.' Powerful as at times it is, the presentation of Lady Mason is never entirely free from such unsettling changes of focus.

What does remain steady throughout is the chivalric devotion of Sir Peregrine, and it is only increased by Lady Mason's refusal to exploit it in the interests of her own self-preservation. The tragic irony is that the old man's love has been so selfless that it has aroused in her an answering affection which ensures that it cannot be reciprocated; she cares for him too much to marry him, since to do so must be to injure him. Even at the end, after the trial and as she prepares for exile, Sir Peregrine still longs for the impossible; in a touching conversation with his daughter-in-law in Chapter LXXVI, he reluctantly accepts that 'it is all over', but Trollope leaves us in no doubt that his love is a sorrow 'that was bringing him to his grave'. The last sentence of the chapter has, in the light of the circumstances, a restraint that gives it power: 'It is seldom that a young man may die from a broken heart; but if an old man have a heart still left to him, it is more fragile.' Despite the laconic understatement, the last four words indicate a particularly intense manifestation of authorial sympathy. The inherent pathos of the whole situation makes the other love stories in *Orley Farm* seem relatively insipid: the transfer of the young lawyer Felix Graham's affections from the girl he has been grooming for matrimony to

Judge Staveley's daughter Madeline is worked through without much excitement, and Lucius's suit to Mr Furnival's daughter Sophia is at first countenanced and then rejected by a girl who knows how to look after her own interests only too chillingly.

Sir Peregrine's farewell to Lady Mason is echoed in an odd way by Trollope's own, which combines loyalty to the character with an uneasy deference to what is taken to be conventional opinion:

> And now we will say farewell to her, and as we do so the chief interest of our tale will end. I may, perhaps be thought to owe an apology to my readers in that I have asked their sympathy for a woman who had so sinned as to have placed her beyond the general sympathy of the world at large. If so, I tender my apology, and perhaps feel that I should confess a fault. But as I have told her story that sympathy has grown upon myself till I have learned to forgive her, and to feel that I too could have regarded her as a friend. Of her future life I will not venture to say anything. But no lesson is truer than that which teaches us to believe that God does temper the wind to the shorn lamb. To how many has it not seemed, at some one period of their lives, that all was over for them, and that to them in their afflictions there was nothing left but to die! And yet they have lived to laugh again, to feel that the air was warm and the earth fair, and that God in giving them ever-springing hope had given everything. How many a sun may seem to set on an endless night, and yet rising again on some morrow –
>
> > 'He tricks his beams, and with new spangled ore Flames in the forehead of the morning sky!'
>
> For Lady Mason let us hope that the day will come in which she also may once again trick her beams in some modest, unassuming way, and that for her the morning may even yet be sweet with a glad warmth. For us, here in these pages, it must be sufficient to say this last kindly farewell. (LXXIX)

In effect, *Orley Farm* ends by asking the question with which *Can You Forgive Her?* begins. In this case the author's exculpatory sympathy for the character has been the result of the process of writing the novel rather than, as in the case of the later book, the consequence of the character's presence in the author's mind over a number of years. What is significant, however, is that the end result is so similar: the impulse to condemn which the study ought to provoke is dissipated by the empathy which that study entails. Even so, the sentimental sermonette which follows Trollope's personal declaration is regrettable; it is hard to feel that Trollope's favourite lines from Milton's 'Lycidas' can have anything to do with Lady Mason's future case, and nothing in his actual portrayal of her suggests that they should. But it is typical of his procedure at such points that the character is admitted to be fictional – she is the 'chief interest of our *tale*' – but treated as if he or she were real, and could look forward to a life beyond the novel: in Trollope's case he or she often could.

One of the reasons why Lady Mason wins her case is that in the court-room itself she, like Phineas Finn, simply does not look guilty – although of course she is and he is not. The analysis of the accused's consciousness during the trial itself is less subtle than in the later novel partly because Trollope has other matters on his mind. One of these is the treatment of the witnesses. The case against Lady Mason rests on the testimony of the two witnesses to the original deed: Bridget Bolster is a dogged reiterator, and even Mr Chaffanbrass cannot do much to shake her, but John Kenneby is timid in manner, his memory not too certain after twenty years, and he does not seem too bright in any case. Mr Furnival has little difficulty in demoralizing him and demolishing his evidence. At the end of the man's cross-examination Trollope briefly flushes with what is obviously an extreme indignation: 'Evidence by means of torture, – thumbscrew and such-like, – we have for many years past abandoned as barbarous, and have acknowledged that it is of its very nature useless in the search after truth. How long will it be before we shall recognize that the other kind of torture is equally opposed both to truth and civilization?' (LXXI) This sudden outcrop of social criticism can not only be related to Trollope's animadversions on lawyers in his then unpublished *The New Zealander* written half a dozen years before *Orley Farm*. Chaffanbrass had already been described as applying 'the thumbscrew, the boots, and the rack to the victim before him' when he first appeared in *The Three Clerks*. The way in which the hapless witness is browbeaten, bullied, threatened, terrified, and held up to the court's contempt by Mr Allwinde in *The New Zealander* also repeats the performance given by the Dublin lawyer Allewinde in Trollope's first novel *The Macdermots of Ballycloran*.

In fact, matters of legal principle are raised sufficiently often in *Orley Farm* for the critic to be tempted to posit an integrating concept, to sense the consoling presence of a structuring theme. Of course, lawyers appear very frequently in Trollope's work – the Gerouldses *A Guide to Trollope* lists over a hundred of them – but in *Orley Farm* several not only have an unusual prominence as characters, but also specifically discuss the question of the relationship between moral principle and professional ethics. Early on in the novel, Lucius Mason refuses to consider going into the law because '"lawyers are all liars"'. (II) Mr Furnival, Lady Mason's lawyer but also a distinguished member of his profession, and the young and idealistic Felix Graham, among others, attend an international legal conference at Birmingham at which the eminent German jurist Von Bauhr gives a protracted and high-minded lecture. Most of the English lawyers naturally find such continental philosophizing insufferably boring, but Graham sees something in him, and so does Trollope, who is tender towards the German's pleasantly absurd private fantasy of a bust inscribed 'To Von Bauhr, who reformed the laws of nations'. Felix's views are clearly close to Trollope's as expressed in *The New Zealander* (as its modern editor points out). The argument is that the English system is fundamentally mistaken in its attitude towards guilt. A patently guilty man is given every chance to escape proper punishment through technicalities which lawyers are therefore encouraged to exploit improperly. Moreover, those lawyers are led to think purely in terms of their client's interest, when they ought to be concerned with establishing the facts: '"It all resolves itself into this,"' Graham says, '"Let every lawyer go into court with a mind resolved to make conspicuous to the light of day that which seems to him to be the truth. A lawyer who does not do that . . . has in my mind undertaken work which is unfit for a gentleman and impossible for an honest man."' (XVIII) Given such views, it is naturally important for Felix to be able to believe in Lady Mason's innocence when he agrees to act as a junior in her defence. His anxiety on the matter embarrasses Furnival, who has become privately convinced of his client's guilt, and is regarded with contempt by Chaffanbrass, who has never doubted it. Felix's intolerance is even reproved by the moderate Judge Staveley, who defends Chaffanbrass and his like: '"Graham, my dear fellow, judge not that you be not judged ... Believe me that as you grow older and also see more of them, your opinion will be more lenient, – and more just."' (LII) Nevertheless, the author's own intruded comments at one point tally exactly with Felix's: of the 'five lawyers concerned, not one of whom gave to the course of justice credit that it would ascertain the truth, and not one of whom wished that the truth should be ascertained ... I cannot understand how any gentleman can be willing to use his intellect for the propagation of untruth, and to be paid for so using it.' (LVI)

Trollope's own ideas about the relationship between truth and legal practice, and his indignation at the way witnesses are treated in court (as he points out in Chapter LXXV they are the only ones present who get nothing out of it), are thus an important element in *Orley Farm*. The discussion is not only carried on at the professional level: the commercial traveller Moulder – who bulks large in the robustly vulgar sub-plot – delights in the professionalism of barristers who can reduce '"some swell dressed up to his eyes"' to the flabbiness of wet paper in ten minutes. As he says, '"That's power ... and I call it beautiful."' (LXI) Arguments about truth do not impress him – '"They're paid for it; it's their duties; just as it's my duty to sell Hubble's and Grease's sugar."' Mr Moulder takes what might be called the Chaffanbrass view of the question, and it is a view of which Trollope himself seems inconsistently to concede the force. He is prepared to acknowledge, in Chapter LXXV, that 'there was a species of honesty about Mr Chaffanbrass which certainly deserved praise. He was always true to the man whose money he had taken.' Trollope couples the barrister's fidelity to his client to that of 'an assassin' he knew in Ireland who prided himself on never failing his customer. The irony is both ponderous and not entirely persuasive. After all, who delights in what Mr Moulder would call Chaffanbrass's 'power' more than its creator? Even allowing for an element of irony in his earlier comment that 'It was pretty to see the meek way in which Mr Chaffanbrass rose to his work' (LXVIII), Trollope clearly relishes the forensic technique of his 'old friend' as it is displayed in *Orley Farm*, even if the exhibition itself is not as masterly as it was to become in *Phineas Redux* (where in Chapter LX we also learn something of Chaffanbrass's private opinions about the law). Even Chaffanbrass's first appearance in *The Three Clerks* was something which, in a proud understatement in the *Autobiography*, Trollope felt he had no cause to be ashamed of. (VI) Trollope instinctively warms to people who set about their work whole-heartedly. It is in this novel (apropos of Mr Furnival's early struggles) that he utters one of his most striking *cris de cœur*: 'There is no human bliss equal to twelve hours of work with only six hours in which to do it.' (XLIX) Mr Furnival himself finds that, as he takes up Lady Mason's cause in court, 'the old fire' returns to him, so that 'it may be doubted whether at moments during these three days he did not again persuade himself that she was an injured woman'. (LXXI) His closing speech for the defence – reported by Trollope extensively with long extracts in direct speech – is a highly eloquent performance. Its energy seems due to a kind of release in the novelist himself, and anticipates the vim of Quintus Slide's disgraceful editorials in the *People's Banner*. As a result the heavily ironic authorial corrective which follows it – pointing out that even when it became clear that the wretched witnesses were in the right, the legal world still regarded Furnival as having done his duty 'in a manner becoming an English barrister and an English gentleman' (LXXII) – lacks complete authority.

As for Felix Graham, who is nearest to being the mouthpiece for Trollope's own views, it seems unlikely that his intransigence will be long sustained, once the responsibilities of marriage to a judge's daughter modify his idealism. The domesticated Isadore Hamel in *Ayala's Angel* had to start sculpting real people for the market rather than allegorical figures for posterity; Felix will similarly adjust to the actual world, and stop writing clever articles on legal reform for the *Quarterly*. It will not be to his discredit when he does so; other men of principle in Trollope's fiction – John Bold in *The Warden* for example, or Phineas Finn – abandon the purity of their original positions and are not pilloried for it. Only the unnaturally obstinate or the mad refuse to accommodate to things as they are. After all, just as Chaffanbrass is honest according to his lights, so Furnival is neither corrupt or culpable, as Trollope on more than one occasion insists. His motives for defending an attractive women are not entirely pure but nor are they vicious. As Trollope reminds us early in the novel when discussing what spurred Mr Dockwrath on to revive the Orley Farm case, 'All our motives are mixed'. (XVI) It is one of those inconspicuous little asides about the self-evident which contribute so much to our sense of both the clarity and the tolerance of the author's vision. And in a way he is as compromised as the rest: after all, it is the author himself who has willed that guilt should in this instance escape the legitimate clutches of the law. Lady Mason's story does not end as it does because Trollope wishes to show that Justice as at present conducted is blind, as Felix teasingly suggests when Judge Staveley consents to join in a game of blindman's-buff during the Christmas festivities at Noningsby. What Trollope has done is to prefer the felt claims of the character who constitutes the tale's 'chief interest' to the stricter demands of poetic as well as natural justice. In theory Trollope constantly hankers after a state of affairs in which transparent straight-forwardness brings its own honest reward, the kind of world which Sir Peregrine Orme fondly imagines to exist; in practice, the novelist's understanding loyalty to the compromised individual case coerces him into a collusion which as constantly subverts his own ideals. His attitude to guilt is thus both genuinely severe and intensely exonerating. That Trollope was as an artist so little incommoded by this discrepancy is an indication of his profound equanimity.

Lady Anna

Ten years after *Orley Farm*, Trollope came back to the idea of a titled mother who would do anything to maintain the claims of her child in *Lady Anna* (written in 1871 during a two-month voyage to Australia, published 1874). In this case, however, the mother only becomes criminal towards the end rather than at the beginning of the story. Guilt is openly led up to, instead of serving as a veiled point of departure, and although *Lady Anna* is relatively slight when compared with the generous scale of *Orley Farm*, the gain in psychological coherence is marked.

The story is initially set on the Cumberland–Westmorland border, a locality which Trollope again associates with a marked intensity of emotion (as he also did in *Can You Forgive Her?*, *Sir*

Harry Hotspur of Humblethwaite, and *The Duke's Children*).
Josephine Murray marries Lord Lovel because she thinks much of
rank. Trollope concedes that her motives were ignoble but hopes
that 'her wrongs may be thought worthy of sympathy, – and may
be felt in some sort to atone' (I) for them; the plea resembles that
made on behalf of Lady Mason. The Countess begins to pay for her
ambition soon enough: after six months of marriage the Earl – an
inveterate womanizer – explains that he already had an Italian wife
when he 'married' her, and so the child she is carrying cannot be his
heir. When he dies, he leaves everything to his latest Italian mistress, cutting out both his nephew Frederick, who at least succeeds
to the title, and Anna, the Countess's daughter. There are thus
three claimants to the large fortune involved (later said to be around
£300,000), and the legal complications are considerable. Trollope
has to go into these – the situation is kept under constant review by
a number of eminent lawyers, from the Solicitor-General downwards – but their main value is that they allow him to monitor the
unceasing struggle by the Countess to establish the validity of her
marriage and the consequent recognition of her daughter as truly
Lady Anna. In her fight she is morally and materially supported by
Thomas Thwaite and his son Daniel, tailors by trade and Radicals
by conviction. Unusually for Trollope, the story is set back in the
earlier part of the century – its main action is intermittently
signalled as taking place in the 1830s although the book feels
contemporary most of the time – and this allows Thwaite *père* to be
acquainted with the Lake poets Wordsworth and Southey. Indeed,
an elderly man referred to as 'the Keswick poet' is subsequently
consulted by Daniel, who is disconcerted to find that he takes a
more worldly view of things than the idealism of his verse might
have led one to expect. Daniel and Anna thus grow up together,
and by the time of the book's main action, have become secretly
engaged. It is this which makes Anna resist the solution proposed
by the collective wisdom of the lawyers: her marriage to her
cousin, Lord Lovel, the young Earl. This would reconcile their
competing claims, give the title the financial support needed for its
proper maintenance and avoid the terrible possibility of the tailor
getting his hands on the ancestral cash (we may remember the
general anxiety lest Burgo Fitzgerald should dissipate Lady Glencora's fortune).

Anna is not immune to the appeal of aristocracy. Frederick has a 'sweet winsome boyishness of face' (X) which is restful after the fire and authority of Daniel's look, and of course his manners are nice. During her stay with the Lovel family in Yorkshire, he organizes an expedition to Wharfedale; Anna is impressed by the ruins of Bolton Abbey, and is successfully encouraged to cross the fast-flowing river by the well-known stepping stones. Her cousin also tempts her to jump across the narrow gully known as The Stryd, but this time Anna hurts herself. These little episodes might be seen as neatly allegorizing the opportunity of crossing the class divide which is being offered to Anna, but they are better left naturally in narrative place as the sort of thing that idle tourists do. When the young Earl formally proposes, however, Anna immediately and almost instinctively rejects him on the grounds that she is already committed to Daniel, a man of proven worth:

> 'He should not have asked for this,' said Lord Lovel hoarsely.
> 'Why not he, as well as you? He is as much a man. If I could believe in your love after two days, Lord Lovel, could I not trust his after twenty years of friendship?'
> 'You knew that he was beneath you.'
> 'He was not beneath me. He was above me. We were poor, – while he and his father had money, which we took. He could give, while we received. He was strong while we were weak, – and was strong to comfort us. And then, Lord Lovel, what knew I of rank, living under his father's wing? They told me I was the Lady Anna, and the children scouted me. My mother was a countess. So she swore, and I at least believed her. But if ever rank and title were a profitless burden, they were to her. Do you think that I had learned then to love my rank?' (XVI)

It is characteristic of the underlying strength of Anna's temperament that although apparently docile she should, when the occasion demands, speak up and out with a forthrightness only emulated in the novel by her fiancé. As the *Autobiography* and Trollope's own letters confirm, it was an essential part of his original conception that her loyalty should prove capable of resisting all the heavy pressures that are put on it. He explained in a letter (21 June 1873) to his friend Lady Wood that 'The story was originated in my mind by an idea I had as to the doubt which would, (or might) exist in a girls mind as to whether she ought to be true to her troth, or true to her leneage [*sic*] when, from early circumstances the one had been given in a manner detrimental to the other – and I determined that in such case she ought to be true all through.' The idea of Lady Anna marrying a tailor is as distressing to most of the characters in the book as it apparently was to some of Trollope's original readers, and they go to unscrupulous lengths to get her to change her mind. It is not only her mother – driven almost mad by a recalcitrance which threatens everything she has fought for during the last twenty years – who persecutes Anna; even the lawyers who ought to be acting for her bully her and are not above bending the truth in order to bring her round.

In fact, a number of those on the establishment rather than the egalitarian side of the question act sufficiently badly to suggest that *Lady Anna* is a work with levelling tendencies. The young Earl, for instance, is for a time thoroughly put off Anna when he learns that she has already been contaminated by the embrace of a common fellow like Daniel Thwaite. Moreover, his suggestion to the Solicitor-General – '"Could we buy the tailor, Sir William?"' (XVIII) – hardly shows him in a pleasant light. On the other hand, he behaves quite well once it is clear that he has no hope of succeeding with Anna, and indeed the Radical Daniel is rather disappointed to find a nobleman capable of being civil. Admittedly, Anna's generosity has given Lord Lovel the prospect of a share of the disputed estate. However, Trollope's letter makes it clear that the social gulf between the two suitors was intended to intensify the girl's dilemma, rather than as a theme in its own right: 'To make the discrepancy as great as possible I made the girl an Earl's daughter, and the betrothed a tailor.' The situation is essentially an extreme version of Trollope's misalliance plot, of which he had by this time (1871) long experience. Given the kind of *sotto voce* tenacity which Anna shares with earlier heroines of deceptively mild demeanour, the only serious narrative uncertainty concerns the actual terms on which she will finally get her subdued but unshaken way.

One has only to compare Daniel's politics with those of the more familiar and more articulate Radical, Felix Holt, to see that Trollope's treatment of them is thin – so thin, in fact, as to make it difficult to see them as essential to the story's interests. (George Eliot's novel, published in 1866, was also set in the 1830s.) Although only a tailor's foreman in Wigmore Street, Daniel is said to be a thoughtful and well-read man whose ideas about the desirability of diminishing 'the distances, not only between the rich and the poor, but between the high and the low' (IV) seem perfectly compatible with Trollope's own – and for that matter with Plantagenet Palliser's. He does tend to dwell on social injustice in a personal way, and thinks of himself as a better man than the aristocrats with whom he and his like have as little in common, he feels, as the Jews and the Christians have in *The Merchant of Venice*. Given the aristocrats on offer in *Lady Anna*, he has some reason to do so. Daniel is a man of principle as well as power (for all his egalitarianism, he is thoroughly masterful – there is an element of fear in Anna's love for him). His integrity is irreproachably solid, as the lawyers who try to insinuate that his attachment to Anna is not unconnected with her wealth quickly find out. In such interviews (in Chapters XXI and XXXIV, for example) Daniel finds the exhilarating fluency common to Trollopian characters when they know that they are in the right and have a favourable opportunity to demonstrate that they are so; there is a kind of exultation in exposing the shabbiness of the opposite party's position while underlining one's own probity. Such successful defiance of conventional authority, however, is more a matter of the kind of temperament Trollope was drawn to (as in the cases of Mr Crawley and Dr Wortle) than an expression of class hostility. Daniel's Radicalism is a function of his personality in relation to his circumstances and his relationship to Anna Lovel. We do not see him in independent political activity deriving from a sense of social obligation. Unlike Felix Holt, he does not grapple with the problems of working-class literacy or get involved in mob violence, and it is hard to imagine Trollope writing in Daniel's name the kind of closely-argued 'Address to Working Men' which George Eliot published as Felix Holt's in *Blackwood's Magazine* (January 1868). The *Saturday Review* thought it 'cowardly' that we hardly glimpse Daniel at his actual trade. His speech does not have regional or proletarian features; he is not related to the provincial society of the period. His letter to

Anna, offering to release her from her engagement if she wishes (given verbatim in Chapter XXV) reveals no betraying solecisms but is written in the manly and transparently straightforward diction shared by Trollope's men of integrity. At the beginning of the novel it is generally assumed that Daniel, being a tailor, cannot be a gentleman; by its end his behaviour and qualities have sufficiently impressed the Solicitor-General for him to prophesy that '"In five years he'll be in Parliament as likely as not"' (XLI), and the Earl recommends Daniel to his ultra uncle on the grounds that '"You'll find he'll make a very good sort of gentleman."' (XLVI) In a concluding but inconclusive conversation the Solicitor-General agrees with Daniel Thwaite that the theory of equality is very grand but observes that human variability will always re-establish inequalities; what Daniel fails to realize is that aristocracy is both the reward and the nursery of public service. Sir William's view of social process is certainly soothing: '"The energetic, the talented, the honest, and the unselfish will always be moving towards an aristocratic side of society, because their virtues will beget esteem, and esteem will beget wealth, – and wealth gives power for good offices."' (XLVII) Daniel's sardonic gloss – '"As when one man throws away forty thousand a year on race-courses"' – puts a less comforting note of reality into the matter (at this date, Silverbridge has not yet dropped £70,000 on the St Leger) – but he is not unimpressed by the argument that thinking of equality as a good does not necessarily mean that all those who most benefit from rank and place must be regarded as bad. At any rate, Daniel does not by the end have to ask Anna to share the life of a poor man, as Felix asks Esther to do in George Eliot's novel; he is no way covets Anna's money but his attitude to it is pragmatic, not quixotic. Besides, he has returned to him the £9,000 which the Thwaites have lent to the Countess over the years. The married couple are last seen leaving for a fact-finding tour of Australia (as Trollope himself was when writing their history). Trollope ends the book with a half-promise of 'further doings' by Daniel and Lady Anna. This may be no more than a graceful coda, but it may also indicate Trollope's sense at the time of future possibilities in the characters. The power of and contradictions within Daniel's personality – Trollope suggestively describes him at one point as 'ambitious, discontented, sullen, and tyrannical' (XXI) as well as showing him as patently honourable and disinterested – might well have been further explored. Perhaps the greatest compliment Trollope pays to Daniel's calibre and dignity is his refusal on this occasion to take the character's origins as a signal for a semi-comic mode, as he does in the case of Ontario Moggs in *Ralph the Heir*. Trollope himself has here transcended those social preconceptions from which many in the book suffer. However, his treatment of the political and historical issues raised by the story is perfunctory. As usual Trollope's creative mind was on the individual case, and was unworried and even careless about the ideology which might be inferred from it.

The most interesting individual situation in *Lady Anna* is that of the heroine's obsessive mother. When the narrator remarks in the first chapter that for the Countess 'it had become her one religion to assert her daughter's right', it may seem not much more than a figure of speech. The novel, however, goes on to show that the phrase is literally accurate; the intensity and absoluteness of her creed leads to a kind of imbalance which reminds us of Mr Kennedy in his later, unstable phase, or of Mrs Bolton, the maternal maniac in *John Caldigate*, who is also unable to tolerate her daughter's marital choice. The Countess's preoccupation with her rank and her rights means that initially it simply does not occur to her that Anna could be seriously attached to Daniel, her childhood playfellow, but infinitely below her in birth. Nor does she realize that her constant insistence on Anna's rightful title makes the girl sick of it. When knowledge of Anna's attachment becomes inescapable, the Countess's reaction is revealingly extreme.

> She would love still, but she would never again be tender till her daughter should have repudiated her base, – her monstrous engagement . . . Sooner than that the tailor should reap the fruit of her labours, – labours which had been commenced when she first gave herself in marriage to that dark, dreadful man, – sooner than that her child should make ignoble the blood which it had cost her so much to ennoble, she would do deeds which should make even the wickedness of her husband child's play in the world's esteem. (XX)

She immediately moves out of the house infected by Daniel's presence and takes lodgings in Keppel Street (the Trollopes' old address again), making her intransigence clear to Anna in tones in

311

which the melodramatic language has the valid function of beginning to register the hysteria within.

Chapter XXXVI presents a strong scene – almost an operatic trio
(of which there is a reprise in Chapter XLII) – with the two lovers
reaffirming their troth in the presence of the baleful Countess, and
ends with these threats from mother to daughter:

> 'Listen to me, Anna. You shall never marry him; never.
> With my own hands I will kill him first; – or you.' The girl
> stood looking into her mother's face, and trembling. 'Do you
> understand that?'
>
> 'You do not mean it, mamma.'
>
> 'By the God above me, I do! Do you think that I will stop
> at anything now; – after having done so much? Do you think
> that I will live to see my daughter the wife of a foul, swel-
> tering tailor? No, by heavens! He tells you that when you are
> twenty-one, you will not be subject to my control. I warn
> you to look to it. I will not lose my control, unless when I see
> you married to some husband fitting your condition in life.
> For the present you will live in your own room, as I will live
> in mine. I will hold no intercourse whatever with you, till I
> have constrained you to obey me.'

The unnerving thing about the Countess's remarks about being
driven mad and killing, so barely reported by the author, is that
they may sound theatrical but are in fact literal guides to what is to
happen. When, a little later, the Solicitor-General tells her she
should get the better of her feeling that she would rather see Anna
die than become Daniel Thwaite's wife, she replies: '"Of course I
should. No doubt every clergyman in England would tell me the
same thing. It is easy to say all that, sir. Wait till you are tried."'
(XXXVII) Sir William's easy pieties are left looking rather wan in
the light of the Countess's fierce and lucid unreason.

The most striking part of Trollope's presentation of the Countess
is the point at which the logic of her obsession pushes her into
action. Her attempt to kill Daniel and thus remove the cause of all
her trouble is given in the watchful and steady narrative manner
that in his mature work serves Trollope so well at times of violent
crisis:

She had let the moment go by, – the first moment, – when he was close to her, and now there would be half the room between them. But she was very quick. She seized the pistol, and, transferring it to her right hand, she rushed after him, and when the door was already half open she pulled the trigger. In the agony of that moment she heard no sound, though she saw the flash. She saw him shrink and pass the door, which he left unclosed, and then she heard a scuffle in the passage, as though he had fallen against the wall. She had provided herself especially with a second barrel, – but that was now absolutely useless to her. There was no power left to her wherewith to follow him and complete the work which she had begun. She did not think that she had killed him, though she was sure that he was struck. She did not believe that she had accomplished anything of her wishes, – but had she held in her hand a six-barrelled revolver, as of the present day, she could have done no more with it. She was overwhelmed with so great a tremor at her own violence that she was almost incapable of moving. She stood glaring at the door, listening for what should come, and the moments seemed to be hours. But she heard no sound whatever. A minute passed away perhaps, and the man did not move. She looked around as if seeking some way of escape, – as though, were it possible, she would get to the street through the window. There was no mode of escape, unless she would pass out through the door to the man who, as she knew, must still be there. Then she heard him move. She heard him rise, – from what posture she knew not, and step towards the stairs. She was still standing with the pistol in her hand, but was almost unconscious that she held it. At last her eye glanced upon it, and she was aware that she was still armed. Should she rush after him, and try what she could do with that other bullet? The thought crossed her mind, but she knew that she could do nothing. Had all the Lovels depended upon it, she could not have drawn that other trigger. She took the pistol, put it back into its former hiding-place, mechanically locked the little door, and then seated herself in her chair. (XLIII)

The last little movement is brilliantly seen, although like the rest of the account completely unobtrusive. As we have already noted, the pot-shot at the hated rival (which is what Daniel is) is an event which Trollope had already studied with some attention, in Vavasor's attempt on John Grey in *Can You Forgive Her?* for instance, and more comparably, given the instability involved, in Mr Kennedy's firing at Finn in *Phineas Redux*, the novel which immediately preceded *Lady Anna* in point of composition. (Phineas was shot at by Kennedy in Judd Street, only a few minutes' walk away from Keppel Street, where the Countess wounds Daniel.) In the latter case, we are given the moment-by-moment sensations of the person with the gun, rather than only those of the intended victim. Trollope's understanding of the Countess's reactions after her attempt are equally plausible. After it becomes clear that Daniel is going to keep quiet about the affair out of consideration for Anna, her mother lapses into a fatalistic passivity (if not into the actual insanity of the murderous mother in *An Eye For An Eye*), from which she only emerges to return to solitude relieved by impulsive good works among the poor in her native Cumberland.

In his description of the Countess's last days, Trollope completely avoids the kind of moral commentary which was so anxious to assure us that Lady Mason in *Orley Farm* had indeed paid the price for her dreadful deed. In *Lady Anna* guilt is again left unpunished by the law, although it again leads to desolation and a kind of exile. Now, however, the overwhelming desire of the mother for her child to inherit has been studied in conditions of much greater narrative isolation and presented more dramatically and objectively. It is in the nature of this dispassionate attention to make us feel that we understand the guilty party better, even though she is put before us with much greater novelistic economy.

Ralph the Heir

As its title indicates, *Ralph the Heir* (written 1869, published 1871) also involves a question of legitimacy, but a situation involving uncertain inheritance is once more chiefly used as a means of studying the individualities of those affected by them. In fact there are two Ralphs, and the narrative issue to be resolved is simply which one of them is to be the heir? In the normal way the pleasant estate of Newton, on the Hampshire–Berkshire borders, must pass from the present squire to his nephew Ralph Newton, given the absence of a legitimate son (as the Meetkerke estate would have passed to Thomas Trollope). There is, however, an illegitimate son – also called Ralph – who lives with his father and to whose interests the old man brings an intense, even fanatical, devotion comparable to Lady Mason's and Countess Lovel's. The squire has not only the usual eagerness to pass on his land to the son he loves, but he also has the added incentive of wanting to see his son thus compensated for his illegitimacy. The entail which frustrates the squire provides a characteristically Trollopian conflict between the freedom of the individual and the inhibitions of the law.

The contrast between Ralph the heir and Ralph who is not the heir understandably strengthens the squire's concern, since the former is an unimpressive if not entirely unamiable drone and the latter everything that an English country gentleman should be. Admittedly Ralph the heir is in a difficult position; as a man 'brought up to great expectations' (X) and with some money of his own, he feels no obligation to settle to anything. On the other hand, he is such a weak – though not vicious – character, that settling to anything is probably beyond his power. Although physically quite energetic, he spends his time in a state of drift which is fundamentally enervated. As his debts begin to get out of hand they oblige him to consider not only marrying beneath him for money, but also selling his right of inheritance to his uncle. The possibility of buying up the heir's interest excites the squire greatly, but his euphoria leads to one of Trollope's many hunting accidents, and he dies before his plans to benefit the illegitimate son can come to fruition. In this novel, the law takes its proper course, and in the end the legitimate nephew is indeed the heir.

When he finally installs himself at Newton, Ralph the heir is lucky not to have become encumbered with a wife who, whatever her personal merits, is undeniably and unapologetically the daughter of a tradesman. Ralph has become sufficiently friendly with, as well as indebted to, the breeches-maker Mr Neefit – not the subtlest of names, but he is not the subtlest of characters – to be invited down to Neefit's rural retreat (as it then was) at Hendon. As with Sexty Parker's relationship with Lopez in *The Prime Minister*, Trollope exploits the interface between the genteel and the common cheerfully. As with the Mrs Greenow areas of *Can You Forgive*

Her?, Trollope's untroubled sense both of his own station and of his audience's attitudes allows him to give vulgarity his full and genial attention. In fact, Neefit stands out as a character with a good deal of vitality in a novel in which energy is in relatively short supply. Highly successful in his trade – so that he can afford to take a haughty line with customers unwise enough to complain – he doesn't know what to do with himself outside it. He buys Alexandrina Cottage to please his wife, and would like to purchase Ralph to please his daughter. Polly is not insensible of the charms of becoming a lady and would do much to gratify her father, but she rightly sees that Ralph's rather tepid proposals are only something that financial exigency and Neefit's pressure have reduced him to, and not the result of a genuine devotion like that of Ontario Moggs, the Radical son of a fashionable boot-maker. Neefit becomes almost 'driven . . . to madness' by 'foiled ambition' (LIII); he pesters Ralph at his lodgings (rather as the money-lenders persecuted Eames and Finn), and writes abusive letters to Ralph's connections. But all his appeals to Ralph – whom he engagingly addresses as 'Captain . . . feeling, no doubt, that Mister was cold between father-in-law and son-in-law, and not quite daring to drop all reverential title' (XVII) – all his efforts to make him act 'on the square', are finally unavailing. He has to accept, with bad grace, the wishes of a sensible daughter who is wise enough, Trollope feels, to stay within her own class and in the care of someone who really loves her. There is thus no question of a *Lady Anna* kind of union between trade and birth, even though Neefit's obsessive parental ambition is in some degree a comic analogue of Countess Lovel's – and in this novel parallels Squire Newton's.

Despite his unsatisfactory performance Ralph the heir is nominally the novel's hero; his mediocrity is defended by Trollope in the antepenultimate chapter with the same arguments used to exonerate Frank Greystock in *The Eustace Diamonds*. However, the case is made so belatedly in this instance that it looks too much like afterthought and too little like settled authorial intention. It hardly seems enough here to say that life is full of men like Ralph even if novels are not; the fictional character must make some claim on our attention beyond a minimal plausibility. To be fair, Ralph is not entirely uninteresting: his aimlessness is something that Trollope understands, even though in this case indecision does not reach any degree of intensity. Ralph is 'not without good instincts' but, as one of the girls to whom he proposes notes, there is about him 'a tone of sustained self-applause' (XXXII) that indicates his basic egocentricity. His behaviour towards Clarissa Underwood is careless and causes her an unhappiness which a more sensitive man would have felt more guilty about; it is typical of a flabbiness of character which Trollope conveys without much censure but also without much artistic enthusiasm.

The other Ralph has an inherent uprightness of nature which is almost too obvious a contrast. His conduct in wooing the beautiful orphan Mary Bonner is scrupulously correct. When he has to vacate the estate his father so nearly succeeded in conveying to him, he buys a farm in East Anglia – the terrain of those other exemplary gentleman-farmers also frustrated in love, Will Belton and John Grey – and buries his sorrows in manly application. Even during his father's lifetime, he constantly tries to cool the old squire's irritability over the iniquitous entail. All the same, he would be inhuman not to care at all about his chances of inheritance, and perhaps the most interesting part of this Ralph's experience for us is his state of mind after his father's death. Here, for instance, Trollope briefly touches on an aspect of mental stress in a way that is unusual:

Ralph sat down to dinner all alone. Let what will happen to break hearts and ruin fortunes, dinner comes as long as the means last for providing it. The old butler waited upon him in absolute silence, fearing to speak a word, lest the word at such a time should be ill-spoken. No doubt the old man was thinking of the probable expedience of his retiring upon his savings; feeling, however, that it became him to show, till the last, every respect to all who bore the honoured name of Newton. When the meat had been eaten, the old servant did say a word. 'Won't you come round to the fire, Mr Ralph?' and he placed comfortably before the hearth one of the heavy arm-chairs with which the corners of the broad fire-place were flanked. But Ralph only shook his head, and muttered some refusal. There he sat, square to the table, with the customary bottle of wine before him, leaning back with his hands in his pockets, thinking of his condition in life. The loneliness of the room, the loneliness of the house, were horrible to him. And yet he would not that his solitude should be interrupted . . . He had watched during the whole of the previous night, and now had slumbered in his chair from time to time. But his sleeping had been of that painful, wakeful nature which brings with it no refreshment. It had been full of dreams, in all of which there had been some grotesque reference to the property, but in none of them had there been any memory of the Squire's terrible death. And yet, as he woke and woke and woke again, it can hardly be said that the truth had come back upon him as a new blow. Through such dreams there seems to exist a double memory, and a second identity. The misery of his isolated position never for a moment left him; and yet there were repeated to him over and over again those bungling, ill-arranged, impossible pictures of trivial transactions about the place, which the slumber of a few seconds sufficed to create in his brain. 'Mr Ralph, you must go to bed; – you must indeed, sir,' said the old butler, standing over him with a candle during one of these fitful dreamings. (XXXIV)

Earlier, under the immediate impact of his father's death, Ralph hates himself because 'he could not keep himself from remembering that he had now lost more than a father'. (XXXI) Such a state of divided mind, torn between sorrow and self-interest, had interested Trollope since the days of Archdeacon Grantly's wrestle with his conscience by the death-bed of his father the Bishop, and its reinvestigation in *Ralph the Heir* provides some of its most closely observed pages.

The most absorbing area of this often relatively routine novel also involves the isolated mind, but in the case of Sir Thomas Underwood the alienation is the product not of crisis but of settled habit and inclination. The terms on which he is introduced are, novelistically speaking, distinctly promising. The first chapter is given over to a full account not only of Sir Thomas's personal history but also, less predictably, of his peculiar temperament – a temperament which 'I, and I hope my readers also, will have to know very intimately'; Trollope writes as if the gaining of that knowledge was the point of the novel. In fact, intimacy in relationship is exactly what Sir Thomas cannot cope with. A widower of sixty, he has no close friend, has largely withdrawn from his profession and the political career which had briefly made him Solicitor-General, and even leaves his daughters largely to their own devices out at Fulham while he keeps to his lawyer's chambers, emerging to take a lonely dinner at his club. He is attended in Southampton Buildings by his long-time clerk; the two live in a symbiotic seclusion that could easily suggest Dickensian eccentricity were it not for the way in which Trollope underlines the self-accusatory sensitivity that makes Sir Thomas's withdrawn life almost as painful to him as a gregarious one would be. He broods over the 'almost insupportable mortification' caused by the readiness of his former political colleagues to drop him, once they had discovered how unconversible he was. No one realizes that despite his public competence in court or in the House of Commons, he was privately 'shy to a degree quite unintelligible to men in general' – though such thinness of skin in unlikely persons is familiar enough to readers of Trollope. Sir Thomas feels permanently guilty about being an absentee parent, but nevertheless slips away from the Fulham villa as much as he can and on the flimsiest excuses. He seems least burdened in the stillness of the small hours:

> He would prowl about the purlieus of Chancery Lane, the Temple, and Lincoln's Inn, till two or even three o'clock in the morning; – looking up at the old dingy windows, and holding, by aid of those powers which imagination gave him, long intercourse with men among whom a certain weakness in his physical organization did not enable him to live in the flesh. Well the policemen knew him as he roamed about, and much they speculated as to his roamings. But in these night wanderings he addressed no word to any one; nor did any one ever address a word to him. Yet the world, perhaps, was more alive to him then than at any other period in the twenty-four hours. (I)

Sir Thomas's potential affinities with hypersensitive and recessed natures – a class of which Plantagenet Palliser is the greatest example – will be immediately obvious. The main disappointment of *Ralph the Heir*, however, is that Trollope fails to find ways of developing and dramatizing the character's difficulties which do justice to his imaginative apprehension of them. The recurring elements in the book's situations are not in this case enough to mobilize fully what seem to be the character's possibilities. For the first third of the novel Sir Thomas does little but worry about his new guardianship of his destitute niece Mary Bonner and about the rudderless Ralph. An invitation then arrives, out of the blue, to stand as a Conservative candidate for the constituency of Percycross in tandem with Mr Griffenbottom, long established as its Tory member but hardly a model of integrity or the type of politician with whom someone of Sir Thomas's fastidiousness would wish to associate. Sir Thomas's readiness to interrupt the noiseless tenor of his way is ascribed by Trollope to 'that renewed ambition in his breast . . . which six months ago he would have declared to be at rest for ever' (XX), but at this point the motivation seems to be thrown in as a matter of authorial convenience.

Sir Thomas has a bad time at Percycross. His experiences are in every way disagreeable and the constituency proves to be hopelessly habituated to bribery (although, as in George Vavasor's campaign in *Can You Forgive Her?*, there is an agent who hates electoral purity with an intensity that has in its turn a kind of perverse integrity which quite wins Trollope's respect). The ultimate disenfranchisement of the borough is obviously just. Sir Thomas even has his arm broken by a stone thrown at him when on the hustings (it is at any rate a change to have a Trollopian fracture not caused by a hunting accident or pistol shot). But at least his injury restores to him some of the privacy which he so sorely misses, and he is, for the moment, one of the members for Percycross. The constituency goes on being tiresome, nevertheless; Mr Griffenbottom proposes a deal to head off an inquiry into electoral malpractice which Sir Thomas indignantly declines, but he still has to go through the mortification of having to protest his innocent intentions in open court. It is natural enough for him to conclude that 'It was all dirt from beginning to end' (XLIV), and equally natural for him to return to his sequestered habits with some relief. What is rather remarkable is that it is only at this late stage that the reader is told what the governing idea of his existence is. For over thirty years, it is now revealed, Sir Thomas has been planning to write the life of Bacon:

Sir Thomas had resolved that he would tell the tale as it had never yet been told, that he would unravel facts that had never seen the light, that he would let the world know of what nature really had been this man, – and that he would write a book that should live. He had never abandoned his purpose; and now, at sixty years of age, his purpose remained with him, but not one line of his book was written. (XL)

Trollope sums up the impasse in which Sir Thomas's combined ambition, indolence and self-doubt has placed him with Johnsonian plangency: 'The dream of youth becomes the doubt of middle life, and then the despair of age.' It may seem odd that so active a man as Trollope was should show so tender an understanding of how easy it is to put things off, but his own compulsive industry may well have been due, at least in part, to the sort of terror of idleness that can only come from a profound susceptibility to its temptations. We are also now told that Sir Thomas had decided to attempt to return to public life in order to still those self-accusations and 'inward disturbances' which the non-completion of his great project has caused him. This is plausible enough in itself, but its *post hoc* introduction only compounds the suspicion that the whole idea of Sir Thomas's great work was something that Trollope was driven to in the actual process of writing the novel. Sir Thomas's academic ambitions – unlike Mr Casaubon's in *Middlemarch* – are not presented from the first as part of the character's *raison d'être*; they are something that Trollope belatedly discovers, or to put it less politely, improvises. As the *Spectator*'s otherwise appreciative reviewer noted, we 'receive hardly any hint of the real drift of Sir Thomas Underwood's intellectual life'.

It was certainly natural for Trollope to associate personal seclusion with doomed scholarship. As a last misguided attempt to repair the family's desperate financial condition, his own father had undertaken the compilation of a reference work which – if not quite as monumental as Casaubon's Key to all Mythologies – had a similarly comprehensive aim. Thomas Trollope's *Encyclopaedia Ecclesiastica* was designed 'to describe all ecclesiastical terms'; at his death, only three parts out of a projected eight had been completed and those, when Anthony came to write the *Autobiography*, had by then been buried, as he feelingly puts it, 'in the midst of that huge pile of futile literature, the building up of which has broken so many hearts' (I). Trollope thus had first-hand knowledge of grandiose intellectual enterprise, and every reason moreover to associate it with the lawyer's chambers where his father worked until forced to give them up. However, Thomas Trollope had the family gift of application – he worked with an irritable single-mindedness that only incessant headaches could interrupt – and in this respect the fictional Sir Thomas hardly resembles him.

The essentially opportunist nature of Trollope's presentation of Sir Thomas is underlined by the fact that the experiences that the lawyer goes through at Percycross are directly based on the novelist's own recent attempt to win the notoriously corrupt seat of Beverley in 1868.[6] As the *Autobiography* candidly reveals, the resemblances between what actually happened there and the election scenes in *Ralph the Heir* are very close. Trollope thought of the period of his canvass in Yorkshire as 'the most wretched fortnight of my manhood' (XVI); his own discomforts and Sir Thomas's agonies are virtually one and the same. The personal feelings emerge all the more strongly because Trollope has made his protagonist one of the Conservative candidates. Since he himself stood as a Liberal (even if the description was eccentrically qualified by the words 'advanced conservative') and as a supporter of Gladstone, he could hardly use his fictional *alter ego* as a political mouthpiece. As far as the expression of political ideas is concerned, the best coverage is given to the Radical Ontario Moggs, Polly Neefit's lover, whose innocent dreams of triumph and naïve relish of applause are presented with amused tolerance if also with some condescension. The air of burlesque which hangs about Moggs throughout the novel, however, prevents even the limited degree of serious consideration given to the Radicalism of Daniel Thwaite in *Lady Anna*.

Trollope's transcription of recent personal experience into fictional form is very uncharacteristic. (He is more ready to take as settings localities just visited, as with his use of the Middle East in *The Bertrams* – and he continually takes advantage of the wide variety of place to which his professional and personal travels had introduced him.) Oddly enough, however, the election scenes in *Ralph the Heir* do not differ greatly, except in some asperity of emphasis, from other pre-Beverley episodes of the same type, such as those in *Can You Forgive Her?* and *Phineas Finn*. The autobiographical investment has not in this case brought an artistically increased rate of return. No doubt this is partly attributable to Trollope's usual disinclination to treat his own experience as privileged, but it is also due to the way in which Sir Thomas's character seems to have been assembled. If indeed memories of his unhappy father are involved as well, Trollope has tried to combine elements of the recent and the more remote past, and some uncertainty of focus is the unintegrated result. Other suggestions of a time much more distant than the mortifications of Beverley may also be present. As already noted, the riverside villa at Fulham in *Ralph the Heir* resembles the earlier house by the Thames in the autobiographical *The Three Clerks* (both households contain three girls of marriageable age).

Another example of the kind of gratuitousness to which Trollope's lack of advance planning and the predetermined lengths of his novels made him liable, is the description of Sir Thomas, re-ensconced in his chambers, reflecting again on his endogenous inertia, accompanied this time by a flute obbligato:

> It was one of those almost sultry days which do come to us occasionally amidst the ordinary inclemency of a London May, and he was sitting with his window open, though there was a fire in the grate. As he sat, dreaming rather than thinking, there came upon his ear the weak, wailing, puny sound of a distant melancholy flute. He had heard it often before, and had been roused by it to evil wishes, and sometimes to evil words, against the musician. It was the effort of some youth in the direction of Staple's Inn to soothe with music the savageness of his own bosom. It was borne usually on the evening air, but on this occasion the idle swain had taken up his instrument within an hour or two of his early dinner. His melody was burdened with no peculiar tune, but consisted of a few low, wailing, melancholy notes, such as may be extracted from the reed by a breath and the slow raising and falling of the little finger, much, we believe, to the comfort of the player, but to the ineffable disgust of, too often, a large circle of hearers.
>
> Sir Thomas was affected by the sound long before he was

aware that he was listening to it. To-whew, to-whew; to-whew, to-whew; whew-to-to, whew-to-to, whew-to-to; whew, to-whew. On the present occasion the variation was hardly carried beyond that; but so much was repeated with a persistency which at last seemed to burden the whole air round Southampton Buildings. The little thing might have been excluded by the closing of the window; but Sir Thomas, though he suffered, did not reflect for awhile whence the suffering came. Who does not know how such sounds may serve to enhance the bitterness of remorse, to add a sorrow to the present thoughts, and to rob the future of its hopes? (LI)

The association of the flute with melancholia may possibly be a reminiscence of the doleful musicianship of Mr Mell in *David Copperfield*, but it is treated in this chapter (titled 'Music Has Charms') at some length, and the precise alignment of scene and mood make one speculate about a more intimate source. Perhaps this vivid sense of loneliness and futility may be traced to those desolate periods of Trollope's youth spent mooching about Lincoln's Inn, left alone with his morose father while the rest of the family were away in America. At any rate, the episode again illustrates the way in which the character of Sir Thomas passes through a series of states which, however interesting in themselves, are not sufficiently amalgamated for us to feel that the personality shows the organic development typical of Trollope's best work. And in a larger sense the same lack of co-ordination is a handicap carried by the novel as a whole. Sir Thomas's passivity is more absorbing than Ralph the heir's, but the parallel between the two – like the connection between the inheritance plot and Sir Thomas's inner history – is fortuitous.

Mr Scarborough's Family

Trollope used uncertainty over inheritance as the main plot element in two further novels written late in his career – indeed, *Mr Scarborough's Family* was the last but one novel he completed. Although *Is He Popenjoy?* (written 1874–5, published 1878) is not without appeal for the hardened Trollopian, the redeployment of

the motif in that case does not lead to those psychological dis-
coveries or to that intensity in the dramatized scene which are the
justification of Trollope's recapitulatory technique. It is, however,
reassuring that Trollope's last treatment of inheritance should show
so strikingly how well his repetitive methods could continue to
serve him. There is little in the materials of *Mr Scarborough's Family*
(written 1881, published 1883) to surprise the loyal reader of Trollope's fiction since it is mostly given over to a reworking of some
of its most entrenched elements. Nevertheless, Trollope has been
led in this case by his recurrent interest in a particular state of affairs
to infer a character of peculiar interest. Mr Scarborough is perhaps
the most impressive as well as the last of the line of Trollopian
testators who wish to pervert the proper course of law.

At stake in *Mr Scarborough's Family*, in fact, are two inheritances,
but any suggestion of too neat a parallelism is offset by the disparity
of calibre between those disposing of them. Harry Annesley, the
novel's nominal – and in Trollopian terms quite predictable – hero,
has been brought up as the acknowledged heir of his bachelor uncle
Mr Prosper, squire of a modest estate in Hertfordshire. Harry
offends his uncle, more by negligence than design, and the piqued
Prosper contemplates marriage and progeny as a means of cutting
Harry out. The initial situation thus has a clear resemblance to the
actual one faced by Trollope's father (whose uncle's property was
also in Hertfordshire), except that the fictional Mr Prosper shies off
matrimony when faced by the fierce bargaining of Miss Thoroughbung, his proposed bride, who does not see why she should give up
either her comforts or her obsequious companion, Miss Tickle. As
her name delicately hints, Miss Thoroughbung – although cheery
in her way – comes from a brewing family and turns out not to be
enough of a lady to suit even so silly a gentleman as Mr Prosper.
The social comedy involved is mildly amusing, though it can
hardly seem so to the nephew heir, threatened with the loss of both
expectations and allowance because his uncle is in a huff. Harry is
the more put out because he needs an income to enable him to
marry Florence Mountjoy, the niece of Mr Scarborough.

Having accepted Harry, Florence proceeds to stick to him with
that intransigent loyalty which has been such a feature of the
Trollopian heroine since the Barsetshire days. In this case, as
usually though not as always, unswerving devotion is eventually

rewarded. In the meantime, however, Florence has to put up with her mother's tireless if unintelligent advocacy of the claims of Captain Mountjoy, another cousin-lover and Mr Scarborough's eldest son. This leads to a long stay in Brussels, enforced on the by now familiar assumption that taking a girl abroad is the best way of getting her over an undesirable attachment. It does not work this time, and Mrs Mountjoy subsides into petulant acquiescence.

The rivalry of Harry and Mountjoy for Florence's hand leads to a late-night street scuffle between the two of them which Mountjoy, being drunk, gets the worst of; he subsequently disappears. Through the insinuations of Augustus, Mr Scarborough's younger son, the episode is made to discredit Harry (Augustus also has his eye on Florence). This minor fracas is closer to Tom Tringle's abortive assault on Jonathan Stubbs in *Ayala's Angel* than to the attempted garrotting of Kennedy and the actual murder of Bonteen in the Phineas books, but its appearance shows again how persistently Trollope can recycle a narrative device that has been part of his repertoire at least since Eames hit Crosbie at Paddington. In *Mr Scarborough's Family*, Harry's relatively insignificant breach of the peace neatly connects the novel's love interest, centring on Florence and his own uncertain status as an heir, with the book's more absorbing concern: the respective claims of the Scarborough brothers on their father's wealth.

The fate of Mr Scarborough's fortune is a more substantial affair than the uncertainty over Mr Prosper's intentions partly because there is so much of it. The value of the estate at Tretton has been greatly enhanced by its proximity to the Staffordshire Potteries. Such appreciation, however, looks like being more than offset by the spectacular gambling debts of the heir. In order to meet them Mountjoy has been obliged to raise such large sums by post-obits from the money-lenders that the estate is bound to fall into their hands when Mr Scarborough dies. That event looks to be not far off since he is seriously ill and can only expect to last a few months. But despite being at death's door, Mr Scarborough succeeds in saving the estate and he does so by means that are in flagrant breach of legal propriety even though he so contrives things that the law cannot touch him.

It is made immediately clear in Trollope's more than usually confident exposition that Mr Scarborough has a long-standing hostility to being bound by legal custom: 'of all things he hated most the entail'. (I) However, Mr Scarborough's wish to defeat the entail is not prompted – as was Squire Newton's in *Ralph the Heir* – by the existence of a preferred and worthy illegitimate son. It is true that Mr Scarborough always retains some regard for his elder – and certainly has no special partiality for his younger – son. But when Mr Scarborough suddenly produces documentary evidence to prove that Mountjoy was not in fact born in wedlock and that Augustus is therefore the true heir, he is not animated by personal affection for either of them but by a disinterested desire to save the estate from Mountjoy's creditors. It appears that Mr Scarborough's wife (now dead) gave birth to Mountjoy before the union was regularized (at Nice). The way is thus clear for the financially prudent Augustus to inherit – a prospect which he greets with an unattractive combination of greed and ingratitude. He argues that his father, by suppressing the fact of Mountjoy's illegitimacy, had intended to cheat him of his due. The best recompense the old man can make for this injury, Augustus feels, is to die soon. Mr Scarborough, who is his own perverse but unselfish way has a strong feeling for natural justice, has made a point of saving enough to leave Augustus an excellent income in the normal course of events, and he is deeply embittered by his younger son's unfilial and unwise words. Nevertheless, the two of them collaborate in buying off the money-lenders (a group of Jews, some of whom appear elsewhere in Trollope and who are broadly though not unsympathetically treated), so that the estate is again unencumbered. Mr Scarborough then produces his ace: Mountjoy is legitimate after all. There was another, earlier, marriage (in Rummelsburg, Prussia). Mountjoy is accordingly restored as heir, and Augustus accepts with bad grace, after Mr Scarborough's death, Mountjoy's offer – suggested in his last moments by his father – of £25,000 as a consolation prize. As for the heir himself, it seems very likely at the end of the novel that his addiction to gambling will re-exert its old sway. This compulsion is analysed by Trollope with an almost clinical understanding, even if the picture of Mountjoy futilely trying to break the bank at Monte Carlo (recently visited by the novelist) does not have the resonance of our last view of Burgo Fitzgerald (whom we know so much better) playing at the tables of Baden-Baden. Mr Scarborough's heroic struggle to save Tretton is clearly going to prove pointless in the end, since Mountjoy will again gamble away its accumulated profits.

In practical terms, therefore, Mr Scarborough finally achieves little, and the terminal irony can obviously be seen as a judgement against his lack of scruple. But Trollope is in practice much more interested in the nature of the temperament capable of planning manoeuvres of such far-sighted deviousness than in moralizing over the vanity that they imply.

Although Mr Scarborough vacillates between one heir and another this is not because, like Indefer Jones in *Cousin Henry*, he cannot decide between what he ought and what he would like to do. He is remarkable for a tenacity of will made more pronounced by his infirmity of body. His cunning in fiddling the marriage registers so long ago is consistent with the cleverness of the testator whose moribund operations the novel actually chronicles. It is the nature of what he calls his 'inner man' to struggle 'to free itself from conventionalities'. (XIX) He is partly attracted by the danger of so doing, but more profoundly by the desire to prove himself stronger than the law. He hates the law because it puts a restraint upon him; he is one of the most extreme examples of that class of men in Trollope's fiction who find the limitation of their will by others intolerable. He is also one of the most interesting because his hatred of restriction exists in an unusually pure form, and because he ensures his freedom of action through the very means that ought to check it. His boast that '"I haven't allowed the law to bind me"' (XL) is part of a larger refusal to accept the orthodox:

> All virtue and all vice were comprised by him in the words 'good-nature' and 'ill-nature'. All church-going propensities, – and these propensities in his estimate extended very widely, – he scorned from the very bottom of his heart. That one set of words should be deemed more wicked than another, as in regard to swearing, was to him a sign either of hypocrisy, of idolatry, or of feminine weakness of intellect ... And law was hardly less absurd to him than religion. It consisted of a perplexed entanglement of rules got together so that the few might live in comfort at the expense of the many. Robbery, if you could get to the bottom of it, was bad, as was all violence; but taxation was robbery, rent was robbery, prices

fixed according to the desire of the seller and not in obedience to justice, were robbery. 'Then you are the greatest of robbers,' his friends would say to him. He would admit it, allowing that in such a state of society he was not prepared to go out and live naked in the streets if he could help it. But he delighted to get the better of the law, and triumphed in his own iniquity, as has been seen by his conduct in reference to his sons. (XXI)

Mr Scarborough's free-thinking, however, by no means precludes being 'kind to many people' and 'having a generous and open hand'. He prides himself on having been an excellent landlord; he has rebuilt all the cottages, and founded a school (insisting, characteristically, that Dissenters should have the right to attend). As the novel proceeds, indeed, Mr Scarborough's good qualities become more and more in evidence. He displays, for instance, a notable serenity in the face of death, despite his dismissal of the usual consolations of religion. He bears the pain of his last months with an exemplary equanimity, so that his medical attendant Merton becomes ever more impressed with his patient's character as well as his courage.

An interest in life helps one to hang on to it, and Mr Scarborough's determination to make his will prevail makes him husband his remaining strength carefully. Much of the novel's interest comes from its close study of the ways in which a man at his last gasp can still outwit everyone else. Mr Scarborough is able to manoeuvre with such freedom, even when bedridden, partly because his wealth gives him the means to command others, but chiefly because he has freed himself from received notions of conduct. Options are open to him which an ordinary man would be too inhibited by propriety to take up. Having lived a life of complete independence – most of it abroad and away from the daily pressure towards social conformity – Mr Scarborough shows not the slightest anxiety about public opinion. He is untroubled by that hypersensitivity as to what the world may think that is such a persistent worry to so many of Trollope's protagonists. But this disregard is more impressive than the brutal indifference of the expatriate Marquis of Brotherton in *Is He Popenjoy?* because it is not simply a device for doing as one likes. As Mr Scarborough explains to Merton, '"I have made efforts on behalf of others, in which I have allowed no outward circumstances to control me."' (XXI) Merton comes to think that the old man 'has within him a capacity for love, and an unselfishness, which almost atones for his dishonesty', and concludes that 'He would rob anyone, – but always to eke out his own gifts to other people. He has therefore to my eyes been most romantic.' (LIII)

No such favourable construction is put on Mr Scarborough's behaviour by his lawyer, Mr Grey. Augustus argues early on in the novel that 'The making of all right and wrong in this world depends on the law' (V), although the superficiality and self-interest of his own character hardly adds much weight to his view. Such orthodoxy is more powerfully expressed in the upright Grey, to whom the law is Holy Writ and who naturally feels that Scarborough's 'utter disregard for law' makes him 'the wickedest man the world ever produced'. (XVII) It is certainly hard on Mr Grey to have the closing stages of his honourable career blighted by a client who regards the lawyer's devotion to his calling with such amiable contempt. As Mr Grey feelingly puts it to his daughter (who is even more of a stickler for legal virtue than himself), '"The light that has guided me through my professional life has been a love of the law . . . I am sure that the law and justice may be made to run on all-fours. I have been so proud of my country as to make that the rule of my life."' (LV) It is not only that he finds Mr Scarborough's fraudulent dealings objectionable in principle: he also feels that his own probity has been contaminated by them, even though he has been as much a victim of his client's duplicity as anyone else. In fact, Mr Scarborough's success in making the law an ass positively drives Mr Grey into premature retirement. He feels that '"my idea of honesty is a mistake"' (LXII), and that the tolerance of such iniquity as Scarborough's shown by his younger and more up-to-date partner Mr Barry (whose offer of marriage his daughter significantly refuses) is little better than collusion. It is also part of Mr Grey's mortification that he himself has been '"a baby"' in Mr Scarborough's hands, so that the latter's 'death-bed triumphs' (LV) seem a personal injury as well as disgraceful in principle.

Mr Scarborough's actual demise is made the occasion for a summing-up that is shared between the narrator and Merton, the choric medical man. It is much more retrospective than those earlier death-bed scenes in which the author's chief attention is reserved for the mixed feelings of those still alive:

> He died with his left hand on his son's neck, and Merton and his sister by his side. It was a death-bed not without its lesson, not without a certain charm in the eyes of some fancied beholder. Those who were there seemed to love him well, and should do so.
>
> He had contrived in spite of his great faults to create a respect in the minds of those around him which is itself a great element of love. But there was something in his manner which told of love for others. He was one who could hate to distraction, and on whom no bonds of blood would operate to mitigate his hatred. He would persevere to injure with a terrible persistency. But yet in every phase of his life he had been actuated by love for others. He had never been selfish, thinking always of others rather than of himself. Supremely indifferent he had been to the opinion of the world around him, but he had never run counter to his own conscience. For the conventionalities of the law he entertained a supreme contempt, but he did wish so to arrange matters with which he was himself concerned as to do what justice demanded. Whether he succeeded in the last year of his life the reader may judge. But certainly the three persons who were assembled around his death-bed did respect him, and had been made to love him by what he had done.
>
> Merton wrote the next morning to his friend Henry Annesley respecting the scene. 'The poor old boy has gone at last, and in spite of all his faults I feel as though I had lost an old friend. To me he has been most kind, and did I not know of all his sins I should say that he had been always loyal and always charitable. Mr Grey condemns him, and all the world must condemn him. One cannot make an apology for him without being ready to throw all truth and all morality to the dogs. But if you can imagine for yourself a state of things in which neither truth nor morality shall be thought essential, then old Mr Scarborough would be your hero. He was the bravest man I ever knew. He was ready to look all opposition

in the face, and prepared to bear it down. And whatever he did he did with the view of accomplishing what he thought to be right for other people. Between him and his God I cannot judge, but he believed in an Almighty One, and certainly went forth to meet Him without a fear in his heart.' (LVIII)

Both summaries are highly characteristic of Trollope's realism at its most unblinking and his reticence at its most tactful. The death-bed is said to be 'not without its lesson', but what is the lesson? Trollope's comment that it had 'a certain charm' seems bafflingly laconic. The reader is called in to make whatever judgement he may feel appropriate because the novelist's appreciation of the character's mixed nature will not allow him to pass a facile verdict. Good and bad in Mr Scarborough are so inextricable in their operation, and our sense of their coexistence is so much a part of our consciousness of his individuality, that Merton's readiness to leave it to God to sort the matter out seems the wisest as well as the most humane plan. The novelist himself agrees with Merton in refusing to anticipate divine judgement: his recapitulation of Mr Scarborough's nature and actions is simply and impartially descriptive. As Merton observes, according to conventional ideas of truth and morality Mr Scarborough must stand condemned, but the whole tendency of Trollope's imaginative immersion in the character's situation and consciousness has been to make censoriousness seem increasingly irrelevant. Similarly, the large questions of legal principle which the story may seem to have invoked dissolve in the light of the *ad hominem* case. Mr Scarborough is clearly in some sense guilty, but it is not a sense the law can get at. This does not mean that the law is futile or that offences against it are allowable or, *pace* Mr Grey (and some modern critics), that society's standards of honesty are in serious decline; it simply underlines the ineffectualness of those abstract categories by which the law attempts to codify the complexity and restrict the autonomy of the self.[7] And paradoxically but typically enough, Trollope has here elicited an exceptionally compelling example of human originality by deploying once more novelistic formulas which he has often used previously. *Mr Scarborough's Family* demonstrates yet again how Trollope renews his art by repeating himself.

Obstinacy and Insanity

Trollope's continued openness to the variousness of human nature is strikingly demonstrated by the even-handedness of his absorption in states of mind quite incompatible with each other. If *Mr Scarborough's Family* shows his persistent fascination by extreme tenacity of will, *Cousin Henry* illustrates an equally intense but opposite compulsion towards the study of almost paralytic weakness. The fact that the situations dramatized are in both cases articulated through plots involving inheritance shows how Trollope used repetition to get at human variety. The familiar in Trollope, therefore, is not necessarily the predictable. *Sir Harry Hotspur of Humblethwaite*, for instance, charts the fate of yet another of those Trollopian girls who refuse to give up the man of their choice despite the strongest parental pressure, but what develops in this particular case is not so much a healthy loyalty to her lover but a faithfulness that proves terminal. The depth of Trollope's interest in situations in which people irrationally refuse to give way is shown by the fact that they involve relationships that are otherwise quite different. In *Sir Harry Hotspur* obstinacy appears as a morbid fidelity; in *Dr Wortle's School*, as impassioned insubordination; in *He Knew He Was Right*, as an insane jealousy. What these cases have in common with each other (and with many others in Trollope's work) is that the intransigence of the protagonists is so determinedly in excess of the facts as they appear.

Dr Wortle's School

Dr Wortle's School is a short, one-volume novel (written in three weeks in 1879, published 1881) whose main purpose is to demonstrate the nature of Dr Wortle's temperament, which combines entrenched obstinacy and impulsive generosity in a way that can easily become highly volatile. The ambiguous mixtures of his character are incisively spelt out by Trollope in the first chapter – indeed, in the first sentence: 'The Rev. Jeffrey Wortle, D.D., was a man much esteemed by others, – and by himself.' The point is elaborated on the next page: 'He liked that people under him should thrive, – and he liked them to know that they throve by his means. He liked to be master, and always was. He was just, and liked his justice to be recognized. He was generous also, and liked that, too, to be known.' The cumulative force of Trollope's 'ands' is tersely suggestive. It is not surprising that successive bishops, unwise enough to cavil at Dr Wortle's conduct as rector or as master of his highly prosperous preparatory school, have retired from the fray with fleas in their ears: 'Dr Wortle . . . was a man who would bear censure from no human being.'

In the present case, however, Dr Wortle's conflict with his bishop is precipitated by the actions not of himself but of his new usher Mr Peacocke. From the Doctor's point of view, Mr Peacocke's availability is an almost unbelievable stroke of luck: he is a gentleman, has been a Fellow of Trinity College, Oxford (as well as, more curiously, Vice-President of a college at St Louis, Missouri), and is in orders. Moreover, the beautiful Mrs Peacocke is obviously a lady, although an American, and is happy to act as matron. The couple's combination of professional skills and patent dignity is irresistible, and the only odd thing about them is the way they insist on keeping themselves to themselves. The mystery behind this is ostentatiously revealed by Trollope in Chapter III, where he tells the reader that (as usual) he will refuse to keep things back: 'You are to know it all before the Doctor or the Bishop, – before Mrs Wortle or the Hon. Mrs Stantiloup, or Lady de Lawle. You are to know it all before the Peacockes become aware that it must necessarily be disclosed to anyone.' This strategy is less artless than it may seem: it privileges the reader but at the same time ingests him into the world of the novel, almost as if he were a character too. At any rate, the secret is a simple one – the Peacockes are not legally married.

It is not their fault, as Trollope hastens to explain. Mrs Peacocke had been married as a girl to a Colonel Ferdinand Lefroy, who had fought for the South in the American Civil War, been dispossessed as a result and had 'fallen by degrees into dishonour, dishonesty, and brigandage'. Mr Peacocke, when in St Louis, established after a journey to Mexico and on the testimony of Lefroy's brother Robert that Ferdinand was dead; only then did his scruples allow him to declare himself to the responsive widow. Their married happiness is marred when six months later the original husband briefly turns up – fit and well although not apparently interested in resuming married life – but promptly disappears again. The Peacockes resolve not to be parted, and indeed their passionate devotion to each other is one of the novel's strongest notes. Trollope immediately moves to deflect the censure which their cohabitation is likely to arouse in the orthodox reader by condemning it himself: 'Every day passed together as man and wife must be a falsehood and a sin.' (Part I, Ch. III) He does so, however, in terms which underline the extreme human cost of separation – 'Though their hearts might have burst in the doing of it, they should have parted' – and thus prepares the way for Dr Wortle's more impulsive response.

Mr Peacocke is obliged to tell the whole story to Dr Wortle when Robert Lefroy arrives in England with blackmail in mind, but he had already decided that his false position had become intolerable to a man of his integrity. When he describes what would have been Mrs Peacocke's plight in St Louis had he abandoned her, Dr Wortle impetuously exclaims '"I would have clung to her, let the law say what it might,"' (Part III, Ch. VIII) even though he was to concede that he might have been wrong to do so. His sympathy for the Peacockes is natural, partly because the two men are strikingly alike; Dr Wortle has always been aware that if he was to keep Mr Peacocke 'no censure, no fault-finding, would be possible'. Even in his present position of disadvantage, Peacocke dislikes being told by the Doctor that 'no man had a right to regard his own moral life as isolated from the lives of others around him' (although as far as he himself is concerned, the Doctor usually behaves as if this were in fact the case). In addition to this affinity of temperament, there is Dr Wortle's obvious admiration for Mrs Peacocke. It is not just that he refuses to cast the first stone. Since to him '"she is as pure as the most unsullied matron in the country"' (Part IV, Ch. X), Dr Wortle proposes that Mrs Peacocke should stay in the school house under his protection while her husband goes off to America, with the younger Lefroy, to find out for certain whether the elder brother still survives.

This has not been an easy decision for the Doctor to take. He has, as Trollope puts it, two consciences in the matter, one of which counsels correctness (severing all connection with the erring couple) and the other recommending humanity (standing by those who have suffered so much and so unjustly). He is aware that conventional opinion – in the form of Mr Puddicombe, a fellow clergyman who acts throughout as a *raisonneur* moderating the Doctor's philanthropy, and as expressed by his own innately respectable wife – will readily find against the Peacockes. He foresees that the Bishop is bound to disapprove and that his school may suffer from parents who, offended by his high-handedness in the past, will now urge others to withdraw their little boys from moral contamination. Nevertheless, he has 'taken the man altogether to his heart', and with some apprehension but also some relish looks forward to braving the matter out.

Dr Wortle's identification with and defence of a couple who have been technically sinful although in highly extenuating circumstances may remind us of Clara Amedroz's loyalty to the Askertons in *The Belton Estate*, another couple under an isolating cloud of ostracizing disapproval. His subsequent conflict with the Bishop is irresistibly reminiscent of the endemic warfare between the Grantly and Proudie factions in the Barchester novels, and, more particularly, of Mr Crawley's defiance of episcopal authority. In both Crawley's and Wortle's cases, the insubordination involved is of an irrational intensity, and the arguments used by the parish priests against their superiors derive their energy as much from a spirit of rebellion as from the justness of their case. Here, after an initial and inconclusive interview, the parties carry on the conflict through a correspondence that, on the Doctor's side, is almost recklessly intransigent as well as compulsive (Wortle being the sort of man who cannot help composing in his head further rejoinders to replies not yet received). Trollope has a sharp sense of epistolary protocol. In the *Autobiography* he recalls that as a Post Office official he 'never scrupled to point out the fatuity of the improper order in the strongest language that I could decently employ'; he 'revelled' in these correspondences, regarding some of them as 'among the great delights of my life'. (VIII) Trollope therefore finds it easy to understand the intense provocation of the Bishop's 'affectionate letter': 'Affection from one man to another is not natural in letters. A

336

bishop never writes affectionately unless he means to reprove severely.' (Part V, Ch. II) He knows that for a bishop to address a clergyman as his 'dear brother in Christ' is invariably a prelude to the kind of censure that Dr Wortle finds intolerable.

The issue is further complicated by another familiar annoyance. With Mr Peacocke in America, Dr Wortle has taken to visiting the lonely wife to administer comfort and support. On one occasion he holds her hand at parting rather longer than he might have done were she less attractively desolate (rather as in *Orley Farm* Mr Furnival over-consoles his still appealing client Lady Mason). A London scandal-sheet, *Everybody's Business*, gets hold of the story and writes it up in a piece, intended merely to be amusing, which suggests that in 'enjoying the smiles of beauty under his own fig-tree' (Part V, Ch. II) while one husband is out of the way looking for the other, the Doctor has distinctly the better deal. Dr Wortle may be susceptible and even indiscreet but is conscious of the purest motives, so that when the Bishop sends him a copy of the offending article in what seems to be an admonitory spirit, he can hardly contain himself. The actual phrases of the article 'stuck to him like the shirt of Nessus, lacerating his very spirit' (Part V, Ch. III) – a response that other Trollopian characters calumniated by the press (Mr Harding, Phineas Finn, Plantagenet Palliser among them) would find entirely natural. Dr Wortle thinks of taking the paper to court for libel, and his sense of injury against the Bishop is so great that he begins to wander about the lanes meditating ways in which he may be 'crushed' (the same word that Mr Crawley uses in his private rehearsals of his duel with his bishop). Dr Wortle's final letter (Part V, Ch. V) is a fine example of the kind of passionate self-justification which Trollope sympathized with so deeply, and the language in it is so strong that although the rector is rather proud of it he is also a little afraid of it. Nevertheless, when the Bishop's diplomatic reply deprives Doctor Wortle of the abject apology that, in his fantasy at least, he clearly hopes for, he feels cheated. The letter is 'beastly' and 'unmanly' because it does not gratify the innate appetite for opposition which the Doctor's obstinacy breeds.

At the end of the novel Wortle is left in command of the field. Like other Trollopian seekers after clinching foreign evidence, Mr Peacocke successfully returns from his mission with a photograph of Ferdinand Lefroy's grave in San Francisco; this enables him and his wife to be definitively remarried by Dr Wortle himself. The Doctor has the further gratification of his daughter's engagement to one of his former pupils Lord Carstairs – another character who despite his youth knows his own mind – and of seeing his school restored to aristocratic approbation.

However, any reader requiring an equally positive resolution of the ethical problems raised by the narrative is likely to be disappointed. The motif of the marriage that may not be a marriage – used elsewhere in connection with doubts about legitimacy and inheritance (as in *Lady Anna, Is He Popenjoy?*, and *Mr Scarborough's Family*) – is here allowed to beg important questions of morality, but they are questions that Trollope has little intention of resolving. As so often, he evades coming to an unambiguous conclusion in principle because in practice there is so much to be said on both sides, all of it perfectly understandable. According to the letter of contemporary moral correctness, Dr Wortle ought to have condemned the Peacockes' conduct rather than colluded with it, but as Trollope says, the Doctor 'hated severity' – indeed, he almost 'hated that state of perfection which would require no pardon. He was thoroughly human.' (Part II, Ch. IV) He sympathizes with Mr Peacocke's situation 'as between man and man', and although Peacocke himself admits that men 'must live together by certain laws', he is moved and heartened, as who would not be, by the Doctor's fellow-feeling. The Bishop argues that the company of the guilty must be shunned 'in our present imperfect condition of moral culture' (Part IV, Ch. XI), but the Doctor asks his wife to be kind to Mrs Peacocke for the sake of charity and the love of Christ; both are advancing arguments in support of positions they have already adopted for reasons that have more to do with character and calculation than with abstract and spiritual considerations. The obstinacy of Dr Wortle in refusing to accept his Bishop's advice is inextricably bound up with the soft-heartedness that made him so vulnerable to the Peacockes' predicament, so that his intransigence becomes the register of his humanity. Moreover, Mr Peacocke's conduct is powerfully defended, as is natural, by Mrs Peacocke who, when roused, has the strong-minded independence of the mature American woman. As far as she is concerned, he is '"the most perfect of human beings"'; in a long outpouring to the bemused Mrs Wortle, Mrs Peacocke even appeals to the Last Judgement, believing that if her husband '"were called to his long account he would stand there pure and bright, in glorious garments, – one fit for heaven, because he has loved others better than he has loved himself, because he has done to others as he might have wished that they should do to him."' (Part V, Ch. VII) Overpowered by several pages of such scriptural rhetoric, Mrs Wortle is won over, even though she finds it difficult to envisage Mrs Peacocke's bizarre history as happening to herself. And it is the very unlikelihood of the whole story that gives Dr Wortle his final escape clause. '"Events like these"', he argues, are '"so altogether out of the ordinary course that the common rules of life seem to be insufficient for guidance."' (Part V, Ch. VII) One has, in fact, to let one's imaginative understanding of the individual case dictate the appropriate attitude. Dr Wortle has sometimes been said, rather fancifully, to be a self-portrait, but character and novelist certainly share an instinctive solidarity with inconsistent human realities rather than with the narrow prescriptions of theory.

He Knew He Was Right

Despite the impressive concentration which Trollope sometimes achieved through brevity, it tends to preclude that almost daily intimacy with a character over a long period that is the ground of his best work. The obstinacy of Dr Wortle is intriguingly presented, but not elaborated, developed and modified as it could have been in a narrative of greater scope, and its psychological interest is consequently underfunded. There are no moments in the novel when we suddenly realize that there is more to the man than we thought, even though what we now see turns out to be entirely consistent with what we have previously been shown. The wilfulness of the main character is energetically demonstrated by an episode rather than discovered over a period through long and patient inquiry. The obstinacy of the hero of *He Knew He Was Right* (written 1867–8, published 1869), on the other hand, is seen as an extended process, in a novelistic environment that at first sight could hardly look more loose and baggy, but which is nevertheless one of Trollope's most powerful achievements.[8]

339

The man who knew he was right is Louis Trevelyan, whose marriage to Emily (the daughter of Sir Marmaduke Rowley, a colonial governor) seems initially to have everything in its favour; by the end of the novel, it has brought him to madness and despair. 'The long, slow process of the conjugal wreck' was recalled by Henry James, in his obituary essay, with an admiration based on the fact that, in this case, Trollope 'has dared to be thoroughly logical; he has not sacrificed to conventional optimism; he has not been afraid of a misery which should be too much like life.' (It will be remembered that Trollope's refusal to accept such a logic on behalf of Lady Glencora had annoyed James in his review of *Can You Forgive Her?* nearly twenty years earlier.) It is a pity Trollope did not live to read a tribute which might have consoled him for what, at the time of writing the *Autobiography*, he regarded as the novel's failure. Nowhere, he felt, had he fallen more completely short of his intention. His purpose had been 'to create sympathy for the unfortunate man' but 'the sympathy has not been created yet'. (XVII) Trollope's disappointment is a striking *ad hominem* reminder of what he thought most important in fiction: he felt he had failed because his readers had not been led to live with Trevelyan so as to understand the character as intimately as he, the author, understood him.

The actual execution of the novel, however, shows no signs of discouragement and indeed is full of energy (it was the first major novel Trollope wrote after his resignation from the Post Office). Trollope's concentration is maintained throughout, and only towards the end of its very considerable length do his recapitulations of how the various narrative situations have developed sometimes seem gratuitous rather than the legitimate means by which he inches the characters forward along the paths their natures dictate. Certainly, the opening chapters give an exposition of the nature and circumstances of the Trevelyan marriage that is masterly in its detail, economy and command. There is not much in its later breakdown that cannot, with hindsight, be seen to have been implied in these early pages. We are told, almost immediately, that Trevelyan 'liked to have his own way', and, more ominously, that '"Emily likes her way too"'. Trevelyan's first words are '"It is my idea that . . ."', and there is plenty of early evidence of his inability to change his mind, apologize, or see things as others see them.

The immediate cause of dispute between husband and wife is her relationship with Colonel Osborne. The Colonel, who is after all middle-aged and an old friend of Emily's father, has 'nothing fiendish' about him; he is known, however, to be 'fond of intimacies with married ladies, and perhaps was not averse to the excitement of marital hostility'. (I) Trevelyan's sense of jealousy is therefore not altogether unnatural, even if his expression of it is clumsy and unreasonable. His wife feels the very harbouring of such thoughts is insufferably offensive; she is prepared to obey commands but will not tolerate insulting misconstructions. Her sister Nora, who has accompanied her to London from the Mandarin Islands, effects an edgy reconciliation that is short-lived, partly because Trevelyan is vacillating and soft-hearted as well as dictatorial, and partly because Emily is truculent and provocative. Domestic life becomes more and more strained, and separation seems the increasingly likely outcome. There is nothing melodramatic in the presentation of these difficulties. Trollope's effortless command of trivial family events – sending and receiving letters, giving instructions to servants, hearing things at the club, chance meetings in Hyde Park – allows him to show how the normality of domestic routine can itself reveal symptoms of incompatibility which make its continuance impossible.

As they indignantly reiterate their cases both parties become more intransigent; neither will accept advice because to do so would weaken a position each believes to be morally impregnable. On both sides, the will towards self-justification is stronger than the desire for reconciliation. Trevelyan will have nothing to do with Lady Milborough's well-meant recommendation of the tried Trollopian remedy: '"Take her to Naples at once."' (XIII) Nor is Emily swayed by the same lady's pleas that as a good wife she should submit: '"He shall not make me say I have been wrong, when I know I have been right."' (XI) As Trollope explains, the fundamental difficulty was that 'there was no decided point which, if conceded, would have brought about a reconciliation . . . each desired that the other should acknowledge a fault, and . . . neither of them would make that acknowledgement'. Emily is therefore sentenced, with the child and for the duration of Trevelyan's displeasure, to exile in Devonshire (not far from the prison on Dartmoor, ironically situated as Trollope drily notes amidst the kind of moorland scenery that always produces a 'delightful sense of romance'). (XVI) Colonel Osborne, his sexual vanity spruced up by the whole affair but still with 'no settled scheme' (XX) of intrigue, visits Mrs Trevelyan on a pretext which is patently flimsy but which she, resenting the tedium of her rural retirement, misguidedly accepts. This meeting is reported to Trevelyan by the private detective he has hired, and the situation inevitably deteriorates yet further.

This detective is an ex-policeman named Bozzle, and the next stage of Trevelyan's decline is dominated by a connection which he knows to be degrading but feels to be necessary. Not only does Bozzle find out the facts, but he also acts on a professional presumption of guilt, unlike Trevelyan's friend Hugh Stanbury, who is increasingly appalled at his irrationality. Trevelyan's humiliating dependence on Bozzle is in some ways an extension of those involuntary associations with social inferiors which other Trollopian characters have to endure, usually for financial reasons: Lopez's partnership with Sexty Parker, for instance, or Ralph the heir's with Neefit, not to mention the embarrassing importunity of a whole series of money-lenders who badger such men as Eames, Finn, and Captain Scarborough. Bozzle also functions, with a daring clash of registers, as a semi-comic Iago (*Othello* is explicitly invoked in Chapter XLV), whose vulgar workaday approach to a predicament Trevelyan feels to be uniquely anguished is an additional cause of pain. During the Bozzle phase, Trollope provides a number of résumés of Trevelyan's internal broodings, and nowhere in his work perhaps is his command of the internal soliloquy more telling. There is an extended example of such increasingly neurotic self-communings in Chapter XXVII. A particularly impressive recapitulation, which in itself effectively mimics the obsessively repetitive nature of Trevelyan's thoughts, can be found in Chapter XXXVIII. By now, Trevelyan has taken himself off to Italy, and thus relies even more on Bozzle for information and interpretation, being detached from other moderating pressures.

Alone in Turin, waiting for Bozzle's latest report, Trevelyan reflects on his situation in the following terms:

> Gradually, as he spent day after day in thinking on this one subject, he came to feel that even were his wife to submit, to own her fault humbly, and to come back to him, this very

342

coming back would in itself be a new wound. Could he go out again with his wife on his arm to the houses of those who knew that he had repudiated her because of her friendship with another man? Could he open again that house in Curzon Street, and let things go on quietly as they had gone before? He told himself that it was impossible; – that he and she were ineffably disgraced; – that, if reunited, they must live buried out of sight in some remote distance. And he told himself, also, that he could never be with her again night or day without thinking of the separation. His happiness had been shipwrecked . . .

His mind was at work upon it always. Could it be that she was so base as this – so vile a thing, so abject, such dirt, pollution, filth? But there were such cases. Nay, were they not almost numberless? He found himself reading in the papers records of such things from day to day, and thought that in doing so he was simply acquiring experience necessary for himself. If it were so, he had indeed done well to separate himself from a thing so infamous . . .

He came to believe everything; and, though he prayed fervently that his wife might not be led astray, that she might be saved at any rate from utter vice, yet he almost came to hope that it might be otherwise; – not, indeed, with the hope of the sane man, who desires that which he tells himself to be for his advantage; but with the hope of the insane man, who loves to feed his grievance, even though the grief should be his death. They who do not understand that a man may be brought to hope that which of all things is the most grievous to him, have not observed with sufficient closeness the perversity of the human mind. Trevelyan would have given all that he had to save his wife; would, even now, have cut his tongue out before he would have expressed to anyone, – save to Bozzle, – a suspicion that she could in truth have been guilty; was continually telling himself that further life would be impossible to him, if he, and she, and that child of theirs, should be thus disgraced; – and yet he expected it, believed it, and, after a fashion, he almost hoped it.

The step-by-step patience of such recapitulations is an important part of their effect. Trollope's own intervention towards the end of this passage has a peculiar authority which more than one critic has noticed: 'They who do not understand that a man may be brought to hope that which of all things is most grievous to him, have not observed with sufficient closeness the perversity of the human mind.' The Johnsonian weight of the sentence is a rebuke to the sloppiness of our habitual assumptions, but does Trollope himself observe Trevelyan's case with 'sufficient closeness'? He did not of course have the advantage of modern vocabularies of mental disturbance, and is not in any case considering the demonstrably deranged, the man 'who may fancy himself to be a teapot, or what not'. The term paranoia – which we would now use for the condition which Trevelyan's symptoms indicate – dates (according to *OED*) from 1857, only ten years before the novel was written. Trevelyan is on the borderline between sanity and insanity, and it is this which Trollope argues is 'imperfectly understood'. The character is indeed 'mad on the subject of his wife's alleged infidelity' (XXXVIII), and at one point Trollope suggests that only a madman could act as cruelly as Trevelyan does, even though he is not, from a clinical point of view, certifiable – or so the doctor thinks when he is finally brought home. Trollope's chief anxiety – in the interests of the 'sympathy' he refers to in the *Autobiography* – seems to be that we should not assume that his character's claims on us could be adequately met by a merely formal acknowledgement of his madness. The details given of Trevelyan's physical deterioration may partly be a way of ensuring that we remain concerned. We are not to think of Trevelyan as someone who, because he is irrational, is beyond the reach of our understanding. Although the presentation of the man in the later stages of his decline is more external and dramatic – and although his wife admits in the end that her husband's mind is 'a mystery' to her – there is no break in the continuity of Trollope's attention. Even though there is no hope for Trevelyan (as there is, for instance, for the intermittently unbalanced Mr Crawley), Trollope refuses to give him up, creatively speaking. This is natural enough, since for all its pathological dimensions, Trevelyan's is a characteristically Trollopian and therefore 'normal' tendency of mind taken to an extremity of stress.

With the rift between husband and wife apparently unbridgeable, the next complication of the quarrel concerns the custody of their child. With the aid of Bozzle, Trevelyan kidnaps the boy and, after a spell in a dreary cottage at Willesden, takes him off to Italy. By this time, Trevelyan is wretchedly haggard, drinks but hardly eats; his hands twitch and his feet shuffle restlessly; he seems on the verge of collapse. But his speech – as indicated by his words to Emily's father at Willesden in Chapter LXIX – are typically lucid and formal, although perverse in their reasoning. In fact, his courtesy and correctness of manner become more studied as his actions become more grotesque. In Italy he settles, with the child, at Casalunga, an isolated hilltop country house within reach of Siena.

It is during this phase of his decline that Trollope's presentation of Trevelyan's state is at its most impressive. Henry James, who had 'always remembered' it, thought it 'a picture worthy of Balzac' – a compliment that given the American's reverence for the French master could hardly be more handsome. In his 1875 essay on Balzac James notes that 'the place in which an event occurred was in his view of equal moment with the event itself; it was part of the action', and he was no doubt struck by the resonance of the descriptions of Trevelyan's desolate retreat in the Casalunga chapters of *He Knew He Was Right*. Trollope's first description of it, as it appears to Emily's father and Mr Glascock (who is connected to Trevelyan by his interest in his wife's sister), is marked by an exactness of visualization in which all the details tell, both concretely and in their implications:

> On this side of the house the tilled ground, either ploughed or dug with the spade, came up to the very windows. There was hardly even a particle of grass to be seen. A short way down the hill there were rows of olive trees, standing in prim order and at regular distances, from which hung the vines that made the coopering of the vats necessary. Olives and vines have pretty names, and call up associations of landscape beauty. But here they were in no way beautiful. The ground beneath them was turned up, and brown, and arid, so that there was not a blade of grass to be seen. On some furrows the maize or Indian corn was sprouting, and there were patches of growth of other kinds, – each patch closely marked by its own straight lines; and there were narrow paths, so

345

constructed as to take as little room as possible. But all that
had been done had been done for economy, and nothing for
beauty. The occupiers of Casalunga had thought more of the
produce of their land than of picturesque or attractive
appearance.

The sun was blazing fiercely hot, hotter on this side, Sir
Marmaduke thought, even than on the other; and there was
not a wavelet of a cloud in the sky. A balcony ran the whole
length of the house, and under this Sir Marmaduke took
shelter at once, leaning with his back against the wall. 'There
is not a soul here at all,' said he.

'The men in the barn told us that there was,' said Mr
Glascock; 'and, at any rate, we will try the windows.' So
saying, he walked along the front of the house, Sir Marmaduke following him slowly, till they came to a door, the
upper half of which was glazed, and through which they
looked into one of the rooms. Two or three of the other
windows in this frontage of the house came down to the
ground, and were made for egress and ingress; but they had
all been closed with shutters, as though the house was
deserted. But they now looked into a room which contained
some signs of habitation. There was a small table with a
marble top, on which lay two or three books, and there were
two arm-chairs in the room, with gilded arms and legs, and a
morsel of carpet, and a clock on a shelf over a stove, and – a
rocking-horse. 'The boy is here, you may be sure,' said Mr
Glascock. 'The rocking-horse makes that certain. But how
are we to get at any one!'

'I never saw such a place for an Englishman to come and
live in before,' said Sir Marmaduke. 'What on earth can he do
here all day!' As he spoke the door of the room was opened,
and there was Trevelyan standing before them, looking at
them through the window. He wore an old red English
dressing-gown, which came down to his feet, and a small
braided Italian cap on his head. His beard had been allowed to
grow, and he had neither collar nor cravat. His trousers were
unbraced, and he shuffled in with a pair of slippers, which
would hardly cling to his feet. He was paler and still thinner
than when he had been visited at Willesden, and his eyes

seemed to be larger, and shone almost with a brighter brilliancy. (LXXVIII)

The solitary rocking-horse is sufficient indication of the 'terrible melancholy' of the child's life, although additional, 'almost unheeded' toys are described later. The understanding shown – both here and in other chapters – of a child's reaction to parental misery is unparalleled in Trollope. Trevelyan's own physical appearance grows more pathetic and bizarre, while the obsessional patterns of his thought intensify (Trollope insists that 'Thought deep, correct, continued, and energetic is quite compatible with madness'). A new element in such further examples of Trevelyan's 'long unspoken soliloquies' as those in Chapters LXXIX and LXXXIV, is his fear of being put away because he is mad, 'shut up in dark rooms, robbed of his liberty, robbed of what he loved better than his liberty, – his power as a man'. It is the attempt, hopelessly enfeebled as he is, to maintain his power as a man that gives Trevelyan a tragic dignity that survives his self-pity and his injustice towards others. After restoring the child to his mother, Trevelyan exclaims:

> 'There is a curse upon me . . . it is written down in the book of my destiny that nothing shall ever love me!'
>
> He went out from the house, and made his way down by the narrow path through the olives and vines to the bottom of the hill in front of the villa. It was evening now, but the evening was very hot, and though the olive trees stood in long rows, there was no shade. Quite at the bottom of the hill there was a little sluggish muddy brook, along the sides of which the reeds grew thickly and the dragon-flies were playing on the water. There was nothing attractive in the spot, but he was weary, and sat himself down on the dry hard bank which had been made by repeated clearing of mud from the bottom of the little rivulet. He sat watching the dragon-flies as they made their short flights in the warm air, and told himself that of all God's creatures there was not one to whom less power of disporting itself in God's sun was given than to him. Surely it would be better for him that he should die, than live as he was now living without any of the joys of life. The solitude of Casalunga was intolerable to him, and yet

there was no whither that he could go and find society. He could travel if he pleased. He had money at command, and, at any rate as yet, there was no embargo on his personal liberty. But how could he travel alone, – even if his strength might suffice for the work? There had been moments in which he had thought that he would be happy in the love of his child, – that the companionship of an infant would suffice for him if only the infant would love him. But all such dreams as that were over. To repay him for his tenderness his boy was always dumb before him. Louey would not prattle as he had used to do. He would not even smile, or give back the kisses with which his father had attempted to win him. In mercy to the boy he would send him back to his mother; – in mercy to the boy if not to the mother also. It was in vain that he should look for any joy in that quarter. Were he to return to England, they would say that he was mad!

He lay there by the brook-side till the evening was far advanced, and then he arose and slowly returned to the house. The labour of ascending the hill was so great to him that he was forced to pause and hold by the olive trees as he slowly performed his task. The perspiration came in profusion from his pores, and he found himself to be so weak that he must in future regard the brook as being beyond the tether of his daily exercise. Eighteen months ago he had been a strong walker, and the snow-bound paths of Swiss mountains had been a joy to him. He paused as he was slowly dragging himself on, and looked up at the wretched, desolate, comfortless abode which he called his home. Its dreariness was so odious to him that he was half-minded to lay himself down where he was, and let the night air come upon him and do its worst. In such case, however, some Italian doctor would be sent down who would say that he was mad. Above all things, and to the last, he must save himself from that degradation. (LXXXIV)

There is a perverse heroism in his tenacity, brought out here by its association with a dried-up and alien version of the waterside location for the rejected that Trollope habitually provides. It is not surprising that Emily's anger gives way to pity, so that at last she gives up trying to justify herself and is ready to admit to anything that will soothe her husband's distorted imaginings: '"I do not think I should answer a word, if he called me the vilest thing on earth."' (XCII) Such accommodation is now too late to be of use. Trevelyan has become so habituated to his role that he even tries out jaunty variations on it, complete with jocose Shakespearean echoes, when visited by his journalistic friend Hugh Stanbury; there is now a self-consciousness in his speech which takes up the suggestions of literary activity in the novel's early pages.

'Sit down and let us two moralise,' he said. 'I spend my life here doing nothing, – nothing, – nothing; while you cudgel your brain from day to day to mislead the British public. Which of us two is taking the nearest road to the devil?'

Stanbury seated himself in a second arm-chair, which there was there in the verandah, and looked as carefully as he dared to do at his friend. There could be no mistake as to the restless gleam of that eye. And then the affected air of ease, and the would-be cynicism, and the pretence of false motives, all told the same story. 'They used to tell us,' said Stanbury, 'that idleness is the root of all evil.'

'They have been telling us since the world began so many lies, that I for one have determined never to believe anything again. Labour leads to greed, and greed to selfishness, and selfishness to treachery, and treachery straight to the devil, – straight to the devil. Ha, my friend, all your leading articles won't lead you out of that. What's the news? Who's alive? Who dead? Who in? Who out? What think you of a man who has not seen a newspaper for two months; and who holds no conversation with the world further than is needed for the cooking of his polenta and the cooling of his modest wine-flask?'

'You see your wife sometimes,' said Stanbury.

'My wife! Now, my friend, let us drop that subject. Of all topics of talk it is the most distressing to man in general, and I own that I am no exception to the lot. Wives, Stanbury, are an evil, more or less necessary to humanity, and I own to being one who has not escaped. The world must be populated, though for what reason one does not see. I have helped, – to the extent of one male bantling; and if you are one who

349

consider population desirable, I will express my regret that I
should have done no more.'

It was very difficult to force Trevelyan out of this humour,
and it was not till Stanbury had risen apparently to take his
leave that he found it possible to say a word as to his mission
there. 'Don't you think you would be happier at home?' he
asked.

'Where is my home, Sir Knight of the midnight pen?'

'England is your home, Trevelyan.'

'No, sir; England was my home once; but I have taken the
liberty accorded to me by my Creator of choosing a new
country. Italy is now my nation, and Casalunga is my home.'

'Every tie you have in the world is in England.'

'I have no tie, sir; – no tie anywhere. It has been my study
to untie all the ties; and, by Jove, I have succeeded. Look at
me here. I have got rid of the trammels pretty well, – haven't
I? – have unshackled myself, and thrown off the paddings,
and the wrappings, and the swaddling clothes. I have got rid
of the conventionalities, and can look Nature straight in the
face. I don't even want the Daily Record, Stanbury; – think of
that!' (XCII)

Trevelyan's spurious but exhilarated brio when so enfeebled (the
dying Mr Scarborough also boasts of having emancipated himself
from 'the conventionalities') is a further example of the way in
which Trollope continually finds new resources of dramatic tone
and novelistic technique in order to convey with an appropriate
intensity and exactness his apprehension of his hero's last days.

Returning to England, after a journey protracted by Trevelyan's
extreme weakness, his wife finally concedes the point that has been
contested so long:

The journey was made first to Dover, and then to London.
Once, as they were making their way through the Kentish
hop-fields, he put out his hand feebly, and touched hers.
They had the carriage to themselves, and she was down on
her knees before him instantly. 'Oh, Louis! Oh, Louis! say
that you forgive me!' What could a woman do more than that
in her mercy to a man?

'Yes; – yes; yes,' he said; 'but do not talk now; I am so tired.' (XCIII)

The period touch about the quality of a woman's mercy is entirely superseded by the dramatic immediacy of Trevelyan's stunningly laconic '"Yes; – yes; yes,"' – words which could not be more simple or more desolatingly ironic in their resigned acknowledgement of the irrelevance, now, of what, formerly, he had wanted more than anything else. Trevelyan's actual death takes place in a riverside cottage at Twickenham (also the scene of a near-fatal illness in the early *The Three Clerks*). By this time, Emily has reverted to her usual sense of injured merit, and is determined to get an acquittal from her husband before the end. In his last moments, 'at length the lips moved, and with struggling ear she could hear the sound of the tongue within, and the verdict of the dying man had been given in her favour'. Shortly after, she says to her sister, '"He declared to me at last that he trusted me"' – 'almost believing', Trollope adds, 'that real words had come from his lips to that effect'. (XCVIII) It is clear from the way Emily construes the event that the natural woman has reasserted herself, but Trollope refuses to underline the point. It is a telling moment of restraint, indicating with a fine economy that some kinds of obstinacy are expert beyond experience.

The whole history of the Trevelyans' tragic incompatibility and the analysis of the husband's instability must have been of the greatest value to Trollope when three years later he came to study the marital miseries of Lady Laura and the madness of Mr Kennedy in *Phineas Redux* (considered above). But the exacerbated obstinacy of both husband and wife is also demonstrated in more benign forms by several of the other characters in *He Knew He Was Right*. There is Miss Stanbury, for instance, down at Exeter – an excellent woman, but one who likes her own way. She is 'a thorough Tory of the old school' (VII) such as Trollope loved to describe. Innovation of all kinds is hateful to her. She maintains, for instance, an utter scepticism as to the reliability of the new iron pillar boxes for letters (though he does not say so in the text, it was Trollope who recommended their introduction in England by the General Post Office).[9] She ceases to subsidize her nephew Hugh because he has taken to writing for a Radical newspaper: in her view, no paper that costs only a penny can possibly be respectable. She is lonely, however, and the fierceness of her manner cannot long conceal an underlying softness of heart. When she takes on her niece Dorothy as a companion, she soon finds that, despite her mouse-like manner, Dorothy is a true Stanbury too, and has a will of her own. Dorothy refuses to accept her aunt's choice of suitor, and finally marries her aunt's heir – an alliance which for complicated personal reasons Miss Stanbury at first regards as quite out of the question. Dorothy's resistance to her aunt is so sweet-natured that the old girl's obstinacy is eventually tamed. The Exeter scenes generally are good examples of Trollope's parochial manner, with its agreeable blend of the ridiculous, the touching, and the ordinary. They include an over-indulged but amusing sub-plot involving the rivalry of two predatory sisters over which of them should get the hapless Mr Gibson, the weak-minded clergyman Miss Stanbury wanted Dorothy to take. Mr Gibson's situation is really a burlesque of the common Trollopian dilemma in which a man cannot decide between two women, both of whom want him.

Hugh Stanbury, Dorothy's brother, shares with her and indeed all the Stanburys, 'the same eager readiness to believe themselves to be right'; the novel's parallels thus seem naturally familial rather than deliberately engineered. 'The same belief in self, – which amounted almost to conceit', is modified by their possessing too 'the same warmth of affection, and the same love of justice'. (XXII) Hugh is 'obstinate and self-reliant' because he has decided on an occupation which brings him a reasonable if raffish living now rather than one which may promise him greater means and respectability later. Like Phineas Finn, he abandons the law, being impatient to get on with the business of life and not content to hang about waiting for briefs. Leader-writing for the *Daily Record* brings him around £500 a year – just enough, in Trollopian terms, to live decently on a modest scale. Stanbury vigorously defends journalism against the charge that it is not gentlemanly by pointing to its practical influence: the editor of the *Jupiter* has more effect on the real world than the Lord Chancellor himself. Stanbury, in fact, is the acceptable alternative to Quintus Slide. In him, a liking for his own way leads, constructively, to a manly readiness to make it.

Hugh needs to be able to support a wife because he wants to marry Nora Rowley, Emily Trevelyan's sister. Nora is yet another

Trollopian heroine who finally wears down parental objection to her choice by sheer persistence of will. It is remarkable how Trollope avoids being bored or becoming boring on such a familiar theme. As James remarked, 'Trollope's heroines have a strong family likeness, but it is a wonder how finely he discriminates between them.' Nora, like others of her kind (such as Clara Amedroz of *The Belton Estate*), is offered a choice between two men, one of whom is eminently eligible and whom she esteems; the other offers less worldly advantage, but exerts a powerful physical appeal. When Mr Glascock proposes, Nora's first thought is that 'he lacked – he lacked; – what was it he lacked? Was it youth, or spirit, or strength; or was it some outward sign of an inward gift of mind?' (XIII) The lack is simply caused by the fact that Nora is in love with someone else. That being so, she has to turn down prospects which could hardly be more attractive: not only is Mr Glascock an obviously nice man but he is also due to become Lord Peterborough (and actually does so before the novel is out). The stages by which Hugh and Nora reach their understanding – including a scene in which Hugh tries to persuade her to cross the rocks of a moorland stream with him and which resembles a similar occaion in *Lady Anna* – are less striking than Nora's tenacity in the face of family opposition once she has committed herself. Like Ayala Dormer, Nora learns some distasteful lessons about life when she has to stay with poor relations (as a result of the Trevelyan quarrel), and she thinks of Mr Glascock's offer with some regret. Her resistance to her parents' disapproval is so resolute, however, that she even contemplates taking lodgings and living on her own until Hugh is ready for her – a Bohemian obstinacy which does much to make her aghast parents give way. As Emily rightly concludes, '"With all her girlish ways, she is like a rock; – nothing can move her."' (XCII)

One of the more agreeable turns in the novel's events is the amiable relationship that develops between Nora and the girl Mr Glascock does marry. While travelling, he falls in with Caroline Spalding, the niece of the American minister at Florence, and Trollope's first attempt at a portrait of the American girl, later studied at full length in *The Duke's Children*. Jonas Spalding is distinctly trying – he practises the high-level oratorical style which Trollope (following Dickens in *Martin Chuzzlewit* though with more subtlety) presents as the American alternative to conversation – and Caroline's friend Wallachia Petrie is clearly impossible. Miss Petrie ('Wally' to her intimates) is the author of those celebrated lines 'Ancient Marbles, while ye crumble', and is known as the Republican Browning. She is an ardent feminist who deeply disapproves of Caroline's marrying a feudal relic like Mr Glascock whom she regards as an oppressor of slaves due to perish before the onward march of American egalitarianism: '"He shall be cut down together with the withered grasses and thrown into the oven, and there shall be an end of him."' (LVI) Mr Glascock (who is on the wrong side of forty) does not much care for being called withered grass, and begins to wonder whether an American bride is such a good idea after all. The same thought occurs to Caroline herself, who is afraid that he will be despised by his relations because of his reckless transatlantic alliance. Mr Glascock recovers his nerve, however, and overrules her scruples with an obstinacy that may be more calmly expressed than that of some other characters in the novel, but which in its polite upper-class way is just as firm. As Caroline concludes, '"You must be master, I suppose . . . a man always thinks himself entitled to his own way."' (LXXXI)

The Italian scenes of cosmopolitan comedy anticipate in some ways Henry James's much more sophisticated exercises, and even such later developments as Forster's early novels. Their integration with the tragic Casalunga chapters is an impressive example of Trollope's effortless changes of fictive gear. Trollope knew the international circle at Florence well since his elder brother Tom had settled there with their mother in 1846 (Mrs Trollope had died in 1863). Like *Can You Forgive Her?*, *He Knew He Was Right* reflects an easy familiarity with modern modes of European travel – a writer who travelled the globe as vigorously as Trollope did naturally takes a relaxed view of routine hazards like crossing the Alps – and famous sights are referred to in an almost offhand way. The Campanile at Florence is said, in passing, to be 'that loveliest of all works made by man's hands' (XL), but it is only mentioned because it is the venue for a moonlight meeting between the Spaldings and Mr Glascock. Nowhere in Trollope does the experience of Italy awaken a character to a new dimension of moral or aesthetic life, as in the cases, for instance, of Dorothea Brooke or Roderick Hudson. On the other hand, Trollope remains faithful to those trivial episodes which in fact make up so much of the tourist's experience. He does not forget how important, at the time, is the excellence of break-fasts at French stations, especially when contrasted with the 'real disgrace of England . . . the railway sandwich, – that white sepul-chre, fair enough outside, but so meagre, poor, and spiritless within, such a thing of shreds and parings . . .' (XXXVII) – a judgement that has a timeless validity.

It was in Florence that Trollope had first met the enthusiastic young American Kate Field, and the caricature of Wallachia Petrie may have been in the nature of a private joke between them, or at least by way of an awful warning to her. Trollope wrote part of *He Knew He Was Right* in the United States (he was negotiating a postal treaty) and he was in renewed contact with Kate. She may even have something to do with one of the novel's most important emphases. Trollope's letters urge her to get the better of her femin-ist craving for independence, and commit herself to matrimony. The question of a woman's place is one on which several characters in the novel have their own views – as you would expect from people who like their own way – and they are not always in agreement with the official authorial line. Admittedly, Wallachia's ideas on the subject cannot be taken seriously, but that is because her absurd picture of the life of English aristocratic women is the product of ideological prejudice. If Caroline has a baby, she won't be allowed to nurse it, but '"they'll let you go and see it two or three times a day"'. (LXXXI) In any case Wallachia has been protected from reality both by her success as a lecturer, and by the way her femininity exempts her from criticism: 'the chivalry of men had given to her sex that protection against which her life was one continued protest'. (LXXVII)

The disadvantages of being a woman, as other female characters in the novel see it, include the fact that marriage is for all practical purposes the only available career, and the fact that marriage itself is such a risk. As early as Chapter IV, Nora Rowley is found reflecting that 'the lot of a woman . . . was wretched, unfortunate, almost degrading. For a woman such as herself there was no path open to her energy, other than that of getting a husband'. How-ever, it is clear, in context, that such feelings are at least partly prompted by the pressure Nora is under to accept the well-born Mr Glascock when she secretly prefers the impecunious Stanbury.

When she compares the two men, Trollope says that 'she had dreamed, if she had not thought, of being able to worship a man . . . she had dreamed, if she had not thought, of leaning upon a man all through life with her whole weight, as though that man had been specially made to be her staff, her prop, her support, her wall of comfort and protection' (XIII) – hardly the sentiments of a convinced feminist. Trollope's use of the word 'worship' to imply sexual feeling is common in his fiction, and the 'dreamed, if she had not thought' formula suggests that what Nora wants sub-consciously (as we should now say) is entirely orthodox. Later on, she says that she would '"sooner write for a newspaper than do anything else in the world"' (XXV), and notes that '"one or two"' women have actually done it, but she does not seriously contem-plate an independent career any more than Alice Vavasor does, in *Can You Forgive Her?*. Her enthusiasm is transparently the expres-sion of her loyalty to the man she loves – something that the novel gives her ample opportunity to demonstrate and which is in due course rewarded. It seems certain that marriage will provide an adequate path for her energies since she identifies herself so com-pletely with her future husband's interests.

Much the same pattern can be seen in the case of Dorothy Stanbury, though in a more subdued way. The greater timidity of her temperament does not prevent a sudden outburst on behalf of the unattached woman: '"She is a nobody, and a nobody she must remain. She has her clothes and her food, but she isn't wanted anywhere. People put up with her, and that is about the best of her luck. If she were to die somebody perhaps would be sorry for her, but nobody would be worse off. She doesn't earn anything or do any good. She is just there and that's all."' (LI) This protest is feeling and generous but is again the result of frustrated emotion. Brooke Burgess, to whom Dorothy is talking, 'understood per-fectly that she was thinking of her own position'; and she too realizes that she is expressing her own fears of becoming one of those lonely old maids (like her Aunt Stanbury) 'who are born and live and die without that vital interest in the affairs of life which nothing but family duties, the care of children, or at least of a husband, will give to a woman'. Such fears by their very expres-sion encourage Brooke Burgess to ensure that they are groundless; Dorothy's self-discipline in regarding herself 'from her earliest years' as 'outside the pale within which such joys are found' thus becomes unnecessary. But her self-training for a 'blank existence' has never precluded her from knowing 'where happiness lay' (LVII), which is in the arms of the right man. Trollope stresses that Dorothy's happiness in love leads directly to a marked increase in confidence and capacity; marriage will clearly bring her out further.

But if Nora, Dorothy and Caroline all joyfully find their place as women by the side of the men they love, they are also aware – as they are bound to be with the domestic misery of Emily Trevelyan staring them in the face – that marriage does not guarantee bliss. Caroline Spalding reflects that becoming Lady Peterborough with a large fortune may not be enough to ensure her happiness; it 'would be a leap in the dark, and all such leaps must needs be dangerous'. (LVI) The same phrase is used earlier when Trollope is rehearsing the arguments for and against marriage as people usually put them to themselves. On the positive side of the question Trollope – while admitting that 'Of course there is a risk' – feels sure that 'that country will be most prosperous in which such leaps in the dark are made with the greatest freedom'. (XXXIII) Such confidence is bound to lack complete authority when it occurs in the middle of a novel whose strongest pages are devoted to the study of a leap which ends in conjugal disaster. Emily's view of the married woman's lot is understandably bitter; by Chapter V she is already beginning to realize that if she separates from her husband society and the law will automatically be against her: '"It is a very poor thing to be a woman,"' she complains to her sister; '"It would be better to be a dog. One wouldn't be made to suffer so much."' Trollope himself shows he is perfectly aware of the inherent injustice of this aspect of Victorian double standards: 'It is all very well for a man to talk about his name and his honour; but it is the woman's honour and the woman's name that are, in truth, placed in jeopardy.' (XI) The peculiar misfortune of Emily, of course, is that she is not merely disadvantaged to the extent that any wife might be by the Victorian husband's rights: she suffers the particular humiliation of being subject to a man who although monstrously irrational is not insane enough to forfeit his control over her. As she understandably complains, '"It is hard that the foolish workings of a weak man's mind should be able so completely to ruin the prospects of a woman's life!"' (LX) It is hardly surprising

357

that she cannot bear the idea of marrying again after Trevelyan's death – 'Anything but that!' (XCIX) Trollope is 'disposed to think' that her revulsion will be permanent.

The obvious way to avoid the risks of marriage is to remain single, and in the character of Priscilla Stanbury Trollope explores (superfluously, so far as the necessities of plot are concerned) the personality of someone who has deliberately taken that decision. As a true Stanbury, she is fond of her own way, but she also has more self-knowledge, perhaps, than anyone else in the book. This, combined with her sense of a social realism, means that she fully understands what, for her, are the limits of the possible. In an arresting conversation with Emily Trevelyan, Priscilla shows how clear-sighted she is about her own social and sexual nature, and also how orthodox she is on the question of wifely obedience:

'I stand alone, and can take care of myself,' said Priscilla. 'I defy the evil tongues of all the world to hurt me. My personal cares are limited to an old gown and bread and cheese. I like a pair of gloves to go to church with, but that is only the remnant of a prejudice. The world has so very little to give me, that I am pretty nearly sure that it will take nothing away.'

'And are you contented?'

'Well, no; I can't say that I am contented. I hardly think that anybody ought to be contented. Should my mother die and Dorothy remain with my aunt, or get married, I should be utterly alone in the world. Providence, or whatever you call it, has made me a lady after a fashion, so that I can't live with the ploughmen's wives, and at the same time has so used me in other respects, that I can't live with anybody else.'

'Why should not you get married, as well as Dorothy?' . . .

'I am not fit to marry. I am often cross, and I like my own way, and I have a distaste for men. I never in my life saw a man whom I wished even to make my intimate friend. I should think any man an idiot who began to make soft speeches to me, and I should tell him so.'

'Ah; you might find it different when he went on with it.'

'But I think,' said Priscilla, 'that when a woman is married there is nothing to which she should not submit on behalf of her husband.' (XVI)

Priscilla's attitude to sexual politics as discussed here has its own convenient integrity: she wants her own way but thinks that wives should not expect to have theirs; since marriage and female independence are not compatible, she won't mix them. Later in the same conversation she reveals an irritable impatience with Emily's problems: '"It seems a trumpery quarrel, – as to who should beg each other's pardon first, and all that kind of thing. Sheer and simple nonsense!"' Having made her marriage-bed, Priscilla thinks, Emily ought to lie on it. But it is easy for her to take this line because she is so detached from those feelings which make people marry. Her 'distaste for men' is not related to a feminist zeal for equality with them. It is a quality in her that Trollope vividly apprehends without seeming to know what to do with. What is one to make, for instance, of this exchange with her brother Hugh? (They have been discussing Priscilla's refusal to let Hugh pay for unnecessarily grand accommodation.)

'But you must not quarrel with me, Hugh. Give me a kiss. I don't have you often with me; and yet you are the only man in the world that I ever speak to, or even know. I sometimes half think that the bread is so hard and the water so bitter, that life will become impossible. I try to get over it; but if you were to go away from me in anger, I should be so beaten for a week or two that I could do nothing.'
'Why won't you let me do anything?'
'I will; – whatever you please. But kiss me.' Then he kissed her, as she stood among Mr Soames's cabbage-stalks. 'Dear Hugh; you are such a god to me!'
'You don't treat me like a divinity.'
'But I think of you as one when you are absent. The gods were never obeyed when they showed themselves. Let us go and have a walk. Come; – shall we get as far as Ridleigh Mill?' Then they started together, and all unpleasantness was over between them when they returned to the Clock House. (XLIII)

The end of the chapter cuts off further authorial comment, but what would Trollope have found to say? This revelation that the only man Priscilla finds she can care about is the one she can never be more than a sister to, is unforeseen and undeveloped – but it must have struck Trollope as a truth, if an enigmatic one.

At the end of the novel, Priscilla looks set to take over from Aunt Stanbury the role of the fierce old maid who does not expect much from life and will not thank anyone who tries to make it better for her. As she says to her sister Dorothy, '"I hate to take things"' – even Hugh's money. When Dorothy suggests that such an attitude is morbid, Priscilla replies '"Of course it is. You don't suppose I really think it grand . . . But I am strong enough to live on, and not get killed by the morbidity."' And when the sisters look forward to Dorothy's marriage, Priscilla contemplates her own lonely future with a stoic puzzlement:

'I wonder why it is that you two should be married, and so grandly married, and that I shall never, never have any one to love.'

'Oh, Priscilla, do not say that. If I have a child will you not love it?'

'It will be your child; – not mine. Do not suppose that I complain. I know that it is right. I know that you ought to be married and I ought not. I know that there is not a man in Devonshire who would take me, or a man in Devonshire whom I would accept. I know that I am quite unfit for any other kind of life than this. I should make any man wretched, and any man would make me wretched. But why is it so?' (XCVII)

Priscilla's question hangs in the air disconcertingly. The bleak life to which her nature commits her makes any easy conclusions about a woman's place look facile. Priscilla's fate, in a small way, like Emily Trevelyan's in a larger one, powerfully qualifies the romantic optimism expressed formally by the three marriages (Nora, Caroline, Dorothy) to which the novel moves.

But although the disparate nature of female experience in *He Knew He Was Right* may beg large questions about a woman's place, the novel is not organized as a symposium on such a topic. It is rather something that naturally comes up as a result of finding out what happens to a particular set of people. The characters are linked more by their own affinities of temperament than by any authorial thesis; the varieties of obstinacy exhibited are more genuinely connective than any theoretical concern with the risks and rewards of marriage. It is not surprising therefore – and not seriously damaging – that the novel should be so inconclusive about a matter on which the author clearly has no monopoly of wisdom. What looks like theme is really side-effect. The novel is essentially open-minded, and the more characteristically Trollopian for that.

It is also in a certain sense open-ended – equally characteristically. The hospitality of *He Knew He Was Right* – the way it accommodates so equally not only a wide range of opinion and experience but also varying levels of tone – owes much to Trollope's mastery of contingency. This novel is typical of Trollope's best work in that it seems to have an entirely natural relationship with the larger fictional world of his continuing imagination. The casual ways in which Bishop Proudie, Lady Glencora and Lord Cantrip are mentioned are significant if fleeting indications of that interconnectedness, and there is too an intriguing moment of covert cross-reference. After Sir Marmaduke Rowley has made an ineffective appearance before a Parliamentary committee, he rather dreads meeting at the Colonial Office 'the young Irish Under-Secretary'. The man turns out to be perfectly civil – as we might expect, since although Trollope does not name him in the text he must be none other than Phineas Finn. However tiny in itself, this kind of interior allusiveness is symptomatic of the way in which the world of a given Trollope novel is imagined by the writer as part of a greater continuum in which it is natural for people from different books to come across each other by chance. This principle operates just as effectively within novels as between them. If it is easy to accept Colonel Osborne's report of a country house party at which Lady Glencora is also a guest ('"and uncommon pleasant she made it"', (LXIV)), there seems no objection to a narrative which however obliquely connects such fictive extremes as the comic vacillation of Mr Gibson at Exeter and the tragic desolation of Mr Trevelyan at Casalunga. Such indiscriminateness may look uncritical, and it certainly overwhelms by sheer proliferation attempts to tidy up the novel by imposing unifying concepts. In practice, however, it satisfies our sense of the random juxtapositions of life.

IV
Character and Authorial Purpose

Trollope's primary allegiance to the character was always liable to get in his way when he wanted to argue a case. As we have seen, both the Barsetshire and the Palliser series repeatedly show his interest in the individual prevailing over any tendency to force the ecclesiastical or political issue; and in other novels – where repetition of situation rather than reappearance of character has been the basis of Trollope's working method – the fact that similar states of affairs can be developed and resolved in such varying ways again indicates a willingness to let the dramatis personae have their head. It may seem perverse to talk of the freedom available to Trollope's characters given the constraints on Victorian conduct both on and off the page, but within the limits of their period and provenance, freedom is what they mostly seem to have. It is a condition of our interest in them. When they are patently coerced by the author's desire to make them accessory to an argument, the novel either suffers from being thus nailed down, or (as D. H. Lawrence put it) gets up and walks away with the nail. The alternatives are clearly demonstrated by the cases of Carry Brattle, the fallen woman in *The Vicar of Bullhampton*, and Augustus Melmotte, the great swindler whose social acceptability illustrates the decadence of *The Way We Live Now*. In both works Trollope's argument is openly advertised, but the novelistic results of his canvassing turn out very differently.

The Vicar of Bullhampton

In *The Vicar of Bullhampton* (begun immediately after completion of *He Knew He Was Right* in 1868, published 1870) Trollope goes to the unprecedented length of adding a Preface to explain and justify his intentions. This was so important to him that he not only inserted it verbatim in the *Autobiography* but also went over the points it and the novel makes yet again. The questions which Trollope felt to be at issue are whether he was right to introduce a girl whom he delicately calls 'a castaway' at all, and whether his treatment of her in the novel is proper. He defends himself by saying that although well-brought-up young persons used not even to be aware of creatures like Carry Brattle, such innocence no longer obtains and cannot therefore be corrupted by his portrayal of her. However, while he has not shown her life of shame to be alluringly luxurious he has also refused to endorse the extreme severity of those who disown women who have lived in sin lest they and their families should be contaminated. Trollope's arguments – such as the fact that it is usually the man who is most to blame, or that rehabilitation is more likely to be effective if not accompanied by compulsory sackcloth and ashes – seem to us so obviously humane that it may need an effort to recall the contemporary strength of the prejudice against which he was protesting. The *Autobiography*'s question 'How is the woman to return to decency to whom no decent door is opened?' (XVIII) was not so unanswerable to Mrs Grundy as it now sounds: she believed in a closed door policy as a deterrent, and was not likely to accept Trollope's further plea that the punishment of social ostracism does not in fact deter because the full horror of it is not known beforehand. At any rate, Trollope's hope that the studied moderation of his presentation of Carry's plight, being as the Preface says 'handled with truth to life', might do good was clearly an earnest one.

In the *Autobiography* Trollope readily concedes that Carry could not be the heroine of the story – she could not be rewarded for her weakness – and he no doubt also felt that to make her so would take him too far from what his audience expected; in this case, the question 'can you forgive her?' had to be put more diplomatically. He needed, therefore, a host plot or plots, and fell back on what James called (with this novel specifically in mind) his 'inveterate system'. James's remarks on *The Vicar of Bullhampton* in his 1883 essay are generous to the point of indulgence, and he gives no sign of being as irritated by Mary Lowther's vacillation as he had earlier been by Alice Vavasor's. Mary's friends want her to marry Harry Gilmore, the squire of Bullhampton; she prefers her second cousin

Walter Marrable, an impecunious soldier. Walter's prospects look so discouraging that he resolves to go back to service in India, and Mary releases him from their engagement to make it easier. Under pressure, she agrees to marry Mr Gilmore, making it clear that she does so from duty rather than inclination. When Captain Marrable is unexpectedly taken up as *de facto* heir by yet another uncle, Mary rushes back to him, leaving the resentful squire to assuage his bitterness by prolonged travel. James found Gilmore interesting – or, more strictly, found Trollope's interest in him interesting. He is another of those Trollopian men in whom constancy is the other side of the coin from obstinacy; their refusal to take no for an answer is given a particular intensity because in them their love and their sense of their lives have become so welded together that the former cannot be abandoned without great damage to the latter. This complaint tends to become more morbid in later Trollope, and we are told that Gilmore was 'verging on to a species of insanity'. (XXXII) There is no question, however, of his receiving the kind of attention paid so extensively to Louis Trevelyan, just as there is no fullness of investigation – by the standards of Trollope's best work – into the psychology of Mary's changes of mind. The best-rendered stages of the relationship between the couple come towards its end, when Trollope has to some degree worked himself into and up to it; their last scene together (in Chapter LXIV) has moments of genuine power.

Other areas of *The Vicar of Bullhampton* involve equally familiar material. The Vicar himself, Frank Fenwick, combines charity and pugnacity in a typically Trollopian way. His quarrel with the silly Marquis who owns most of his parish is an amusing but light-weight version of that opposition of the self to authority which Trollope found so sympathetic. As the Vicar wryly admits when manoeuvred into reconciliation, '"The truth is, that the possession of a grievance is the one state of human blessedness."' (LXI) The sectarian dispute about building a hideous Wesleyan church on top of the parsonage is more in the manner of the small beer of *Rachel Ray* than the diocesan warfare of Barchester. Mr Fenwick's compassionate provision for Carry Brattle owes something to her beauty and it is misconstrued in a way that hints at the fuller development of the idea later in *Dr Wortle's School*. Carry's brother is suspected of being accessory to a murder, and this leads to his appearance at a trial during which Trollope airs his old grouse about the bullying of witness by counsel, but his heart hardly seems in it. The Vicar has to spend an aimless day in London which distantly but perfunctorily recalls the Warden's attempt to kill time, long ago. Such echoes and cross-references – which also include such stand-bys as the timely prospect of inheritance and, of course, waterside love scenes (in an early chapter Mary Lowther actually falls in) – are Trollope's way of keeping the novel respectably going in order to give himself the opportunity of interesting us in Carry's plight.

His actual mode of doing so is both circumspect and uncharacteristic. Carry's home is an old mill by the stream, pastoral in presentation as well as setting. It is dominated by Jacob Brattle, whose strong sense of self-respect has been sorely tried by the seduction of his daughter and to a lesser extent the insubordination of his son. Trollope finds his emotions easier to deal with than Carry's and the portrait has its integrity, although Trollope writes of the miller's way of life with an unusual sense of social distance. Trollope's purpose on this occasion naturally precluded any of the geniality he customarily brought to common life, and in any case Brattle's own unremitting severity could not encourage Trollope to relax.

Although Jacob is said to have virtually torn Carry's seducer limb from limb, we learn almost nothing of the original circumstances of her fall, or of the emotions and the relationship which led to it. Carry herself is not introduced in person until as late as Chapter XXV. By then she is clearly imbued with the same sense of shame about her condition that everybody else has; when the Vicar offers her his hand, she replies, '"Oh, Mr Fenwick, I ain't fit for the likes of you to touch."' We are given no real understanding of her interior life at any stage, although a generalized pathos accompanies her throughout. We never come to know as much about her as about, say, Hetty Sorrel in *Adam Bede* (although Trollope has the restraint to eschew the normally obligatory pregnancy). In fact, Trollope treats his character so externally that he deprives himself of his best means of achieving his intention of what the *Autobiography* calls exciting 'not only pity but sympathy for a fallen woman'. (XVIII) In *He Knew He Was Right* his aim had also been to 'create sympathy' for its principal character, and it depended absolutely on that close attentiveness to a suffering consciousness which is here lacking. The most imaginatively rendered part of Carry's story is perhaps her return on foot to the mill, begun as an aimless wandering but gradually yielding to a homing instinct. 'Nothing could be more truly tragical than the utterly purposeless tenour of her day' (LII) is Trollope's comment, and for a couple of pages his fictive world seems to touch Hardy's, morally as well as geographically. But the scene following Carry's return to her parents is oddly conventional, and so is the moment when Jacob brings himself to extend to his child that forgiveness which Trollope hoped also to arouse in his readers:

> 'Father,' she said, looking up into his face. Then she fell on the ground at his feet, and embraced his knees, and lay there sobbing. She had intended to ask him for forgiveness, but she was not able to say a word. Nor did he speak for awhile; but he stooped and raised her up tenderly; and then, when she was again standing by him, he stepped on as though he were going to the mill without a word. But he had not rebuked her, and his touch had been very gentle. 'Father,' she said, following him, 'if you could forgive me! I know I have been bad, but if you could forgive me!'
>
> He went to the very door of the mill before he turned; and she, when she saw that he did not come back to her, paused upon the bridge. She had used all her eloquence. She knew no other words with which to move him. She felt that she had failed, but she could do no more. But he stopped again without entering the mill.
>
> 'Child,' he said at last, 'come here, then.' She ran at once to meet him. 'I will forgive thee. There. I will forgive thee, and trust thou may'st be a better girl than thou hast been.'
>
> She flew to him and threw her arms round his neck and kissed his face and breast. 'Oh, father,' she said, 'I will be good. I will try to be good. Only you will speak to me.'
>
> 'Get thee into the house now. I have forgiven thee.' So saying he passed on to his morning's work. (LXVI)

Read in context, the passage is touching enough, but it is curiously anonymous. Although Carry's embracing of her father's knees parallels Lady Mason's winding her arms round the knees of Sir

Peregrine in *Orley Farm*, the scene might have been written by any competent novelist – or illustrated by any competent painter – of the period. There is more of Trollope's normal insight in the miller's confession of his feelings to the Vicar:

> 'But I can't look no man square in the face now; – and as for other folk's girls, I can't bear 'em near me, – no how. They makes me think of my own.' Fenwick had now turned his back to the miller, in order that he might wipe away his tears without showing them. 'I'm thinking of her always, Muster Fenwick; – day and night. When the mill's agoing, it's all the same. It's just as though there warn't nothing else in the whole world as I minded to think on. I've been a man all my life, Muster Fenwick; and now I ain't a man no more.' (LXIII)

The point about not being able to bear other men's girls is small enough, but psychologically plausible and true to the character, and Jacob's feeling of being unmanned has a wounded masculine pride which leaves the Vicar lost for any words of either comfort or reproof. The imbalance between our vivid sense of the father's affliction and our rather formal apprehension of the daughter's situation further modifies Trollope's success in achieving his novelistic purpose, humane as it is. A preoccupation with the effect he is making does not at this date lead Trollope to that self-consciousness more typical of his earlier work, but here it still weakens his concentration on the individual character and therefore distracts him from what is artistically his most valuable activity.

The Way We Live Now

The Way We Live Now (written 1873, published 1875) may seem to owe its prodigious length to the author's desire to provide comprehensive evidence for the thesis clearly signalled by the title, but the longer it goes on the more his habitual and involuntary centres of interest reassert their appeal to his imagination. It was the first work Trollope began after settling again in the centre of London (at 39 Montague Square), and perhaps he felt it an appropriate moment to tackle a major theme. The *Autobiography* retrospectively defines the book's subject as 'the commercial profligacy of the age', which is most obviously embodied in the figure of Augustus Melmotte, the forger financier, whose brief ascendancy is taken as symptomatic of the general deterioration. Modern commentary – greatly reassured by the prospect of a Trollope novel which seems ostensibly and incontrovertibly to address itself to large social and moral issues – has tended to assume that the book actually delivers the promised critique.[1] In fact, the argument becomes more and more blurred by the inconvenient autonomy that the characters insist on assuming. Sadleir notes, in reproducing Trollope's advance lay-out for the novel (which is simply an annotated list of characters), that Melmotte is not there envisaged as its central figure. 'The chief character' is to be Lady Carbury, a still attractive widow who is trying to offset the depredations caused by her worthless son Felix through hack-work masquerading as literature. The excellently written first chapter, which reproduces her letters begging various editors to puff her forthcoming book *Criminal Queens*, certainly shows that she lacks that integrity in literary dealings which Trollope prized so highly, and indeed exemplified so admirably himself. Although there are some sharp points made about the standards of periodicals later on (Trollope was no doubt able to draw on his experience of editing the *St Paul's Magazine* between 1867 and 1870, the full-scale study of corruption in literary life which our introduction to Lady Carbury seems to promise never in fact arrives; *The Way We Live Now* is not a precursor of Gissing's *New Grub Street*. During most of Trollope's novel, Lady Carbury is studied as a doting mother whose foolish indulgence of the callously selfish Felix is accompanied by her continuous irritation with the obstinacy of her daughter Henrietta, who refuses to marry their relative Roger Carbury, a Suffolk squire and head of the family. Lady Carbury's experience of life has taught her that girls ought not to be too fussy. Her main hope is that Felix will succeed in marrying Melmotte's daughter Marie, and thus be able to call on funds magnificent beyond even his powers of depletion. The idea that access to Melmotte's cash will solve their problems is one that a considerable number of the novel's characters have in common, but most of them have nothing to do with literature – in fact, some of the aristocratic drones at the Beargarden Club who are most desperately in need of subvention seem hardly able to read and write.

Lady Carbury's other worry is the attentions of Mr Broune. As editor of the *Morning Breakfast Table*, he is of course literary. His partiality for Lady Carbury makes him compromise his professional ethics to some extent, but he knows well enough that she has no real talent. Nevertheless, Mr Broune not only proposes, but continues as an increasingly close friend after he has been rejected. The development of their middle-aged romance is possible because Lady Carbury refuses to think of it as such; her trust in his constant support depends on her feeling thankful that all that sort of thing is out of the way. This paradoxically leads to an intimacy that at the end of the novel she cannot evade. Mr Broune's second proposal is made in an unflustered tone quite unlike his first, and Lady Carbury finds herself 'kneeling at his feet, with her face buried on his knees'. (XCIX) It is an unexpectedly touching moment because Trollope sees the scene not in genre terms (as with Carry Brattle and Lady Mason) but as involving inappropriate individuals: 'Considering their ages perhaps we must say that their attitude was awkward. They would certainly have thought so themselves had they imagined that any one could have seen them.' However, as he explains, 'It is not that Age is ashamed of feeling passion and acknowledging it, – but that the display of it is without the graces of which Youth is proud, and which Age regrets.' Such an understanding presentation hardly suggests satire, and when, in the later stages of the story, we are again told something of Lady Carbury's literary production, there is a further modification of the initial severity. Immediately after finishing her dubious *Criminal Queens*, she turns to the novel because it seems more likely to sell. But although *The Wheel of Fortune*, the resulting title, is obviously rubbish, her discipline in writing it is praiseworthy; she shows the kind of application that Trollope himself (as well as his mother before him) regularly practised: 'From day to day, with all her cares heavy upon her, she had sat at her work, with a firm resolve that so many lines should be always forthcoming, let the difficulty of making them be what they might'. (LXXXIX) She takes a Trollopian pleasure in having completed her work 'exactly in the time fixed'. Even more curiously, Trollope lends Lady Carbury an experience which as he later revealed in the *Autobiography* (VI) had been his own. In the novel her publisher's advice is '"whatever you do, Lady Carbury, don't be historical. Your historical novel, Lady

Carbury, isn't worth a —"'; Trollope himself was told, '"Whatever you do, don't be historical; your historical novel is not worth a damn."' There was more point in such a tip in the late 1850s, when the long buoyant market in pseudo-Scott was fading, than in the world of the early 1870s, which *The Way We Live Now* ostensibly satirizes. Trollope's transfer of this little incident is typical of his lack of superior self-regard, and his readiness to allow Lady Carbury authorial perseverance if not literary merit indicates how constitutionally unable he was to sustain the kind of astringency which comes naturally to the true satirist. The acquaintance with Lady Carbury that writing the novel has deepened has nurtured a fellow-feeling which inhibits censure. The sustained hostility of, say, a Wyndham Lewis, was something of which Trollope was too innately generous to be capable.

This magnanimous handicap substantially affects his treatment of Melmotte, seen by everybody as the essential sign that things are not now as once they were. Like Madame Max Goesler and Ferdinand Lopez, Augustus Melmotte emerges from a continental background which seems inadequately accounted for. In Melmotte's case, there are those who think that his sudden arrival and mushroom prosperity in the City justifies putting the worst constructions on his previous career, but he quickly establishes a commanding commercial position all the same. Trollope's main point is that it is 'society' that takes Melmotte up. Lord Alfred Grendall and his son Miles for instance willingly submit to being patronized by and readily run errands for the great financier for the sake of what they hope to get out of him. Mr Longestaffe, who takes immense if fatuous pride in his lineage and gentility, is nevertheless sufficiently hard up to sell to the vulgar Melmotte one of the ancestral houses and to act as a dummy director on the board of Melmotte's greatest enterprise. This is the South Central Pacific and Mexican Railway, a project originally brought over from San Francisco by a sharp American called Hamilton K. Fisker. It is quite understood though not openly admitted that the company does not exist actually to build the railway – a transcontinental task of herculean difficulty and unlikely to make money – but is rather a speculative affair designed to float shares and talk them up into dizzy profitability. Most of the aristocratic characters in *The Way We Live Now* are only too eager to associate themselves with such an unprincipled venture. By the middle of the novel, Melmotte has become the acclaimed exemplar of commercial enterprise, rumoured to be the key figure in a series of vast enterprises all over the globe – a man who has risen, of course, 'above any feeling of personal profit'. (XLIV) He is chosen as the Conservative candidate in the forthcoming Westminster by-election, and selected as an outstanding example of British mercantile greatness to entertain the visiting Emperor of China at a banquet of spectacular expense. This period of Melmotte's life represents a kind of Balzacian apogee from which he can only decline. It is the period when Melmotte is most useful to Trollope as far as satirical purpose is concerned, since it shows in so diagrammatic a way that collusion between money and rank which is such an indictment of the way we live now. But the point at which Melmotte's empire begins to crumble is also the point at which Trollope begins to pay him a more detailed and less theoretical kind of attention; the character becomes progressively less of a portent and more of a person.

It has been 'part of the charm of all dealings' with Melmotte that 'no ready money seemed ever to be necessary for anything'. (XLV) He has perfected the art of implying that 'everything necessary had been done, when he had said that it was done.' The shaky foundations of Melmotte's aggrandizement are put under increasing stress as his projects pile up, and he becomes more and more vulnerable to a loss of confidence. It is a pleasant irony – though perhaps one of rather unnerving implication – that the Melmotte bubble is pricked by someone who, in business matters, would never claim to be more than a child. Dolly Longestaffe is the most engaging of the Beargarden Club set (it is not surprising that Trollope brought him back in *The Duke's Children*), and although – as he would be the first to admit – his intelligence is limited, he is bright enough to know the difference between promises and cash in hand. The gambling at the Beargarden, carried on largely by means of worthless IOUs, is to be seen as analogous to speculative dealings in the real market of the City, but while Dolly may accept paper from Felix Carbury or Miles Grendall out of good nature and a wish not to spoil the game, he only agrees to sell Melmotte his share in the family property for real money. As he artlessly puts it, '"A cheque upon his bank which I can pay in to mine is about the best thing going."' (XLV) Dolly's inopportune simplicity finds Melmotte unable to put his hands on the required amount, and the collapse of confidence begins, helped along by resentment at his increasing arrogance and by the rumour that he has attempted to tide things over by forgery.

It is when Melmotte thus has his back to the wall that Trollope's interest quickens – an interest that is far more psychological than commercial. We are never given an exact or even plausible account of Melmotte's business affairs in the kind of detail that Balzac readily supplies when accounting for the rise of figures like Birotteau or Nucingen. Round sums are casually introduced but not totted up. What is clearly shown is the kind of hubris which clouds Melmotte's judgement and precipitates his downfall, as he himself comes to realize. At one point, Trollope notes, Melmotte 'came almost to believe in himself'. (LVI) However, in the unprecedentedly full account of Melmotte's thoughts during and after the great banquet, Trollope's increased command of the twists and turns of the financier's mind is presented as a new dimension of self-knowledge: 'Perhaps never in his life had he studied his own character and his own conduct more accurately, or made sterner resolves, than he did as he stood there smiling, bowing, and acting without impropriety the part of host to an Emperor.' (LXII) He determines to brave things out, and Trollope adds, 'I think he took some pride in his own confidence as to his own courage, as he stood there turning it all over in his mind.' Trollope's interjection of 'I think' is not only often used as an indication that a person's motives are more interestingly and justifiably mixed than might be conventionally supposed, but also tends to imply the achievement of that familiarity with a character's interior life which it is the overriding purpose of Trollope's art to promote. Here, it is an indication that satire is giving way to a kind of sympathy. As a result, we begin to see the Melmotte that no one else sees. In the next chapter he is shown privately destroying some obviously incriminating documents, and we are given an hour-by-hour report of Melmotte's activities on the day of the election, which he wins by a slim majority. Ignorant as he is, Melmotte is as elated and awed as other successful Parliamentary candidates in Trollope's fiction at 'the magnitude of the achievement'. After an evening's drinking in solitary triumph, he goes up to bed 'with careful and almost solemn steps'. (LXIV) Although his party are by now embarrassed by their

375

newest recruit, Melmotte happens to meet its leader as he arrives at the House, and is chivalrously accompanied by him. His first impressions of the Commons are not dissimilar from those of such other new members as Phineas Finn, and, like Phineas, he is humiliated by his lack of ready words when he rashly attempts to make a premature first speech.

The more interior presentation of Melmotte does not involve any softening of the character's harsher features. His physical violence against his daughter Marie when she refuses to let him draw on the money he had put away in her name against the rainy day which has now arrived, is not glossed over (though not closely described); we also witness the forging of further signatures (the crime is of the same type as Lady Mason's in *Orley Farm*, although the motives are different). Nevertheless, the last phase of Melmotte's career is described with that concentration and neutral objectivity so characteristic of Trollope's art when he is most engaged in his material.

As ruin looks more and more imminent, Melmotte's self-communings are given at increasing length. Chapter LXXXI for instance shows him mulling over his chances of survival and gives a full report of his self-condemnation. Melmotte's judgement of himself has 'a certain manliness' because it is unsparing and objective, but it never crosses his mind that he should 'repent of the fraud in which his whole life had been passed'. His dishonesty is so axiomatic that it has a perverse kind of integrity which Trollope refrains from overtly condemning; indeed, most of the passage in question remains strictly within Melmotte's point of view.

Melmotte's last day begins with the defection of his loyal clerk and the knowledge that a City colleague, Mr Brehgert, will not help him out because he has rumbled Melmotte's forgeries. He resolves that although 'he was about to have a crushing fall . . . the world should say that he had fallen like a man' (LXXXII), and therefore goes down to the House nevertheless. His entry causes a sudden silence in the chamber, and for the rest of the evening he has briefly to endure a sense of isolation almost as intense, in its way, as that felt by such alienated characters as Mr Crawley and Louis Trevelyan. Melmotte may be a crook, but he has the Trollopian sensitivity to social ostracism all the same. His self-consciousness is carefully registered through details of his dress and appearance – his hat 'a little more cocked than usual', his coat-lapels 'thrown back a little wider', his step always slow and now 'almost majestic' – which seem the result of an ever closer authorial scrutiny. No one will sit next to him; the waiters are reluctant to serve him at dinner, when he drinks heavily; the Speaker himself tries to ignore the new MP's attempts to catch his eye, but has finally to let him speak:

> Melmotte standing erect, turning his head round from one side of the House to another, as though determined that all should see his audacity, propping himself with his knees against the seat before him, remained for half a minute perfectly silent. He was drunk, – but better able than most drunken men to steady himself, and showing in his face none of those outward signs of intoxication by which drunkenness is generally made apparent. But he had forgotten in his audacity that words are needed for the making of a speech, and now he had not a word at his command. He stumbled forward, recovered himself, then looked once more round the House with a glance of anger, and after that toppled headlong over the shoulders of Mr Beauchamp Beauclerk, who was sitting in front of him.
>
> . . . There was much commotion in the House. Mr Beauclerk, a man of natural good nature, though at the moment put to considerable personal inconvenience, hastened, when he recovered his own equilibrium, to assist the drunken man. But Melmotte had by no means lost the power of helping himself. He quickly recovered his legs, and then reseating himself, put his hat on, and endeavoured to look as though nothing special had occurred. The House resumed its business, taking no further notice of Melmotte, and having no special rule of its own as to the treatment to be adopted with drunken members. But the member for Westminster caused no further inconvenience. He remained in his seat for perhaps ten minutes, and then, not with a very steady step, but still with capacity sufficient for his own guidance, he made his way down to the doors. His exit was watched in silence, and the moment was an anxious one for the Speaker, the clerks, and all who were near him. Had he fallen some one, – or rather some two or three, – must have picked him up and

carried him out. But he did not fall either there or in the
lobbies, or on his way down to Palace Yard. Many were
looking at him, but none touched him. When he had got
through the gates, leaning against the wall he hallooed for his
brougham, and the servant who was waiting for him soon
took him home to Bruton Street. That was the last which the
British Parliament saw of its new member for Westminster.
(LXXXIII)

It is hard to say why this almost farcical episode is so oddly
impressive. It might be argued that Melmotte's actual fall is simply
an emblem of his metaphorical one, that his rejection by the House
at this point is symbolic of the Establishment's refusal, in the end,
to tolerate the corruption he represents. Such a reading, however,
would indicate that society is not deteriorating as badly as Trollope
seems to be implying earlier on. In fact Trollope explicitly dissoci-
ates himself from Carlylean pessimism in the *Autobiography*, and
indeed his views coincide with those expressed by the Bishop of
Elmham in Chapter LV in the novel itself. His settled conviction
that on the whole things were getting better, that the age was
indeed one of improvement even though certain kinds of public
dishonesty were disgracefully flagrant, meant that – as polemic –
The Way We Live Now was always likely to run out of steam. Here
the truth is surely that Trollope has preferred his intuitive understanding of the character to the logic of his argument. The close
physical observation of Melmotte's movements in the paragraphs
quoted – such little touches as the way he leans against the wall
while waiting for the brougham – do not suggest the kind of
attention that has more than half an eye on allegorical significance.
The actual death of Melmotte by prussic acid is reported at the end
of the chapter in a laconic, almost police-court manner which not
only indicates Trollope's habitual refusal to sensationalize, but also
reveals no wish to gloss the event through any kind of generalizing
comment. Trollope's extreme restraint allows Melmotte to retrieve
in death the dignity he has compromised earlier by tumbling over
Mr Beauclerk. As in the analogous case of Lopez, Trollope refrains
from offering to interpret the character's last thoughts; instead –
and with generous novelistic tact – we are left to make the appropriate inferences from his actions. One has only to look back to

Trollope's handling of Sir Henry Harcourt's suicide in *The Bertrams* to register the gain in delicacy and suggestiveness. There is a kind of respect for the character in allowing him his privacy at such a time. Moreover, Trollope later maintains a posthumous loyalty to Melmotte by a suddenly vigorous protest against the inquest's vindictive refusal to consider a verdict of suicide while temporarily insane: 'it may be imagined, I think, that during that night he may have become as mad as any other wretch, have been driven as far beyond his powers of endurance as any other poor creature who ever at any time felt himself constrained to go'. (LXXXVIII) Melmotte is entitled to the same imaginative compassion as anyone else.

The strong sense that we finally have of Melmotte as an individual – and as therefore something more interesting than a mere symptom of a social malaise – is established partly by his finding himself in a fictional environment that despite Trollope's intention (as recalled in the *Autobiography*) 'to take the whip of the satirist into my hand' (XX) is not unlike the novelist's normal world. This is not just because Melmotte's Parliamentary experience and his suicide are situations that can be paralleled in that world – as can be the attempt to stave off disaster by terrorizing womenfolk into handing over money properly theirs (compare Harcourt's and Lopez's bullying of their wives with Melmotte's violence towards his daughter). It is also due to the fact that many features of the world of *The Way We Live Now* are also to be found in novels written without any proclaimed thesis. Trollope is quite ready to think of its personnel as moving in that imaginative continuum on which the Palliser series draws, and the novel has a good deal in common with its immediate successor, *The Prime Minister*. As already noted, some characters appear briefly in later books (Lady Carbury and Mr Broune, Dolly Longestaffe); others are mentioned who are already known (Sir Orlando Drought, Mr Bideawhile of Slow and Bideawhile, and Glencora's uncle the Marquis of Auld Reekie, whose son Lord Nidderdale is Melmotte's favoured suitor for Marie).

The other main areas of plot interest in *The Way We Live Now* offer more substantial examples of Trollopian repetition. They are plausibly co-ordinated with the Melmotte affair, but on a basis of loose contingency rather than thematic corroboration. For instance, Melmotte's most vocal critic is the Suffolk squire Roger Carbury, often taken to be an authorial mouthpiece; it is Roger who most strenuously insists that the rise of the great swindler is a sign of the deplorable decadence of the times. When Lady Carbury explains her scheme to solve the problem of Felix by marrying him to Marie Melmotte, Roger's reaction is trenchant:

> 'You will never get me to say that I think the family will be benefited by a marriage with the daughter of Mr Melmotte. I look upon him as dirt in the gutter. To me, in my old-fashioned way, all his money, if he has it, can make no difference. When there is a question of marriage, people at any rate should know something of each other. Who knows anything of this man? Who can be sure that she is his daughter?'
>
> 'He would give her her fortune when she married.'
>
> 'Yes; it all comes to that. Men say openly that he is an adventurer and a swindler. No one pretends to think that he is a gentleman. There is a consciousness among all who speak of him that he amasses his money not by honest trade, but by unknown tricks, – as does a card-sharper. He is one whom we would not admit into our kitchens, much less to our tables, on the score of his own merits. But because he has learned the art of making money, we not only put up with him, but settle upon his carcase as so many birds of prey.' (XV)

Admittedly, Roger has quixotically high standards in these matters: 'To him it seemed that a gentleman was disgraced who owed money to a tradesman which he could not pay' (VII) – a disgrace which would attach itself to a considerable number of characters in Trollope who are certainly gentlemen in other respects. But although Roger may look at first as if he is to function as an exemplary upholder of values which are a standing reproach to the way we live now, it soon becomes clear that his conservatism is the natural expression of an eccentric kind of temperament with which readers of Trollope nevertheless become very familiar. During most of his appearances in the novel he is preoccupied with private concerns rather than public morals. As another lover who is also a cousin, Roger is likely to be disappointed in Hetta Carbury since she is in love with Roger's younger friend and former protégé Paul

Montague. Nevertheless he maintains his passion with that fanatical constancy recently seen in Harry Gilmore in *The Vicar of Bullhampton*. He thinks of this love '"always, often despising myself because I think of it so much"' since '"a man should not allow his love to dominate his intellect"'. (XIX) As he himself realizes, Roger's obsession is related to his solitariness, but he is a more rewarding character than Gilmore because he is seen in a richer variety of relations. In Suffolk his style of antique gentility puts the neighbouring *nouveaux riches* in their place; he maintains a stolid Anglicanism against the importunate Romanism of a local Catholic priest whom he befriends; he is ready to come up to town on other people's affairs (such as his mission on behalf of the miller John Crumb, whose devotion to the flighty Ruby Ruggles is, as he realizes, an analogue of his own); he is scrupulous in some of his dealings with Paul, even though his love makes him unjust in other respects. He also adjusts, finally, to Hetta's preference for Montague with a startling kind of emotional logic: '"As you will not be my wife, you shall by my daughter . . . I will hurry to grow old that I may feel for you as the old feel for the young. And if you have a child, Hetta, he must be my child."' (XCIII) Roger has at least found an answer, if a self-punishing one, to the constant but rejected lover's problem, and it is one that seems consistent with the curious mixture of uprightness and imbalance in his nature. He provides one of the more interesting of Trollope's variations on a recurrent psychological state (a motif that Trollope was still deploying in his last completed novel *An Old Man's Love*), but – as its appearance elsewhere indicates – it is an interest that has no necessary connection with Melmottism.

Much space in *The Way We Live Now* is also given over to the dilemma of Paul Montague, which is classically Trollopian. Paul has tried to make his way in America, and his partnership with Fisker leads to his involvement with the great Mexican railway speculation. Although he accepts his share of the profits, he becomes increasingly uneasy about Melmotte's manner of treating directors as rubber stamps and makes himself awkward at board meetings. A similar mixture of weakness and principle is evident in his emotional life, which is given proportionately more attention than his business affairs (the 'glimmerings' of Radicalism mentioned in Trollope's advance notes come to nothing). While in the

States Paul has had what clearly amounts to an affair with Mrs Winifred Hurtle. It was only when that was safely behind him, as he thought, that he addressed himself to Hetta Carbury. Mrs Hurtle, however, is too strong-minded a woman to give up the man she genuinely loves without a struggle, and pursues him to London where her presence cannot but be embarrassing. Paul can hardly refuse to see her, but every time he does, Mrs Hurtle renews an attack which is alternately recriminatory and suppliant but always energetic. The mature Mrs Hurtle is quite different from the bright but compliant American girls who marry English aristocrats in *He Knew He Was Right* and *The Duke's Children* – she is rather a less respectable alternative to Mrs Peacocke in *Dr Wortle's School*. She is connected with the West rather than the East, and is even rumoured to have shot a man in Oregon. The latent violence of the frontier with which she is associated is indeed part of her powerful erotic appeal. As with Mrs Peacocke, there is some uncertainty about her marital status; she claims to be divorced according to the laws of the state of Kansas, but it is not clear whether what is good enough for Kansas is acceptable elsewhere nor is it certain whether Mr Hurtle is alive or dead. Unlike Mrs Peacocke, Winifred Hurtle is not a lady; she admits that she is 'wild' where Paul is 'sleek' and 'tame', and one can easily see why Paul found her both irresistible in the short term and impossible in the long. The difficulty is that she is not 'a woman whom a man might ill-treat or scorn with impunity' (XXVI), and Paul is partly afraid of her. He is less than firm with Winifred, however, principally because he shrinks 'from subjecting her to the blank misery of utter desertion'. Trollope's intervention in order to exonerate Paul from the charge of cowardice is expressed in terms rich in implication for that moral imagination on which his own art relies:

> In social life we hardly stop to consider how much of that daring spirit which gives mastery comes from hardness of heart rather than from high purpose, or true courage. The man who succumbs to his wife, the mother who succumbs to her daughter, the master who succumbs to his servant, is as often brought to servility by a continual aversion to the giving of pain, by a softness which causes the fretfulness of others to be an agony to himself, – as by any actual fear which

the firmness of the imperious one may have produced. There is an inner softness, a thinness of the mind's skin, an incapability of seeing or even thinking of the troubles of others with equanimity, which produces a feeling akin to fear; but which is compatible not only with courage, but with absolute firmness of purpose, when the demand for firmness arises so strongly as to assert itself. (XLVII)

As so often, Trollope is concerned to point out that what is conventionally thought of as inconsistent is not really so, that 'masculine' and 'feminine' traits are not mutually exclusive but coexist in the same nature. His subtle sense of the intermixture of qualities which ought in theory to be distinct is one of the main reasons why he seems to have so much more flexibility and openness in his response to human reality than his contemporaries. Moreover, Trollope's unequalled capacity for conveying the sufferings of the thin-skinned has as its noble corollary that 'incapacity of seeing or even thinking of the troubles of others with equanimity', as he here puts it with characteristic restraint. Like other sensitive Trollopian men caught between two women – like, most notably, Phineas Finn – Paul Montague finds it painful to cause others pain, and his vacillation is the result. It also to some degree makes matters worse. Had he been firmer in casting Mrs Hurtle off, she might have suffered less. However, Paul's manifest kindness does at length prevail over Winifred's desire for revenge, and arouses her residual good nature in three moving scenes of resignation. At first the conflicting impulses within her are expressed in two letters which she writes but does not send. One magnanimously releases him; the other threatens grievous bodily harm. In the end, after showing him both letters, she lets him go. As Paul kneels at her feet in tears, she puts her hand on his forehead and pushes back his hair in a tender gesture reminiscent of Lady Laura's farewell to Phineas. (LI) On the second occasion Mrs Hurtle summons Hetta Carbury to an interview which might easily have become a conventional *scène à faire* – as the chapter title, 'The Rivals', indicates. It is saved in the event by the secure understanding of the character that Trollope has by now established, so that even a suspiciously stagey paradox like Winifred's "'I am strong enough to acknowledge that I have nothing to forgive in you; – and weak enough to forgive all his

383

treachery"' makes Hetta's 'weeping, she knew not why' sympathetic. (XCI) The final parting with Paul is accompanied by an embrace and an echo of Lily Dale's cry, '"My love; – my love"', and is followed by a more arresting and private moment:

> She stood still, without moving a limb, as she listened to his step down the stairs and to the opening and the closing of the door. Then hiding herself at the window with the scanty drapery of the curtain she watched him as he went along the street. When he had turned the corner she came back to the centre of the room, stood for a moment with her arms stretched out towards the walls, and then fell prone upon the floor. She had spoken the very truth when she said that she had loved him with all her heart. (XCVII)

A criticism looking for the emblematic might align Mrs Hurtle's collapse with Melmotte's fall in the House (noting that she is an enthusiastic admirer of his), but what matters to Trollope's dramatic imagination is the sudden exacerbation of wordless pain (conveyed by a sequence of actions similar to those which follow an earlier separation described in Chapter XLVII). In any case, the emotional predicament of a highly unassimilable outsider like Mrs Hurtle does not seem immediately relevant to a satire on the venality of English society, and the more interesting she becomes in her own right, the more the novel's grip on its announced theme weakens.

The situation of Georgiana Longestaffe, however, is more germane and must be what Trollope refers to in the *Autobiography* when he writes of the novel's castigation of 'other vices' such as 'the intrigues of girls who want to get married'. (XX) Georgiana's manoeuvres are expressed in unequivocal market terms:

> She had now been ten years at the work, and was aware that she had always flown a little too high for her mark at the time. At nineteen and twenty and twenty-one she had thought that all the world was before her. With her commanding figure, regular long features, and bright complexion, she had regarded herself as one of the beauties of the day, and had considered herself entitled to demand wealth and a coronet. At twenty-two, twenty-three, and twenty-four any young

peer, or peer's eldest son, with a house in town and in the country, might have sufficed. Twenty-five and -six had been the years for baronets and squires; and even a leading fashionable lawyer or two had been marked by her as sufficient since that time. But now she was aware that hitherto she had always fixed her price a little too high. On three things she was still determined, – that she would not be poor, that she would not be banished from London, and that she would not be an old maid. (LX)

At twenty-nine, Georgiana is no longer in a strong position, and her attempts to find a man prepared to put up with her disagreeable temper as well as meet her minimum residential conditions grow more and more desperate. When the family withdraws from London in order to retrench, she is ready to stay with the despicably vulgar Melmottes so as to have a base from which to carry on her campaign. She is even prepared to accept the proposal of a middle-aged Jewish widower from the City who already has children. Her family are appalled by the very idea of an alliance with someone like Mr Brehgert, and their reactions to him are hardly to their credit. Georgiana's attempts to make them see that 'it is no good going on with the old thing' and that on the matter of marriages between Christians and Jews there has been 'a general heaving-up of society' in the direction of tolerance or at least indifference, are not successful. When introduced half-way through the novel, Mr Brehgert is presented in terms of his type as conventionally rendered; he is fat and greasy, his hair is dyed (as for that matter is Mr Longestaffe's), his eyes are too close together, and at first his speech has the stereotyped mannerisms of Jewish moneylenders found elsewhere in Trollope. These soon wear off, and the character gains in dignity at each appearance, perhaps as a result of a growing appreciation by Trollope of his possibilities (he is not listed at all in the advance lay-out). His good humour and even temper show to advantage as Georgiana wriggles to negotiate the best contract she can. After her father tells Mr Brehgert in offensive terms of his disapproval, the banker sends her a letter which leaves it to her to stand by or recede from their engagement. As the novelist says, it is 'a plain-spoken and truth-telling letter' of 'single-minded genuine honesty' (LXXIX), and as such thrown away on

Georgiana. In it Brehgert explains that because of the losses he has
sustained through his dealings with Melmotte he cannot now
afford to maintain a house in London as well as his present home
out at Fulham, as originally agreed. Georgiana thinks that in view
of 'her own value as a Christian lady of high birth and position
giving herself to a commercial Jew' she is in a position to insist, but
as usual she tries for more than the market will bear. Brehgert
withdraws from the engagement, on the grounds – expressed with
a delicate but deadly irony which will certainly be lost on his
former fiancée – that 'of course I have no right to ask you to share
with me the discomfort of a single home'. When, later on, Mr
Longestaffe needs Mr Brehgert's professional assistance, he is made
speechless by the Jew's assertion that throughout the Georgiana
affair he has behaved '"like a gentleman"' (LXXXVIII) and an
honest man, but any unbiased reader must agree. Mr Brehgert's
integrity not only shows up the Longestaffes' shabbiness, but also
offsets the crimes of the other City Jews, Melmotte and his associate Cohenlupe; his upright conduct is a rebuke both to aristocratic
rapacity and to the facile idea that the way we live now can be put
down to Semitic penetration. Brehgert argues that in thinking of
Society as closed against Jews Mr Longestaffe 'has hardly kept pace
with the movements of the age' (LXXIX), and although Roger
Carbury might think such movements retrogressive, it would be
hard to maintain on this evidence that Trollope does so. As so often
in Trollope's work, things tend to balance out; on the one hand,
Melmotte – on the other, Brehgert. Such states of equipoise (the
term applied by the historian W. L. Burn to Trollope's age as a
whole) are inherently inimical to satire. Similarly, although Georgiana herself is in the end perfunctorily allowed to find whatever
happiness she can by eloping with a local curate, Trollope shows
elsewhere that he can be intensely sympathetic to the plight of girls
who work the marriage market year after year without success. His
defence in a letter (17 February 1877) of Arabella Trefoil, the
determined husband-hunter in *The American Senator*, is playful in
tone, but implies a serious creative commitment, as his scrupulous
presentation of her in the novel itself shows: 'I have been, and still
am very much afraid of Arabella Trefoil . . . Think of her virtues;
how she works, how true she is to her vocation, how little there is
of self indulgence, or of idleness. I think that she will go to a kind of

third class heaven in which she will always be getting third class husbands.' Miss Trefoil, however, struck *The Times'* reviewer as 'playing a more unblushing game than is even compatible with "the way we live now"'.

Trollope was unable to settle whole-heartedly to the satirist's task because for him the necessity of making a strong rhetorical effect interfered with the representation of the complex human truth. He had long felt that the exaggeration necessary to its method was likely to lead to artistic dishonesty. In *The Way We Live Now* it admittedly leads Trollope to deal with some of the recurring material less ambivalently than usual. Sir Felix Carbury functions in the novel as the incarnation of that selfishness which the theory of the book postulates as the endemic contemporary condition. The only thing for which he can summon up any energy is immediate gratification: 'he did not know how to get through a day in which no excitement was provided for him. He never read. Thinking was altogether beyond him. And he had never done a day's work in his life.' Beyond eating, drinking, lying in bed, and playing cards, there was only amusing himself with women, and 'the lower the culture of the women, the better the amusement' (LXVII). He is quite unable to put a future benefit before an immediate pleasure. The planned elopement with Marie Melmotte, which would have been profitable in that she has money in her own right, is aborted because Felix cannot tear himself away from the card table. Even his attempt to seduce Ruby Ruggles, which ends in his being beaten up by John Crumb, is relatively languid. He thus compares unfavourably in fictive interest with other disreputable young men elsewhere in Trollope. Although as 'beautiful' as Burgo Fitzgerald in appearance, he is never felt to have the genuine glamour and grace which offsets Burgo's fecklessness; although addicted to gambling like Captain Scarborough, he has none of those traces of good feeling which make Scarborough refuse to think ill of his dead mother; he does not even vacillate weakly but plausibly in the manner of Ralph the heir. The roughness of the justice he receives from Crumb – in yet another nocturnal street assault – is appropriate to the relatively crude terms of the portrayal. In his case, as with the offstage and offhand disposal of Georgiana Longestaffe, an arbitrary end to his career seems to be the result of the pressure Trollope has felt under to justify his thesis:

Felix is last reported in penitential exile in Eastern Prussia under the unlikely guardianship of a clergyman. The diminished expectations finally visited on both characters are ethically retributory rather than artistically logical, and underline the fact that the novel is at its weakest when it keeps most closely to the author's original purpose.

At its best, however, *The Way We Live Now* is a striking and significant demonstration of Trollope's inability – even when consciously and conspicuously addressing himself to the problems of his age – to prevent his concern for the particularity of individuals from prevailing over all other considerations. The effective source of authorial energy in this novel, as in all his work, is not the impulse to make public statements but the private desire to know his characters – those characters which the *Autobiography* insists the novelist must live with 'in the full reality of established intimacy'. As Henry James put it, in the essay which still remains the truest short account of what he does not hesitate to call Trollope's genius: 'We care what happens to people only in proportion as we know what people are. Trollope's great apprehension of the real, which was what made him so interesting, came to him through his desire to satisfy us on this point – to tell us what certain people were and what they did in consequence of being so.'

Bibliographical Notes

I Living with Characters

1. Henry James's essay on Trollope was included in his *Partial Portraits* (1888). It is conveniently reprinted in Donald Smalley's *Trollope: The Critical Heritage* (London, 1969), which also includes James's earlier reviews of *Miss Mackenzie*, *Can You Forgive Her?*, and *The Belton Estate*. Other quotations from periodical reviews are also taken from *The Critical Heritage* volume. *The Novel Machine: The Theory and Fiction of Anthony Trollope* by Walter M. Kendrick (Baltimore and London, 1980) includes a stimulating study of the *Autobiography*.

2. On Trollope's representation of Irish English, see John W. Clark's *The Language and Style of Anthony Trollope* (London, 1975). The importance and quality of *The Macdermots of Ballycloran* is vigorously defended in R. C. Terry's *Anthony Trollope: The Artist in Hiding* (London, 1977).

II Reappearing Characters

1. A recent summary of the controversial background to *The Warden* can be found in Bill Overton's *The Unofficial Trollope* (Brighton, 1982).

2. Michael Sadleir's *Trollope: A Commentary* was first published in 1927 (revised 1945).

3. Comparisons between *Doctor Thorne* and *Felix Holt* are made by Raymond Williams in *The English Novel from Dickens to Lawrence* (London, 1970).

4. Chapter XVI of *The Small House at Allington* is interestingly discussed by A. O. J. Cockshut in *Anthony Trollope: A Critical Study* (London, 1955).

5. In *Trollope's Palliser Novels: Theme and Pattern* (London, 1978) Juliet McMaster argues that Lily's self-inflicted suffering is part of the general theme of perversity in *The Small House at Allington*.

6. On the extent to which the Barsetshire novels can be correlated with historical events, see P. D. Edwards's *Anthony Trollope: His Art and Scope* (Hassocks, 1978).

389

7. The relation between 'two separate and distinct kinds of consciousness' in Trollope's fiction is illuminatingly explored in Bill Overton's *The Unofficial Trollope*.

8. For an extraordinary attack on Madame Goesler as 'one of the most repulsive characters in fiction' see Rebecca West's *The Court and the Castle* (London, 1958).

9. On the question of historical originals for Trollope's politicians see, for example, A. O. J. Cockshut, op. cit.; John Halperin's *Trollope and Politics* (London, 1977); P. D. Edwards, op. cit.

10. Tenway Junction has been variously interpreted by modern critics. For Robert M. Polhemus (*The Changing World of Anthony Trollope*, Berkeley and Los Angeles, 1968) it is a 'metaphoric vision of modern existence . . . the new pandemonium' of a 'fragmented humanity'; for Geoffrey Harvey (*The Art of Anthony Trollope*, London, 1980) it is 'a potent symbol of an industrial age' and represents 'the subterranean world of the working classes'; for Robert Tracy (*Trollope's Later Novels*, Berkeley, Los Angeles, London, 1978) it is a metaphor that sums up Trollope's structural technique and 'also an image of order in society'.

III Recurring Situations

1. Quotations are from James R. Kincaid's *The Novels of Anthony Trollope* (Oxford, 1977), Ruth apRoberts's *Trollope: Artist and Moralist* (London, 1971 – published in the USA as *The Moral Trollope*), and J. Hillis Miller's *The Form of Victorian Fiction* (Notre Dame, 1968).

2. On the relationship between the realistic and the sensational, see the scholarly discussion in P. D. Edwards, op. cit.

3. Lizzie's house party at Portray is described by James Kincaid, op. cit., as 'symptomatic of a world which has lost direction and control'.

4. J. Hillis Miller's remarks on the relationship between the self and falling in love in his discussion of *Ayala's Angel*, op. cit., can be applied widely beyond it.

5. On law, justice, and guilt in *Orley Farm*, see the rewarding discussions by A. O. J. Cockshut, Geoffrey Harvey, P. D. Edwards, and Bill Overton, op. cit.

6. On Percycross and Beverley, see 'Trollope's Political Novels' by Arthur Pollard (University of Hull, 1968).

7. On *Mr Scarborough's Family*, Andrew Wright (*Anthony Trollope: Dream*

and Art, London, 1983) states that 'it is certainly not improper to read the novel as the picture of a corrupt age'. A. O. J. Cockshut, op. cit., suggests that Trollope's satirical aim was similar to that of Sir Thomas More. Ruth apRoberts, op. cit., argues that the novel shows that 'no generalisation will ever hold in all cases'. Bill Overton, op. cit., claims that 'the novel, as well as the society it represents, is treated in part as a game'. Overton has some interesting details of Trollope's manuscript revisions.

8. On the form of *He Knew He Was Right*, see Walter M. Kendrick's highly suggestive account of Trollope's handling of fictional space and time, op. cit.

9. On pillar boxes and Trollope's professional career generally, see R. H. Super's *Trollope in the Post Office* (Ann Arbor, 1981).

IV Character And Authorial Purpose

1. Robin Gilmour notes that '*The Way We Live Now* has been so widely admired and written about . . . because it seems to lend itself readily to the kind of moral and thematic analysis with which modern criticism is most at home' ('A Lesser Thackeray? Trollope and the Victorian Novel', in *Anthony Trollope*, ed. Tony Bareham, London, 1980). The moral complexities involved in the novelist's and the reader's relationship with some of the principal characters are penetratingly discussed in Douglas Hewitt's *The Approach to Fiction: Good and Bad Readings of Novels* (London, 1972).

Index

For principal characters discussed see under individual novel(s) in which they appear: *Ayala's Angel* (Imogene Docimer, Ayala & Lucy Dormer, Isadore Hamel, Frank Houston, Jonathan Stubbs); *Barchester Towers* (Mr Arabin, Mrs Bold, Archdeacon Grantly, Mr Harding, Madeline Vesey Neroni, Mrs Proudie, Mr Slope, Bertie Stanhope); *The Belton Estate* (Clara Amedroz, Mrs Askerton, Captain & Lady Aylmer, Will Belton); *Can You Forgive Her?* (Burgo Fitzgerald, John Grey, Lady Glencora & Plantagenet Palliser, Alice Vavasor, George Vavasor); *The Claverings* (Harry Clavering, Lady Julia Ongar); *Cousin Henry* (Mr Apjohn, Isabel Brodrick, Henry Jones); *Doctor Thorne* (Miss Dunstable, Lady Arabella Gresham, Frank Gresham, Dr Thorne, Mary Thorne, Sir Roger Scatcherd); *Dr Wortle's School* (Mr & Mrs Peacocke, Dr Wortle); *The Duke's Children* (Isabel Boncassen, the Duke of Omnium, Mrs Finn, Lady Mabel Grex, Lady Mary Palliser, Francis Tregear, Lord Silverbridge); *The Eustace Diamonds* (Mrs Carbuncle, Mr Emilius, Lady Lizzie Eustace, Frank Greystock, Lucy Morris); *Framley Parsonage* (Mr Arabin, Mr Crawley, Miss Dunstable, Griselda Grantly, Archdeacon Grantly, Lady Lufton, Lord Lufton, Mrs Proudie, Lucy Robarts, Mark Robarts, Mr Sowerby, Dr Thorne); *He Knew He Was Right* (Mr Glascock, Colonel Osborne, Nora Rowley, Caroline Spalding, Hugh, Dorothy & Priscilla Stanbury, Miss Stanbury, Louis & Emily Trevelyan); *Lady Anna* (Lady Anna Lovel, Countess Lovel, Daniel Thwaite); *The Last Chronicle of Barset* (Mr & Mrs Crawley, Grace Crawley, Adolphus Crosbie, Lily Dale, Madalina Demolines, John Eames, Archdeacon Grantly, Major Grantly, Mr Harding, Mrs Proudie, Bishop Proudie, Mr Toogood); *Miss Mackenzie* (John Ball, Lady Ball, Miss Mackenzie); *Mr Scarborough's Family* (Harry Annesley, Mr Grey, Mr Scarborough, Captain & Augustus Scarborough); *Orley Farm* (Mr Chaffanbrass, Mr Furnival, Felix Graham, Lady Mason, Sir Peregrine Orme, Mrs Orme); *Phineas Finn* (Lord Chiltern, Violet Effingham, Phineas Finn, Mme Max Goesler, Mr Kennedy, Mr Monk, the Duke of Omnium, Quintus Slide, Lady Glencora Palliser, Lady Laura Standish); *Phineas Redux* (Mr Chaffanbrass, Lord & Lady Chiltern, Phineas Finn, Mme Max Goesler, Lady Laura & Mr Kennedy, Mr Monk, the Duke of Omnium, Lady Glencora & Plantagenet Palliser, Quintus Slide); *The Prime Minister* (Lady Rosina De Courcy, Lady Lizzie Eustace, Mr & Mrs Finn, Arthur Fletcher, Ferdinand Lopez, the Duke & Duchess of Omnium, Quintus Slide, Emily Wharton, Mr Wharton); *Ralph the Heir* (Ontario Moggs, Mr Neefit, Ralph Newton [illegitimate], Ralph Newton ['the heir'], Sir Thomas Underwood); *The Small House at Allington* (Adolphus Crosbie, Lily Dale, Lady Alexandrina De Courcy, Lady Dumbello, John Eames, Plantagenet Palliser); *The Vicar of Bullhampton* (Carry Brattle, Jacob Brattle, Frank Fenwick, Harry Gilmore); *The Warden* (Archdeacon Grantly, Mr Harding); *The Way We Live Now* (Mr Brehgert, Mr Broune, Felix, Hetta & Roger Carbury, Lady Carbury, Winifred Hurtle, Georgina Longestaffe, Augustus Melmotte, Marie Melmotte, Paul Montague).

Index